The good
web site
guide 2004

The good
web site
guide 2004

GRAHAM EDMONDS

ORION

First published in 2003 by Orion Media
An imprint of Orion Books Ltd
Orion House, 5 Upper St Martin's Lane,
London WC2H 9EA

A CIP catalogue record for this book is
available from the British Library.

ISBN 0 75285 993 5

Designed by Staziker Jones, Cardiff

Printed by Clays Ltd, St Ives plc

Introduction

Welcome to the fourth edition of the Good Web Site Guide and we've sold over 150,000 copies of the first three. This edition is fully updated, all the sites have been checked and rechecked and I've added over one thousand new ones!

This year I've introduced a couple of important new sections, the first one of which is Disability Information. Here the internet is particularly useful and you can find a huge amount of information and help. The second is Security. I get lots of e-mails asking about this subject and I've tried to cover all the questions by offering a selection of sites that will help you keep your PC safe. I've also added sections on Consumer Information, Dance and Party Organising.

To select sites for inclusion in the book, I search out and review the very best sites in each category, then look for those sites that offer something unique or have features that make them stand out and recommend those too. I also list alternatives, especially in the popular genres such as music, shopping or finance. Essentially, I concentrate on what's really useful and encourage people to see the Internet as a tool like any other and not be intimidated by it.

So what has changed in a year since the last edition? Generally, sites have improved in speed and design and in ease of use, more thought and care is being taken. I've now taken speed out of my ratings as it's much less of an issue these days.

There are some truly great sites that I've added to the book this year, here are a few of the best ones, they represent the myriad of ways that the internet can be used and set new standards of site design and usage.

http://earthobservatory.nasa.gov – outstanding photography and a grand concept.

www.50ways.org – a lesson in how to involve people in giving to charity.

www.africatravelresource.com – if only all travel sites where as good or as helpful as this.

www.becominghuman.org – the best broadband site I've seen, beautifully illustrated and genuinely interesting.

www.cool–reads.co.uk – produced by children for children, excellent design and content.

www.historyworld.net – incredibly wide ranging, ambitious and entertaining.

www.kevinsplayroom.co.uk – what an education site should be like.

www.playingwithtime.org – a new way of looking at the world.

www.thebanmappingproject.com – beautifully designed ancient history site with excellent attention to detail.

Most of the major information sites have been busily improving their content while it seems that most retailers have cut back on content now they realise people only visit their site to shop. Some sites are so big now as they follow the 'one-stop, one site does all' policy in their field. Sites such as **www.bbc.co.uk**, **www.amazon.co.uk** and **www.about.com** are huge and are great examples of how to become authoritative, entertaining and all encompassing.

Quality is still a big issue. The cost and time involved in maintaining a good site is sometimes prohibitive, the result being that many sites are not updated as frequently as they should be, while others just die through lack of interest and funding. Still, hundreds of sites go live every day showing that creativity and entrepreneurialism are alive and kicking on the Net.

Unfortunately, lack of time and resource often results in site names (URLs) being turned over to directories, search engines or even adult entertainment sites. I got caught out again in the last guide when a site ceased to exist, their ownership lapsed and disturbingly, they were rented out to an adult entertainment company while awaiting re-sale. There should be some sort of 'cooling off' period introduced to avoid this, but I fear that while there is little or no regulation of the Internet that's pretty unlikely.

Please do let me know if you find any major changes to the sites recommended in this book, I can assure you that all the reviews are accurate at the time of writing this book. Send comments to: **goodwebsiteguide@hotmail.com**

KEEPING SAFE

Some people are worried about using their credit card to shop on the Net. In theory it's safer than giving credit card details over the phone because on most sites the information is encrypted. Before giving out card details, check that you are on a secure line, a small padlock icon will appear on your toolbar, and the http:// prefix will change to https:// Providing you shop from UK sites you are fully covered by the same fair trade laws that cover every form of shopping in the UK, but buying from abroad could have some risk attached. If in doubt, shop from reputable firms and known brand names.

There's also a great deal of concern about cookies. A cookie is the popular name of a file which holds some information about your machine and, only if you give it out, about you. They have a sinister reputation but they enable web site owners to monitor traffic and find out who is visiting their sites. In theory, this means they can tailor their content to their customers or provide a better service. If you're worried about cookies, you can easily delete them or set your computer to not receive them. Be aware however, that many sites do need cookies to function, especially shopping sites.

If you are concerned about security check out our new Security Section on page 320 where you'll find a selection of the best security sites.

USING THE BOOK

Ratings

ORIGIN UK
INFO ✓✓✓✓✓
VALUE ✓✓✓✓✓
EASE ✓✓✓✓✓

✓ = slow/poor   ✓✓✓✓✓ = fast/good

I don't pretend to be a judge and jury, my ratings are just my opinion, that of a customer and consumer.

Info – this gives you a gauge of how much information is available, with respect to how much you are entitled to expect. It's also a measure of the number and quality of links they provide.

Value – value for money. The higher the score the better value you can expect. In some cases this is not relevant.

Ease – this is intended to give an indication of how easy the site is to use. Is it logical, easy to navigate and well signposted?

Origin – a site's country of origin is not always obvious. This can be important, especially if you are buying from abroad. There may be restrictions, taxes or delivery charges that aren't obvious at the time of purchase. Also information that is shown as general may apply to one part of the world and not another. For instance, gardening advice on a US site may not be appropriate in the UK.

If you have any suggestions as to how I can improve the Good Web Site Guide or have a site you think should be included in the 2005 edition then please e–mail me at **goodwebsiteguide@hotmail.com**

Acknowledgements

I'd just like to end in thanking a few important people:

Firstly, a big thank you to all those people who have written in with suggestions and sites for me to check out, over 100 sites have been included in the book as a result of people e–mailing me. I'd especially like to thank Billi–Jo for all her suggestions and David Wilkinson for his help too.

Orion, especially the sales team and Jo Carpenter who did a great job with the other books and I know will with this one.

In particular to Deborah Gray for great patience and excellent advice and ever increasing contributions to the book.

All my many friends and colleagues for their support and suggestions.

Anyone who bought the first books and the booksellers who supported them.

Lastly to Michaela for all else that matters.

Aircraft and Aviation

www.flyer.co.uk

AVIATION IN THE UK

ORIGIN UK
INFO ✓✓✓✓✓
EASE ✓✓✓✓

A well established portal with comprehensive news, views and information about the world of aviation from the *Flyer Magazine* site. There's a good section on aviation links, a club and school guide and info on how to buy and sell an aircraft, classified ads and even free Internet access.

www.flightinternational.com

AVIATION NEWS

ORIGIN UK
INFO ✓✓✓✓
VALUE ✓✓✓
EASE ✓✓✓✓

An online version of the best selling magazine with articles, information and news all laid out in a slick site. It basically gives you a taster of what's in the mag and you have to subscribe to get the best out of it, but there's good information on events, a bookshop and a jobs section.

www.aeroflight.co.uk

AVIATION ENTHUSIASTS

ORIGIN UK
INFO ✓✓✓✓✓
EASE ✓✓✓✓

This site attempts to offer an 'information stop' for all aviation enthusiasts. It's well laid out and has details on international air forces, a section on the media including specialist books and bookshops, a discussion forum, as well as details of air shows and museums.

www.f4aviation.co.uk

AIR SCENE UK

ORIGIN UK
INFO ✓✓✓✓
EASE ✓✓✓✓

A weekly e-zine provided by F4 Aviation, a group of dedicated enthusiasts, this site has lots of information, nostalgia, links to related sites and personal flying accounts. It's also got an air show listing with reports, previews and some good photography.

www.landings.com

THE BUSIEST AVIATION HUB IN CYBERSPACE

ORIGIN US
INFO ✓✓✓✓✓
EASE ✓✓✓

A huge amount of information on offer from this site with everything from the latest news to history and masses of links; use the directory to navigate this massive site. Also check out **www.thisisaviation.org.uk**

www.raf.mod.uk

ROYAL AIR FORCE

ORIGIN UK
INFO ✓✓✓✓
EASE ✓✓✓✓

This site features lots of information on the RAF. The history section is particularly good with data covering aircraft from the very first planes to the latest illustrated by a gallery of pictures; however, the time-line section only reaches 1989 at time of writing. You can also find out what the Red Arrows are up to, get career advice and technical information. See also **www.rafmuseum.org.uk** for the sites dedicated to the museums at Hendon and Cosford.

www.wpafb.af.mil/museum

US AIR FORCE MUSEUM

ORIGIN US
INFO ✓✓✓✓✓
EASE ✓✓✓✓

A superbly detailed site with masses of data on the aircraft and their history from the first planes to space flight, the archive section is particularly good with features on particular types of aircraft and weapons, with information on how they were developed.

http://theaerodrome.com

WW1

ORIGIN UK
INFO ✓✓✓✓
EASE ✓✓✓✓

Devoted to the aircraft and aces of the First World War, this site offers lots of background information, personal experiences and details about the pilots who fought above the trenches. For WWII aircraft try **www.compsoc.man.ac.uk/~wingman/** while at **www.fighter-collection.com** you can find out about the remaining airworthy 'war birds' in Europe.

www.thunder-and-lightnings.co.uk

BRITISH POST WAR MILITARY AIRCRAFT

ORIGIN UK
INFO ✓✓✓✓
EASE ✓✓✓✓

You won't find Spitfires here, but you will learn about great British military planes produced since the war, each has a linked page which is very detailed. There's also a spotter's guide, links, events and a photo quiz. If you do want to know about Spitfires try the excellent site **www.spitfiresociety.demon.co.uk/**

http://catalogue.janes.com/jawa.shtml

JANES DEFENCE INFORMATION

ORIGIN UK   Janes are the authority on military information, and
INFO ✓✓✓✓✓   you can download (with monthly updates) their
VALUE ✓✓✓   *All the World's Aircraft* list for £950 annually, or buy
EASE ✓✓✓   it on CD-Rom for £865. For their homepage go to
                 www.janes.com

http://cloud.prohosting.com/hud607

THE UGLY AND UNCOMMON AIRCRAFT

ORIGIN UK   We couldn't resist this one, with its devotion to
INFO ✓✓✓✓   uncommon and ugly aircraft, each with a page devoted
EASE ✓✓✓✓   to why it existed in the first place. You can contribute
                 to the annual survey too and take part in their quizzes.

www.airdisaster.com

NO.1 AVIATION SAFETY RESOURCE

ORIGIN US   A rather macabre site that reviews each major air
INFO ✓✓✓✓✓   crash, and looks into the reasons behind what
EASE ✓✓✓✓   happened. It's not for the squeamish, but the cockpit
                 voice recordings and eyewitness accounts make fasci-
                 nating, if disturbing, reading. There are some really
                 annoying pop-up adverts on this site which spoils the
                 visit. See also **www.aaib.gov.uk** for the Air Accident
                 Investigation Branch which has a monthly bulletin
                 with details of crashes and current investigations.

www.ukaircraftsales.com

BUY A PLANE

ORIGIN UK   OK so now you've passed all the exams, saved up
INFO ✓✓✓✓   your pennies and naturally want to own your own
EASE ✓✓✓✓   plane, here's where to go, prices start at £20,000,
                 and don't forget the VAT!

www.gliderpilot.net

GLIDER PILOT NETWORK

ORIGIN UK   Weather, news, links and information on all forms
INFO ✓✓✓✓   of gliding, plus chat and classified ads.
EASE ✓✓✓✓

www.iac.org

AEROBATICS

ORIGIN USA
INFO ✓✓✓
EASE ✓✓✓✓

The site of the International Aerobatic Club and the place to go for information on the sport. See also **www.aerobatics.org.uk** for the British Aerobatic Association.

http://avia.russian.ee

HELICOPTERS

ORIGIN ESTONIA
INFO ✓✓✓✓
EASE ✓✓✓✓

A comprehensive guide to the world's rotorcraft with pictures, information and even articles on the theory of flying helicopters.

www.ufosightingsuk.co.uk

UFOS IN THE UK

ORIGIN UK
INFO ✓✓✓✓
EASE ✓✓✓✓

Couldn't resist adding this one, it's a great catalogue of eye witness accounts of encounters with UFOs in the UK. Whether you believe in it or not makes for an interesting read.

Antiques and Collectibles

The Internet is a great place to learn about antiques, it's also full of specialist sites run by fanatical collectors. If you want to take the risk of buying over the Net, then the best prices are found on the big auction sites such as Ebay and icollector.

www.antiques.co.uk

FIND AND BUY ONLINE

ORIGIN UK
INFO ✓✓✓✓
EASE ✓✓✓✓

An attractive and well-designed site, which is basically an online showroom dedicated to most aspects of art and antiques. The emphasis is on quality and experts vet all items and you can arrange viewings too. There's also a news and reviews section with interesting articles on the latest fashionable antiques. Value for money is of course purely subjective.

www.antiquesbulletin.co.uk
INTERACTIVE WORLD OF ANTIQUES

ORIGIN UK
INFO ✓✓✓✓✓
EASE ✓✓✓✓

A well laid out site with loads of information and links to more specialist sites and dealers. It aims to cover every aspect of antiques and does a great job, there are details on auctions, advice on how to buy and sell and a bookshop. You can also buy and sell from the site. To access the articles archive, you need to purchase a site licence.

www.invaluable.com
ART MARKET INTELLIGENCE

ORIGIN UK
INFO ✓✓✓✓✓
EASE ✓✓✓

Get the latest word on antiques, plus contact details and links to hundreds of dealers, catalogues and auction houses world-wide. The links section is particularly good.

www.antiquesworld.co.uk
AN ALADDIN'S CAVE FOR THE ENTHUSIAST

ORIGIN UK
INFO ✓✓✓✓✓
EASE ✓✓✓

Catch up on the latest news, obtain details on major and local fairs and events, book a course or indulge your interests by linking to a specialist online retailer or club. You can't buy from this site but the links and information are very good.

www.antiquestall.com
ONLINE ANTIQUES STALL

ORIGIN UK
INFO ✓✓✓✓
EASE ✓✓✓

A no-nonsense site devoted to selling antiques at fixed prices rather than by auction. There's a good search facility and each item has a picture and details of shipping.

www.antiquegems.net
ANTIQUE JEWELLERY

ORIGIN UK
INFO ✓✓✓✓
VALUE ✓✓✓
EASE ✓✓✓✓

A fine site from a Birmingham dealer and restorer with a good selection of gems and jewellery as well as watches and a selection of bargains. You can't buy online but there's a contact service for the pieces that you're interested in.

www.dmgantiquefairs.com
FOR THE LARGEST ANTIQUES FAIRS

ORIGIN UK

INFO ✓✓✓✓

EASE ✓✓✓✓

DMG run the largest fairs in the UK. Their attractive site gives details of each fair, including dates, location and local tourist information. For a site that simply lists antiques and collectors fairs in date order with links to organiser's web sites go to www.antiques-web.co.uk/fairs.html

www.portobelloonline.com
THE PORTOBELLO ROAD

ORIGIN UK

INFO ✓✓✓✓

EASE ✓✓✓✓

The traders from London's well known antiques market have got together a great site which not only gives information about Portobello Road itself, but also offers excellent links and a directory.

www.lapada.co.uk
ASSOCIATION OF ART AND ANTIQUE DEALERS

ORIGIN UK

INFO ✓✓✓

EASE ✓✓✓✓

Get information on their fairs, advice on buying and selling antiques and useful links.

www.bafra.org.uk
ANTIQUE FURNITURE RESTORERS ASSOCIATION

ORIGIN UK

INFO ✓✓✓✓

EASE ✓✓✓✓

If you have an antique that is in need of restoration, then this is a useful place to visit as it helps you find the right restorer. Apart from the usual links page, there's also information and articles on caring for antiques and how to find a course if you want to become a restorer.

www.collectiques.co.uk
COLLECTIBLES

ORIGIN UK

INFO ✓✓✓✓✓

EASE ✓✓✓✓

Despite its fairly naff name, Collectiques is a good resource if you're searching for information or that elusive piece for your collection. It covers an impressive array of areas of interest from toys to models, kits and architectural antiques, it's easy to use and it's great for background info and links.

www.collectorcafe.com
ONLINE COLLECTING COMMUNITY

ORIGIN UK   A portal site which is great for classified ads, links,
INFO ✓✓✓✓   articles and chat covering most of the major areas
EASE ✓✓✓✓   of collecting.

www.worldcollectorsnet.com
BY COLLECTORS FOR COLLECTORS

ORIGIN US   Great for discussion groups, collector's message
INFO ✓✓✓   boards and general chat about collecting. There's
VALUE ✓✓✓   also a good online magazine plus plenty of advice and
EASE ✓✓✓✓   links. See also www.collectors.com which is great for
Americana and also www.collectingchannel.com

www.finds.org.uk
THE PORTABLE ANTIQUITIES SCHEME

ORIGIN UK   An interesting site devoted to volunteered
INFO ✓✓✓   archaeological and antiquity finds made by
EASE ✓✓✓✓   individuals who register them so that they can
be researched properly.

Ceramics

www.ukceramics.org
A CERAMICS SHOWCASE

ORIGIN UK   An excellent showcase site for new and established
INFO ✓✓✓✓   artists. It has beautiful pictures of the ceramics with
EASE ✓✓✓✓✓   good biographical information. The site enables you
to contact artists to buy their work.

www.studiopottery.com
THE POTTERY STUDIO

ORIGIN UK   Divided into 3 sections: pots, potters and potteries,
INFO ✓✓✓✓✓   this site gives information on the history of studio
EASE ✓✓✓✓   pottery. It's a huge site with over 4,200 pages and
it's continually being updated. Everything is cross-
referenced with good explanations and photographs.

www.claricecliff.com

THE FIRST LADY OF CERAMIC DESIGN

ORIGIN UK   A must for fans of Clarice Cliff pottery. There is
INFO ✓✓✓✓✓   information on auctions, biographical details, patterns,
VALUE ✓✓   shapes; also a newsletter and forum for related chat. The
EASE ✓✓✓✓   site offers reproductions and related merchandise for sale.

www.chinasearch.uk.com

REPLACING LOST CHINA

ORIGIN UK   A company specialising in finding china to match
INFO ✓✓✓✓   services and lost pieces, they also buy unwanted
EASE ✓✓✓✓   tableware. The site is easy to use and they have over one
               million pieces in stock so they should be able to help.

Apple Mac Users

*The following sites specialise in Apple Mac technology and
programs. See also the general sections on Computers, Software
and Games which may also have relevant information.*

www.apple.com or www.uk.euro.apple.com

HOME OF THE ORIGINAL

ORIGIN US   Get the latest information and advances in Apple
INFO ✓✓✓✓   computers at this beautifully designed site. You
VALUE ✓✓✓   can buy from the Applestore but don't expect huge
EASE ✓✓✓✓   discounts, although they do offer finance deals.

www.cancomuk.com

APPLE MAC HARDWARE AND SOFTWARE

ORIGIN UK   A well-designed site offering a wide selection of
INFO ✓✓✓✓   hardware, peripherals and software all developed for
VALUE ✓✓✓✓   Apple computers. There are plenty of deals and free
EASE ✓✓✓✓   delivery on all orders over £100 before VAT.

www.macwarehouse.co.uk

GREAT PRICES ON MACS

ORIGIN UK   Part of the Microwarehouse group, they specialise
INFO ✓✓✓✓   in mail order supply with a reputation for excellent
VALUE ✓✓✓✓   service. Good prices and a wide range make this a good
EASE ✓✓✓   first port of call if you need a new PC or an upgrade.

www.macintouch.com
THE ORIGINAL MAC NEWS AND INFORMATION SITE

ORIGIN US
INFO ✓✓✓✓✓
EASE ✓✓

If you have a Mac then this is the site for you. It has lots of information, bug fixes and software to download, but it is a little overwhelming and it takes a while to get your bearings. Once you've done that, for the Mac user this is invaluable.

In the unlikely event that you can't find what you're looking for here try any of the following sites:
www.macaddict.com – very comprehensive, one for the experts.
www.macfixit.com – fix your problems.
www.macinstein.com – which has a good directory, even a quiz.
www.maclaunch.com – the latest news.
www.macnn.com – the Mac News network, lots of ratings.
www.macobserver.com – more news, tips and forums.
www.macupdate.com – the latest hot software and updates.

www.macassist.co.uk
APPLE HELP

ORIGIN UK
INFO ✓✓✓✓
VALUE ✓✓✓
EASE ✓✓✓✓✓

A great looking site from a British company that specialises in Macintosh computers with advice on the latest hardware, plus forums, classified ads and virus information.

www.ihateapple.com
IF YOU REALLY DON'T LIKE APPLE

ORIGIN US
INFO ✓✓✓✓
EASE ✓✓✓

An entertaining anti-Apple web site devoted to 'debunking' and exposing Apple faults – it's actually quite informative and funny too.

Games for Macs

Here are three great sites to help you if you feel restricted by having an Apple Mac.

www.macgamer.com
MAC GAMER MAG

ORIGIN US   A great looking online magazine with all the usual
INFO ✓✓✓✓   features we've come to expect: news, reviews, links
EASE ✓✓✓✓   and even a few giveaways. It's all neatly packaged
            on an attractive website.

www.macgamefiles.com
MAC GAME FILE LIBRARY

ORIGIN US   To quote them 'Macgame files.com is the one-stop
INFO ✓✓✓✓✓   source for Macintosh game files. The web site features
EASE ✓✓✓✓   lively libraries of Macintosh demos, shareware,
            updaters, tools, add-ons, and more'. And they're
            right; it's a very good site with some really good
            games and useful stuff.

www.insidemacgames.com
IMG MAGAZINE

ORIGIN US   A magazine devoted to Mac games where you can
INFO ✓✓✓✓   find the latest demos, updates for the games, loads
EASE ✓✓✓✓   of shareware games, news and reviews.

Architecture

www.greatbuildings.com
ARCHITECTURE ONLINE

ORIGIN US   This site shows over 1,000 buildings and features
INFO ✓✓✓✓   hundreds of leading architects, with 3D models,
EASE ✓✓✓   photographic images and architectural drawings,
            commentaries, bibliographies and web links. It's
            all well packaged, easy to use and you can search
            by architect, building or location.

www.skyscrapers.com
SKYSCRAPERTASTIC!

ORIGIN US   This really entertaining and award-winning site has
INFO ✓✓✓✓   many thousands of images of skyscrapers and major
EASE ✓✓✓✓   buildings from around the world, and more are being

added constantly. There are also features, chat and
you can search by region as well as by architect or
building. See also www.skyscrapernews.co.uk for
news of what's going on in the UK.

www.architecture.com
THE ROYAL INSTITUTE FOR BRITISH ARCHITECTS

ORIGIN UK
INFO ✓✓✓✓✓
EASE ✓✓✓✓

A massive site from the RIBA with some 250,000
pages on all aspects of architecture including history,
jobs, events and features on great buildings.

www.buildingconservation.com
CONSERVING ASSETS

ORIGIN UK
INFO ✓✓✓✓
VALUE ✓✓✓✓
EASE ✓✓✓✓

They claim to be the online information centre for
the conservation and restoration of historic buildings,
churches, gardens and landscapes; the site seems to
live up to its billing providing plenty of quality
information.

Also check out the following sites:
www.aabc-register.co.uk – the register of architects
accredited in building conservation.
www.archibot.com – news and forums dedicated to
all things architectural.
www.archidose.org – an entertaining and informative
weekly magazine devoted to contemporary architecture run by an American expert.
www.architectureforall.com – a collaborative venture
between the Victoria & Albert museum and the
RIBA to promote understanding of architecture.
www.retropolis.net – Art Deco architecture, a labour
of love.
www.spab.org.uk – home of the charity The Society
for the Protection of Ancient Buildings.

Art and the Arts

*One of the best things about the Internet is the ability to showcase
things that otherwise would be quite obscure or inaccessible. Now
working artists can show their wares to excellent effect and we can
view their art before we buy. In addition, we can now 'visit' some*

*of the world's great galleries and museums. Here are the best
sites for posters, online galleries, museums, cartoons, exhibitions,
showcases for new talent and how to get the best clip-art for your
own use.*

Resources, shops, museums, galleries and exhibitions

www.artlex.com
THE VISUAL ARTS DICTIONARY

ORIGIN US   From abbozzo to zoomorphic, there are over 3,000 defi-
INFO ✓✓✓✓   nitions of art-related terms with links to related articles
EASE ✓✓✓   other sites; however, some of the links aren't reliable.

www.artcyclopedia.com
THE FINE ART SEARCH ENGINE

ORIGIN CANADA   A popular resource for finding out just about
INFO ✓✓✓✓✓   anything to do with art, it's quick, nicely designed
EASE ✓✓✓✓✓   and informative. At time of writing they had indexed
1,200 leading arts sites, and offer more than 32,000
links directly to an estimated 100,000 works by 7,500
different artists. See also the economically designed
www.artincontext.com and **www.artswire.org** home
of the New York Foundation of the Arts.

www.artandculture.com
THE EVER EXPANDING WORLD OF ART AND CULTURE

ORIGIN US   A site devoted to everything from design, visual arts,
INFO ✓✓✓✓   music to literature. It's full of articles and biographical
EASE ✓✓✓✓   detail, but the highlight has to be the way it links all
aspects of the arts and encourages you to look for
more information with book recommendations and
other related web sites. You need the latest Flash
software for it to run properly, this can easily be
downloaded free from **www.macromedia.com**

www.accessart.org.uk
MAKING ART ACCESSIBLE

ORIGIN UK   A really good, colourful site dedicated to helping
INFO ✓✓✓✓   students, children and teachers get to grips with the
EASE ✓✓✓✓   art world and the meaning behind art. There are good
online workshops on topics such as sculpture, use of
colour and photography.

http://wwar.com
THE WORLD-WIDE ART RESOURCE
ORIGIN US   This is an effective search vehicle with links to artists,
INFO ✓✓✓✓✓   exhibitions, galleries and museums, it is now much
EASE ✓✓✓✓✓   better designed and easier to use as a result. Plenty
of pop-up adverts spoil it though.

www.design-council.org.uk
PROMOTING THE EFFECTIVE USE OF DESIGN
ORIGIN UK   This good looking site effectively promotes the work
INFO ✓✓✓   of The Design Council through access to their archive
EASE ✓✓✓✓   of articles on design and details of their work with
government; also gives feedback on design issues.

www.artguide.org
THE ART LOVER'S GUIDE TO BRITAIN AND IRELAND
ORIGIN UK   Organised by artist, region, exhibition or museum
INFO ✓✓✓✓   with more than 4,500 listings in all. This site is easy
EASE ✓✓✓✓   to navigate with a good search engine and cross-
referencing making it simple to find out about events
in a particular region, aided by annotated maps.

www.thegallerychannel.com
WORLD'S MOST COMPREHENSIVE ARTS LISTING
ORIGIN UK   The Gallery Channel provides information on exhibi-
INFO ✓✓✓✓   tions, with online cross-referencing for over 19,000
EASE ✓✓✓✓   artists and 650 museums; there are also comprehensive
exhibitions listings for the UK. The site is continually
updating and there's always something new to look
at along with plenty of articles, news and previews.

www.artchive.com
MARK HARDEN'S ARTCHIVE
ORIGIN UK   Incredible, but seemingly the work of one art fanatic,
INFO ✓✓✓✓✓   this superb site not only has an excellent art
EASE ✓✓✓✓   encyclopaedia, but also the latest art news and galleries
with special online exhibitions. The quality of the
pictures is outstanding. There's also a section on
theory and good links.

www.surrealism.co.uk

ONLINE GALLERY

ORIGIN UK
INFO ✓✓✓
EASE ✓✓✓✓

Not as way out as you'd expect, this site gives an overview of surrealism and features contemporary artists. The online gallery is OK without being that exciting, but as a showcase it works.

www.graffiti.org

THE WRITING ON THE WALL

ORIGIN UK
INFO ✓✓✓✓
EASE ✓✓✓✓

If you're fascinated by graffiti then here's the place to go – it's got a gallery of the best examples, history and links to other graffiti sites.

www.the-artists.org

20TH CENTURY ART

ORIGIN UK
INFO ✓✓✓✓
EASE ✓✓✓✓

This site is easy to use, with minimalist design and details of every major artist of the last century.

www.culture.gov.uk

THE GOVERNMENT'S VIEW

ORIGIN UK
INFO ✓✓✓✓
EASE ✓✓✓✓

A dense site giving information on how the Government is supporting the arts and museums. There are plenty of facts, figures and reports to download, as well as links and information on libraries, the creative industries and even sport.

The major museums and galleries

www.museums.co.uk

MUSEUM SEARCH

ORIGIN UK
INFO ✓✓✓✓
EASE ✓✓✓✓✓

MuseumNet is a simple search engine which allows you to search either by subject or location, each entry has a short description and a map. There's also industry information and a jobs page for those who want to work in a museum.

www.museumstuff.com
MUSEUM GATEWAY

ORIGIN	US
INFO	✓✓✓✓✓
EASE	✓✓✓✓

An outstanding portal devoted to museums. There's information on virtually any topic you can name plus thousands of links to specialist sites and museums. They also provide a list of museum shops, chat rooms and forums plus links to the fun sections on museum sites.

www.24hourmuseum.org.uk
OPEN ALL HOURS

ORIGIN	UK
INFO	✓✓✓✓✓
EASE	✓✓✓✓

Run by the Campaign for Museums, this site aims to give high quality access to the UK's galleries, museums and heritage sites – and it succeeds. The graphics are clear, it's easy to use and really informative. There's a museum finder, links, a magazine, resources for research and a link to **www.show.me.uk** which is the sister site for children. See also the rather pretentious **www.artmuseum.net** which is supported by Intel.

www.tate.org.uk
THE ARCHETYPAL GALLERY SITE

ORIGIN	UK
INFO	✓✓✓✓
VALUE	✓✓✓
EASE	✓✓✓✓✓

A real treat with good design and quality pictures, the site covers all the Tate galleries and offers information about exhibitions, relevant articles, webcasts and also a good shop.

www.nationalgallery.org.uk
THE NATIONAL COLLECTION OF WESTERN EUROPEAN PAINTING

ORIGIN	UK
INFO	✓✓✓✓✓
VALUE	✓✓✓
EASE	✓✓✓✓✓

A very comprehensive site, with sections on the permanent collection and exhibitions. There's also a shop with a wide range of books and gifts as well as information for schools on what they can get out of working with the gallery. For access to all the Scottish National Galleries on a similar site, go to **www.natgalscot.ac.uk** who have a similarly informative and enjoyable site.

www.thebritishmuseum.ac.uk

ILLUMINATING NEW CULTURES

ORIGIN UK
INFO ✓✓✓✓
VALUE ✓✓✓
EASE ✓✓✓✓

Whether you explore the world's cultures with interactive mapping, understand and educate yourself or just browse the collection, this is a beautifully illustrated site. The online shop stocks a selection of gifts and goods based on museum artefacts. Delivery cost depends on weight of purchases. They also arrange museum tours.

www.npg.org.uk

THE NATIONAL PORTRAIT GALLERY

ORIGIN UK
INFO ✓✓✓✓✓
VALUE ✓✓
EASE ✓✓✓✓

With over 16,000 works on view, this is one of the biggest online galleries. It shows the most influential characters in British history portrayed by artists of their time. You can search by sitter or artist, and buy the print. The online shop offers gifts plus pictures with options on print size, framing and delivery, including overseas.

www.royalacademy.org.uk

WHERE ART IS MADE, SEEN AND DEBATED

ORIGIN UK
INFO ✓✓✓✓
EASE ✓✓✓✓

An interestingly designed and modern gallery site with all the information you need on the Royal Academy as well as ticket information and a shop. There's support for schools, colleges and teachers, plus information and previews of exhibitions.

www.vam.ac.uk

VICTORIA & ALBERT MUSEUM

ORIGIN UK
INFO ✓✓✓✓
VALUE ✓✓
EASE ✓✓✓✓

The world's largest museum has a plain functional web site, with information on visiting, learning and how you can help support the museum. The online shop offers gifts, reproductions and books. You can also explore the museum virtually, visiting most of the galleries with back-up information explaining their exhibits with details of what they contain.

www.moma.org
THE MUSEUM OF MODERN ART IN NEW YORK

ORIGIN US
INFO ✓✓✓✓✓
VALUE ✓✓
EASE ✓✓✓

A comprehensive and minimally attractive site that covers the collection and offers much in the way of information on the works and artists. There's also an excellent gift shop, although shipping to the UK is expensive. It can be quite slow at times.

www.metmuseum.org
THE METROPOLITAN MUSEUM OF ART IN NEW YORK

ORIGIN US
INFO ✓✓✓✓
VALUE ✓✓✓
EASE ✓✓✓✓

A beautiful and very stylish site, featuring lots of great ideas, with quality illustrations and photographs, you can view any one of 3,500 exhibits, become a member, or visit a special exhibition. The shop offers a great range of products, many exclusive, and there's a handy gift finder service. Delivery costs to the UK depend on how much you spend.

www.uffizi.firenze.it/welcome.html
THE UFFIZI GALLERY IN FLORENCE

ORIGIN ITALY
INFO ✓✓✓
EASE ✓✓✓✓

It's the quality of the images of the paintings that make this site stand out. They are superb and it's a shame that there are not more of them to view, although more are being digitised, meaning the site can go offline occasionally. Navigating is easy and quicker than most. There is also gallery information and a tour.

www.louvre.fr
FRANCE'S TREASURE HOUSE

ORIGIN FRANCE
INFO ✓✓✓✓
VALUE ✓
EASE ✓✓✓✓

Similar to the UK's National Gallery site:
1. You can take a virtual tour.
2. View the collection.
3. Learn about its history.
4. Check out the latest exhibitions and buy advance tickets.
5. The shop has interesting items and delivery to the UK is about £8.

www.guggenheim.org
VANGUARDS OF ARCHITECTURE AND CULTURE

ORIGIN US
INFO ✓✓✓✓
VALUE ✓✓
EASE ✓✓✓✓

There is the promise of a unique virtual museum, but while we wait, the other five – Berlin, Bilbao, Venice, New York and Las Vegas can be visited here.

1. You can find out about exhibitions and collections, projects, tours, events and developmental programs.
2. Join. Membership entitles you to free entry and a store discount.
3. The store is stocked with a wonderful selection of unusual goods and gifts, and is not bad value. Delivery to the UK starts at £18.

www.hermitagemuseum.org
THE STATE HERMITAGE MUSEUM

ORIGIN RUSSIA
INFO ✓✓✓✓✓
EASE ✓✓✓✓

Another beautifully presented museum site with features on the highlights of the collection with a section of superb digital photographs, details of the museum itself, exhibitions and an education centre.

www.artgalleries-london.com
GUIDE TO LONDON'S TREASURES

ORIGIN UK
INFO ✓✓✓✓
EASE ✓✓✓✓

An attractive site that offers a directory of the capital's museums, galleries and relevant links to related sites.

Sites featuring the top artists:
http://arthistory.about.com/library/blartists.htm – biographies of over 150 artists plus loads of art history information.
www.chez.com/renoir/indexe.html – Renoir
www.daliuniverse.com – Dali
www.lucidcafe.com/library/96jun/gauguin.html – Gauguin
www.mark-rothko.com – Rothko
www.marmottan.com – Monet
www.mos.org/leonardo – Da Vinci
www.musee-matisse-nice.org/ – Matisse
www.tamu.edu/mocl/picasso – Picasso
www.vangoghgallery.com – Van Gogh.

Clipart

These sites are loaded with pop-ups and advertising which is really irritating, you may just try Google (www.google.co.uk) which has an excellent image search facility. If you know of a site that is ad free please let me know.

www.clipart.net
THE PLACE TO START IF YOU NEED CLIP-ART

ORIGIN US
INFO ✓✓
EASE ✓✓✓✓

A clip-art search facility, you should quickly find the perfect image. Many linked sites have free art for use, otherwise cost varies enormously depending on what you want.

See also:
www.321clipart.com – some 12,000 images.
www.barrysclipart.com – a huge resource with
    hundreds of categories.
www.clipartcastle.com – sections on photos and
    animation as well as clip art. Registration is a
    right pain though.

Cartoons

www.cartoonbank.com
WORLD'S LARGEST CARTOON DATABASE

ORIGIN US
INFO ✓✓✓
EASE ✓✓✓✓

Need to find a cartoon for a particular occasion? Then there's a choice of over 20,000 mostly from *New Yorker* magazine. You can send e-cards, but they only supply products to the USA. For a massive set of links to cartoon and humorous sites then try the excellent Norwegian search site www.cartoon-links.com

www.cartoon-factory.com
BUYING CARTOON CELS

ORIGIN US
INFO ✓✓✓✓
VALUE ✓✓
EASE ✓✓✓✓✓

Buy cartoon cels, mainly from Disney and Warner cartoons; you can search by subject or artist. Delivery is expensive, although they are flexible about payment. See also the Open Directory Projects section on Animation. It offers over 18,000 links at
http://dmoz.org/arts/animation

Buying art

www.artrepublic.co.uk
BOOKS, POSTERS AND WHAT'S ON WHERE

ORIGIN	UK
INFO	✓✓✓✓
VALUE	✓✓✓
EASE	✓✓✓✓✓

A nicely designed, easy-to-use site, which sections on Posters – choose from thousands of posters, use the glossary of art terms or peruse artist's biographical data. Free shipping world-wide and What's on world-wide – details of the latest exhibitions, competitions and travel information for over 1,250 museums around the world.

www.onlineposters.com
POSTER SHOPS ONLINE

ORIGIN	UK
INFO	✓✓✓✓
EASE	✓✓✓✓

Simply a ranked list of shops that sell posters, from the generalist to the very specialised retailers.

www.barewalls.com
INTERNET'S LARGEST ART PRINT AND POSTER STORE

ORIGIN	US
INFO	✓✓✓✓
VALUE	✓✓
EASE	✓✓✓✓✓

This site backs its claim with a huge range, it's also excellent for gifts and unusual prints and posters but be aware that the shipping costs are high – $29 for the UK. There's also a gift voucher scheme. See also www.art.com which is excellent and does a great line in movie posters as well as art. Delivery is expensive.

www.postershop.co.uk
FINE ART PRINTS AND POSTERS

ORIGIN	UK
INFO	✓✓✓✓
VALUE	✓✓✓
EASE	✓✓✓✓✓

There are over 22,000 prints and posters available to buy, covering the work of over 3,900 artists. There's also a framing service and a good user-friendly search facility where you can search by subject as well as artist. In the museum shop there's a range of art-related gifts to choose from. Delivery costs £3 for the UK.

www.totalposter.com

GET THE BIG PICTURE

ORIGIN	UK
INFO	✓✓✓✓
VALUE	✓✓✓
EASE	✓✓✓

Excellent poster store, specialising in photographic posters with a very wide selection. Extra services include: printing up your own photos to poster size, plus pictures of recent key sporting and news events in their 'Stop Press' section. Delivery costs vary.

www.easyart.com

FINE ART PRINTS AND POSTERS

ORIGIN	UK
INFO	✓✓✓✓
VALUE	✓✓✓✓
EASE	✓✓✓✓

Excellent art shop selling posters, limited editions, photographs and etchings. They provide inspiration too with advice on the best place to hang art in your home and a custom art section where you can turn pictures of your friends in to pop icons.

www.eyestorm.com

BUYING CONTEMPORARY ART

ORIGIN	UK
INFO	✓✓✓
VALUE	✓✓✓
EASE	✓✓✓✓✓

A really attractive and well-designed site, which show-cases contemporary art and photography, you can buy online as well.

www.whitecube.com

WHITE CUBE GALLERY

ORIGIN	UK
INFO	✓✓✓✓
VALUE	✓✓✓
EASE	✓✓✓✓

Outstanding design makes this site stand out, it show-cases top artists in an original way and highlights what can be done when web site development technology is used at its best. Although influential in developing the careers of some of the best artists working today, you can buy art here at reasonable prices too.

Other online art showcase sites and stores worth visiting:

www.art4deco.com – attractive site offering several hundred works for sale; good search facility.

www.artandparcel.com – messy site that boasts the largest gallery on the web.

www.artlondon.com – well designed art store with an emphasis on the UK, value for money and quality.

www.artuk.co.uk – a slightly confusing site but well worth a visit as there's some interesting art and articles.

www.axisartists.org.uk – a very good showcase site for contemporary artists with lots of content and information as well as links and exhibitions. It claims over 17,000 pieces of work by over 4,000 artists.

www.britart.com – good looking site concentrating on the work of 400 British artists.

www.fineart.co.uk – the home of the Fine Art Trade Guild.

www.insidespace.com – clutter free design, original prints and photographs from contemporary artists for sale.

www.modernbritishartists.co.uk – a gallery and shop catering for those of us who love and covet the work of modern British artists, including those from early in the last century.

www.newartportfolio.com – another showcase site for new artists with an intriguing design, offering plenty of information and a money back guarantee – useful if you find you can't live with your purchase after all.

www.saa.co.uk – the society for all artists, help, advice and a good shop.

www.artloss.com

THE ART LOSS REGISTER

ORIGIN US
INFO ✓✓✓✓
EASE ✓✓✓✓

The register of stolen and lost art featured thefts and recoveries makes for interesting if rather sad reading.

Creating art

www.kurzweilcyberart.com

CYBER ART

ORIGIN US
INFO ✓✓✓✓
EASE ✓✓✓✓

Once you download the program, watch in fascination as art is created for you as a screen saver. It's free and great fun too.

www.arthouse.uk.com

WATERCOLOURS ON THE WEB

ORIGIN UK
INFO ✓✓✓✓
VALUE ✓✓
EASE ✓✓✓

Learn about watercolour techniques, go on a course, find out about exhibitions, seek out designers or book an artistic holiday. There are also several galleries devoted to artists with work for sale and many pictures to view.

For more watercolour sites try:
http://painting.about.com/cs/watercolours/index.htm
  – pages of advice from **www.about.com**
www.paintdoodles.com – an interactive course on
  CD-Rom.
www.wasp-art.skynow.co.uk – a simple online course
  by Peter Saw.

www.simplypainting.com
FRANK CLARK

ORIGIN	UK	Learn how to paint with leading art teacher
INFO	✓✓✓✓	Frank Clark, the site has free lessons, tips plus
VALUE	✓✓✓	a shop and gallery.
EASE	✓✓✓	

Astrology

www.astrology.com
ALL ABOUT ASTROLOGY

ORIGIN	UK	A very comprehensive site offering free advice from the
INFO	✓✓✓✓✓	stars, you can buy a personalised reading and chart or
EASE	✓✓✓✓	just browse the more general horoscopes. You can find

celebrity horoscopes too, and learn about the history
and techniques of astrology. See also
www.horoscope.co.uk home of *Horoscope Magazine*.

www.live-astro.com
RUSSELL GRANT

ORIGIN	UK	Now is your chance to buy a horoscope from a real
INFO	✓✓✓✓	celebrity, costs range from £3.99 upwards. This site
VALUE	✓✓	has been expanded to include dream interpretations,
EASE	✓✓✓✓	tarot and other astrological resources as well as the

various horoscopes.

www.easyscopes.com
ASTROLOGY SEARCH ENGINE

ORIGIN	US	Here you can get as many different free horoscopes
INFO	✓✓✓✓✓	as you can handle, the site contains direct links to the
EASE	✓✓✓✓	daily, weekly, monthly and yearly horoscopes for each

zodiac sign. You just have to select your zodiac sign
and you are presented with a large list of horoscopes
to choose from. It's amazing how different they all
are for the same sign!

www.lovetest.com
ARE YOU COMPATIBLE?

ORIGIN US
INFO ✓✓✓
VALUE ✓✓✓✓
EASE ✓✓✓✓

It's a bit long winded to use but enter your birthday
and your partner's and you get a compatibility score
based on the star signs. There are also quizzes, chat,
classified ads, links, not forgetting the love test
thermometer.

Auctions and Classified Ads

*Before using these sites be sure that you are aware of the rules and
regulations surrounding the bidding process, and what your rights
are as a seller or purchaser. If they are not properly explained
during the registration process, then use another site. They
should also offer a returns policy as well as insurance cover.*

*Whilst there are plenty of bargains available, not all the products
on offer are cheaper than the high street or specialist vendor, it's
very much a case of buyer beware. Having said that, once you're
used to it, it can be fun, and you can save a great deal of money.*

www.ebay.co.uk
YOUR PERSONAL TRADING COMMUNITY

ORIGIN UK
INFO ✓✓✓✓
VALUE ✓✓✓
EASE ✓✓✓✓

With over 3 million items you are likely to find what
you want here. The emphasis is on collectibles and it
is strong on antiques of all sorts, although there's
much, much more. There is a 24-hour support facility
and automatic insurance cover on all items up to £120.
Previous clients have reviewed each person who has
something to sell, that way you can check up on
their reliability.

www.ebid.co.uk

NO CHARGE TO LIST AN ITEM

ORIGIN UK	Divided into auctions, wanted and swap sections.
INFO ✓✓✓✓	The auctions can easily be accessed and browsed;
VALUE ✓✓✓	its strengths are in computing, electronics and music,
EASE ✓✓✓✓	although there has been a great increase in the number
	of collectibles available.

www.icollector.com

REDEFINING THE ART OF COLLECTING

ORIGIN US	An attractive site bringing together the wares of
INFO ✓✓✓✓	some 950 auction houses and dealers, icollector is an
VALUE ✓✓✓	ambitious project that works well. The emphasis is on
EASE ✓✓✓✓	art, antiques and collectibles. Be sure that the auction
	house you're dealing with ships outside the USA.

www.qxl.com

A PAN-EUROPEAN AUCTION COMMUNITY

ORIGIN UK/EUROPE	This wide-ranging site offers anything from airline
INFO ✓✓✓✓	tickets and holidays to cars, collectibles and electronics
VALUE ✓✓✓✓	(in several languages). The quality of merchandise
EASE ✓✓✓✓	seems better than most sites. Another site worth check-
	ing out is www.CQout.co.uk it has over 80,000 lots,
	a wide selection of categories and a nice design.

www.sothebys.com

QUALITY ASSURED, BUT JUST FOR THE CONNOISSEURS

ORIGIN UK/US	You can bid in their online auctions, find out about
INFO ✓✓✓✓	their normal auctions or enlist their help with one
VALUE ✓✓	of the many extra services they offer. The emphasis
EASE ✓✓✓✓	here is on high quality and the arts and you can buy
	catalogues too.

www.christies.com

FOR THOSE WITH DEEP WALLETS

ORIGIN UK	Christies have a slowish site with info on their
INFO ✓✓✓	programme of auctions and on how to buy and sell
VALUE ✓✓	through them, but you can't carry out transactions
EASE ✓✓✓	from the site. The LotFinder service searches their
	auctions for that special item – for a fee. There's also
	a good specialist bookstore and lots of information
	on how to buy and sell.

www.ad-mart.co.uk
AWARD WINNING

ORIGIN UK
INFO ✓✓✓✓
VALUE ✓✓✓✓
EASE ✓✓✓✓✓

Excellent design and ease of use makes this site stand out; there are fourteen sections, all the usual suspects plus personal ads, boating and pets. See also www.nettrader.co.uk which is also really well designed and easy to use.

www.exchangeandmart.co.uk
EXCHANGE & MART

ORIGIN UK
INFO ✓✓✓✓
VALUE ✓✓✓✓
EASE ✓✓✓✓✓

Everything the paper has and more, great bargains on a massive range of goods found with good search facility, all packaged in a bright easy-to-use site. It is split into three major sections: home and leisure, motoring and business.

www.loot.com
FREE ADS ONLINE

ORIGIN UK
INFO ✓✓✓✓
VALUE ✓✓✓✓
EASE ✓✓✓

Over 70,000 ads make Loot a great place to go for a bargain. It's an interesting site to browse with seventeen sections covering the usual classified ad subjects supplemented by areas featuring students, jobs, accommodation and personals. Go to Loot café for a chat.

Beauty

Beauty product retailers are popular on the Internet so we've featured a few of the best ones for advice, help and shopping!

www.beautyconsumer.com
COMPLETE GUIDE TO SKIN CARE

ORIGIN UK
INFO ✓✓✓✓
EASE ✓✓✓✓

An excellent web site with help and information on all forms of skin care as well as beauty tips and product information, there's even a section especially for men. Two people experienced in the field put it together and the information is very easy to access.

www.avonshop.co.uk

SHOP WITHOUT THE DROP

ORIGIN UK	A very good online shop from the traditional leaders
INFO ✓✓✓✓	in direct selling of cosmetics, with clear design and
VALUE ✓✓✓✓	lots of offers.
EASE ✓✓✓✓✓	

www.lookfantastic.com

LOOK FANTASTIC

ORIGIN UK	Not as much fun as it was when it started, but it's
INFO ✓✓✓✓	still a well-designed online retailer offering some really
VALUE ✓✓✓✓	good discounts, while shipping costs start at £2.50.
EASE ✓✓✓✓	It also offers advice guides on how to use make-up,

shampoo and conditioners, in fact virtually everything a girl needs – it's war out there after all.

www.fragrancenet.com

WORLD'S LARGEST DISCOUNT FRAGRANCE STORE

ORIGIN US	A massive range of perfumes for men and women,
INFO ✓✓✓✓	every brand is represented and there are some excellent
VALUE ✓✓✓✓	offers. However, the site is American with shipping
EASE ✓✓✓✓	costs from $19 dollars and more depending on

what you buy. See also **www.perfumeshopping.com** who offer 1,000 perfumes and fragrances from a well-designed site.

www.directcosmetics.com

WIDE RANGE AND THE BEST PRICES

ORIGIN UK	They claim to offer a **wide range** of perfumes with up
INFO ✓✓✓✓	to 90% off UK **recommended retail** prices plus the
VALUE ✓✓✓✓✓	latest news from the **big brand** names. The site is quick
EASE ✓✓✓✓	and easy-to-use and **the offers** are genuine; however,

delivery costs £3.95.

See also:
www.allbeautyproducts.com – excellent site from
   the Allcures camp.
www.beauty4you.co.uk – slow and not very up to date.
www.beautynaturals.com – attractive all round
   beauty site.
www.beautyserve.com – home of the Guild of
   Professional Beauty Therapists.

www.beautyspy.com – a German company with a nice
site and a good range, all the prices are in Euros but
it seems good value, watch out for the shipping costs
though.

www.benefitcosmetics.com – trendy cosmetics from
the US, worth it to be different…

www.cosmetics.com – American skincare specialists.

www.folica.com – great site on hair care.

www.skinstore.com – good looking site selling
premium skincare products.

www.stillroom.com – 100% natural cosmetics, the
site is slow and not that easy on the eye.

The High Street online

www.bodyshop.co.uk
ISSUES, SELF-ESTEEM AND COSMETICS

ORIGIN UK · · · · · Balancing the rights of the under-privileged with the
INFO ✓✓✓✓✓ demands of a commercial cosmetics company. There
EASE ✓✓✓✓ is good product information but you can't buy online.

www.lush.co.uk
SOAP WITHOUT THE SCENT

ORIGIN UK · · · · · Lush offer a wide range of soaps and associated
INFO ✓✓✓✓ products from their site, it's easy to shop and if you
VALUE ✓✓✓✓ like their soap but find the smell of the high street
EASE ✓✓✓✓ shops over powering, then it's perfect. Postage &
packing starts at £2.95.

See also:

www.spacenk.co.uk – nicely designed store featuring
their excellent cosmetics.

www.wellbeing.com – strong offering from Boots,
easier to shop than the real store!

Books and Booksellers

Books were the first products to be sold in volume over the Internet, and their success has meant that there are many online booksellers, all boasting about the speed of their service and how many titles they can get. In the main, the basic service is the same wherever you go, just pick the bookshop that suits you.

www.bookbrain.co.uk

BEST PRICES FOR BOOKS

ORIGIN UK
INFO ✓✓✓✓✓
EASE ✓✓✓✓

All you do is type in the title of the book and Bookbrain will search out the online store that is offering it the cheapest (including postage). You then click again to get taken to the store to buy the book – simple. It's also worth checking out the American site **www.bestbookbuys.com**

www.amazon.co.uk

MORE THAN JUST A BOOKSTORE

ORIGIN UK
INFO ✓✓✓✓✓
VALUE ✓✓✓
EASE ✓✓✓✓

Amazon is the leading online bookseller and most online stores have followed their formula of combining value with recommendation. Amazon has spent much on providing a wider offering than just books and now has sections for music, gifts, travel, games, software and DVD/video. It also offers an auction service, there's an excellent kids' section, aimed at parents and you can download e-books which can be read on your PC or handheld computer. There are also auctions and zshops where Amazon act as a guarantor for the stores it recommends. For books, there are better prices elsewhere, although they have the odd very good offer. See also **www.waterstones.co.uk** who have abandoned their site in favour of Amazon, as has Borders **www.borders.com**

www.bol.com

THE EURO-BOOKSELLER

ORIGIN UK/EUROPE
INFO ✓✓✓✓✓
VALUE ✓✓✓
EASE ✓✓✓✓

Owned by Bertlesmann the German media giant, you can get access to books in seven European countries. Slightly dull, it appeals to the true book lover, with lots of recommendations but recently they've increased the number of offers. Like Amazon it has expanded to include music, video, DVD and games, and you can also download audio books.

www.bookshop.co.uk
THE INTERNET BOOKSHOP

ORIGIN UK
INFO ✓✓✓✓
VALUE ✓✓✓✓
EASE ✓✓✓✓

Owned by W.H.Smith, this follows the usual Internet bookshop pattern, but it is slightly clearer with a variety of offers. Also sells videos, CDs and games, with links to other magazines and, unusually, stationery.

www.ottakars.co.uk
RECOMMENDS ONLY

ORIGIN UK
INFO ✓✓✓✓
EASE ✓✓✓✓

Ottakars' site is clear and easy to use with some nice personal touches; it offers a mix of store information, recommendation, competitions and they offer free online magazines on a variety of genres that are very entertaining. There's even a web page for each store giving information on the locale and events. There are no facilities to buy books from the site.

http://bookshop.blackwell.co.uk
FOR ACADEMICS AND THE SERIOUS MINDED

ORIGIN UK
INFO ✓✓✓✓✓
VALUE ✓✓✓
EASE ✓✓✓✓

Blackwells are best known for academic and professional books, but their site offers much more, with the emphasis on recommendation and help finding the right book rather than value for money. For more academic books, a good place to try is **www.studentbookworld.com** or **www.swotbooks.co.uk**

www.countrybookshop.co.uk
YOUR LOCAL BOOKSHOP

ORIGIN UK
INFO ✓✓✓✓✓
VALUE ✓✓✓✓
EASE ✓✓✓✓

A small bookseller attempting to take on the corporate giants and largely succeeding if this site is anything to go by. It's very comprehensive and although it may not offer the cheapest books it's easier and more enjoyable to use than many sites. Another triumph of content and good design is at the Book Pl@ce **www.thebookplace.com** who offer the usual online bookshop but with the addition of a magazine devoted to books and an 'Ask a Bookseller' facility if you can't decide what you want.

www.bn.com
THE WORLD'S BIGGEST BOOKSELLER

ORIGIN	US
INFO	✓✓✓✓✓
VALUE	✓✓✓
EASE	✓✓✓✓

Barnes and Noble's site boasts more books than any other online bookseller. In style it follows the other bookshops with an American bias, and looks very similar to Amazon. It has a good out-of-print service; you can also buy software, prints and posters as well as magazines and music. Unusual features include an e-book shop and their online university where you can take courses in anything from business to learning a language.

www.bookpeople.co.uk
INCREDIBLE DISCOUNTS

ORIGIN	UK
INFO	✓✓✓
VALUE	✓✓✓✓✓
EASE	✓✓✓✓

Offers a limited range of discounted books with up to 75% off the r.r.p. It's strong on children's titles and certain types of fiction, but low on recommendations. Some books vary from shop editions – using cheaper paper or are paperback editions. Delivery is free if you spend over £25, plus point-based loyalty scheme.

See also www.etsp.co.uk and www.worldbooks.co.uk both from the same company, offering large discounts but as they are book clubs you have to commit to further purchases to get the great offers in the first place.

www.powells.com
MASSIVE

ORIGIN	US
INFO	✓✓✓✓✓
VALUE	✓✓✓
EASE	✓✓✓

A huge and impressive site which is well designed and relatively easy to use, Powells seems to occupy most of Portland in Oregon and for once the cost of shipping isn't prohibitive for UK customers. A good place to go if you're looking for something unusual.

www.abebooks.com
ADVANCED BOOK EXCHANGE

ORIGIN	US
INFO	✓✓✓✓✓
EASE	✓✓✓

A network of some 10,000 independent booksellers from around the world claiming access to 40 million used, rare, and out-of-print books, just use the excellent search engine to find your book and they'll direct you to the nearest bookseller.

www.literature-awards.com

BOOK AWARDS

ORIGIN US
INFO ✓✓✓✓
EASE ✓✓✓✓

A comprehensive listing of the major book awards throughout the world, who won them and why they exist.

http://classics.mit.edu

THE CLASSICS ONLINE

ORIGIN US
INFO ✓✓✓✓✓
EASE ✓✓✓✓

A superb resource offering over 440 free books to print or download, there's also a search facility and help with studying.

www.bibliomania.com

WORLD LITERATURE ONLINE

ORIGIN UK
INFO ✓✓✓✓✓
VALUE ✓✓✓
EASE ✓✓✓✓

Another superb resource, Bibliomania has changed to a more commercial and attractive site. You can search the entire site for quotes, for a specific book, get help with research or subscribe to the magazine. There's also a shop which is well categorised with excellent use of reviews and biographies.

www.shakespeare.sk

COMPLETE WORKS

ORIGIN US
INFO ✓✓✓✓✓
EASE ✓✓✓✓

This is a straightforward site featuring the complete writings of Shakespeare, including biographical details and a glossary explaining the language of the time.

http://promo.net/pg/

PROJECT GUTENBERG

ORIGIN US
INFO ✓✓✓✓✓
EASE ✓✓✓✓

I can't think why I've missed this out of the guide so far, it's one of the most famous Internet projects ever and one of the first web sites to post free e-books. There are over 6000 listed. You can't do it justice in a small review, suffice to say it's well worth a visit for any book lover.

www.booklovers.co.uk

QUALITY SECOND-HAND BOOKS

ORIGIN UK
INFO ✓✓✓✓✓
EASE ✓✓✓✓

If you can't find the book you want, then this is worth a try. There is an excellent search facility or you can leave them a request. They give a quote if you want to sell a book or arrange a swap. There's also an events listing for book fairs. If you can't find what you're looking for here it's worth checking out three very good sites www.shapero.com www.bookfinder.com and www.bibliofind.com (part of Amazon) who all have very fast search facilities. www.hp-bookfinders.co.uk are also worth a look.

www.cool-reads.co.uk

CHILDREN'S BOOK REVIEWS

ORIGIN UK
INFO ✓✓✓✓✓
EASE ✓✓✓✓

Books for 10- to 15-year olds, reviewed by 10- to 15-year-olds. An outstanding site both for its design and content. The books are well categorised and reviewed using a star rating system. If you're stuck for something to read or give then a trip here is well worthwhile. There are also games, quizzes and chat.

www.achuka.co.uk

CHILDREN'S BOOKS

ORIGIN UK
INFO ✓✓✓✓✓
EASE ✓✓✓✓

Achuka are specialists in children's books and offer a comprehensive listing of what's available from a fairly boring site. There's plenty of information on the latest news and awards as well as reviews, author interviews, a chat section and links to booksellers. For shopping you are directed to Amazon.

Other children's book sites:

www.carolhurst.com – good design and great for book reviews.

www.childrensbookshop.com – very traditional site from a shop based in Hay on Wye.

www.ucalgary.ca/~dkbrown/ – home of the excellent Children's Literature Web Guide.

www.ukchildrensbooks.co.uk – basically a list of links to sites listed by author, illustrator, publisher and a miscellaneous section.

www.wordpool.co.uk – good advice on what to read.

www.wordsofdiscovery.com – a children's bookshop that stocks books aimed at giving children a positive and more spiritual view on life.

www.worldbookday.com – find out about this great event that happens every March.

www.audiobooks.co.uk

THE TALKING BOOKSHOP

ORIGIN UK
INFO ✓✓✓✓✓
EASE ✓✓✓✓

Specialists in books on tape, they have around 6,000 titles in stock and can quickly get another 10,000. They also stock CDs but no MP3 yet. Search the site by author or reader, as well as by title. There are some offers, but most stock is at full price with delivery being £2 per order. Also uses the address www.talkingbooks.co.uk

See also www.isis-publishing.co.uk who offer thousands of unabridged audio books, and more in the way of CDs, but for a really unusual audio experience go to www.totallyword.com

www.bookbrowser.com

BOOK REVIEWS

ORIGIN US
INFO ✓✓✓✓✓
EASE ✓✓✓

A site offering over 8,000 book reviews and author interviews, albeit fiction oriented. It's a little cluttered but makes for an interesting browse. For participation in over 1,000 online reading groups go to www.readinggroupguides.com

www.bookaid.org

BOOKS FOR CHARITY

ORIGIN US
INFO ✓✓✓✓✓
EASE ✓✓✓

A charity dedicated to giving unwanted books to places where books are scarce and needed. Find out about their activities and how you can get involved.

Book specialists

The following sites specialise in one form or genre of book:

www.compman.co.uk – computer manuals.
www.crimeboss.com – crime comic books.
www.firstbookshop.com – one of the few to offer book tokens.
www.lotrfanclub.com – Lord of the Rings fanclub.
www.poems.com – home of Poetry Daily.
www.poetrybooks.co.uk – the Poetry Book Society.
www.stanfords.co.uk – excellent site from the UK's leading travel and map retailers.
www.swotbooks.co.uk – low cost books for clever dicks.

Resources for writers

www.author.co.uk

FOR AUTHORS EVERYWHERE

ORIGIN UK
INFO ✓✓✓✓✓
EASE ✓✓✓

A good place to start if you think you've got a book in you (haven't we all?) with sections, articles and links to help. Worth a visit even for experienced authors. With a slightly messy site **www.writersservices.com** offers just as much if not more help and advice.

See also:
www.thenewwriter.com – online magazine for writers.
www.theromancereader.com – lots of romantic reviews and links.
www.wordpool.co.uk – writing for children.

Cars

Whether you want to buy a car, check out your insurance or even arrange a service, it can all be done on the Net. If you want to hire a car see page 443.

Information and motoring organisations

www.dvla.gov.uk

DRIVER AND VEHICLE LICENSING AGENCY

ORIGIN UK
INFO ✓✓✓✓✓
VALUE ✓✓✓
EASE ✓✓✓✓

Excellent for the official line in motoring, the driver's section has details on penalty points, licence changes and medical issues. The vehicles section goes through all related forms and there's also a 'What's New' page. It's clearly and concisely written throughout and information is easy to find.

www.smmt.co.uk

SOCIETY OF MOTOR MANUFACTURERS &TRADERS

ORIGIN UK
INFO ✓✓✓✓
EASE ✓✓✓✓

The SMMT support the British motor industry by campaigning and informing the trade and public alike. Here you can get information on topics like the motor show and the tax regime based on exhaust emissions as well as links to other industry sites.

www.theaa.co.uk

THE AA

ORIGIN UK
INFO ✓✓✓✓✓
EASE ✓✓✓

A very comprehensive motoring site with a route planner, new and used car info, travel information, insurance quotes, shop and a car data checking facility.

www.rac.co.uk

THE RAC

ORIGIN UK
INFO ✓✓✓✓
VALUE ✓✓✓✓
EASE ✓✓✓✓

A much clearer site than The AA's, with a very good route planner and traffic news service. There's also information about buying a car, getting the best finance and insurance deals and a small shop.

www.greenflag.co.uk

GREEN FLAG

ORIGIN UK
INFO ✓✓✓✓✓
EASE ✓✓✓✓

The usual route planner and car buying advice all packaged on a nice looking and very green site, there's a particularly good section on European travel and motoring advice.

See also **www.internationalbreakdown.com** who offer a wide range of cover across the UK and Europe.

www.autoindex.org

WORLD CAR CATALOGUE

ORIGIN US
INFO ✓✓✓✓✓
EASE ✓✓✓✓

An amazing directory of the world's car makers illustrated by some 35,000 pictures. There is detailed information on each manufacturer and what they produce. You can search by maker, country, category or body style.

www.carsurvey.org

CAR REVIEWS BY THEIR OWNERS

ORIGIN UK
INFO ✓✓✓✓✓
EASE ✓✓✓✓

Don't let the basic design fool you, this is an impressive collection of reviews on hundreds of cars, by those most important people – their owners. It's easily searchable and genuinely useful if you're looking for unbiased opinion.

TV tie-in sites

www.topgear.beeb.com

TOP GEAR

ORIGIN UK
INFO ✓✓✓✓
VALUE ✓✓✓
EASE ✓✓✓✓

A new look site to go along with the new TV series, it has everything you'd expect along with features on new and used cars, competitions, classifieds and a shop. See also **www.bbc.co.uk/lifestyle/motoring/** which is great for advice on buying and owning.

www.4car.co.uk

DRIVEN

ORIGIN UK
INFO ✓✓✓✓
EASE ✓✓✓✓

News, sport, reviews, advice, chat and games – it's all here, and you can find out what's been and is being featured on each of their main motoring programmes.

www.channel5.co.uk/5thgear

5TH GEAR

ORIGIN UK
INFO ✓✓✓
EASE ✓✓✓✓

All the old Top Gear presenters seem to have washed up here which is no bad thing, there's plenty of advice, news and articles from them.

Traders, magazines and buying guides

www.parkers.co.uk

REDUCING THE GAMBLE

ORIGIN UK
INFO ✓✓✓✓✓
EASE ✓✓✓✓✓

The premier buying guide with a premier site, this covers all the information you'll need to select the right car for you. There are five sections:
Pricing – a complete list of cars from 1982 and what you should be paying.
Choosing – advice on the right car for you.
Buying – with details of used cars and finance deals.
Owning – insurance, warranties and advice on how to sell.
Advice – legal, important contacts and chat.

www.autoexpress.co.uk

THE BEST MOTORING NEWS AND INFORMATION

ORIGIN UK
INFO ✓✓✓✓✓
EASE ✓✓✓✓

Massive database on cars, with motoring news and features on the latest models, you can check prices too. It also has classified ads and a great set of links. You have to register to get access to most of the information; lots of advertising makes the site a bit annoying to use.

www.whatcar.co.uk

BRITAIN'S NUMBER 1 BUYER'S GUIDE

ORIGIN UK
INFO ✓✓✓✓
EASE ✓✓✓✓

A neatly packaged, one-stop shop for cars with sections on buying, selling, news, features and road tests, the classified section has thousands of cars and an easy-to-use search facility.

www.carnet.co.uk

ONLINE CAR MAGAZINE

ORIGIN UK
INFO ✓✓✓✓✓
EASE ✓✓✓✓

Car Net is a well designed and fun site with the latest news and new car reviews as well as feature micro-sites and links to deals on cars and insurance, statistics (on over 6,000 cars) and classifieds. You can also visit the specialist chat sections and have a go at the trivia quizzes.

www.hoot-uk.com

IT'S A HOOT!

ORIGIN UK
INFO ✓✓✓✓
EASE ✓✓✓✓

A fun, simple site with a marque-by-marque news listing and the latest headlines. There are also sections with car tests, some good writing and chat at the aptly named 'Gas Station'.

www.carkeys.co.uk

INFORMATION SERVICE STATION

ORIGIN UK
INFO ✓✓✓✓
EASE ✓✓✓✓

A wide-ranging magazine-style site with lots of data on current and new models as well as launch reviews and motoring news.

www.womanmotorist.com

MOTORING ISN'T JUST FOR MEN

ORIGIN UK
INFO ✓✓✓✓
EASE ✓✓✓✓

A well laid out and interesting magazine-style site that dispels the myth that motoring is just for men. Lots of advice, buying information, a glossary and car reviews.

www.testcar.com

TEST REPORTS

ORIGIN UK
INFO ✓✓✓✓
EASE ✓✓✓✓

With test reports on a large number of cars and free Internet access, this site is very useful if you're not sure what to buy. It's also got classified ads and an irreverent column called 'Let's be Frank'. See also the new car review site www.new-car-net.co.uk which is attractive and has a good car magazine. A good feature is that you can compare up to three car specifications at the same time.

www.motortrak.com

USED CAR SEARCH

ORIGIN UK
INFO ✓✓✓✓
EASE ✓✓✓✓✓

A hi-tech site where, in theory, you can find the right used car. Just follow the search guidelines and up pops your ideal car! It's easy to use and very fast.

www.autobytel.co.uk

WORLD'S LEADING CAR BUYING SERVICE

ORIGIN US/UK
INFO ✓✓✓✓✓
VALUE ✓✓✓✓
EASE ✓✓✓✓

The easy way to buy a car online, just select the model you want then follow the online instructions, they've improved information on used and nearly new cars and will get quotes from local dealers. All cars featured have detailed descriptions and photos. There's also financial information and aftercare service.

www.eurekar.com

SAVE MONEY BY IMPORTING FROM EUROPE

ORIGIN UK
INFO ✓✓✓✓
VALUE ✓✓✓✓✓
EASE ✓✓✓✓

Eurekar is a venture set up by the ISP Totalise to import cheaper right-hand drive cars from Europe. They claim to save up to 40% off UK prices. The choice of cars is limited, but all are inspected by Green Flag and have a warranty. Totalise offer quotes inclusive of VAT, delivery and duties.

www.oneswoop.co.uk
SMART WAY TO BUY

ORIGIN	UK
INFO	✓✓✓✓
VALUE	✓✓✓✓
EASE	✓✓✓✓

A straightforward and very popular site that concentrates on making the process of importing and buying a car from Europe as painless as possible. You can choose a car through one of three methods: buy what's available quickly; have a bit more choice; or be really picky. There are also some good special offers and a finance section.

www.jamjar.com
DIRECT LINE

ORIGIN	UK
INFO	✓✓✓✓
VALUE	✓✓✓✓✓
EASE	✓✓✓

One of the most hyped sites for car buying, Jam Jar is a big investment for Direct Line Insurance and they want to make it work well. The design is OK, and if you persevere there are some fantastic offers and they're also improving the service by branching into other merchandise related to driving such as personal leasing and insurance.

For more car buying information and cars for sale try:

http://uk.cars.yahoo.com – the excellent Yahoo has a used car search engine, specialist car database and directory.

www.autolocate.co.uk – great for links, good new car guide and review section, also good for used cars.

www.autopoint.ie – Ireland's leading online car retailer and auction house.

www.autoseek.co.uk – thousands of cars for sale, great for links.

www.autotrader.co.uk – claiming to be Britain's biggest car showroom with 200,000 listed. Nice, clear design.

www.broadspeed.com – car import specialists with a nicely designed and fast site.

www.carseller.co.uk – free advertising if selling and good links.

www.carsource.co.uk – great for data and online quotes, lots of cars for sale.

www.carsupermarkets.co.uk – a useful list of the UK's car supermarkets with lots of information and how to find them.

www.contracthireandleasing.co.uk – a portal site for all the UK's contact and leasing companies.

www.fish4cars.co.uk – over 250,000 cars on their database, plus hundreds of other vehicles. Comprehensive.

www.importanewcar.co.uk – good site if you fancy importing a car from Europe, they help you all the way and there's the potential to save wads of cash in the process.

www.motability.co.uk – the scheme that helps disabled people become more mobile.

www.showroom4cars.com – bright, brash and fast.

www.tins.co.uk – sophisticated and with a large selection of new and used cars, not always the cheapest though.

www.topmarques.co.uk – luxury vehicles only, some 6,000 for sale.

www.vanbuy.co.uk – vans and more vans of all shapes and sizes.

www.virgincars.com – good savings and speedy delivery, nice design and good features such as a car servicing service.

www.wannavan.com – specialist in supplying vans for business and personal use.

www.carpricecheck.com

WHERE TO GET THE BEST DEAL

ORIGIN UK	If you can't be bothered with trawling around the
INFO ✓✓✓✓	different car dealers, just put in the model you want
EASE ✓✓✓✓	and after you've given a few details 'Car Price Check'
	will get back to you with the best deal. See also the car
	price checker at **www.uk.kelkoo.com**

www.hpicheck.com

DON'T BE RIPPED OFF...

ORIGIN UK	Before you buy a second-hand car it's wise to pay out
INFO ✓✓✓✓✓	£35.95 on an HPI check which will tell you about
VALUE ✓✓✓✓	what mileage the car should have, whether it's been in
EASE ✓✓✓✓	an accident or damaged and also if there's any
	outstanding finance against it.

Car registrations

WWW.DVLA-SOM.CO.UK

CHERISHED AND PERSONALISED NUMBERS

ORIGIN UK
INFO ✓✓✓✓
VALUE ✓✓✓
EASE ✓✓✓✓

Here's the first port of call if you want that special number plate. They sell by auction but there's plenty of help and you search for un-issued, select registrations in both new and old styles. Order over the phone using their hotline.

For more sites try:
www.alotofnumberplates.co.uk – good search engine, over 5 million combinations.
www.statreg.co.uk – lots of cheap plates.
www.newreg.co.uk – the first online directory of cherished registration marks.

Insurance

Most of the general finance sites (page 122) and motoring organisations (page 45) will offer links to insurance companies, but these are worth a try.

www.easycover.com

CAR INSURANCE

ORIGIN UK
INFO ✓✓✓✓
EASE ✓✓✓✓

Quotes from a large number of insurance suppliers, you just fill in the form, and they get back to you with a quote.

See also:
www.cheapest-motor-insurance.co.uk
www.eaglestar.co.uk
www.swinton.co.uk
www.diamond.co.uk and **www.girlmotor.co.uk** – specialists in insurance for women drivers who are statistically a safer bet.

Looking after and repairing your car

www.ukmot.com
M.O.T.

ORIGIN UK
INFO ✓✓✓✓
EASE ✓✓✓✓✓

Find your nearest M.O.T. test centre, get facts about the test and what's actually supposed to be checked, there's also a reminder service. You can also run an HPI check from the site and find out about the foibles of specific models.

www.carcareclinic.com
LOOKING AFTER YOUR CAR

ORIGIN UK
INFO ✓✓✓✓
EASE ✓✓✓

If you need advice with car repairs or faults, then help is at hand here. There are discussion forums on all sorts of problems and, if you post a message or ask for advice, there's always someone to answer. They also provide a glossary of terms and a good set of links. See also **www.autosite.com/garage/garmenu.asp** which is from a large American site, here you can find a maintenance encyclopedia.

www.haynes.co.uk
HAYNES MANUALS

ORIGIN UK
INFO ✓✓✓✓
EASE ✓✓✓✓

Unfortunately they've stopped the download service, so now you have to buy the books – there's 2,500 available so there should be one for you.

Car accessories and kits

www.kitcars.org
BUILD YOUR OWN

ORIGIN UK
INFO ✓✓✓✓
EASE ✓✓✓✓

All you need to know about kit cars, this site is excellent for links, information, pictures and classified ads for all things to do with them. It was being updated when we visited so you could also try **www.kitcar.com** and **www.kitcars.com** two big American sites truly devoted to the subject.

www.autofashion.co.uk

ACCESSORISE YOUR CAR

ORIGIN	UK
INFO	✓✓✓✓
VALUE	✓✓✓
EASE	✓✓✓✓

An entertaining site where you can buy body kits and accessories for many makes of car, including custom made. See also Motech at **www.motech.uk.com** who specialise more in performance enhancement.

www.caraudiocentre.com

IN CAR AUDIO SYSTEMS

ORIGIN	UK
INFO	✓✓✓✓
VALUE	✓✓✓✓
EASE	✓✓✓✓

Here you can get loads of advice and offers on a wide range of stereos with a price promise and low delivery costs. See also **www.toade.com** who have a highly interactive site and can also supply security, multi-media and navigation equipment on top of audio, and **www.incar-discount.co.uk** who specialise in CD changers.

See also:

www.autostore.co.uk – specialists in car storage solutions, slow site though.

www.caralarms-security.co.uk – every type of car alarm and security device.

www.gttowing.co.uk – for tow bars, roof racks and trailers, good site.

Specialist car sites

www.classicmotor.co.uk

FOR CLASSIC CARS

ORIGIN	UK
INFO	✓✓✓✓✓
EASE	✓✓✓

By far the best classic car site. Design wise it's a jumble (it's better to use the no frames version), but it's comprehensive, including clubs, classifieds and books; here you can buy anything from a car to a headlight bulb.

See also:

www.classic-car-directory.com which is a well categorised links site.

www.motorbase.com – a growing site with lots of potential, good for links but a little slow.

www.vintage-car-world.com – a German owned site offering news, event information and classifieds.

www.pistonheads.com

SPEED MATTERS

ORIGIN UK
INFO ✓✓✓✓
EASE ✓✓✓✓

Pistonheads is a British site dedicated to the faster side of motoring and is great for reviews of the latest cars and chat. It's passionate and very informative.

www.krbaker.demon.co.uk/britcars

HISTORY OF BRITISH CARS TO 1960

ORIGIN UK
INFO ✓✓✓✓
EASE ✓✓✓

An amateur site with a good make-by-make history of the British car industry, it includes a glossary and information on tax and other historical references. Unfortunately it's not well illustrated.

www.conceptcar.co.uk

AUTOMOTIVE DESIGN

ORIGIN UK
INFO ✓✓✓✓
EASE ✓✓✓✓

A really interesting, comprehensive and well laid out site devoted to car design and new concepts, it's great for links and you can tell that it's used by the industry itself.

Learning to drive

www.learners.co.uk

LEARNER'S DIRECTORY

ORIGIN UK
INFO ✓✓✓✓
EASE ✓✓✓✓

The point of this site is to help you find the right driving school, just type in your postcode and the schools will be listed along with helpful additional information such as whether they have a female instructor or that they train for motorway driving. There is plenty of supplementary information on things like theory tests and how to buy a car.

www.2pass.co.uk

THEORY AND PRACTICAL TESTS

ORIGIN UK
INFO ✓✓✓✓✓
EASE ✓✓✓✓

A learner driver's dream, this site helps with your tests in giving advice, mock exams plus other interesting snippets of information such as why the British drive on the left. There are also articles on driving abroad, on motorbikes and driving automatics. There's also plenty of fun with top stories, even poems and crash of the month!

www.driving-tests.co.uk
THE DSA

ORIGIN UK
INFO ✓✓✓✓
EASE ✓✓✓✓

Get the official line from the Driving Standards Agency where you can book an online driving theory test, get advice for learners and instructors and learn about government schemes to promote better driving. For the Highway Code faithfully reproduced as a website go to www.highwaycode.gov.uk

www.iam.org.uk
INSTITUTE OF ADVANCED MOTORISTS

ORIGIN UK
INFO ✓✓✓✓
EASE ✓✓✓✓

A site from IAM to give you all the encouragement you need to become an advanced driver.

Driving issues

www.speed-trap.co.uk
THE SPEED TRAP BIBLE

ORIGIN UK
INFO ✓✓✓✓✓
EASE ✓✓✓✓

While not condoning speeding, this site gives the low down on speed traps, the law and links to police forces. There's even data on the types of cameras used and advice on dealing with the courts and police. However, remember that they are sponsored by a speed trap detector company. See also www.ukspeedcameras.co.uk

www.parkingticket.co.uk
PARKING PROBLEMS

ORIGIN UK
INFO ✓✓✓✓
EASE ✓✓✓✓✓

This site gives details of parking regulation and free advice on how to challenge a parking ticket that you feel has been issued unfairly. For those wanting up to date information on how to keep one step ahead of over-zealous parking attendants there is a free monthly e-zine.

www.abd.org.uk
CAMPAIGNING FOR THE DRIVER

ORIGIN UK
INFO ✓✓✓✓
EASE ✓✓✓✓

The Association of British Drivers aims to be the lobbying voice of beleaguered drivers in the UK. Here you can find out about their campaigns against speed traps, speed limits, the environment and the road infrastructure.

www.rospa.co.uk/cms/

ROYAL SOCIETY FOR THE PREVENTION OF ACCIDENTS

ORIGIN UK
INFO ✓✓✓✓✓
EASE ✓✓✓✓

An excellent site from ROSPA with loads of information about road safety with fact sheets available on most issues and problems that affect every driver and pedestrian. See also www.cic.cranfield.ac.uk where all the crash testing goes on.

www.reportroadrage.co.uk

ROAD RAGE ISSUES

ORIGIN UK
INFO ✓✓✓✓✓
EASE ✓✓✓✓

A site supported by the RAC that looks into every aspect of road rage, including its causes and how to prevent it. There's lots of advice, stories and information to help you become a safer and calmer driver.

www.cclondon.com

LONDON CONGESTION CHARGES

ORIGIN UK
INFO ✓✓✓✓
EASE ✓✓✓✓

All you need to know about the congestion charge and how to pay it.

Celebrities

Find your favourite celebrities and their web sites using these sites. A word of caution though – there are many celebrity search engines available on the web and while it's easy to find your favourite, it's also very easy to unwittingly access adult-orientated material through them.

www.celeblink.com

LINKS TO THE STARS

ORIGIN US
INFO ✓✓✓✓✓
EASE ✓✓✓✓

Just about the best celebrity directory in terms of lack of advertising and dodgy links. There's also some good articles, gossip and entertainment news.

www.celebhoo.com

FOR EVERYTHING CELEBRITY

ORIGIN US
INFO ✓✓✓✓
EASE ✓✓✓✓

A very good fan site directory plus information, birthdays, chat and gossip.

www.peoplenews.com

WHERE GOSSIP IS GOOD FOR YOU

ORIGIN US
INFO ✓✓✓✓
EASE ✓✓✓✓

The place to go for breaking celebrity news with sections on music and the movies, chat and where the rich and famous hang out.

www.celebrityemail.com

E-MAIL THE STARS

ORIGIN US
INFO ✓✓✓
EASE ✓✓✓✓

E-mail addresses to over 22,000 of the world's most famous people. It's quite biased towards Americans but give it a try anyway, you might get a reply.

www.debretts.co.uk

POSH CELEBRITY GOSSIP

ORIGIN UK
INFO ✓✓✓✓✓
EASE ✓✓✓✓

An excellent site from Debretts who have been tracking the lives of celebrities for many years longer than the likes of *OK* and *Hello*. There are sections on people in the news plus a good celebrity search engine. There are also sections on the royal family, a guide to the season, charities and a fun search section where you can match birthdays.

www.hellomagazine.com

THE WORLD IN PICTURES

ORIGIN UK
INFO ✓✓✓✓
EASE ✓✓✓

Hello magazine's web site features pictures and articles from current and previous issues with loads of celebrities. You can't search by celebrity but you can have fun trawling through the pictures.

www.glamourmagazine.co.uk

LOSE YOURSELF IN GLAMOUR

ORIGIN UK
INFO ✓✓✓✓
EASE ✓✓✓

Gossip, fashion, beauty tips, chat, competitions and, of course, celebrities are the mainstay of *Glamour* magazine's site. Its main function though is to plug the real magazine.

www.famousnamechanges.com

WHO WAS WHO

ORIGIN US
INFO ✓✓✓
EASE ✓✓✓✓

Find out what name celebrities where born with and what they changed it to – great for trivia quizzes.

www.amiannoyingornot.com

VOTE FOR MOST ANNOYING CELEBRITIES

ORIGIN US
INFO ✓✓✓
EASE ✓✓✓✓

You can spend ages on this site; it's easy to vote and fun to use. Each celeb gets a page with biographical details and reasons why they could be annoying or not...

www.bbc.co.uk/celebdaq

CELEBRITY STOCK EXCHANGE

ORIGIN UK
INFO ✓✓✓✓
EASE ✓✓✓✓

The BBC's entertaining show on BBC 3 monitors the rise and fall of many celebrities and allocates a 'stock price' to them. Great fun.

Charities

The Internet offers a great opportunity to give to your favourite charity or support a cause dear to your heart. There are so many that we're unable to list them all, but here are some top sites with directories to help you find the ones that interest you. For charity cards see page 195.

www.charitychoice.co.uk

ENCYCLOPAEDIA OF CHARITIES

ORIGIN UK
INFO ✓✓✓✓✓
EASE ✓✓✓✓

A very useful and well-put together directory of charities with a good search facility and a list in over 30 categories, there's also the excellent 'Goodwill Gallery' where you can post up a service or a donation you're willing to give to charity.

www.caritasdata.co.uk

CHARITIES DIRECT

ORIGIN UK
INFO ✓✓✓✓✓
EASE ✓✓✓✓

A support site for charities with information on how to raise funds and run a charity, there's also a good directory of UK charities and you can rank them by expenditure, revenue and fund size.

www.charitycommission.gov.uk
THE CHARITY COMMISSION

ORIGIN UK
INFO ✓✓✓✓✓
EASE ✓✓✓✓

The Charity Commission's mission is to give the public confidence in the integrity of charities in England and Wales, and their site lists over 180,000 charities. There's also lots of advice for charities.

See also:
www.50ways.org – an outstanding American site devoted to ways of giving money to save the world's children from suffering.
www.bcconnections.org.uk – businesses can find out how they can get involved in charity donations and charities can find out how they can get businesses involved in their work.
www.charitychallenge.com – raise money for your chosen charity by taking an adventure holiday through Charity Challenge.
www.thehungersite.com – just one click and you'll donate a cup of food to the world's hungry via registered sponsors, a brilliant idea and one that works – over 300 million cups have been donated to date. There are now sister sites for breast cancer, saving rain forests and animal rescue.
www.makethatdifference.com – similar principle to the previous entry except that donations are made when you visit the sponsor's site making it a little less effective.

www.justgiving.com
GIVE EFFECTIVELY

ORIGIN UK
INFO ✓✓✓✓✓
EASE ✓✓✓✓

A newsy and informative site devoted to making the process of giving to charity as easy as possible whether you're an individual donor, charity or a company. See also **www.allaboutgiving.org** which is especially informative about unusual ways of donating such as using tax and shares.

www.free2give.co.uk
GIVE WHEN YOU SHOP

ORIGIN UK
INFO ✓✓✓✓
VALUE ✓✓✓✓✓
EASE ✓✓✓✓

An excellent service that enables you to donate to charity when you shop online as the participating retailers have agreed to give a percentage of their profits to the charity you select. See also www.ushopugive.co.uk

www.careinternational.org.uk
HELPING THE WORLD'S POOREST

ORIGIN UK
INFO ✓✓✓✓
EASE ✓✓✓✓

Care are all about helping the world's most stricken people, here you can learn about their work and donate. See also www.givewater.org to help get water to where it's most needed and the well named www.sendacow.org.uk who will get livestock to those who really need it in East Africa.

Chat

There are literally thousands of chat sites and rooms on the web covering many different topics. However, this is the area of the Net that people have the most concerns about. There have been loads of cases where people have been tricked into giving out personal information and even arranged unsuitable meetings.

But at its best, a chat program is a great way to keep in contact with friends, especially if they live miles away. So chat wisely by following our top tips for keeping safe.

CHAT – OUR TOP TIPS

1. Be wary, just like you would be if you were visiting any new place.
2. Don't give your e-mail address out without making sure that only the person you're sending it to can read it.
3. People often pretend to be someone they're not when they're chatting; unless you know the person, assume that's the case with anyone you chat with online.
4. Don't meet up with anyone you've met online - keep your online life separate. Chances are they'd be a let down anyway, even if they were genuine.

5. If you like the look of a chat room or site, but you're not sure about it, get a recommendation first.
6. If you want to meet up with friends online, arrange a time and place beforehand.
7. If you don't like someone, just block 'em.
8. Check out the excellent **www.chatdanger.com** (see below) for more info on how to chat safely.

www.chatdanger.com
KEEP SAFE IN CHAT ROOMS

ORIGIN US	A great site devoted to the perils of using chat rooms,
INFO ✓✓✓✓✓	full of advice and sensible information, it can be a little
EASE ✓✓✓✓	slow though, but it's worth persevering.

The following are the major chat sites and programs:

www.aim.com
AOL INSTANT MESSENGER

ORIGIN UK	One of the most popular, it's pretty safe and anyway
INFO ✓✓✓✓	you can easily block people who are a nuisance, or
EASE ✓✓✓✓	just set it up so that only friends can talk to you.

http://web.icq.com
ICQ – I SEEK YOU

ORIGIN US	There are lots of chat rooms here. It's quick and
INFO ✓✓✓✓	easy to use combined with a mobile phone. There
EASE ✓✓✓✓	are lots of features such as games, money advice,
	music and lurve.

http://communities.msn.com/people
MICROSOFT MSN MESSENGER

ORIGIN US	Easy to use but it can be confusing as Microsoft are
INFO ✓✓✓✓	so keen for you to use other parts of their massive site
EASE ✓✓✓✓	you'll often find yourself suddenly transferred. The
	best bet is to customise it so that there's no mistake.

www.mirc.com
IRC – INTERNET RELAY CHAT

ORIGIN US	Recently improved and updated, this remains a
INFO ✓✓✓	straightforward chat program that is easy to use.
EASE ✓✓✓✓	Generally it's been overtaken by the likes of MSN
	and AOL but some web sites may opt to use it.

www.trillian.cc
COMMUNICATE WITH FLEXIBILITY AND STYLE

ORIGIN US
INFO ✓✓✓✓
EASE ✓✓✓✓

Trillian is a newish site that enables connections to all the major chat programs through one interface. The reader looks good and you can personalise it too. An excellent idea that works well.

www.paltalk.com
VERSATILITY

ORIGIN US
INFO ✓✓✓✓
EASE ✓✓✓✓

A feature laden system with everything from video conferencing to instant messaging – all free!

www.habbohotel.com
FOR UK TEENS

ORIGIN UK
INFO ✓✓✓✓
EASE ✓✓✓✓

Lots of recommendation from users has meant the inclusion of this site in the book, flexibility, fun graphics and an excellent monitoring policy make it popular.

Children

There's been a continuing growth in the number of sites in this category. You can save pounds on children's clothes and toys by shopping over the Net; it's easy and the service is often excellent because the sites are put together by people who really care. The Internet is also an excellent way to educate and entertain children. They are fascinated by it and quickly become experts. Listed here are some of the best sites anywhere. For ideas for days out with children see the British travel listings page 434, for educational sites see page 100 and for parenting concerns see page 274.

Shopping for children

www.toy.co.uk
FIND THAT TOY

ORIGIN UK
INFO ✓✓✓✓
EASE ✓✓✓✓

A very useful toy search engine, you can search by type, company or age. Once searched, it lists the toys with details, price and where you can buy it online.

www.elc.co.uk

EARLY LEARNING CENTRE

ORIGIN UK
INFO ✓✓✓✓✓
VALUE ✓✓✓
EASE ✓✓✓✓✓

A well-designed and user-friendly site that offers a wide range of toys for the under-fives in particular, it's strong on character products and traditional toys alike. Delivery costs £2.95 per order and you can expect goods to arrive in 5 days.

www.toymania.com

RAVING TOY MANIAC

ORIGIN UK
INFO ✓✓✓✓✓
VALUE ✓✓
EASE ✓✓✓✓

A toy magazine full of details and news on all the latest toys along with an online shop. It's an enjoyable site to browse, the selection is vast and it's a good place to start if you're looking for something you can't get in the UK. Shipping costs depend on the weight of your order.

www.hamleys.co.uk

FINEST TOY STORE IN THE WORLD

ORIGIN UK
INFO ✓✓✓
VALUE ✓✓✓
EASE ✓✓✓✓

Hamley's has improved its site and you can search for toys by gender, price or age. There's also an okay selection of character areas within the store as well as the more traditional range, which is their main strength. Delivery starts at £4.95 free if you spend over £100.

www.toysrus.co.uk

NOT JUST TOYS

ORIGIN UK/US
INFO ✓✓✓✓
VALUE ✓✓✓✓
EASE ✓✓✓✓

Good site with all the key brands and 'in' things you'd expect – you can even buy a mobile phone. Has links to key toy manufacturer's sites and a sister site called **www.babiesrus.co.uk** which covers younger children. Delivery is £3.50 for the UK.

www.thetoyshop.com

THE ENTERTAINER

ORIGIN UK
INFO ✓✓✓✓
VALUE ✓✓✓✓
EASE ✓✓✓✓

The online spin-off from the Entertainer high street stores; it offers much in the way of bargains and this bright and breezy site is easy to navigate. You can search by toy, age, price or category. Shipping to the UK is £3.50 flat rate while international rates vary.

www.newcron.com

CHARACTER PRODUCTS

ORIGIN UK/US
INFO ✓✓✓✓
VALUE ✓✓✓✓
EASE ✓✓✓✓

Newcron has taken over the Character Warehouse site to produce an online store that offers a wide range of mainstream and unusual character products. You can search by character, product or price; delivery starts at £3.99. See also www.shop4toys.co.uk which has a similar offer.

www.dawson-and-son.com

FOR TRADITIONAL WOODEN TOYS

ORIGIN UK
INFO ✓✓✓✓
VALUE ✓✓
EASE ✓✓✓✓

Specialists in the art of making simple, traditional, wooden toys, Dawson and Son offer a wide range of beautifully made items from rattles to sophisticated games. Delivery depends on the value and weight of order. See also the very well put together www.woodentoysonline.co.uk who have a wide range.

www.outdoortoysdirect.co.uk

LOW PRICES ON OUTDOOR TOYS

ORIGIN UK
INFO ✓✓✓✓✓
VALUE ✓✓✓✓✓
EASE ✓✓✓✓

Excellent value for money with free delivery, a money back guarantee, plus a wide range of goods. The selection consists of everything from trampolines to swings, slides and play houses. To complete your outdoor experience you can always pay a visit to www.kiteshop.co.uk who offer a wide range of kites and advice from an excellent site.

www.krucialkids.com

ALL ABOARD THE KRUCIAL KIDS EXPRESS

ORIGIN UK
INFO ✓✓✓✓
VALUE ✓✓✓
EASE ✓✓✓✓

Annoying name, but not an annoying site. It specialises in developmental toys for children up to eight years old, providing detailed information on the educational value of each of the 200 or so toys. The prices aren't bad either. Delivery is free if you spend over £60. For educational toys see also www.ticktocktoys.co.uk

www.mailorderexpress.com

SHOP IN THE COMFORT OF YOUR HOME

ORIGIN UK
INFO ✓✓✓✓
VALUE ✓✓✓✓
EASE ✓✓✓✓

Excellent toy store with games and models too. Shop by brand or by category, with some good prices and special offers. The design is a little old fashioned but effective nonetheless.

Other toy stores worth a visit are:

www.huggables.co.uk – specialists in teddies and other cute soft toys.

www.modelmegastore.co.uk – excellent for models of all types, especially remote control cars, shipping is good value.

www.orchardtoys.co.uk – specialists in fun, educational toys.

www.theoldtoyshop.com – mainly vintage and collectible toys.

www.totalrobots.com – all sorts of robots, probably one for dads really.

www.toycentre.com – a sparse site with some good prices, most brands represented.

www.toysdirecttoyourdoor.co.uk – good design, specialists in Brio among other things.

www.toys-n-ireland.com – excellent Irish store with some 20,000 lines available.

www.toywiz.com – an American site where you can get unusual and new toys, even those that are no longer produced, toys are generally cheaper but shipping is costly.

Other than toys

www.jojomamanbebe.co.uk

FASHIONABLE MOTHERS AND THEIR CHILDREN

ORIGIN UK
INFO ✓✓✓✓
VALUE ✓✓✓
EASE ✓✓✓✓

Excellent for everything from maternity wear and designer children's clothes to gifts for newborn babies. Also has sections on toys, maternity products and special offers. All the designs are tested and they aim to be comfortable as well as fashionable. Delivery costs £3.50, free if collected from the warehouse in Newport. For babywear go to **www.overthemoon-babywear.co.uk** who include a section on natural fibre clothing with free postage in the UK; while for older children **www.tots2teens.co.uk** is a good bet.

www.gltc.co.uk

THE GREAT LITTLE TRADING COMPANY

ORIGIN UK
INFO ✓✓✓✓✓
VALUE ✓✓✓
EASE ✓✓✓✓

A good looking site offering a wide range of child safety products, furniture and baby equipment, you can search the site by age and by product category. Delivery starts at £3.95.

www.urchin.co.uk

WORTH HAVING A BABY FOR

ORIGIN UK
INFO ✓✓✓✓
VALUE ✓✓✓
EASE ✓✓✓✓

Urchin has some 300 products available: cots and beds, bathtime accessories, bikes, clothes, for baby, travel goods, toys and things for the independent child who likes to personalise their own room. They boast a sense of style and good design, and they succeed. Also have a bargains section. Delivery is £3.95 per order with a next day surcharge of £3.

Things to do

www.mamamedia.com

THE PLACE FOR KIDS ON THE NET

ORIGIN US
INFO ✓✓✓✓
EASE ✓✓✓✓

This versatile site has everything a child and parent could want, there is an excellent selection of interactive games, puzzles and quizzes, combined with a great deal of wit and fun. Best of all it encourages children to communicate by submitting a message and gets them voting on what's important to them. There's a superb 'Grown-ups' section with information on getting the best out of the Net with your children.

www.bonus.com

THE SUPER SITE FOR KIDS

ORIGIN US
INFO ✓✓✓✓✓
EASE ✓✓✓✓✓

Excellent graphics and masses of genuinely good games make a visit to Bonus a treat for all ages. There are quizzes and puzzles, with sections offering a photo gallery, art resource and homework help. Access to the web is limited to a protected environment. Shame about the annoying pop-ups.

www.yucky.com
THE YUCKIEST SITE ON THE INTERNET

ORIGIN US
INFO ✓✓✓✓✓
EASE ✓✓✓✓

Find out how to turn milk into slime or how much you know about worms – yucky lives up to its name. Essentially this is an excellent, fun site that helps kids learn science and biology. There are guides for parents on how to get the best out of the site and links to recommended sites. Try this URL if you can't get access on the usual one **http://yucky.kids.discovery.com**

www.wonka.com
THE WILD WORLD OF WONKA

ORIGIN UK
INFO ✓✓✓✓✓
EASE ✓✓✓✓

Ingenious site sponsored by Nestlé with great illustrations and a fun approach, it has several sections all with lots of interactivity, as well as an online club. There's the Invention Room with lots of trivia, Planet Vermes which is about space, Loompaland takes you into the animal kingdom and so on. You can also send postcards and get involved in competitions.

www.switcheroozoo.com
MAKE NEW ANIMALS

ORIGIN US
INFO ✓✓✓
EASE ✓✓✓

Over 6,500 combinations of animals can be made at this very entertaining web site, you need Shockwave and a decent PC for it to work effectively.

www.magictricks.co.uk
THE UK'S LEADING ONLINE MAGIC TRICKS STORE

ORIGIN UK
INFO ✓✓✓✓✓
EASE ✓✓✓✓

A site chock full of tricks, sets and accompanying equipment. You can send in suggestions for new tricks and even find a magician. There's also a section on TV magicians and a bookstore. See also **www.magicweek.co.uk** which is well-designed but more adult.

Other activity sites worth checking out:
http://web.ukonline.co.uk/conker – The Kids Ark – Join Captain Zeb gathering material on the world, strange animals, myths and facts – before it all disappears.

www.24hourmuseum.org.uk/24kids.html – good quality, (if a little boring) online educational kids' content from the 24-hour Museum site with interactive journeys, a Harry Potter trail and arts activities.

www.alfy.com – excellent for young children, with lots of games and plenty of things to do and see.

www.ex.ac.uk/bugclub – bugs and creepy crawlies for all ages.

www.globalgang.org.uk – a Christian Aid sponsored activity and magazine site mainly covering world issues.

www.headbone.com – part of Bonus with chat and games.

www.hotwheels.com/kids – a good looking, but slow site from a model car maker that has some good features and games.

www.kiddonet.com – download the interactive play area for games and surfing in a safe environment. Masses to do and good links.

www.kids.warnerbros.com – a links page to their children's productions, when you consider what they produce it's a shame they can't do more.

www.kidscastle.si.edu – a pretty average kids educational magazine site from the Smithsonian museum. Useful for homework.

www.kidscom.com – play games, post a message on the message board and write to a pen friend (unfortunately the safe chat lines are open during our night-time). A bit dull.

www.kidsdomain.com – masses to download, from colouring books, music demos and homework help and games. Split into 3 age ranges.

www.kidsjokes.co.uk – over 12,000 jokes...

www.kidskorner.net – great use of cartoons to introduce and play games – stealthily educational.

www.kidsreads.com – an American site all about kids' books, with games and quizzes. Good for young Harry Potter fans.

www.kzone.com.au – excellent activity site from Australia.

www.lego.co.uk – games, product information, adventures with their leading characters, lots of interactive features make this site something of a gem.

www.lemonadegame.com – how much lemonade can you sell? Learn about market forces in this oddly fascinating game.

www.matmice.com – create your own web site home page and add it to the internet the easy way.

www.missdorothy.com – The good looking *Dot Comic*, which has loads of activities and is fun to use. Takes a while to download and you need the latest Flash downloads to get the best out of it.

www.neopets.com – look after a multitude of virtual pets, play games and even trade them.

www.planit4kids.co.uk – activities plus what to do when you're short of ideas. Good design.

TV, book and character sites

www.citv.co.uk
CHILDREN'S ITV

ORIGIN	UK	✓✓✓✓
INFO	✓✓✓✓✓	
EASE	✓✓✓✓	

Keep up-to-date with your favourite programmes and talk to the stars of the shows. There's lots to occupy children here including chat with fellow fans, play games, find something to do, enter a competition, e-mail a friend and join the club.

www.nickjr.com
THE NICKELODEON CHANNEL

ORIGIN	US
INFO	✓✓✓
VALUE	✓✓
EASE	✓✓✓✓

Ideal for under-eights, this has a good selection of games and quizzes to play either with an adult or solo. The 'Red Rocket Store' has an excellent selection of merchandise, but beware of shipping costs. For activities aimed at a wider age range check out www.nick.co.uk where there is chat, gossip, games and plenty of background info on the shows.

www.sesamestreet.com
THE CHILDREN'S TELEVISION WORKSHOP

ORIGIN	US
INFO	✓✓✓✓
VALUE	✓✓✓
EASE	✓✓✓✓

Enter Elmo's world which is very colourful, with lots to do. There are games to play, art and music to create and friends to talk to. There's plenty for parents too.

www.bbc.co.uk/cbbc
CHILDREN'S BBC

ORIGIN UK
INFO ✓✓✓✓
EASE ✓✓✓✓

Lots of activities here, you can catch up on the latest news, play games and find out about the stars of the programs. There are also web guide links to other recommended children's sites. See also **www.bbc.co.uk/cbeebies** which is for the very young with printable colouring pages, stories and games.

www.bbc.co.uk/newsround
KEEP UP TO SPEED

ORIGIN UK
INFO ✓✓✓✓✓
EASE ✓✓✓✓

One of the best bits of CBBC is Newsround, here you can get all the latest news, do quizzes, chat and join their club.

www.disney.com
WHERE THE MAGIC LIVES

ORIGIN US
INFO ✓✓✓✓
VALUE ✓✓✓
EASE ✓✓✓✓

A mega site that is split into eight sections:

1. Entertainment – details of films, activities and a Disney A–Z.
2. Kids Island Home – lots of games and music.
3. Playhouse – games and character sites for younger children.
4. Blast – the online kids' club.
5. Family fun – party planners, recipes and craft ideas.
6. Vacations – Information on the theme parks.
7. Shopping – the Disney store and auctions.
8. Main Street – more retail opportunities.

The British version **www.disney.co.uk** is more compact with less about vacations and more emphasis on activity. You should be aware that it's very commercial with lots of pop-up adverts and we even found it difficult to move on to other sites after loading it, you have to close the browser.

www.cooltoons.com
RUGRATS, STRESSED ERIC AND MORE

ORIGIN UK
INFO ✓✓✓
EASE ✓✓✓✓

Each character has their own section where you can find lots to do and see. There's also an eight-step guide on how to become an animator. The store has all the related merchandise.

www.foxkids.co.uk

FOX TV

ORIGIN UK
INFO ✓✓✓✓
EASE ✓✓✓✓

All the characters and shows are featured on this bright and entertaining site with added extras like a games section, competitions, a sports page and a magazine. There's also a shopping facility where you earn Brix by using the site, they can then be spent on goodies in the 'Boutik'. The graphics can be a little temperamental.

www.aardman.com

HOME OF WALLACE AND GROMMIT

ORIGIN UK
INFO ✓✓✓✓
EASE ✓✓✓✓

This brilliant site takes a while to download but it's worth the wait. There's news on what the team are up to, links to their films, a shop and an inside story on how it all began.

www.gosh.org

HOME OF PETER PAN

ORIGIN UK
INFO ✓✓✓✓
EASE ✓✓✓✓

A good site from Great Ormond Street Hospital's charity with a section devoted to Peter Pan – all proceeds from the sale of the books go to the hospital. There's also lots to do on the site with competitions, links and information about the hospital itself.

www.guinnessrecords.com

GUINNESS WORLD RECORDS

ORIGIN US
INFO ✓✓✓✓✓
EASE ✓✓✓✓

An outstanding site that offers much in the way of entertainment with footage of favourite records and informative sections on key areas of record breaking such as sport, nature, the material world and human achievements.

Here's where the best children's characters and shows hang out:
Action Man – www.actionman.com and
    www.thunderbirdsonline.com
Animal Ark – www.animalark.co.uk
Art Attack – www.artattack.co.uk
Artemis Fowl – www.artemisfowl.co.uk
Bagpuss – www.smallfilms.co.uk/bagpuss
Barbie – www.barbie.com

Batman – www.batmantas.com (animated series)
Batman – www.batmanbeyond.com
Beano – www.beano.co.uk
Bill and Ben – www.bbc.co.uk/cbeebies/character-pages/billandben
Bob the Builder – www.bobthebuilder.org
Boohbahs – www.boohbah.com
Buffy – www.buffy.com and www.buffyguide.com
Danger Mouse – www.dangermouse.org
Dragonball Z – www.dragonballz.com or www.dbzgtlegacy.com
Fimbels – www.bbc.co.uk/cbeebies/fimbles
Goosebumps – www.scholastic.com/goosebumps
Lemony Snicket – www.lemonysnicket.com
Letter Land – www.letterland.com
Mary Kate and Ashley – www.marykateandashley.com
Mr Men – www.mrmen.com
Noddy – www.noddy.com
Paddington – www.paddingtonbear.co.uk
Pokemon – www.pokeland.yorks.net or www.pokemon.com
Roald Dahl – www.roalddahlclub.com
Robot Wars – www.robotwars.co.uk
Sabrina – www.paramount.com/television/sabrina/
Spiderman – www.spiderman.sonypictures.com or www.spiderman.com
Teletubbies – www.teletubbies.com
Thomas the Tank Engine – www.thomasthetankengine.com
Thunderbirds – www.thunderbirdsonline.co.uk
Tintin – www.tintin.be
Toontown – www.toontown.com
Tweenies – www.bbc.co.uk/tweenies
Winnie the Pooh – www.winniethepooh.co.uk
Yu-Gi-Oh – www.yugiohkingofgames.com

Harry Potter

Harry Potter deserves a special mention and with loads of web sites springing up, here are the official ones. You might want to keep checking the Warner Brothers site for information on the next film at http://harrypotter.warnerbros.co.uk

www.bloomsbury.com/harrypotter

WHERE IT ALL BEGAN

ORIGIN UK
INFO ✓✓✓✓
EASE ✓✓✓✓

You have to enter using a secret password known only to witches and wizards everywhere, then you get to find out all about the books, meet JK Rowling and join the Harry Potter club. 'Howlers and Owlers' – e-mail insults and compliments – is great, but don't worry if you're a 'Muggle', all is explained.

www.scholastic.com/harrypotter

HARRY AMERICAN STYLE

ORIGIN US
INFO ✓✓✓✓
EASE ✓✓✓✓

Here's wizard trivia, quizzes, screensavers, information about the books and an interview with JK Rowling, all on a fairly boring web site.

www.mugglenet.com

THE ULTIMATE HARRY POTTER SITE

ORIGIN US
INFO ✓✓✓✓✓
EASE ✓✓✓✓

An outstanding fan site put together by some teenage fans, it has features on the books and the films plus links, games and the latest news. The Wall of Shame is particularly entertaining.

Search engines and site directories

www.yahooligans.com

THE KID'S ONLINE WEB GUIDE

ORIGIN US
INFO ✓✓✓✓
EASE ✓✓✓✓

Probably the most popular site for kids, yahooligans offers parents safety and kids hours of fun. There are games, articles and features on the 'in' characters, education resources and sections on sport, science, computing and TV. It has an American bias. See also **www.ipl.org/div/kidspace/** which is the children's section of the Internet Public Library, useful for homework as well.

www.ajkids.com

ASK JEEVES FOR KIDS

ORIGIN US
INFO ✓✓✓✓
EASE ✓✓✓✓

A search engine aimed at children, it's simple, safe and is excellent for homework enquiries and games.

www.surfmonkey.com

SURFING FOR KIDS

ORIGIN US
INFO ✓✓✓✓
VALUE ✓✓✓
EASE ✓✓✓✓

A very well designed site where you can download the Surf Monkey browser, then your children can surf over 5,000 sites in safety, it's also great for beginners, but it is $3.95 per month.

Competitions

www.loquax.co.uk

THE UK'S COMPETITION PORTAL

ORIGIN UK
INFO ✓✓✓✓✓
EASE ✓✓✓✓

This site doesn't give away prizes but lists the web sites that do. There are hundreds of competitions featured, and if you own a web site they'll even run a competition for you. There are daily updates and special features such as 'Pick of the Prizes' which features the best the web has to offer, with links to the relevant sites.

See also:
www.compaholics.co.uk – competitions and gambling too, heavy on the advertising.
www.myoffers.co.uk – which is a slow site, with as the name suggests lots of offers.
www.theprizefinder.com – offer a wide range of prizes in lots of categories, you have to register though.
www.theprizefinder.com – excellent site, they claim someone actually won £1,000,000 there.

Computers

It's no surprise that the number one place to buy a computer is the Internet. With these sites you won't go far wrong, and it's also worth checking out the price checker sites on page 295 before going shopping and checking the software sites on page 336 Mac users should also check out the section on Apple Macs page 18.

www.itreviews.co.uk

START HERE TO FIND THE BEST

ORIGIN UK
INFO ✓✓✓✓✓
EASE ✓✓✓✓

IT Reviews gives unbiased reports, not only on computer products, but also on software, games and related books. The site has a good search facility and a quick visit may save you loads of hassle when you come to buy. For other excellent information sites try www.zdnet.co.uk or www.cnet.com both have links to good online stores.

www.pcadvisor.co.uk

EXPERT ADVICE IN PLAIN ENGLISH

ORIGIN UK
INFO ✓✓✓✓✓
EASE ✓✓✓✓

A derivative from *PC Advisor* magazine, the site offers much in the way of reviews and information on how to find the best PC. It also allows you to pick up advice from experts on technical queries. There's a games room, a place from which you can download programs and a consumer section where you can air your praises and gripes.

www.pcworld.co.uk

THE COMPUTER SUPERSTORE

ORIGIN UK
INFO ✓✓✓✓
VALUE ✓✓✓✓
EASE ✓✓✓✓

A very strong offering from one of the leading computer stores with lots of offers and star buys. They sell a wide range of electronics from cameras to the expected PCs and peripherals.

www.simply.co.uk

SIMPLY DOES IT

ORIGIN UK
INFO ✓✓✓✓
VALUE ✓✓✓✓
EASE ✓✓✓✓

An award-winning site and company that offers a wide range of PCs and related products, their strengths are speed, quality of service and competitive prices. They also sell mobile phones.

www.dabs.com

500,000 CUSTOMERS LATER...

ORIGIN UK
INFO ✓✓✓✓
VALUE ✓✓✓✓
EASE ✓✓✓✓

One of the most successful online computer product retailers, there are loads of offers and a wide range of goods. It's a big site and not that easy to navigate, but there are rewards for those who persevere in the guise of dabspoints which can be converted to airmiles.

www.tiny.com
LATEST TECHNOLOGY AT UNBEATABLE PRICES

ORIGIN UK
INFO ✓✓✓✓
VALUE ✓✓✓
EASE ✓✓✓✓

A businesslike site that includes all the details you'd need on their range of computers and peripherals for home and office use. Tiny are the UK's largest computer manufacturer and have a history of reliability and good deals. Shipping costs vary according to what you buy and where you live.

Other PC manufacturers' site addresses:
Apple – **www.apple.com**
Dell – **www.dell.co.uk**
Elonex – **www.elonex.co.uk**
Evesham – **www.evesham.com**
Gateway – **www.gateway.com/uk**
Hewlett Packard – **www.hp.com/uk**
Time – **www.timecomputers.com**
Viglen – **www.viglen.co.uk**

Computer accessories and specialist retailers

www.totalpda.co.uk
PERSONAL DIGITAL ASSISTANTS

ORIGIN UK
INFO ✓✓✓✓
VALUE ✓✓✓✓
EASE ✓✓✓✓

Good looking site specialising in PDAs and related products with a wide range and some good bargains. See also **www.expansys.com** which is also very good for bargains.

www.oink-oink.com
CARTRIDGES, REFILLS AND PAPER

ORIGIN UK
INFO ✓✓✓✓
VALUE ✓✓✓✓
EASE ✓✓✓✓

One of many sites specialising in supplying peripheral products, we particularly liked this one because it's fun and some of the proceeds go to supporting the RSPCA. See also **www.ukcra.com** and **www.tonik.co.uk** who both offer good prices and a wide range.

www.cex.co.uk
COMPUTER EXCHANGE

ORIGIN UK
INFO ✓✓✓✓
VALUE ✓✓✓✓
EASE ✓✓✓✓

Computer Exchange buy and sell used electronics, computers and games. The process is pretty straightforward, so if you have an old PC give them a call.

www.pcmech.com

PC MECHANIC

ORIGIN US
INFO ✓✓✓✓✓
EASE ✓✓✓✓✓

Plain English explanations of all the bits that make up a computer, it's easy to follow and use with lots of background information and support. Excellent.

The following sites are useful if you want to keep up with the latest developments, need help when your PC goes wrong or you just need to learn something.

www.compinfo.co.uk – a bewildering number of computer related links all set out in a large directory.

www.driverguide.com – advice on finding and installing the right drivers for your PC.

www.help.com – part of the high quality CNET site it has the most up-to-date information on new products and articles and advice. It assumes some knowledge.

www.maximumpc.co.uk – lots of tutorials, useful programs to download and reviews galore.

www.pcpitstop.com – a host of programs to get your PC running on top form. They can even test how well your PC is running and offer advice on how to improve its performance.

www.wired.com – all the latest news and product information.

Consumer Information and Advice

A new section following requests from readers, these sites help with the latest consumer law and provide answers or give guidance on what to do if you've been wronged.

www.which.net

WHICH MAGAZINE

ORIGIN UK
INFO ✓✓✓✓✓
EASE ✓✓✓✓✓

Excellent spin off from the magazine with everything from consumer advice to product reviews. You need to be a member to get the best out of it.

www.consumers.gov.uk
THE CONSUMER GATEWAY

ORIGIN UK
INFO ✓✓✓✓✓
EASE ✓✓✓✓✓

A consumer advice site run by the government that offers links and information across all the major areas where issues occur from cars, to shopping to home improvements. A good place to start if you have issues you feel strongly about.

See also:

www.adviceguide.org.uk – the old Citizens Advice Bureau offers a wide range of tips and advice on the most common problems and how to solve them, plus how to get in touch if you have specific issues.

www.consumer-rights.org.uk – handy hints and tips all designed for you to get the best service.

www.howtocomplain.com – find out how to make a complaint at this easy to follow site which even provides specially designed forms to make your complaint even more effective.

www.oft.gov.uk – home of the Office of Fair Trading.

Crime

This section was introduced last year and we've added a few more sites in this edition. It is intended to be of help to victims of crime or it may even help solve one. Hopefully you won't need it.

www.police.uk
THE POLICE ONLINE

ORIGIN UK
INFO ✓✓✓✓
EASE ✓✓✓✓

Here you can notify the police of minor crimes and get essential information on the organisation and how it works. There are sections on specific crimes or appeals, recruitment and information on related organisations. The site is easy to navigate and use.

See also:

www.nationalcrimesquad.police.uk – the fight against organised crime.

www.pca.gov.uk – the Police Complaints Authority.

www.fbi.gov – the Federal Bureau of Investigation.

www.cia.gov – the Central Intelligence Agency.
www.interpol.com – the fight against international crime.

www.cjsonline.org
THE CRIMINAL JUSTICE SYSTEM
ORIGIN UK
INFO ✓✓✓✓✓
EASE ✓✓✓

A helpful site that tells what happens when someone gets arrested, and provides information about the trial procedure, how a court works and what you need to do if you're a witness. There's a guide to who does what in the legal profession and a section on related links. See also the Crown Prosecution Service at www.cps.gov.uk

www.crimestoppers-uk.org
KEEP 'EM PEELED
ORIGIN UK
INFO ✓✓✓✓✓
EASE ✓✓✓

Information on the Crimestoppers trust and how you can get involved in their fight against crime with information on the latest campaign and initiatives, links and, of course, their phone number 0800 555 111. See also www.crimereduction.gov.uk which has been set up by the government to become the number one resource for the crime prevention practitioner. It's not there yet, but the site is growing.

www.localhomewatch.co.uk
NEIGHBOURHOOD WATCH
ORIGIN UK
INFO ✓✓✓✓
EASE ✓✓✓✓

A directory of neighbourhood watch schemes by county with advice on preventing crime and how you can set up a neighbourhood watch scheme in your area.

www.victimsupport.com
VICTIM SUPPORT
ORIGIN UK
INFO ✓✓✓✓
EASE ✓✓✓✓

An independent charity that supports the victims of crime throughout the UK with help and advice. It also advises witnesses on the justice system and campaigns for equal opportunities. You can also find out about how you can help or give funds.

www.fraud.org

NATIONAL FRAUD INFORMATION CENTER

ORIGIN UK   Find out about the many ways you can be defrauded
INFO ✓✓✓✓   and how to spot a fraud on the Internet. See also
EASE ✓✓✓✓   **www.fraudbureau.com** and **www.scambusters.com**

www.secureyourmotor.gov.uk

SECURITY TIPS FOR MOTORISTS

ORIGIN UK   Pretty straightforward site detailing the best steps to
INFO ✓✓✓✓   guard against your car, bike or truck being stolen. You
EASE ✓✓✓✓   can take tests to see how secure your car is or test your
         security knowledge.

Cycles and Cycling

See page 435 for cycling holidays and tours and page 349 for information on cycling as a sport.

www.cycleweb.co.uk

THE INTERNET CYCLING CLUB

ORIGIN UK   A great attempt to bring together all things cycling.
INFO ✓✓✓✓✓   Aimed at a general audience rather than cycling as a
VALUE ✓✓✓   sport, it has masses of sections and links on everything
EASE ✓✓✓   from the latest news to clubs, shops and holidays.

www.bikemagic.com

BIKE MAGIC!

ORIGIN UK   There's plenty here on the world of bikes, it has
INFO ✓✓✓✓   forums on hot bike topics, reviews of equipment,
VALUE ✓✓✓   buying advice, classifieds, the latest news, links and an
EASE ✓✓✓   events calendar.

www.bicyclenet.co.uk

UK'S NUMBER 1 ONLINE BICYCLE SHOP

ORIGIN UK   Great selection of bikes and accessories, there's
INFO ✓✓✓✓   also good advice on how to buy the right bike and
VALUE ✓✓✓   assembly instructions on all that they sell. Delivery
EASE ✓✓✓✓   starts at £3.75. See also **www.cyclestuff.co.uk** who
         have a good range of accessories, as does the
         wonderfully named **www.wiggle.co.uk**

See also:

www.a-nelson.dircon.co.uk/cyclingprelycra – cycling as it used to be before the Lycra clad hordes took to the roads, nicely done and with a great nostalgic feel.

www.bikeweek.org.uk – find out about Bike Week which is in mid-June.

www.tandem-club.org.uk – a pretty basic site devoted to the world of the tandem with discussion groups, classifieds, buying advice, events and a newsletter.

Dance

Here are a few sites for those who dance or think they can...

www.danceart.com

DANCE!

ORIGIN US
INFO ✓✓✓✓
EASE ✓✓✓✓

A slightly messy but enthusiastic site centred on the US dance scene, it has lots of links, articles and interviews.

See also:

http://scarecrow.caps.ou.edu/~hneeman/dance_hotlist.html – a hotlist of dance sites.

www.dancebooks.co.uk – where to go for specialist dance titles.

www.dancescape.com – a good Canadian dance magazine site.

www.dancesport.uk.com – the UK ballroom dancing scene covered.

www.folkdancing.org – home of the Folk Dance Association.

www.istd.org – home of the Imperial Society of Teachers of Dancing.

www.pearldata.co.uk/dance/paul/cool.htm – good for dancing-related links.

www.the-ballet.com – a good e-zine all about ballet.

www.young-dancers.org – dedicated to helping teenagers learn to dance.

Dating

Using the Net has become an accepted means to meet people, but be careful about how you go about meeting up; many people aren't exactly honest about their details. If in doubt, err on the side of caution.

www.wildxangel.com

THE LOW DOWN

ORIGIN US	An American site that tells it like it is and gives advice
INFO ✓✓✓✓	about using chat and dating sites, it also gives awards
EASE ✓✓✓	for the best ones and there are links too.

www.uksingles.co.uk

FOR ALL UK SINGLES

ORIGIN UK	Not just about dating, this site is devoted to helping
INFO ✓✓✓✓✓	you get the most out of life. There are several sections:
EASE ✓✓✓	accommodation, sport and activities, holidays, help for

single parents, and listings for matchmaking and dating services. All the companies that advertise in the directories are vetted too.

www.faceparty.com

BIGGEST PARTY ON EARTH

ORIGIN UK	A combination of dating agency, party organiser and
INFO ✓✓✓✓	chat site. You download your details and photo to
EASE ✓✓✓✓	create your own profile, then just join in.

Here are some additional sites, there's not much to choose between them, it's all a matter of taste. All are secure and allow you to browse and participate in relative safety.

www.dateline.co.uk – 30 years experience at the dating game gives Dateline lots of credibility and it's a good site too, easy to use and reassuring.

www.datingdirect.com – claims to be the UK's largest agency with over 450,000 members, the site is not as sophisticated as some, though they seem to have lots of success stories.

www.dinnerdates.com – one of the longest established and most respected dining and social events clubs for unattached single people in the UK; find out how you can get involved here.

www.ivorytowers.net – where unattached alumni and undergraduates from the 'leading' universities get together.

www.love-exchange.co.uk – upmarket profiles for busy professionals, you can chat without revealing your proper e-mail address.

www.match.com – leading site in the US, get your profile matched to someone or join in the chat, there's an excellent magazine too.

www.singles121.com – good site, easy to use with, on the whole, good quality photos.

www.tiggle.com – seven days free registration and a nice site, but you have to register to gain access.

www.udate.com – US site for over 25s only, an attractive site with a good search facility.

www.soyouvebeendumped.com
HOW TO COPE...

ORIGIN UK	An interesting way to help yourself after you've split
INFO ✓✓✓✓	up, lots of advice and help to get you through it all.
EASE ✓✓✓✓	

Disability Help and Information

In this section you'll find some sites which may help if you are disabled or care for someone with a disability. The sites listed are portals, e-zines or general information sites, it's worth checking your local council's site as they tend to have good local information on the help that is available in your area. Thanks should go to David Wilkinson for his help on this section.

www.disability.gov.uk
THE GOVERNMENT'S VIEW

ORIGIN UK	Information and help on rights for the disabled
INFO ✓✓✓	with links to related departments. You can't
EASE ✓✓✓✓	help thinking that there could have been more
	information across a broader spectrum. See
	www.dwp.gov.uk/lifeevent/benefits/index.htm
	for an index of benefits and services available.

www.bcodp.org.uk

THE BRITISH COUNCIL OF DISABLED PEOPLE

ORIGIN UK
INFO ✓✓✓✓
EASE ✓✓✓✓

An action-oriented site that has information on how the council works, useful articles and helpful information. It shows how you can get involved whether you are disabled or not, and most importantly, how you can contribute. See also www.youreable.com which is full of useful advice.

For more advice check out the following sites; they're not great design wise but the information they contain may be useful.
http://members.aol.com/adaip/ – home of the Alliance of Disability Advice and Information Providers.
www.dialuk.org.uk – the Disability Advice Network.
www.diabilityuk.com – a portal site with a large number of useful links.

www.dlf.org.uk

THE DISABLED LIVING FOUNDATION

ORIGIN UK
INFO ✓✓✓✓✓
EASE ✓✓✓✓✓

A charity devoted to helping people who need equipment to live life to the full. This excellent site has information on how to choose the best equipment, masses of links to self-help groups, a bookshop, training information and of course a section on how you can contribute.

See also:
www.disabledgo.info – a directory of places that have good access and businesses that are sympathetic to disabled people.
www.independentliving.co.uk – equipment and advice on making life easier.
www.motability.co.uk – the scheme that helps you contract hire a car or powered wheelchair or scooter.
www.webable.com – lots of links and information on access.
www.wheelchair-travel.co.uk – self drive wheelchairs and cars for hire.

www.ncb.org.uk/cdc/

COUNCIL FOR DISABLED CHILDREN

ORIGIN UK
INFO ✓✓✓✓
EASE ✓✓✓

From the National Children's Bureau, this site is basically a forum devoted to helping parents and children cope with disability. It's a good starting point if you need information, but it's not an easy site to navigate so patience is required. Help can also be found at **www.childcarelink.gov.uk** and **www.cafamily.org.uk** where you can find advice on caring for a disabled child.

www.techdis.ac.uk

HELP FOR STUDENTS WITH A DISABILITY

ORIGIN UK
INFO ✓✓✓✓✓
EASE ✓✓✓

A site containing masses of help and information designed to enable disabled students to have the opportunity to learn effectively. Most of it is free, so an excellent resource. See also **www.skill.org.uk** who help promote opportunities for post-16 year olds in education and **www.nasen.org.uk** the National Association for Special Educational Needs.

www.opportunity.org.uk

CAREER HELP FOR THOSE WITH DISABILITIES

ORIGIN UK
INFO ✓✓✓✓✓
EASE ✓✓✓✓

A good site from Employment Opportunities with sections for jobseekers and employers, the aim being to help people get and retain jobs. See also **www.remploy.co.uk www.shaw-trust.org.uk** and **www.rehab.ie/uk** who can also help the fight on the job front.

www.jobability.com

LEADING JOB SITE FOR DISABLED PEOPLE

ORIGIN UK
INFO ✓✓✓✓
EASE ✓✓✓✓

A straightforward site designed to help disabled people find employment; it covers the UK by region plus Europe. There's also advice on careers and how to find a job. See also **www.yourable.com** who have a good jobs section.

www.drc-gb.org

DISABILITY RIGHTS

ORIGIN UK
INFO ✓✓✓✓
EASE ✓✓✓

A helpful site offering links and views on rights issues for the disabled. The site doesn't always load properly and it's not easy to find your way around, but useful nonetheless - at least there's a search facility.

www.disabilityview.co.uk

DISABILITY VIEW

ORIGIN UK
INFO ✓✓✓✓
EASE ✓✓✓✓

Inspired by the magazine of the same name, this site sets out to be the best source of information for all those who have to cope with a disability, and it largely succeeds. There are loads of links and useful sections such as travel, guides, sports and an events guide. See also www.disabilitynow.org.uk which is a more newsy magazine and www.mainstream-mag.com.

www.carers.gov.uk

FOR THOSE WHO CARE

ORIGIN UK
INFO ✓✓✓
EASE ✓✓✓✓

A barely useful resource from the government for carers, there are links and details of their policies concerning care. For more useful sites go to www.aqu.co.uk/carers/ and look up the long-winded www.royalgeorgetintern.com/carersunited/index.htm and also www.caringmatters.dial.pipex.com/ all of which have articles, chat and useful links.

Do-It-Yourself

The web doesn't seem a natural home for do-it-yourself, but there are some really useful sites, some great offers on tools and equipment and plenty of sensible advice.

Superstores

www.diy.com

THE DIY SUPERSTORE

ORIGIN	UK
INFO	✓✓✓✓
VALUE	✓✓✓✓
EASE	✓✓✓✓

B&Q has a bright and busy site with lots of advice, inspiration, tips and information on projects for the home and garden. It also has an excellent searchable product database. There are also plenty of offers and the store has a good selection of products covering all the major DIY areas. Delivery costs vary according to how much you buy and how fast you want it. Returns can be made to the stores. You need to be able to accept cookies before the site can operate effectively or you want to place an order.

www.homebase.co.uk

CREATE YOUR IDEAL HOME, FROM HOME

ORIGIN	UK
INFO	✓✓✓✓✓
VALUE	✓✓✓✓
EASE	✓✓✓✓

A good looking and logically laid out site, with a fairly large selection of products to buy, you can also get help with projects, plenty of inspirational ideas and decorating tips for each room of the house, as well as offers and competitions. Delivery times and charges vary, although the minimum is £4.95, up to £45 for garden sheds. You can return unwanted or faulty goods to your nearest store.

www.wickes.co.uk

DIY SPECIALISTS

ORIGIN	UK
INFO	✓✓✓✓
EASE	✓✓✓✓

Good ideas, inspiration and help are the key themes for this site, it's easy to use and genuinely helpful with well laid out project details. You can visit their show-rooms for product information and even take a 3-D tour of a conservatory. There's a handy calculator section where you can work out how many tiles or rolls of wallpaper you may need.

www.focusdoitall.co.uk

FOCUS DO-IT-ALL

ORIGIN	UK
INFO	✓✓✓✓✓
VALUE	✓✓✓✓
EASE	✓✓✓

A functional site, which attempts to put over lots of ideas and inspiration, it also carries a wide range of products at good prices. Delivery is £4.99 minimum and you can return unwanted goods to the store.

Other DIY stores worth checking out are:

www.decoratingdirect.co.uk – functional and easy-to-use site that concentrates on home décor products at excellent prices.

www.jewson.co.uk – Jewson's site is more corporate than anything but it does have a small section on each part of the house and how they can help.

Buying tools and equipment

www.screwfix.com

PRODUCTS FOR ALL DIY NEEDS

ORIGIN UK
INFO ✓✓✓✓✓
VALUE ✓✓✓✓✓
EASE ✓✓✓✓

Rightly considered to be one of the best online stores, Screwfix offer excellent value for money with free delivery and wholesale prices on a massive range of DIY products. You need cookies enabled for it to work effectively.

www.cooksons.com

TOOLS A-PLENTY

ORIGIN UK
INFO ✓✓✓✓
VALUE ✓✓✓✓
EASE ✓✓✓✓

An award-winning site from this Stockport firm, it has a huge number of tools and related products available, with free delivery on orders over £38.29 ex VAT. There are plenty of special offers and a loyalty scheme for regulars.

www.draper.co.uk

QUALITY SINCE 1919

ORIGIN UK
INFO ✓✓✓✓
VALUE ✓✓✓
EASE ✓✓✓

An attractive but relatively slow site from Draper tools with advice sections and an online shop which seems to have a life of its own.

www.diytools.co.uk

MORE TOOLS

ORIGIN UK
INFO ✓✓✓✓
VALUE ✓✓✓✓
EASE ✓✓✓✓

Another well-designed and extensive tool store with a huge range of products, there's also free delivery for orders over £50. Also check out **www.blackanddecker.co.uk** who have lots of advice on how to use power tools correctly, and also the slow but thorough **www.worldofpower.co.uk** who also supply garden equipment.

DIY help and advice

www.fmb.org.uk/consumers

THE FEDERATION OF MASTER BUILDERS

ORIGIN UK
INFO ✓✓✓✓✓
EASE ✓✓✓✓

Get help to avoid cowboys and advice on getting the best out of a builder. There's information and articles on most aspects of home maintenance, plus hints on finding reputable help. For similar information see **www.qualitymark.org.uk** which covers the government's scheme to ensure the reliability of tradesmen. See also **www.buildersguild.co.uk** who have a helpful section on their site.

www.homepro.com

THE HOME IMPROVEMENT SPECIALISTS

ORIGIN UK
INFO ✓✓✓✓✓
EASE ✓✓✓✓✓

An excellent and very helpful site split into four major sections, a 24-hour emergency call out service for your area, a 'Find a Professional' service for any household job, a help and advice section and lastly a superb inspirational section where you can go for ideas for your home. You can access via WAP or call the help lines too. See also the similarly helpful **www.tradanet.co.uk**

www.improveline.com

FIND A CONTRACTOR AND IDEAS

ORIGIN UK
INFO ✓✓✓✓✓
EASE ✓✓✓✓

Well-designed site offering information and inspiration for home improvements, there's also a service that puts you in touch with someone to do small jobs on the house within the hour, they have some 150,000 people registered. Inspiration comes in the form of thousands of categorised pictures which are easily pulled up via a good search facility. You can also ask an expert and get advice on financing your project.

www.buildadvice.com

THE RIGHT ADVICE FIRST TIME

ORIGIN UK
INFO ✓✓✓✓
EASE ✓✓✓✓

An award winning advice site from a family firm with sections on each major DIY job, there are clear instructions on how to go about them. They choose to cover some unusual areas such as disabled access, disaster recovery and asbestos.

www.hometips.com

EXPERT ADVICE FOR YOUR HOME

ORIGIN US
INFO ✓✓✓✓
EASE ✓✓✓

American the advice may be, but there is plenty here for every homeowner. The site is well laid out and the advice good. See also www.naturalhandyman.com which is fun or there is the well-designed forum site http://homedoctor.net/main.html where you can discuss your DIY problems; or the extensive www.doityourself.com which is very detailed.

www.diyfixit.co.uk

ONLINE DIY ENCYCLOPAEDIA

ORIGIN UK
INFO ✓✓✓✓
EASE ✓✓✓

Get help with most DIY jobs using the search engine or browse by room or job type. The information is good but some guidance and more illustrations would help.

See also:

www.diynot.com – a good all-rounder, encyclopedia, forums and DIY help.
www.finddiy.co.uk – a list of DIY sites.
www.fourwalls.co.uk – DIY sites listed and reviewed.
www.freddyfixit.co.za – DIY help from South Africa.
www.homedoctor.net – tips and advice from experts and contributors who've actually done the work, advice from the neighbour essentially. It can be a bit hit and miss.
www.ukdiyguide.co.uk – a messy but useful DIY portal site.

www.howtocleananything.com

STAIN REMOVAL PAR EXCELLENCE

ORIGIN CANADA
INFO ✓✓✓✓✓
EASE ✓✓✓✓

A group of cleaners have got together to produce a site that contains over 1,000 cleaning tips for outside or inside the house, the car – you name it basically.

Building

www.architect-net.co.uk

ARCHITECTS AND BUILDING CONTRACTOR'S DIRECTORY

ORIGIN UK
INFO ✓✓✓
EASE ✓✓✓

Find an architect to design your next home using the regional directory. Not a great site, but useful for good links to related sites.

www.ebuild.co.uk

BUILD YOUR OWN HOUSE

ORIGIN UK
INFO ✓✓✓✓✓
EASE ✓✓✓

All the information and contacts you need if you're thinking of buying that plot of land and getting stuck in. There's also a continually updated list of what plots of land are available and where.

The following sites will also prove useful if you're out to build your own:
www.builditthisway.co.uk – a good overview on what it takes to build your own house from a retired builder.
www.homebuilder.co.uk – good design and services, with a Scottish bias.
www.planning.odpm.gov.uk – the Office of the Deputy Prime Minister has information on the latest government initiatives on planning.
www.selfbuildcentre.com – pretty annoying design but lots of links and advice make it worth a visit.
www.selfbuildit.co.uk – help for first timers.

www.conservatoriesonline.co.uk

ALL YOU NEED TO KNOW ABOUT CONSERVATORIES

ORIGIN UK
INFO ✓✓✓✓✓
EASE ✓✓✓✓

A good portal site which offers links and advice on conservatories, sunrooms, garden rooms and solariums. There's a buyer's guide plus information on materials, styles, even on pools and orangeries.

See also:
www.conservatories-direct.co.uk – a good, comprehensive site from this specialist.
www.diy-conservatories-uk.co.uk – all you need if you want to erect your own.

Plumbing, bathroom and kitchen

www.plumbworld.co.uk
AN ONLINE PLUMBING SHOP

ORIGIN UK
INFO ✓✓✓
EASE ✓✓✓

Good selection of plumbing tools at competitive prices. Not exactly the most informative site as you have to assume much, for example, there's very little information about shipping which, incidentally, is free to most of the UK when you spend £50 or more.

See also:
www.plumbers.co.uk – if you need to find a plumber try the directory of plumbers.
www.plumbnet.com – for information on how to do work yourself.
www.registeredplumber.com – home of the Institute of Plumbing with a member directory and their code of practise.

www.bathroomexpress.co.uk
BETTER BATHROOMS

ORIGIN UK
INFO ✓✓✓✓
VALUE ✓✓✓✓
EASE ✓✓✓✓

A wide range of bathrooms and accessories are available at decent prices, with some interesting luxury items such as après-shower driers and some unique toilet seats. Delivery is based on how much you spend. See also www.bathroom-association.org and www.thebathroomaccessoryshop.com

www.alarisavenue.co.uk
KITCHENS AND CANE

ORIGIN UK
INFO ✓✓✓✓
VALUE ✓✓✓✓
EASE ✓✓✓✓

A beautifully designed store that offers much in the way of inspiration and quality products for the kitchen.

Doors

www.handlesdirect.co.uk
HANDLES GALORE

ORIGIN UK
INFO ✓✓✓✓
VALUE ✓✓✓
EASE ✓✓✓

A functional site where you can buy, well, handles. It's also got a selection of locks, switches and sockets that match certain handles. The emphasis is on contemporary style, and there's a good advice section which shows you how to fit them. See also **www.knobsandknockers.co.uk** who offer a wide range including security products.

www.doorsdirect.co.uk
DOORS AND HANDLES

ORIGIN UK
INFO ✓✓✓✓
VALUE ✓✓✓
EASE ✓✓✓✓

Features replacement doors for kitchens and bathrooms, you can order made-to-measure or standard and there's a selection of fittings as well.

Salvage

www.salvo.co.uk
SALVAGE AND RECLAMATION

ORIGIN UK
INFO ✓✓✓✓✓
VALUE ✓✓✓
EASE ✓✓✓✓

Salvo provides information on where to get salvaged and reclaimed architectural and garden antiques. The site is comprehensive and easy-to-use with interesting information such as what buildings are due to be demolished and when, so you can be ready and waiting.

Paint and wallpaper

www.decoratingdirect.co.uk
DECORATING MATERIALS

ORIGIN UK
INFO ✓✓✓✓
VALUE ✓✓✓
EASE ✓✓✓✓✓

A really well designed store offering a very wide range of decorating products, it's simple to use and fast. Orders are free when you spend more than £50 and it will save a trip to one of those huge DIY stores, or is it just me that hates them? Check out the refund policy before you buy though.

www.dulux.co.uk

DULUX

ORIGIN UK
INFO ✓✓✓✓✓
EASE ✓✓✓✓

A good looking and interesting site from Dulux, with a 'mouse painter' that you can use to redecorate a number of pre-selected rooms, there's also product information, a kids' zone and top tips on painting techniques. You can't buy from the site although there is a list of stockists. Crown has a similar but less interactive site that can be found at **www.crownpaint.co.uk**

www.farrow-ball.co.uk

TRADITIONAL PAINT AND PAPER

ORIGIN UK
INFO ✓✓✓✓
VALUE ✓✓✓
EASE ✓✓✓✓

Excellently designed web site featuring details on how their paint and paper is manufactured – something they obviously take pride in. You can also order from the site or request samples. For that traditional Mediterranean look try **www.casa.co.uk** who have a good selection and a nice site.

www.sanderson-online.co.uk

WILLIAM MORRIS AMONGST OTHER WALLPAPER

ORIGIN UK
INFO ✓✓✓✓
EASE ✓✓✓

Find out about the company, its heritage and what designs they have - new and old. You can also order a brochure and visit the Morris & Co pages where they have all the favourite designs. For more information on William Morris try visiting **www.morrissociety.org**

www.thedesignstudio.co.uk

GET THE RIGHT DESIGN

ORIGIN UK
INFO ✓✓✓✓
EASE ✓✓✓

This is an excellent database of wallpaper and fabric samples, which is easy-to-use and good fun. Once you've selected your swatch you can then find the nearest supplier. You need some patience, as it can be quite slow.

Inspiration, design and interiors

www.design-gap.co.uk
DESIGNER DIRECTORY

ORIGIN UK
INFO ✓✓✓✓✓
EASE ✓✓✓

A directory of UK-based designers and manufacturers with some 300 pages to browse through. They are arranged alphabetically by first name or company name as well as by category. The illustrations are excellent.

www.design-online.co.uk
NEED A DESIGNER?

ORIGIN UK
INFO ✓✓✓✓
EASE ✓✓✓

Design Online's mission is to put buyers and suppliers in touch with each other and to use the Internet to promote the use of well-designed products and services. You just search for the service you want and a list of suitable suppliers with contact details quickly appears. Could do with some illustrations and examples of the work that they are trying to promote. See also www.bida.org home of the newly formed British Interior Design Association.

www.geomancy.net
FENG SHUI

ORIGIN UK
INFO ✓✓✓✓
EASE ✓✓

What a mess of a site! Considering that it's supposed to promote the principles of light and harmony, it isn't very well designed. However, there's an excellent set of links and you can learn all you need to know about Feng Shui.

Stores for design

www.habitat.co.uk
HABITAT STORES

ORIGIN UK
INFO ✓✓✓✓
EASE ✓✓✓✓

An information only site with lots of details about their product range all wrapped up in a funky design.

www.ikea.com

IKEA STYLE

ORIGIN SWEDEN
INFO ✓✓✓✓
EASE ✓✓✓✓

You can't buy from the site but you can check whether a store has the item you want to buy in stock before you go, it would be great if more stores did this. Otherwise the site is more the usual store fare with plenty of ideas, articles and product lists.

www.maelstrom.co.uk

CONTEMPORARY SELECTION

ORIGIN UK
INFO ✓✓✓✓
VALUE ✓✓✓
EASE ✓✓✓

A wide selection of contemporary gifts, accessories, gadgets and furniture in a good-looking site. Delivery is 10% of the value of order with a flat charge of £10 if you spend more than £100. For more designer furniture see www.interiorinternet.co.uk

www.next.co.uk

NEXT HOME WARE

ORIGIN UK
INFO ✓✓✓✓
VALUE ✓✓✓
EASE ✓✓✓✓

A good selection of Next homeware with an excellent next day delivery service that costs £2.95 whatever you buy.

www.bhglive.com

BETTER HOMES AND GARDENS

ORIGIN US
INFO ✓✓✓✓✓
EASE ✓✓✓

There's more to this than DIY, but superb graphics and videos give this site the edge. It's American, so some information isn't applicable to the UK. The 'How-to Encyclopaedia' is excellent.

www.bluedeco.com

DESIGN ONLINE

ORIGIN UK
INFO ✓✓✓✓
VALUE ✓
EASE ✓✓✓

This site offers a good selection of designer products for the home, from furniture to ceramics, with free delivery to the UK. Unfortunately, returns have to go to Luxembourg.

www.fig.co.uk
FURNITURE, INTERIORS AND GARDENS

ORIGIN UK	A good looking and useful site that aims to act as an
INFO ✓✓✓✓	umbrella for retailers and information covering furni-
VALUE ✓✓✓	ture, interior design and garden design. It has a very
EASE ✓✓✓✓	useful directory and an unusual store where you can

shop by room, product or by style. They offer free delivery in the UK.

www.simplyfurnishings.com
SOFT FURNISHING

ORIGIN UK	All you need to know about making and buying soft
INFO ✓✓✓✓✓	furnishing with plenty of advice for all levels and a
EASE ✓✓✓✓	good store directory.

TV and celebrity designers

www.llb.co.uk
LAURENCE LLEWELYN-BOWEN

ORIGIN UK	Join the fan club, view Laurence's designs from
INFO ✓✓✓✓	greeting cards to cutlery to wall paper, then find
EASE ✓✓✓✓	out how to buy them. There's lots here, even

competitions. www.bbc.co.uk/homes/changingrooms also has top tips, articles, biographies and links to related shows.

www.mccloud.co.uk/kevin/kevin.htm
KEVIN MCCLOUD

ORIGIN UK	A straightforward site from the presenter of
INFO ✓✓✓✓	Grand Designs showing his work and how you
EASE ✓✓✓✓	can commission his team to create something for

you; principly it's about his specialist area, contemporary lighting.

E-Mail

Here's a selection of the best free e-mail providers, there are hundreds to chose from, but hopefully these sites should help you find the one that's right for you, whether you're after efficiency or a trendy @ moniker.

www.fepg.net

FREE E-MAIL PROVIDERS GUIDE

ORIGIN UK
INFO ✓✓✓✓
EASE ✓✓✓

Here's the place to start, it lists over 1,400 providers in 85 countries, including over 40 from the UK, so it's pretty comprehensive. It tends to just list them with a few details but there are recommended sites too. There's also a news section and a FEPG best of the best selection.

www.sneakemail.com

SNEAK E-MAIL

ORIGIN UK
INFO ✓✓✓✓
EASE ✓✓✓✓

Sneak e-mail provides an e-mail protection service whereby you can maintain a level of anonymity, stop spam or unsuitable e-mails getting to you, avoid unwanted soliciting or prevent others from selling your e-mail address to marketing companies, for example.

www.twigger.co.uk

ANYWHERE IN THE WORLD

ORIGIN UK
INFO ✓✓✓✓
EASE ✓✓✓✓

An excellent service that enables you to use your chosen e-mail address wherever you may be. One advantage is that you can see attachments before you download them onto your PC. The service is subscription based.

www.emailaddresses.com

E-MAIL ADDRESS DIRECTORY

ORIGIN UK
INFO ✓✓✓✓
EASE ✓✓✓✓

A useful directory of e-mail services and programs to help you manage your e-mail and mail to your site if you own one, there are also tips on how to find an e-mail address and a directory of address directories.

www.spamcop.com

STOP SPAM

ORIGIN US
INFO ✓✓✓✓
VALUE ✓✓✓
EASE ✓✓✓✓

Spam is a term used to describe unsolicited commercial e-mail, we all get bombarded by it and at this site you can download a useful little program that will help you minimise it.

Education

Using the Internet for homework or study has become one of its primary uses; these sites will help enormously, especially alongside the reference and encyclopaedia sites listed on page 302. There is also a section aimed at students on page 373.

Homework help

www.a-levels.co.uk

A LEVELS – A DODDLE?

ORIGIN UK
INFO ✓✓✓
EASE ✓✓✓✓

Great links providing masses of information on key topics. Most of the popular A level subjects are now completed – worth checking out.

www.atschool.co.uk

PRIMARY EDUCATION

ORIGIN UK
INFO ✓✓✓
EASE ✓✓✓✓

Specialising in Key Stage 1 and 2 this site is fun as well as educational and while the content is strong you do have to subscribe. Rates start at £9.99 for a quarterly subscription. This site does seem quite slow, so probably one for the broadband users.

www.bbc.co.uk/education

GET EQUIPPED FOR LIFE

ORIGIN UK
INFO ✓✓✓✓
EASE ✓✓✓✓

Good looking site covering learning at school, college and adult education, each section tends to be tied to a particular programme rather than subject, but there is masses here and the quality of content is particularly good. The revision sections are excellent.

www.thebigbus.com

HOORAY FOR THE BIG BUS!

ORIGIN UK
INFO ✓✓✓✓
EASE ✓✓✓✓

Excellent animation and content make this stand out, it can be a little slow and you have to subscribe to the CD magazine to get the best out of it (you get a free demo one as a trial). Excellent for younger children.

www.bigchalk.com

HOMEWORK CENTRAL

ORIGIN US
INFO ✓✓✓✓
EASE ✓✓✓

Go to the appropriate area and you get put through to the chalkboard, which has well categorised links to lots of excellent information, web sites and school subjects. There's help and information for parents and a teacher's section full of good resources in spite of the US bias. A more obvious cost structure would help, you waste time trying to find out what's free and what you have to pay for.

www.cln.org/int_expert.html

ASK AN EXPERT

ORIGIN CANADA
INFO ✓✓✓
EASE ✓✓✓

This site lists almost a hundred sites by subject, where you can ask an expert your homework question – what a doddle! North American bias though. Another US site that could be of help is ERIC at http://ericir.syr.edu

www.discoveryschool.com

ANSWERS TO HOMEWORK, FREE

ORIGIN US
INFO ✓✓✓✓
EASE ✓✓✓✓

This huge database is one of the biggest online homework sites, with some 700 links to a variety of reference sites and the provision to ask questions too. Layout has been improved and you can more easily access the information, it also has an excellent clip art gallery.

www.essaybank.co.uk

ESSAY HELP

ORIGIN UK
INFO ✓✓✓✓
EASE ✓✓✓✓

Claiming to be the UK's largest database of quality essays by students from 14 year olds to those at university, they cover a wide variety of subjects and there's no charge! See also www.sparknotes.com who offer their range of study guides free to download if you register.

www.examaid.co.uk

COPING WITH EXAMS

ORIGIN UK
INFO ✓✓✓
EASE ✓✓✓

Not a great web site but it does give an insight into how students cope with exams (or not) and how to help get through them successfully.

www.gridclub.com

FOR 7 TO 11 YEAR OLDS

ORIGIN UK
INFO ✓✓✓✓✓
EASE ✓✓✓✓✓

An excellent site which is backed by the government and several high profile contributors including Channel 4. It uses entertaining educational games to do most of its tutoring but there are links to the more traditional stuff available too. It's been built with safety in mind and it encourages children proactively. All in all, what an educational site should be.

www.homeworkelephant.co.uk

LET THE ELEPHANT HELP

ORIGIN UK
INFO ✓✓✓✓✓
EASE ✓✓✓✓✓

Rightly considered one of the top educational sites with some 5,000 resources and straightforward layout, all aimed at helping children achieve great results, there's help with specific subjects, hints and tips, help for parents and teachers. The agony elephant is great if you get really stuck. It's constantly being updated, so worth checking regularly.

www.homeworkhigh.co.uk

LEARN WITH CHANNEL 4

ORIGIN UK
INFO ✓✓✓✓✓
EASE ✓✓✓✓

Split into six learning sections: history, geography, science, maths, English and languages. There's also news and a chat room plus a personal help section that covers topics like bullying. They even provide teachers online for live sessions to help you out. You can ask questions, track down lots of information and chat with fellow homework sufferers. All in all, this is one of the better-looking homework sites. Excellent.

www.kevinsplayroom.co.uk

AWARD WINNING PORTAL

ORIGIN UK
INFO ✓✓✓✓✓
EASE ✓✓✓✓

An excellent site which is put together with the heavy involvement of pupils. It's won numerous awards and is a favourite among teachers and pupils alike. It has over 2,000 approved sites and they are well cate- gorised. There's also a translation service and a links page for teachers.

www.learn.co.uk
LEARN WITH THE GUARDIAN

ORIGIN UK
INFO ✓✓✓✓✓
EASE ✓✓✓✓✓

A curriculum based site that has much to offer in terms of content. They work closely with schools and it shows, that and access to the *Guardian* content means this is one of the best sites from which to learn. The down side is that it's all a bit clinical and not much fun.

www.learningalive.co.uk
FOR PRIMARY AND SECONDARY

ORIGIN UK
INFO ✓✓✓✓
EASE ✓✓✓

The 'Living Library' is a useful resource for homework help for both primary and secondary students while 'Pathways' provides over 4,000 links to a variety of reference sites. There are loads of resources for teachers too.

www.pupilline.net
FOR US BY US

ORIGIN UK
INFO ✓✓✓✓✓
EASE ✓✓✓✓

A massive, comprehensive site by pupils for pupils, it doesn't stop at education either, it covers social issues as well, in fact everything any pupil would want to know. As it's put together by them it speaks in their language – a cool site then.

www.samlearning.com
EXAM REVISION

ORIGIN UK
INFO ✓✓✓✓✓
VALUE ✓✓✓
EASE ✓✓✓

SAM stands for self-assessment and marking, on this brilliant site you can do just that, it has mock exams covering every major subject and key stage plus GCSE and A level. There are top tips on taking exams and the chance to win some great prizes when you register. There is a 14-day free trial then there are various payment options. See also **www.courseshop.co.uk** who offer a wide range of courses from GCSE upwards.

www.schoolsnet.com
THE EDUCATION SUPER SITE

ORIGIN UK
INFO ✓✓✓✓✓
EASE ✓✓✓✓

An incredibly impressive site that covers all aspects of education; there are school and site guides, jobs pages, book and computer shops, chat rooms, information on revision and exams, the latest news and, of course, plenty of chat. See also **www.educate.org.uk** which is similar but organised slightly differently.

www.schoolzone.co.uk
UK'S TOP EDUCATIONAL SEARCH ENGINE

ORIGIN UK
INFO ✓✓✓✓✓
EASE ✓✓✓

With over 40,000 sites and bits of resource all checked by teachers, Schoolzone has masses of information. It is clearly designed and easy to use with all the sites and information rated according to how useful they are. There is free software to download, plus homework help, career advice, teacher support (they do need it apparently) and much more. Don't be put off by the confusing layout; it's worth sticking with. See also **www.ukeducationguide.co.uk** who offer hundreds of links.

www.brainpop.com
LEARN BY ANIMATION

ORIGIN US
INFO ✓✓✓✓✓
EASE ✓✓✓✓✓

A wonderful example of how the internet should be used. Here you can download animations that cover and explain specific aspects of maths, health, technology, science, English and more. The site is American but very useful for UK students too.

www.happychild.org.uk
PROJECT HAPPY CHILD

ORIGIN UK
INFO ✓✓✓✓
EASE ✓✓✓

A mess of a site but one that aims to provide an index of educational resources for schools, parents and children. There's loads to see and do and it does a good job of highlighting charities for example, but the poor design gets in the way of its objectives. Well worth a visit, but be patient.

http://mathworld.wolfram.com
MATHS WORLD

ORIGIN US
INFO ✓✓✓✓✓
EASE ✓✓✓✓

An outstanding site devoted to the world of mathematics, it explains the complexities really well and is great for homework. It also has sections on chemistry, physics and astronomy.

www.3d-i.org

DESIGN

ORIGIN US
INFO ✓✓✓✓
EASE ✓✓✓

A beautifully designed site on Design and it's many forms in particular fashion, architecture and product design. It aids the student by enabling them to have a go at designing products plus advice on the basic principles.

Pre-school and infant education

www.enchantedlearning.com

FROM APES TO WHALES

ORIGIN UK
INFO ✓✓✓
EASE ✓✓

It's messy, uncool and largely aimed at young children, but there's loads of good information and activities hidden away, especially on nature. Use the search engine to find what you need.

www.underfives.co.uk

WEB RESOURCE FOR PRE-SCHOOL

ORIGIN UK
INFO ✓✓✓✓✓
EASE ✓✓✓✓

Loads of things to do and see here, from games and activities to download to help and advice for parents. Like the best educational sites its educational bias is not obvious or overwhelming, the tone is just right, it's also simple to use and fast.

National Curriculum and government policy

www.nc.uk.net

NATIONAL CURRICULUM REVEALED

ORIGIN UK
INFO ✓✓✓✓
EASE ✓✓✓✓

Very detailed explanation of the National Curriculum and prescribed standards.

See also:

www.ace-ed.org.uk – help for parents at the Advisory Centre for Education. **www.becta.org.uk** – information on technology and ICT education.

www.dfee.gov.uk – the government's site if you want a more overall picture on education.

www.dfes.gov.uk/parents/discover – for parents who want to be proactive in their child's education.

www.ngfl.gov.uk – National Grid for Learning,

outstanding for links. Some very good content too.

www.ofsted.gov.uk – The Office for Standards in Education, if you have a problem go here first.

www.qca.org.uk – more information on the national curriculum.

www.sqa.org.uk – for information on the Scottish education system.

Specialist education publishers

Below are listed some of the key education publishers, they often have competitions, online help and free books.

www.activerevision.com – from Harper Collins, at this site you can test yourself to see how likely you are to pass your exams. It then recommends which books would help you to get a pass.

www.bbc.co.uk/revisewise – excellent section for those doing their National Tests.

www.cgpbooks.co.uk – a basic online shop with details of their popular study guides which you can buy online.

www.hodderheadline.co.uk/index.asp?area=ed – one of the biggest education publishers offers a fairly staid but useful site. Teachers can order inspection copies of their books.

www.letts-education.co.uk – excellent site with lots of resources, news and explanatory notes about their books. Plus the Letts Challenge for schools and shop.

www.nelsonthornes.co.uk – a typical publishing site with good background on their titles and how to order them. Some books are available as online resources if you register.

Post 16 and adult education

www.ngfl.gov.uk

THE NATIONAL GRID FOR LEARNING

ORIGIN UK
INFO ✓✓✓✓
EASE ✓✓✓

The official government education site with sections on every aspect of learning. There's something for everyone, whatever your needs. It is particularly good for info on further and adult education. There are also

details on school web sites, a features section that
covers current news and events, plus advice on
Internet safety. See also **www.lsc.gov.uk** home of the
Learning and Skills Council which provides education
for over 16 year olds.

www.learndirect.co.uk

ADULT LEARNING

ORIGIN UK
INFO ✓✓✓✓
EASE ✓✓✓✓

A government backed site which aims to bring
education to everyone whatever their needs. The site
explains the background to the initiative plus details
of courses and how you can find one that meets your
requirements. There's also help for businesses and a
jobs advice section.

See also:

www.coursesuseek.com and **www.want2learn.com** –
sister sites devoted to offering a wide variety of
online courses.

www.niace.org.uk – a non-government organisation
formed to 'support an increase in the total numbers
of adults engaged in formal and informal learning in
England and Wales; and at the same time to take
positive action to improve opportunities and widen
access to learning opportunities for those communities under-represented in current provision'.

www.support4learning.org.uk – a wide ranging
resource aimed at helping people support their
education needs in a more holistic way.

www.wea.org.uk – the Worker's Educational
Association helps provide learning opportunities for
everyone but especially those who had missed out or
been disadvantaged in some way.

Teacher resources

www.theteachernet.co.uk

ALL A TEACHER NEEDS

ORIGIN UK
INFO ✓✓✓✓✓
EASE ✓✓✓✓

An excellent site that pulls together all the education
resources that a teacher is likely to need from advice
on how to use the Internet to getting a job and, of
course, forums; there's even a certificate generator.

See also:

www.byteachers.org.uk – a collection of useful
websites created by teachers for teachers.

www.eteach.com – recruitment for teachers.

www.everythingeducation.org – like an education
swap shop this site brings education and business
together. A great place to find equipment for schools
at a decent price.

www.qualityteachingresources.co.uk – similar to the
Teacher Net but aimed at Primary school and
student teachers.

www.tes.co.uk – educational resources and news from
the *Times Educational Supplement.*

Electrical Goods, Gadgets and Appliances

*This section covers stores that sell the usual electrical goods but
also offer a bit more in terms of range, offers or service. There's
also the odd spy camera and gadget shop.*

www.comet.co.uk

ALWAYS LOW PRICES, GUARANTEED

ORIGIN	UK	A pretty messy site these days with masses of offers
INFO	✓✓✓✓✓	on the front page, having said that it's a great place
VALUE	✓✓✓✓	to view the widest range of goods at excellent prices.
EASE	✓✓✓	

www.dixons.co.uk

OFFERS GALORE

ORIGIN	UK	The Dixons site has plenty of offers and reflects what
INFO	✓✓✓✓	you'd find in their stores very well. It has a similar
VALUE	✓✓✓✓	but slightly wider product range to Comet, with an
EASE	✓✓✓✓	additional photographic section. Delivery costs vary.

www.maplin.co.uk

ELECTRONICS CATALOGUE

ORIGIN	UK	Maplin is well established and it's a bit of an event
INFO	✓✓✓✓✓	when the new catalogue is published. Now you can
VALUE	✓✓✓	always have access to the latest innovations and basic
EASE	✓✓✓✓	equipment at this well put together site. It features the

expected massive range with online ordering, delivery
over £30 is free.

www.hed.co.uk

HOME ELECTRICAL DIRECT

ORIGIN	UK
INFO	✓✓✓
VALUE	✓✓✓✓✓
EASE	✓✓✓✓

Their motto is 'the lowest prices guaranteed all year round, and that's a promise'. They have a very large range of goods covering all the key product categories. Delivery is free on orders over £100.

See also:

www.24-7electrical.co.uk – which is well designed and looks strong on customer service judging by the number of times they ask you to contact them.

www.bbha.co.uk – nice design and free delivery.

www.electricaldiscountuk.co.uk – a pretty straightforward site with some good offers and a wide range www.we-sell-it.co.uk – is also worth a visit for good prices on kitchen and other domestic appliances.

www.empiredirect.co.uk – good looking site with lots of offers and a wise range.

www.pluggedin.co.uk – an attractive site with usefully big illustrations and some good prices too; free delivery in the UK.

www.pure-digital.com – specialists in digital products such as radios, PC, audio and home entertainment.

www.vacuumcleanersdirect.co.uk – some 200 models to choose from, some great prices too.

www.richersounds.com

LOWEST PRICES GUARANTEED

ORIGIN	UK
INFO	✓✓✓
VALUE	✓✓✓✓
EASE	✓✓✓✓

Bargain hunters will want to include this site on their list, similar to the other electrical goods retailers but with a leaning towards music and TVs, with plenty of offers and advice. There is a search facility and the products are obviously good value, however, they are vague about delivery charges, although products are delivered within 5 working days.

www.appliancespares.co.uk

FIX IT YOURSELF

ORIGIN UK
INFO ✓✓✓
EASE ✓✓✓

Ezee-Fix has thousands of spare parts for a massive range of products, nearly all illustrated, including fridges, cookers, microwaves, vacuum cleaners, etc. All it needs is online fitting instructions, and more details on the products and it would be perfect.

www.flyingtoolbox.com

IF YOU CAN'T FIX IT YOURSELF

ORIGIN UK
INFO ✓✓✓✓
VALUE ✓✓✓
EASE ✓✓✓✓

With Flying Toolbox you can find someone to repair your faulty item. Type in your location and details of the repair and they will provide a list of repairers in your area with information on charges and a rating from previous customers. Good though it is, could it be just a way of selling insurance policies?

www.bull-electrical.com

FOR THE SPECIALIST

ORIGIN UK
INFO ✓✓✓✓
VALUE ✓✓✓✓
EASE ✓✓✓

Fascinating to visit, this mess of a site offers every sort of electronic device, from divining rods to radio kits to spy cameras. There are four basic sections:
1. Surplus electronic – scientific and optical goods, even steam engines.
2. Links to specialist shops – such as spy equipment and hydroponics.
3. Free services.
4. Web services – shopping cart technology, for example.

www.innovations.co.uk

NEW TECHNOLOGY

ORIGIN UK
INFO ✓✓✓✓
VALUE ✓✓✓
EASE ✓✓✓

Several hundred innovative, unusual or just plain daft items for sale, all on a neat web site, the best bit is probably the gift wizard, which helps you find the perfect gift when you're stuck for something to buy. Other places for technology geeks to get their kicks are **www.thegadgetshop.co.uk** who have free delivery on orders over £10 and a free returns policy, **www.firebox.com** for a really wide range of gadgets amongst other boy's toys.

www.simplyradios.com
RADIOS SPECIALIST

ORIGIN UK	An excellent site devoted to radios and the first place
INFO ✓✓✓✓	to go if you want something groovy or the latest thing
VALUE ✓✓✓✓	in digital.
EASE ✓✓✓✓	

Fashion and Accessories

The big brands have never been cheaper. Selling fashion and designer gear is another Net success, as customers flock to the great discounts that are on offer. Many people still prefer to try clothes on before buying but the good sites all offer a convenient returns policy.

Fashion

www.fuk.co.uk
FASHION UK

ORIGIN UK	All you ever need to know about the latest in UK and
INFO ✓✓✓✓✓	world fashion, updated daily. There's also a section on
EASE ✓✓✓	beauty, a good links library, competitions, chat and,
	of course, shopping. It's all packaged into a really
	attractive site, which initially looks cluttered but is
	OK once you get used to it.

www.vogue.co.uk
THE LATEST NEWS FROM BRITISH VOGUE

ORIGIN UK	An absolute must for the serious follower of fashion.
INFO ✓✓✓✓	There's the latest catwalk news and views, and a handy
EASE ✓✓✓✓	who's who of fashion. There's also a section on jobs,
	and you can order a subscription too.

For a similar experience try **www.elle.com** or the slightly less fashion-oriented but more fun **www.cosmomag.com** For access to the top designers' most recent collections and a glimpse at what could be available in the shops the following season try **www.firstview.com**

www.ftv.com

FASHION TV

ORIGIN FRANCE
INFO ✓✓✓✓
EASE ✓✓✓✓

The 24 hour fashion station, so popular in gyms and bars, has a good site offering the latest from around the world. Features include video clips, radio interviews with designers plus links, gossip and horoscopes.

www.net-a-porter.com

PRET A PORTER

ORIGIN UK
INFO ✓✓✓✓
VALUE ✓✓✓
EASE ✓✓✓✓

A great looking site that is easy to use with information on the latest fashions, plus catwalk reports and shopping where you can browse by designer or product type. Delivery costs vary according to what you buy. For an alternative try **www.theclothesstore.com** who also have a good selection of clothes and accessories.

www.fnmare.com

FASHION NIGHTMARE

ORIGIN UK
INFO ✓✓✓✓
VALUE ✓✓✓✓
EASE ✓✓✓✓

Outstanding graphics and creative look make this site stand out, but that's not all, the Fashion Nightmare team will keep you up-to-date with all the latest trends and fashion no-nos too. Annoyingly you can get access until you give your e-mail address.

www.fashionmall.com

FASHION STORE DIRECTORY

ORIGIN US
INFO ✓✓✓✓
EASE ✓✓✓✓

A huge number of stores listed by category, packed with offers and the latest new designs. Most stores are American and their ability to deliver outside the US and delivery charges vary considerably. The site is well-designed and easy to browse.

www.fashion.net

GUIDE TO FASHION

ORIGIN US
INFO ✓✓✓✓
EASE ✓✓✓✓

A good fashion search engine and directory with the added advantage that it carries the latest fashion news too.

www.yoox.com

TOP DESIGNERS

ORIGIN UK	Great looking site with top offers from the top design-
INFO ✓✓✓✓	ers, it's well laid out and easy to navigate with a good
VALUE ✓✓✓✓	returns policy. You can search by designer or category
EASE ✓✓✓✓	and the quality of the photos is good. Offers range
	from a few pounds to massive discounts.

www.haburi.com

CUT-PRICE DESIGNER CLOTHES FOR ALL

ORIGIN UK	Not a big range of clothes but excellent prices.
INFO ✓✓✓	Clear, no-nonsense design makes the site easy to use.
EASE ✓✓✓✓	

www.apc.fr

FRENCH CHIC FROM A.P.C.

ORIGIN FRANCE	Unusual in style and for something a little different
INFO ✓✓✓	A.P.C.'s site is worth a visit. Delivery is expensive in
VALUE ✓✓	line with the clothes, which are beautifully designed
EASE ✓✓✓✓	and well presented. For more of the French look go
	to **www.redoute.co.uk**

www.gap.com

FOR US RESIDENTS ONLY

ORIGIN US	A clear, uncluttered design makes shopping here easy
INFO ✓✓✓✓	if you live in the United States! For UK residents it's
EASE ✓✓✓✓	window-shopping only.

www.next.co.uk

THE NEXT DIRECTORY

ORIGIN UK	The online version of the Next catalogue is available
INFO ✓✓✓✓	including clothes for men, women and children as
VALUE ✓✓✓	well as products for the home. Prices are the same as
EASE ✓✓✓✓	the directory, next day delivery is £2.50 and return
	of unwanted goods is free. You can order the full
	catalogue for £3.

www.extremepie.com

EXTREME FASHION FROM EXTREME SPORTS

ORIGIN UK
INFO ✓✓✓✓
EASE ✓✓✓✓

A brand led selection of clothes from the world of BMX, surf, skate and other so-called sports. The site is excellent with clear visuals and delivery costs start at £2.95.

www.pop-boutique.com

BUY SOMETHING THAT'S ALREADY OUT OF DATE!

ORIGIN UK
INFO ✓✓✓✓
VALUE ✓✓✓
EASE ✓✓✓✓

A fantastic site devoted to fashion chic from the 60s, 70s and 80s, it can be a little slow but worth the wait if you're into the period. It also sells accessories and offers a good set of related links.

Other fashion sites worth a peek...

www.girlonthestreet.com – home to a New York trend agency with some top tips and a sneak preview on what's coming up.

www.girlprops.com – another New York based site with masses of accessories to choose from. Delivery is expensive to the UK though.

www.hintmag.com – a well designed fashion e-zine with regular features, news and links. The photography is especially good.

www.japanesestreets.com – the latest on Japanese street fashion.

www.lucire.com – another fashion magazine, this one is well thought of and it covers everything from catwalk style to skincare.

www.toastbypost.co.uk – good mail order catalogue with the latest designs.

Where the top designers hang out:

www.alexandermcqueen.net – Alexander McQueen.

www.armaniexchange.com – cheap Armani.

www.bensherman.co.uk – Ben Sherman.

www.chanel.com – Chanel.

www.christian-lacroix.fr – Christian Lacroix.

www.gucci.com – Gucci.

www.hugo.com – Hugo Boss.

www.jpgaultier.fr – Jean Paul Gaultier.

www.kenzo.com – Kenzo.

www.paulsmith.co.uk – Paul Smith.
www.tedbaker.co.uk – Ted Baker.
www.tommy.com – Tommy Hilfiger.

General clothes stores

www.arcadia.co.uk

THE UK'S LEADING FASHION RETAILER

ORIGIN UK
INFO ✓✓✓✓
VALUE ✓✓✓✓
EASE ✓✓✓✓

The Arcadia Group has over 1,200 stores in the UK and the web sites are accessible, easy to use and offer good value for money. Each site has its own personality that reflects the high street store. Delivery charges vary.

www.burtonmenswear.co.uk – men's clothes.
www.dorothyperkins.co.uk – women's clothes.
www.evans.ltd.uk – women's clothes.
www.topman.co.uk – men's clothes.
www.tops.co.uk – Topshop.
www.zoom.co.uk – fashion and lifestyle portal.

www.kaysnet.com

KAYS CATALOGUE

ORIGIN UK
INFO ✓✓✓✓
VALUE ✓✓✓✓
EASE ✓✓✓✓

Massive range combined with value for money is the formula for success with Kays. While they lead with clothes there are plenty of other sections outside of that: jewellery, home entertainment, toys, etc. Delivery charge depends on how much you spend.

www.freemans.co.uk

FREE DELIVERY IN THE UK AND GOOD PRICES

ORIGIN UK
INFO ✓✓✓✓
VALUE ✓✓✓✓
EASE ✓✓✓✓

A similar site to Kays, not the full catalogue but there's a wide range to choose from including top brands. Split into five major sections; women, men, children, home and sports, they offer free delivery for UK customers. There are also prizes to be won, a special feature on the latest trends and fashions and information on how to get the full catalogue. See also **www.grattan.co.uk** for Grattan's catalogue. The excellent Shoppers Universe has closed but they recommend **www.aboundonline.com** which is a similar catalogue site with a very good choice and offers a style guide and outfit finder service.

Specialist clothes stores

www.asseenonscreen.com

BUY WHAT YOU SEE ON FILM OR TV

ORIGIN UK
INFO ✓✓✓✓
VALUE ✓✓✓
EASE ✓✓✓✓

Now you can buy that bit of jewellery or cool gear that you've seen your favourite TV or film star wearing, As Seen on Screen specialises in supplying just that. You can search by star or programme, it isn't cheap but you'll get noticed. They also have a handy gift ideas section if you're looking for inspiration.

www.bloomingmarvellous.co.uk

MATERNITY WEAR

ORIGIN UK
INFO ✓✓✓✓
VALUE ✓✓✓✓
EASE ✓✓✓✓

The UK's leading store in maternity and babywear has an attractive site that features a good selection of clothes and nursery products. There are no discounts on the clothes, but they do have regular sales with some good bargains. Delivery in the UK is £3.95 per order.

www.tienet.co.uk

THE INTERNET TIE STORE

ORIGIN UK
INFO ✓✓✓✓✓
VALUE ✓✓✓✓
EASE ✓✓✓✓

Hundreds of ties in seemingly every colour and design, there are sections on fashion ties, bow ties, tartan and character ties. Selection and payment is simple and delivery charge depends on size of order though it starts at 99p.

www.shoe-shop.com

EUROPE'S BIGGEST SHOE SHOP

ORIGIN UK
INFO ✓✓✓✓✓
VALUE ✓✓✓✓
EASE ✓✓✓✓

A massive selection of shoes and brands to chose from, the site is nicely designed with good pictures of the shoes, some of which can be seen in 3-D, a facility they are expanding. Delivery is included in the price and there's a good returns policy. For an alternative try the straightforward www.shoesdirect.co.uk who have a similar offer, and the excellently named www.voodooshoes.com who are a bit more fashion oriented. Women could try the popular www.shoetailor.com

Underwear and lingerie

www.smartbras.com

BRAS, BASQUES AND BRIEFS

ORIGIN	UK	The easy, embarrassment-free way to buy underwear.
INFO	✓✓✓✓	Choose from a selection of around 200 lingerie
VALUE	✓✓✓	products including brand names at high street
EASE	✓✓✓✓	prices. Delivery is £2.50 for the UK.

See also:
www.assetsco.co.uk – for men's underwear.
www.brieflook.co.uk – wide range including
  wedding lingerie.
www.figleaves.com – for wide range and value
  for money.
www.kiniki.com – more men's underwear.
www.mylingerie.net – the Simone Perele range.
www.rigbyandpeller.com – for up-market lingerie.
www.victoriassecret.com – for designer style.

Accessories and jewellery

www.jewellers.net

THE BIGGEST RANGE ON THE NET

ORIGIN	UK	Excellent range of products, fashion jewellery, gifts,
INFO	✓✓✓✓	gold and silver, the watch section is particularly strong.
VALUE	✓✓✓	There is also information on the history of gems, the
EASE	✓✓✓✓	manufacturers and brands available. Delivery to the

UK is free for orders over £50, and there is a 30-day
no quibble returns policy.

Also check out:
http://argenteus.co.uk – odd site but good for designer
  jewellery.
www.jewellerycatalogue.co.uk – guarantee low prices.
www.madaboutjewellery.com – costume jewellery with
  designer style.
www.tateossian.com – great contemporary jewellery
  and accessories.

WATCH HEAVEN

ORIGIN UK	A large range of watches including Swatch, Casio,
INFO ✓✓✓✓	G Shock, Baby G and Seiko are available here. The site
VALUE ✓✓✓✓	is fast and easy-to-use, but a better search facility
EASE ✓✓✓✓	would save time. Delivery is free for the UK, but prices
	appear to be similar to the high street.

Finance, Banking and Shares

The Internet is proving to be a real winner when it comes to personal finance, product comparison and home share dealing; with these sites you will get the latest advice and may even make some money.

General finance information sites, directories and mortgages

www.fsa.gov.uk

FINANCIAL SERVICES AUTHORITY

ORIGIN UK	The regulating body that you can go to if you need
INFO ✓✓✓✓✓	help with your rights or if you want to find out about
EASE ✓✓✓✓	financial products; it will also help you to verify that
	the financial institution you're dealing with is
	legitimate. See also **www.oft.gov.uk** for the
	Office of Fair Trading and its informative site.

www.financial-ombudsman.org.uk

FINANCIAL OMBUDSMAN SERVICES

ORIGIN UK	When you have a complaint about a financial service
INFO ✓✓✓✓✓	this is a good point of call for sensible advice and help
EASE ✓✓✓✓	on how to go about getting a fair hearing.

www.checkmyfile.com

IS YOUR CREDIT GOOD?

ORIGIN UK	For just under a tenner you can get a basic online
INFO ✓✓✓✓	credit rating on yourself, or if you pay more, they'll
VALUE ✓✓✓✓	send you a more detailed report. Very useful and
EASE ✓✓✓✓	informative, they even keep updating your file for a
	yearly sum. You can also work out your likely credit
	score using their online calculator for free. Data
	protection is guaranteed too.

www.find.co.uk
INTERNET DIRECTORY FOR FINANCIAL SERVICES

ORIGIN UK
INFO ✓✓✓✓✓
EASE ✓✓✓✓

Access to thousands of financial sites; split into nine sections: life and pensions, investment, insurance, information, advice and share dealing, banking and saving, mortgages and loans, information services and a centre for Independent Financial Advisers. Superb. See also **www.financelink.co.uk**

www.ft.com or www.ftyourmoney.com
FINANCIAL TIMES

ORIGIN UK
INFO ✓✓✓✓
EASE ✓✓✓✓

FT.com offers up to date news and information. The 'Your Money' section is biased towards personal finance. Although it looks daunting, it is easy-to-use and provides sound, independent advice for everyone.

www.moneyextra.com
THE UK'S PERSONAL FINANCE GUIDE

ORIGIN UK
INFO ✓✓✓✓✓
EASE ✓✓✓✓

A very comprehensive personal finance guide; there are comparison tables for mortgages, loans and other financial services, advice for investors, an excellent financial glossary, tax and mortgage calculators. There's also an online mortgage broker with support from several leading lenders. In fact, it seems to cover everything financial.

www.fool.co.uk
THE MOTLEY FOOL

ORIGIN UK
INFO ✓✓✓✓✓
EASE ✓✓✓✓

Finance with a sense of fun, The Fool is exciting and a real education in shrewdness. It not only takes the mystery out of share dealing but gives great advice on investment and personal finance. You need to register to get the best out of it, unfortunately, it has got very advert laden.

www.thisismoney.com
MONEY NEWS AND ADVICE

ORIGIN UK
INFO ✓✓✓✓✓
EASE ✓✓✓✓

Easy-to-use, reliable, 24-hour financial advice from the *Daily Mail* group. It has loads of information on all aspects of personal finance and is particularly good for comparison tools, especially mortgages, and there's a good 'Ask the Experts' section.

www.iii.co.uk

INTERACTIVE INVESTOR INTERNATIONAL

ORIGIN UK
INFO ✓✓✓✓✓
VALUE ✓✓✓✓
EASE ✓✓✓✓

Now known as Ample, the emphasis is on investment and share dealing with some personal finance thrown in. It retains the interactivity of the original site but with some additional investment information. Also can be reached through **www.ample.com**

www.blays.co.uk

BLAYS GUIDES

ORIGIN UK
INFO ✓✓✓✓✓
EASE ✓✓✓✓

Excellent design and impartial advice make the Blays guide a must visit site for personal finance. It has all the usual suspects: mortgages, savings etc, plus very good sections for students. There's also a comparative section for phone services and utilities.

www.moneynet.co.uk

IMPARTIAL AND COMPREHENSIVE

ORIGIN UK
INFO ✓✓✓✓
EASE ✓✓✓✓

Rated as one of the best independent personal finance sites, it covers over 100 mortgage lenders, has a user-friendly search facility plus help with conveyancing and financial calculators. It now also covers medical and life insurance well too.

For other similar sites go to:

www.advfn.com – a really ugly site but comprehensive if you can put up with the design.

www.adviceonline.co.uk – independent financial advice on a logically designed site.

www.bbc.co.uk/yourmoney – outstanding and ever changing site from the BBC, best for keeping up to date with the latest financial news.

www.digitallook.com – one of the leading providers of financial information, excellent site.

www.marketplace.co.uk – 'independent' advisers from Bradford & Bingley help you make the right financial choices from mortgages to investments and pensions.

www.moneybrain.co.uk – a slick site offering a wide range of financial products and independent advice.

www.moneyfacts.co.uk – a no-nonsense information site which shows the cheapest and best value financial products with lots of authority, it's also a comparatively fast site and less tricky than some. It also covers annuities and offshore banking.

www.moneysupermarket.com – a very good all-rounder with help in most of the important areas of personal finance; good site layout and lots of practical advice add to the package.

www.sexymoney.co.uk – a good attempt at making money fun, in reality it offers solid advice on most aspects of finance.

www.unbiased.co.uk

FIND AN INDEPENDENT FINANCIAL ADVISER

ORIGIN UK
INFO ✓✓✓✓
EASE ✓✓✓✓

A good independent financial adviser is hard to come by, if you need one, then here's a good place to start. Just type in your postcode and the services you need and up pops a list of specialists in your area. See also **www.financialplanning.org.uk** for the Institute of Financial Planning and **www.sofa.org** for the Society of Financial Planners, both sites give information on how to get a financial adviser and plan your finances.

Mortgage specialists

www.charcoalonline.co.uk

JOIN CHARCOAL

ORIGIN UK
INFO ✓✓✓✓
EASE ✓✓✓✓

This established mortgage adviser owned by Bradford & Bingley offers over 500 mortgages from over 45 lenders. There are also sections on pensions, investments and insurance.

It's worth shopping around so check out these sites too:

www.mortgageman.co.uk – aimed at the self-employed or those having difficulty getting a mortgage from the usual lenders, or with CCJs.

www.mortgagepoint.co.uk – geared towards first time buyers and those with a less than perfect credit history.

www.mortgageshop.com – independent financial advice about which is the best mortgage for you, a somewhat messy site though.

www.mortgages-online.co.uk – good independent source of information.

www.yourmortgage.co.uk – *Your Mortgage* magazine.

www.mortgagecode.org.uk

MORTGAGE CODE COMPLIANCE BOARD

ORIGIN UK
INFO ✓✓✓✓✓
EASE ✓✓✓✓

The role of the mortgage board is to ensure that consumers are protected. They have a code of conduct that the lenders sign up to and they back that up by continually monitoring them. The site is packed with sensible information and help.

Insurance

www.insurancewide.com

HOME OF INSURANCE ON THE WEB

ORIGIN UK
INFO ✓✓✓✓✓
EASE ✓✓✓✓

Claiming to be the fastest way to get insurance cover, they offer a wide range of insurance policies covering life, travel, transport, home and business.

www.easycover.com

UK'S BIGGEST INDEPENDENT INSURANCE WEB SITE

ORIGIN UK
INFO ✓✓✓✓✓
EASE ✓✓✓✓✓

Here you can get a wide range of quotes just by filling in one form. The emphasis is on convenience and speed.

www.warrantydirect.co.uk

EXTENDED WARRANTIES

ORIGIN UK
INFO ✓✓✓✓
VALUE ✓✓✓
EASE ✓✓✓✓

Here you can get cover for the important things in life, your car, appliances and your computer.

Other sites worth checking out:

www.eaglestardirect.co.uk – a sparse but useful site from one of the market leaders.

www.elephant.co.uk – instant quotes on a wide selection of policies although they mainly specialise in car insurance.

www.inspop.com – choose the specially selected policy and buy online.

www.morethan.com – hyped with the 'Where's Lucky' ads, this site is from Royal Sun Alliance and it's good for quotes in most areas including pets.

www.quotelinedirect.co.uk – quotes on a wide range of insurance areas.

www.screentrade.co.uk – the right deal on your motor, home and travel insurance.

www.soreeyes.co.uk – a wide range of policies and options.

www.theaa.com/services/insuranceandfinance/ – AA Insurance covers travel, cars and home.

www.ukinsuranceguide.co.uk – a good place to find specialist insurers.

For advice on insurance or problems with insurance:

www.abi.org.uk – Association of British Insurers, lots of advice on all aspects of insurance plus industry information.

www.gisc.co.uk – General Insurance Standards Council, where to go if you have a problem, it is responsible for a code of conduct amongst insurers.

Investing and share dealing

www.schwab-world-wide.com/Europe/

CHARLES SCHWAB EUROPE

ORIGIN US
INFO ✓✓✓✓✓
EASE ✓✓✓✓

Although you'll need to register and put up a deposit, this is the biggest and probably the most reliable Internet share dealer for the UK. You can trade online from various different accounts depending on how much you trade and your level of expertise.

Any of the following are worth checking out, they are all good sites, each with a slightly different focus, so find the one that suits you.

www.barclays-stockbrokers.co.uk – good value for smaller share deals and possibly the best for beginners. Can be slow.

www.deal4free.com – unusual and highly rated dealing site offering spread betting, share dealing and currency trading. You need a good understanding of finance to get the best out of it.

www.ethicalinvestment.org.uk – if you want to invest your money in business that have a moral conscience, then here's the site that will lead you in the right direction.

www.freequotes.co.uk – an all singing and dancing site with the latest share information, tips and links to related and important sites.

www.gni.co.uk – award winning trading and investment site, good design.

www.hemscott.com – one of the more comprehensive offerings with good use of other technologies such as SMS.

www.investorschronicle.co.uk – this established magazine offers a useful site for share information and dealing, especially good for data on medium-sized and large companies.

www.itsonline.co.uk – a well-designed site that concentrates on explaining and campaigning for investment trusts.

www.morningstar.co.uk – a very dense site with huge amounts of information, part of its service is to collate and interpret the output of financial journalists, which must be a job in itself.

www.sharepeople.com – owned by American Express, it has a nice design, is easy to use with lots of explanation on how it all works. Costs vary depending on the size of trade.

www.sharexpress.co.uk – the Halifax share dealing service that is a good beginner's site and charges competitively.

www.tdwaterhouse.co.uk – slightly more expensive than Barclays, but still quite good value, well designed with good information to back it all up.

www.investmentguide.co.uk

FOR THOSE WHO GO IT ALONE

ORIGIN UK
INFO ✓✓✓✓✓
EASE ✓✓✓✓✓

An outstanding site that gives you access to three books from Harold Baldwin which are regularly updated and contain high quality information regarding share dealing and other investments; suitable for beginners or experts. Some information is by subscription.

See also:

www.investmentuk.org – home of the Investment Management Association where you can find out about how the investment industry is managed and works with government, as well as some useful advice.

www.citywire.co.uk – advice and analysis from a well regarded source, some information is subscription only.

www.investopedia.com – described as the investment education site, it's packed with information and helps to navigate the investment minefield.

Pensions

www.pensionsorter.com

FIND A PENSION

ORIGIN UK
INFO ✓✓✓✓
EASE ✓✓✓✓✓

Excellent site if you need help around the pensions minefield, with lots of jargon-free and independent information. It tells you how to buy one, how much you should be paying and advice on what you should be saving if you want a golden retirement.

www.pensionguide.gov.uk

KNOW YOUR OPTIONS

ORIGIN UK
INFO ✓✓✓✓✓
EASE ✓✓✓✓✓

An impartial guide to pensions from the government, which aims to help you choose the right option, there's also information for employers and current pension holders.

www.PensionsNetwork.com

STAKEHOLDER PENSIONS

ORIGIN UK
INFO ✓✓✓✓
EASE ✓✓✓✓

A good site dedicated to bringing you the best value stakeholder pensions. It's easy to use and comes with a good pensions calculator.

For more information on pensions see:
www.opas.org.uk – the Office of the Pensions
 Advisory Service helps when things go wrong.
www.opra.gov.uk – the Occupational Pensions
 Regulatory Authority ensures pension schemes are
 run properly.
www.thepensionservice.gov.uk – the Department for
 Work and Pensions represents the government line
 on pensions and gives good advice and the latest
 news.

Banks and building societies

www.bankfacts.org.uk

BRITISH BANKERS ASSOCIATION

ORIGIN UK
INFO ✓✓✓✓✓
EASE ✓✓✓✓

Answers to the most common questions about banking, advice about Internet banks, the banking code and general information. There's also a facility that helps you resurrect dormant accounts. See also **www.bankingcode.org.uk** where you can find details of the standards of service that all the banks have signed up to. For information on building societies go to the Building Society Association at **www.bsa.org.uk** and also the portal site **www.buildingsocieties.com** which offers a useful regional guide.

Here are the high street and Internet banks, building societies and the online facilities they currently offer:
www.abbeynational.co.uk – full service up and running including a very competitive Internet-only savings account. Following the trend for high street banks to set up Internet-only banks with wacky names, Abbey National have set up Cahoot at **www.cahoot.com** and they also offer a competitive service wrapped up in a neat web site.
www.alliance-leicester.co.uk – a comprehensive service offering mortgages, insurance and banking.
www.banking.hsbc.co.uk – straightforward and easy-to-use site offering online banking alongside the usual services from HSBC, like most other big banks they've also launched a trendier Internet bank called **www.firstdirect.co.uk** which offers all the expected features plus WAP banking from an impressive site.
www.bankofscotland.co.uk – good all-rounder with business banking included on the site, along with services for students and young people.
www.barclays.co.uk – one of the original innovators in Internet banking, they offer an exhaustive service covering all aspects of personal and small business banking.
www.bradford-bingley.co.uk – the site defaults to **www.marketplace.co.uk** – see page 120.
www.citibank.co.uk – very impressive site with a complete Internet personal banking service with

competitive rates. Citibank have few branches and this is their attempt at a bigger foothold in the UK.

www.co-operativebank.co.uk – acknowledged as the most comprehensive of the banking sites and it's easy to use. Excellent, but they have also launched the trendier and more competitive Smile banking site **www.smile.co.uk** which is aimed at a younger audience.

www.egg.co.uk – A new look site with banking, insurance, investment advice even shopping.

www.halifax.co.uk – comprehensive range of services via an easy-to-use and well-designed site and you'll find a great deal of advice and information all clearly explained. Their Internet-only banking offshoot is called Intelligent Finance, which is excellent and can be found at the memorable **www.if.com**

www.lloydstsb.co.uk – combined with Scottish Widows, Lloyds offer a more rounded and comprehensive financial service than most. The online banking is well established and efficient. They provide help for small businesses too.

www.nationwide.co.uk – don't be put off by the dated appearance of the Nationwide site, they offer a complete online banking service as well as loans and mortgages.

www.natwest.com – NatWest offer both online and WAP banking and share dealing, with good sections for students and small businesses. It's got a nice design, and it's straightforward to use.

www.newcastlenet.co.uk – a nice-looking and easy-to-use site from one of the smaller banking/building societies, offering all the usual services including online mortgage applications.

www.standardchartered.com – good looking and user-friendly site from this small bank.

www.virgin-direct.co.uk – access to Virgin's comprehensive financial services site featuring a share dealing service, pension advice, banking, mortgages and general financial advice.

www.woolwich.co.uk – online banking and a WAP mobile phone banking service plus all the other usual personal financial services make the Woolwich site a little different.

www.ybs.co.uk – a good all-rounder from the Yorkshire Building Society.

www.switchwithwhich.co.uk

SWITCH BANK ACCOUNTS EASILY

ORIGIN UK
INFO ✓✓✓✓
EASE ✓✓✓✓

Which? Magazine's site devoted to a campaign to encouraging people to switch to less costly bank accounts. There is advice on the best account for you and how to move your account to the recommended account one painlessly.

Tax   Insurance

www.inlandrevenue.gov.uk

TALK TO THE TAXMAN

ORIGIN UK
INFO ✓✓✓✓✓
EASE ✓✓✓

The Inland Revenue has a very informative site where you can get help on all aspects of tax. You can even submit your tax return over the Internet and there's a good set of links to other government departments.

www.tax.org.uk

CHARTERED INSTITUTE OF TAXATION

ORIGIN UK
INFO ✓✓✓✓✓
EASE ✓✓✓

A great resource, they don't provide information on individual questions but they can put you in touch with a qualified adviser. It's a good place to start if you have a problem with your tax. For the latest tax news go to **http://e-tax.org.uk** which is comprehensive and has an excellent set of links. For a list of sites all relating to tax go to **www.taxsites.com**

http://listen.to/taxman

THE TAX CALCULATOR

ORIGIN UK
INFO ✓✓✓✓
EASE ✓✓✓✓✓

Amazingly fast, just input your gross earnings and your tax and actual earnings are calculated.

Business

www.economist.com

THE ECONOMIST MAGAZINE

ORIGIN UK
INFO ✓✓✓✓✓
EASE ✓✓✓✓

The airports' best-selling magazine goes online with a wide-ranging site that covers business and politics world-wide. You can get access to the archive and also

their excellent country surveys. If you're in business
you need this in your favourites box.

See also www.businessweek.com who offer a wide
range of business news and information.

www.startinbusiness.co.uk
AN ONLINE BUSINESS STARTER KIT

ORIGIN UK
INFO ✓✓✓✓✓
EASE ✓✓✓✓

An excellent portal site on all things to do with
business including a good guide to help you start a
business. There are plenty of links plus listings of
businesses for sale, property, services and potential
opportunities.

See also:

www.businesslink.org – the National Business
   Advice Service has a comprehensive site backed
   up by a hotline.
www.clearlybusiness.com – offers the same
   information as above but is a more commercial
   affair along with pop-up ads and the annoying
   'doubleclick' monitoring cookie.
www.companies-house.co.uk – a useful site if you
   want to research companies and get information
   and guidance on most aspects of business and the
   regulations surrounding it.
www.whichfranchise.com – a slightly messy site that
   offers the information you need on all the available
   franchises in the UK, and how to go about
   getting one.

www.uk.sage.com
BUSINESS SOFTWARE

ORIGIN UK
INFO ✓✓✓✓
VALUE ✓✓✓
EASE ✓✓✓✓

If you need accounting software to solve virtually any
sort of problem or provide a new service, you should
find it here. Sage has a good reputation for helping
small businesses.

www.asiannet.com
BUSINESS INFORMATION ON ASIA

ORIGIN US
INFO ✓✓✓✓
EASE ✓✓✓

Market information, news, services and links all
geared to the main Asian markets each of which has a
feature site. There are company profiles as well as an
online shop where you can contact companies to get
product samples.

Debt management

www.nacab.org.uk
CITIZENS ADVICE BUREAU

ORIGIN UK
INFO ✓✓✓✓✓
EASE ✓✓✓✓

Often the first port of call for people with debt issues, the site offers useful information and the latest campaigns. There's a search facility to find your nearest office and a link to **www.adviceguide.org.uk** which contains basic advice and information on your rights.

See also:
www.debtadvicecentre.co.uk – lots of useful advice and information on what to do if you find yourself in debt; excellent for links.
www.debtcounsellors.co.uk – specialists in advising people on what to do if they get into financial difficulty and dealing with creditors.

Miscellaneous

www.young-money.co.uk
ONLINE MONEY GAME SHOW

ORIGIN UK
INFO ✓✓✓✓
EASE ✓✓✓✓

Combines general knowledge and financial games aimed at turning the little ones into financial whiz-kids of the future. There's a lot that most adults can learn from the site as well as it's a fun way of learning about the world of finance. You need Shockwave for it to work.

www.ifs.org.uk
INSTITUTE OF FISCAL STUDIES

ORIGIN UK
INFO ✓✓✓✓
EASE ✓✓✓✓

Independent analysis of all things financial especially the tax system, surprisingly interesting but a pretty dull site.

www.paypal.com
SEND AND RECEIVE MONEY ONLINE

ORIGIN UK
INFO ✓✓✓✓
EASE ✓✓✓✓

A genuinely useful service, especially for small businesses and online auction junkies; it's very easy and straightforward to use. There's a directory of over 25,000 web sites that use paypal and details of how your site can get involved.

www.paytrust.com
MANAGE YOUR BILLS

ORIGIN	US
INFO	✓✓✓✓
VALUE	✓✓✓
EASE	✓✓✓✓

If you find managing your household bills a complete chore, then it might be worth a visit here. Apparently they will manage your household accounts for you – for a fee.

Finding Someone

Following the success of Friends Reunited, there's been a massive explosion of sites dedicated to finding old friends and colleagues. Here we've listed all the best sites, and also the place to go to find a phone number, contacts for business and the home.

Directory sites

www.yell.co.uk
YELLOW PAGES ONLINE – JUST YELL!

ORIGIN	UK
INFO	✓✓✓✓✓
EASE	✓✓✓✓✓

There are basically three sections:

1. Its primary service is the search engine – this enables you to search for the business or service you want by region, type or name. It is very quick, and you get plenty of details on each entry.
2. Offers a number of guides which provide links on films, health, motoring, shopping, property, weather and weddings.
3. Business – provides sections on international trading, UK business, recruitment and financial information.

See also **www.bigyellow.com** for the USA.

www.scoot.co.uk
THE SIMPLE WAY TO FIND A BUSINESS

ORIGIN	UK
INFO	✓✓✓✓✓
EASE	✓✓✓✓✓

Register, type in the person's name or profession then hit the scoot button and the answer comes back in seconds. Oriented towards finding businesses but useful nonetheless. There's also a cinema finder.

www.thomweb.co.uk
THE ANSWER COMES OUT OF THE BLUE

ORIGIN UK
INFO ✓✓✓✓✓
EASE ✓✓✓✓

Thomson's offer an impressive site and provide local directories online. It's divided up into five major categories:

1. A business finder – search using a combination of name, type of business or region.
2. People finder – track down phone numbers and home or e-mail addresses.
3. Comprehensive local information – available on the major cities and regions.
4. News.
5. Net search and directory.

www.phonenumbers.net
VIRTUALLY EVERYONE WHO'S LISTED

ORIGIN EUROPE
INFO ✓✓✓✓
EASE ✓✓✓✓

Start by clicking on the country or area you need, then you can easily find the phone, fax or e-mail address of anyone who is in the book. It also has a section with a number of links to other search engines such as Yell.

www.bt.com
BRITISH TELECOM SERVICES

ORIGIN UK
INFO ✓✓✓✓
EASE ✓✓

BT offers a site that gives a very thorough overview of its services. To get the best out of it you need to register; have your account number handy and you can view your telephone bill. It's pretty slow and access to the main services isn't exactly obvious.

See also:

www.anywho.com – straightforward American-oriented search site.

www.emailaddresses.com – a free e-mail directory plus other information relating to e-mails.

www.infospace.com – another good search engine with yellow (business) and white (people) pages sections, it offers much more though including a good web directory.

www.royalmail.co.uk – The mail may have a silly name nowadays but this site offers a useful address finder and you can track your recorded deliveries too.

www.ukphonebook.com – simple to use, quick with a no-nonsense design, also has mapping, a business finder and lots of adverts.

www.192.com
THE UK'S LARGEST DIRECTORY SERVICE

ORIGIN UK
INFO ✓✓✓✓
VALUE ✓✓✓✓
EASE ✓✓✓✓

Plenty available for non-fee payers such as people and business finders, directories and route planning. There are also various subscription options, providing access to other databases such as the electoral role, company reports and the UK-info CD.

Finding old friends

www.friendsreunited.co.uk
THE ONE STOP SITE TO REUNITE

ORIGIN UK
INFO ✓✓✓✓
EASE ✓✓✓✓✓

Possibly the UK's most visited web site nowadays. It's a phenomenal success story and millions of people have made contact with old friends using the site. To get the best out of it you have to register which costs £5. For that you get access to the schools and workplace data base and the ability to contact people through the site. It's very easy to use and you'll quickly find yourself.

See also:
www.friendsfaraway.com – Friends Reunited for ex-pats and people who've worked abroad.
www.gradfinder.com – good site covering much of the world's schools and universities.
www.school-friends.co.uk – similar to Friends Reunited but with a very good search facility.

Three very similar sites dedicated to re-uniting old service colleagues:
www.armedforcesfriends.co.uk
www.servicepals.com
www.the-ex-forces-network.org.uk

Try also:
www.ariadne.ac.uk/issue20/search-engines/#lycos – another page of tips, advice and links on finding people using the internet.

www.arielbruce.com – Ariel Bruce is an ex-social
worker with a good track record of finding missing
people.

www.journalismnet.com/people – a tips sheet that
contains links and advice on how to find people.

www.missing-you.net – free message posting designed
to help find lost friends thought to be in the UK.

www.peopletracer.co.uk – people traced for a
fee – from £15.

www.andys-penpals.com
FIND A PENPAL

ORIGIN UK	A site devoted to penpals around the world, covering
INFO ✓✓✓✓	95 countries. It's easy to use and free; there are also
EASE ✓✓✓✓	links to similar sites and a chat room.

Flowers

www.interflora.co.uk
TURNING THOUGHTS INTO FLOWERS

ORIGIN UK	Interflora can send flowers to over 140 countries,
INFO ✓✓✓✓	many on the same day as the order. They'll have a
VALUE ✓✓✓	selection to send for virtually every occasion and
EASE ✓✓✓✓	they offer a reminder service. The service is excellent,

although they are not very up front on delivery costs,
which can be high. If you can't get what you need
here then try www.teleflorist.co.uk who offer a
similar service.

www.flyingflowers.com
EUROPE'S LEADING FLOWERS BY POST COMPANY

ORIGIN UK	Freshly picked flowers flown from Jersey to the UK
INFO ✓✓✓✓	from £8.99. All prices include delivery and you save
VALUE ✓✓✓	at least £1 on all bouquets against their standard
EASE ✓✓✓✓	advertised off-line prices. They'll also arrange next

day delivery in the UK. The site is simple and there's
a reminder service just to make sure you don't
forget anyone.

www.clareflorist.co.uk
STYLISH BOUQUETS AND PRETTY PICTURES

ORIGIN UK	Easy to use site with good customer services and free
INFO ✓✓✓✓	delivery to UK with surcharge for same day delivery.
VALUE ✓✓✓✓	Cost reflects the sophistication of the flowers.
EASE ✓✓✓✓	

www.daisys2roses.com
MAKE YOUR OWN BOUQUET

ORIGIN UK	A simple, step-by-step approach to making up a
INFO ✓✓✓✓	bouquet of your choice. You can select from a large
VALUE ✓✓✓	range of flowers and there's help to get you started,
EASE ✓✓✓✓	you can even search by flower type. Delivery is free
	in the UK.

Food and Drink

*Whether you want to order from the comfort of your own home,
indulge yourself, find the latest food news or get a recipe, this
collection of sites will fulfil your foodie desires. It features supermarkets, online magazines and information sites, specialist food
retailers, vegetarian and organic stockists, drinks information and
suppliers, where to go for kitchen equipment and help in finding
the best places when eating out.*

Supermarkets and general food stores

www.iceland.co.uk
FROZEN FOOD SPECIALIST DELIVERS

ORIGIN UK	Iceland's online service is considered one of the best
INFO ✓✓✓✓	with nearly all of the UK covered. Easy to navigate,
VALUE ✓✓✓✓	but can be ponderous to use. Your order is saved each
EASE ✓✓✓✓	time, which then acts as the basis for your next order.
	Information on the products is good, and there's a
	wide range available; orders must be £40 or more.
	They also offer deals on home appliances.

www.waitrose.com

IF YOU ARE REALLY INTO FOOD

ORIGIN	UK
INFO	✓✓✓✓✓
VALUE	✓✓✓
EASE	✓✓✓✓✓

Waitrose is offering a very good comprehensive and well designed site that oozes quality, so it's a pleasure to do your grocery shopping online. You can buy wine, gifts, organics and some John Lewis products. In addition it also has all the features you'd expect from an Internet Service Provider, including the Waitrose *Illustrated Food Magazine*, an excellent gift shop, plus party, flowers and travel sections and even one on competitions and puzzles.

www.tesco.co.uk

THE LIFESTYLE SUPERSTORE

ORIGIN	UK
INFO	✓✓✓✓
VALUE	✓✓✓✓✓
EASE	✓✓✓✓

This functional site has a comprehensive offering and they've improved it visually. Food aside, there's a wide range of goods on offer though, including electrical goods, clothes and books. There's also a section on personal finance, other shops, parenting advice and healthy living. Offers now abound with some great savings all aimed at capturing your e-mail address and future custom.

www.sainsburys.co.uk

NOT JUST GOOD TASTE

ORIGIN	UK
INFO	✓✓✓✓
VALUE	✓✓✓✓
EASE	✓✓✓✓

Sainsbury's site is sparser than Tesco, with the emphasis being on good food, cooking, recommendation and taste, and of course the Nectar loyalty card. The facility to place an advance order at their Calais store, which you can then pick up, and pay for in France, will appeal to those who wish to save time on their booze run.

www.somerfield.co.uk

MEGADEALS

ORIGIN	UK
INFO	✓✓✓✓
VALUE	✓✓✓✓
EASE	✓✓✓✓

The emphasis is firmly on offers with a rolling feature, which changes every few seconds, but there's also a recipe finder, wine guide and essential food facts. Delivery covers most of the UK and it's free if you spend more than £25, provided you live near enough to the store.

www.asda.co.uk

PERMANENTLY LOW PRICES

ORIGIN UK
INFO ✓✓✓✓
VALUE ✓✓✓✓✓
EASE ✓✓✓✓

There's lots of information about the company and what it stands for plus links to its online shop. There are also sections on insurance, health and offers plus the clothing brand George. Delivery is £4.25, but free if you spend more than £99.

www.safeway.co.uk

FOR THE FAMILY WITH YOUNG CHILDREN

ORIGIN UK
INFO ✓✓✓✓
EASE ✓✓✓✓

A good all rounder the Safeway site provides much in the way of information on lifestyle subjects including cookery advice, recipes, a drinks guide and advice on healthy eating. There's no online shopping though there is information on savings and their cheap petrol scheme. As Safeway are up for sale at time of writing this may change soon.

www.heinz-direct.co.uk

DELIVERING MORE THAN 57 VARIETIES OF FOOD

ORIGIN UK
INFO ✓✓✓
VALUE ✓✓✓✓
EASE ✓✓✓✓

To get the best value for money it's best to order in bulk, as delivery charges can be high. It can be very slow to use and is split into product feature sections: Weightwatchers, canned grocery, Heinz and Farley's baby food, hampers, and sauces and pickles.

www.homefarmfoods.com

DELICIOUS FROZEN FOOD DELIVERED FREE

ORIGIN UK
INFO ✓✓✓
VALUE ✓✓✓✓✓
EASE ✓✓✓✓

Good selection of frozen foods and huge range of ready meals with a good use of symbols indicating whether the product is low fat, microwavable, vegetarian etc. With free delivery, it's especially good value, and there is no minimum order. See also **www.foodhall.co.uk** who have a good selection of specialist stores to choose from.

www.farmersmarkets.net

NATIONAL ASSOCIATION OF FARMERS' MARKETS

ORIGIN UK
INFO ✓✓✓✓
EASE ✓✓✓✓

A farmers' market sells locally produced goods, locate your nearest market or get advice on how to set one up.

Asian and Indian cookery

www.curryhouse.co.uk

EVERYTHING YOU NEED TO KNOW ABOUT CURRY

ORIGIN UK	Curryholics can get their fill of recipes,
INFO ✓✓✓✓✓	recommendations, taste tests, interviews with famous
VALUE ✓✓✓	chefs and a restaurant guide, good for links too.
EASE ✓✓✓✓✓	

See also:
www.currybox.com – spices for curry delivered
 to your door postage paid, some recipes too.
www.currysauce.com – get all the sauces delivered
 and even win a year's supply.
www.curryworld.com – the home of National
 Curry Day.

www.straitscafe.com

RECIPES FROM SINGAPORE

ORIGIN SINGAPORE	A straightforward site with lots of recipes not only
INFO ✓✓✓✓	from Singapore, but also Japan and China, there's also
EASE ✓✓✓✓	a good set of links and a gallery. For Indonesian cook-
	ing go to the enjoyable Henks Hot Kitchen which can
	be found at **www.indochef.com**

www.japanweb.co.uk

JAPANESE CUISINE

ORIGIN JAPAN	An interesting and growing site covering the basics of
INFO ✓✓✓✓	Japanese cooking along with recipes and a UK restau-
VALUE ✓✓✓	rant guide. It also has a glossary and tips on etiquette.
EASE ✓✓✓✓	'Itadakimasu' as they say. See also **www.yosushi.com**
	who offer a hi-tech site which feature their restaurants
	and a sushi ordering service.

www.thaifood2.com

DIRECTORY AND RECIPES

ORIGIN US	A directory of Thai food around the world with links
INFO ✓✓✓	to related sites. See also **www.thaicuisine.com** which
EASE ✓✓✓✓	is a more rounded site with recipes and ingredient
	information, and **www.tat.or.th/food/** which has a
	good overview.

www.chinavoc.com/cuisine/index.asp

CHINESE COOKERY

ORIGIN US
INFO ✓✓✓✓
EASE ✓✓✓✓

Lots of tips and background information on Chinese cookery with advice on techniques and recipes. www.chinavista.com/culture/cuisine/recipes.html is worth checking out for its list of regional recipes. Our old favourite www.chopstix.co.uk was being revamped at time of writing. Also www.chinatown-online.co.uk is dedicated to what's going on in London's China Town; it has an excellent food section.

See also:
www.asiarecipe.com – a messy site with a range of recipes and ingredients covering the whole of Asia.
www.spiceadvice.com – useful spice encyclopaedia from this American spice retailer who doesn't ship outside the US.

Barbecues

www.barbecuen.com

BARBECUES

ORIGIN US
INFO ✓✓✓✓✓
EASE ✓✓✓✓

In the unlikely event that our weather will be good enough to have a barbecue, then here's a site with all you need to know on the subject. See also www.britishbarbecue.co.uk

British and Irish cookery

www.hwatson.force9.co.uk

BEST OF BRITISH

ORIGIN UK
INFO ✓✓✓✓
EASE ✓✓✓✓

Helen Watson is a champion of British cuisine and here you'll find her online cookbook, there's also a magazine and a guide to regional cooking. The site is slow but the content is very good.

See also:
www.greatbritishkitchen.co.uk – sparse site from the British Food Trust
http://pages.eidosnet.co.uk/cookbook/index.html – a tribute to British cooking with some fifty recipes.
www.recipes4us.co.uk – who have over 2,000 recipes although some are international.

www.btinternet.com/~scottishcookery/

CLASSIC SCOTTISH COOKERY

ORIGIN UK   You need patience with this site but again the
INFO ✓✓✓   recipes are well worth the wait, some of which are
EASE ✓✓✓✓ well illustrated.

www.tasteofireland.com

A TASTE OF IRELAND

ORIGIN UK   Recipes, a restaurant guide and a shop all in one,
INFO ✓✓✓   it's not that comprehensive but well worth a
EASE ✓✓✓✓ visit nonetheless.

www.red4.co.uk/recipes.htm

WELSH RECIPES

ORIGIN UK   Here are over 120 traditional recipes including lava
INFO ✓✓✓   bread, wines, cawl and Welshcakes.
EASE ✓✓✓✓ See also **www.hookerycookery.com/welsh-menu.htm**
            where there's a similar list.

www.baxters.co.uk

TRADITIONAL FARE

ORIGIN UK   An old Scottish firm offering their range of soups,
INFO ✓✓✓✓ jams, sauces, hampers and gift foods online through
VALUE ✓✓✓ a well-designed and easy-to-use site; there are also
EASE ✓✓✓✓ recipes from top chef Nick Nairn. Shipping charges
            vary according to destination.

Celebrity chefs and TV

www.delia.co.uk

DELIA SMITH

ORIGIN UK   The queen of British cookery has a clean, well-
INFO ✓✓✓✓ designed site with lots of recipes, which can be
EASE ✓✓✓✓ accessed by the good search facility. If you join you get
            added features such as daily tips, competitions and the
            chance to chat to Delia. There's also a section on what
            Delia is up to and you can ask questions and get advice
            at the cookery school. In the past year a shop has been
            added to the site, it has a wide range of products
            which are supplied via other online retailers.

www.jamieoliver.net
WHAT HE'S ABOUT

ORIGIN UK
INFO ✓✓✓
EASE ✓✓✓

A new look site that is a big improvement on the old one from a cookery point of view; there is plenty about cookery and Jamie himself. The kids club is a good idea but a bit lightweight.

www.garyrhodes.com/
GARY RHODES

ORIGIN UK
INFO ✓✓✓✓
VALUE ✓✓✓✓
EASE ✓✓✓✓

Recipes, tips and seasonal suggestions here at Rhodes' official site. See also **www.bbc.co.uk/food/garyrhodes** a page from the BBC web site, tied to his TV program, it offers seasonal recipes and links to related sites.

www.rickstein.co.uk
PADSTOW, STEIN AND SEAFOOD

ORIGIN UK
INFO ✓✓✓✓
VALUE ✓✓✓
EASE ✓✓✓✓

Information on Rick, his restaurants and cookery school all wrapped up in a tidy web site. You can also book a table or a room as well as order products from the online deli.

www.ukfood.tv
UK FOOD

ORIGIN UK
INFO ✓✓✓✓
EASE ✓✓✓✓

Very attractive site from this specialist TV channel with lots of recipes, tips and features based on their programming. See also **www.bbc.co.uk/food** where you can find the latest from the BBC.

www.foodtv.com
FOOD NETWORK

ORIGIN US
INFO ✓✓✓✓
EASE ✓✓✓

A rather strange but quite appealing site devoted to TV cooks. It has some video footage and a search engine that covers 20,000 recipes, plus some good articles.

Cheese

www.cheese.com
IT'S ALL ABOUT CHEESE!

ORIGIN US
INFO ✓✓✓✓✓
EASE ✓✓✓✓

Not a shop, but a huge resource site about 652 types of cheese. There's advice about the best way to eat cheese, a vegetarian section, a cheese bookshop and links to other cheese-related sites and online stores. You can even find a suitable cheese searching by texture, country or type of milk. For more cheese information try the attractive Cheesenet site at **http://cheesenet.wgx.com** it has an excellent search facility, or the American Dairy Association's **www.ilovecheese.com** which also offers a cheese guide and lots of recipes.

www.cheesemongers.co.uk
OPULENT SITE FROM UK'S OLDEST CHEESEMONGERS

ORIGIN UK
INFO ✓✓✓✓
VALUE ✓✓
EASE ✓✓✓✓

Paxton and Whitfield, the royal cheesemongers, provide a very clear and easy-to-use online shop but charge £7.50 to ship goods. A superb selection of cheese and luxury produce, with hampers, cheese kitchen, accessories and wine. A pleasure to browse and it's tempting to buy; you can also join the Cheese Society. See also the British Cheese Board at **www.britishcheese.com** where you can learn about our cheeses, get some recipes and general cheese propaganda.

www.teddingtoncheese.co.uk
BRITISH AND CONTINENTAL CHEESEMONGERS

ORIGIN UK
INFO ✓✓✓✓
VALUE ✓✓✓
EASE ✓✓✓✓

Much-acclaimed site offering over 130 types of cheese at competitive prices. The sections are split by country and there's a good system for showing whether the cheese is suitable for vegetarians, pregnant women, etc. There is also a small selection of wine and other produce; you can even design your own hamper. When buying you can stipulate how much cheese you want in grams (150 minimum), shipping from £5.95 for the UK.

www.fromages.com
TRADITIONAL FRENCH CHEESE

ORIGIN FRANCE
INFO ✓✓✓✓
VALUE ✓✓
EASE ✓✓✓✓

French cheese available to order and delivered within 24 hours along with wine recommendations and express shipping from France. Delivery is included in the price but if you're worried about cost you probably shouldn't be shopping here.

Confectionery, cake and chocolate

www.hotelchocolat.com
DEDICATED TO GOOD CHOCOLATE

ORIGIN UK
INFO ✓✓✓✓
VALUE ✓✓✓✓
EASE ✓✓✓✓

An excellent and well-illustrated site from an experienced retailer, they also offer lots of choice and a wide range of chocolate-related gifts and you can even buy in bulk! There's a really good selection facility and the chocolate tasting club. Delivery to UK included in the price and they will guarantee that it's delivered by a specified date. Formerly called www.chocexpress.co.uk

www.thorntons.co.uk
WELCOME TO CHOCOLATE HEAVEN

ORIGIN UK
INFO ✓✓✓
VALUE ✓✓✓
EASE ✓✓✓✓

Thorntons offer a comprehensive and easy-to-use site, with an emphasis on gifts. The range is extensive and they supply world-wide – at a cost. Orders costs start at £3.99 for the UK. There are product sections for continental, premier, gifts and hampers plus flowers and wine.

www.chocolate.co.uk
THE CHOCOLATE SOCIETY

ORIGIN UK
INFO ✓✓✓
EASE ✓✓✓✓

A slightly odd site about chocolate. It's not the most up-to-date, but there is information on the history of chocolate, links and events.

www.cakeandcookie.co.uk
FOR ALL SPECIAL OCCASIONS

ORIGIN UK
INFO ✓✓
VALUE ✓✓
EASE ✓✓✓✓

Order a selection of cakes and cookies, personalise them and send them to any one of 86 countries. Delivery charges vary and there's also a corporate service. See also www.clickthecookie.co.uk who offer a wide range of cookies and gift options

www.thecakestore.com
CAKES, CAKES AND MORE CAKES

ORIGIN UK
INFO ✓✓✓✓
VALUE ✓✓✓✓
EASE ✓✓✓✓

Very good online cake store with a huge selection, good prices and the ability for you to have tailor-made cake too. Sadly they only deliver in London and parts of the South East.

www.janeasher.co.uk
JANE ASHER CAKES

ORIGIN UK
INFO ✓✓✓✓
VALUE ✓✓✓
EASE ✓✓✓✓

A pretty workman-like affair, you can order personalised cakes (which have to be collected), select from a range of mail order cakes and you can buy equipment too.

www.pastrywiz.com
PASTRY HEAVEN

ORIGIN US
INFO ✓✓✓✓
EASE ✓✓✓✓

A general food site with the emphasis on pastry in all its forms, there are plenty of recipes and links to keep all cake fans happy.

www.oldsweetshop.com
SWEETS THE WAY THEY USED TO BE...

ORIGIN UK
INFO ✓✓✓✓
VALUE ✓✓✓
EASE ✓✓✓✓

Sweets from an old fashioned sweet shop, stacked with favourites like Dolly Mixtures, sugared almonds and Parma Violets, a visit here is a nostalgia trip as much as anything. Delivery is charged to you at whatever they get charged by weight. See also **www.sugarboy.co.uk** who offer a wide range of goodies.

Diet and nutrition

www.3fatchicks.com
THE SOURCE FOR DIET SUPPORT

ORIGIN US
INFO ✓✓✓✓
EASE ✓✓✓✓

The awesome Three Fat Chicks have produced one of the best food web sites. It's entertaining and informative about dieting or trying to stay healthy. There are food reviews, how to live on fast food, recipes, links to other low fat sites, a section for chocoholics, diet tips and 'tool box' which has calorie tables and calculators; also getting started, on losing weight and how to get free samples.

www.cookinglight.com
THE BEST FROM COOKING LIGHT MAGAZINE

ORIGIN US
INFO ✓✓✓✓
EASE ✓✓✓✓

One of the world's best-selling food magazines, their slow site offers a huge selection of healthy recipes and step-by-step guides to cooking. There are also articles on healthy living.

www.weightwatchers.co.uk
WELCOME TO WEIGHTWATCHERS UK

ORIGIN UK
INFO ✓✓✓
VALUE ✓✓✓
EASE ✓✓✓✓

A much improved site with more information on how to lose weight, keep motivated, keep fit, chat and, of course, where to find your local group. There's also a shop where you can buy specially selected foods and related diet products – delivery starts at £2.

http://atkinscenter.com
DR ATKINS

ORIGIN US
INFO ✓✓✓
VALUE ✓✓✓
EASE ✓✓✓✓

The world's best selling dietician's site that gives the background to his low carbohydrate diet and how you can lose weight and get healthy on it. For a more straightforward approach try **www.low-carb.com** who have a good online shop.

www.mynutrition.co.uk
ONLINE GUIDE TO HEALTHY EATING

ORIGIN UK
INFO ✓✓✓✓
VALUE ✓✓
EASE ✓✓✓✓

Find out what you really should be eating from this cool British site, which has been put together by a professional nutritionist. Its features include an a–z of ailments and diseases, dietary advice, newsletter, relevant articles and of course shopping. Delivery is £1.50 for the UK. For all its beauty and efficiency, you can't help thinking that this is just a very good vehicle for selling vitamins and supplements.

www.weightlossresources.co.uk
FAD FREE TOOLS FOR HEALTHY WEIGHT LOSS

ORIGIN UK
INFO ✓✓✓✓✓
EASE ✓✓✓✓

Excellent place to go for information on weight loss and diets; you can keep a weight loss diary, find out about exercise, get advice on what to eat and catch up on the latest research. You can share your experience with others too; you also have to register to get the best out of it.

See also:

http://lowfatcooking.about.com/ – a well presented and informative section from the About website.

www.caloriecontrol.org – low fat information from the Calorie Control Council.

www.coolmeals.co.uk – food facts for kids.

www.cyberdiet.com – a good all rounder with a wide range of advice, including specialist diets.

www.eatwellcard.co.uk – personal dietary advice.

www.fatfree.com – almost 5,000 recipes all fat free or very low fat.

www.fatfreekitchen.com – Indian vegetarian and low fat recipes.

www.foodag.com – the food additives guide with information on what additives are bad for you and are derived from animals.

www.nutrition.org.uk – home of the British Nutrition Foundation, a site with masses of advice and infor-mation, especially useful for parents.

www.realslimmers.com – a well designed site with good advice and practical help.

www.rosemary-conley.co.uk – all about Rosemary and her healthy lifestyle.

Special dietary needs

Also refer to the section on health, page 196.

www.diabeticgourmet.com
DELICIOUS FOR DIABETICS

ORIGIN UK
INFO ✓✓✓✓
EASE ✓✓✓✓

Lots of recipes and ideas to make food palatable without endangering your blood sugar levels from *Diabetic Gourmet* magazine, see also www.diabetic.com/cookbook/ where there's a great archive of recipes.

www.gfcfdiet.com/
GLUTEN FREE

ORIGIN UK
INFO ✓✓✓✓
EASE ✓✓✓

Not a great site but it has very good information on gluten free products and food. See also www.celiac.com who have some good recipes and www.glutenfreemall.com whose temperamental site has lots of information on products, although they don't deliver to the UK at time of writing.

French food

www.gourmet2000.co.uk

LE GOURMET FRANÇAIS

ORIGIN UK	High quality French ingredients and recipes, combined
INFO ✓✓✓✓	with a nicely designed site and convenient shopping.
VALUE ✓✓	Delivery is very pricey at £7.99 for the minimum £20
EASE ✓✓✓✓	order, but once you spend £100 it's free.

http://frenchfood.about.com

FRENCH CUISINE

ORIGIN US	About.com have created a superb resource at this site
INFO ✓✓✓✓✓	with a huge amount of data, articles and recipes. Every
EASE ✓✓✓✓	aspect of French cooking seems to be covered from the
	ingredients to the shops and presentation.

See also:
www.afrenchkiss.com – make your own gourmet
   meals with this fun French recipe creation program.
www.manoir.com – world class recipes from Raymond
   Blanc as well as details of his hotels and restaurants.

Hygiene and food safety

www.foodsafety.gov/~fsg/fsgadvic.html

FOOD SAFETY

ORIGIN UK	A government site with basic advice on handling foods
INFO ✓✓✓✓	in all sorts of situations from product-specific advice
EASE ✓✓✓✓	to helping those with special needs; there's also good
	links to related topics. See also
	www.foodstandards.gov.uk home of the Food
	Standards Association who have lots of information on
	what is safe to eat.

Italian food

www.mangiarebene.net

EAT WELL

ORIGIN	US
INFO	✓✓✓✓✓
EASE	✓✓✓✓

An award-winning site that covers everything to do with Italian cookery. Its aim is to give a grand tour of Italian cuisine – and it succeeds, including some 600 recipes in the English language section, but over 1,600 overall. See also **http://italy1.com/cuisine** which has good regional cooking and food information as well as lots of recipes, while for Italian food shopping try **www.esperya.com**

www.ilovepasta.org

US NATIONAL PASTA ASSOCIATION

ORIGIN	US
INFO	✓✓✓✓✓
EASE	✓✓✓✓

250 recipes, tips, fast meals and healthy options all wrapped up in a clear and easy-to-use site. There's also information on the different types of pasta and advice on the right sauces to go with them.

www.getoily.com

OLIVE OIL

ORIGIN	UK
INFO	✓✓✓✓
VALUE	✓✓✓
EASE	✓✓✓✓

All you need to know about olive oil, cooking with it, health benefits and history, oh and you can buy it too, along with a good selection of other Mediterranean products.

www.dominos.co.uk

PIZZA DELIVERY

ORIGIN	UK
INFO	✓✓✓
VALUE	✓✓✓
EASE	✓✓✓✓

Order your pizza online and get it delivered to your home providing you live near enough to one of their outlets that is. It's a nicely designed site, which also has a few games if you get bored waiting.

Kitchen equipment

www.lakelandlimited.co.uk

EXCELLENT CUSTOMER SERVICE

ORIGIN	UK
INFO	✓✓✓✓
VALUE	✓✓✓
EASE	✓✓✓✓

Lakeland pride themselves on service and it shows, they aim to get all orders dispatched in 24 hours and delivery on orders over £40 is free. The product listing for both kitchen and homeware is comprehensive too.

See also:

www.alessi.com – a tour round the kitchen design powerhouse that is Alessi, the best bit is that you can now buy from this site too.

www.divertimenti.co.uk – Divertimenti are also worth a look, they go for quality and they are good for gifts.

www.japaneseknifecompany.co.uk – specialists in Japanese cutlery, fantastic quality, some recipes too.

www.kingsofhagley.co.uk – excellent cookware shop with lots of choice and a personal service.

www.kitchenware.co.uk – have a good range, with postage for the UK being £2.95 per order.

www.pots-and-pans.co.uk – Scottish company offering kitchen equipment through a good online store; it's good value but delivery charges may vary.

Kosher cookery

www.koshercooking.com

JEWISH CUISINE

ORIGIN UK	Lots of recipes and links covering all forms of kosher
INFO ✓✓✓✓	cookery and occasions. For more Jewish cookery try
EASE ✓✓✓✓	www.jewishcuisine.com

Luxury food, deli and gift sites

www.stgeorgessquare.com

A VIRTUAL VILLAGE MARKET SQUARE

ORIGIN UK	St Georges Square features an expanding range of
INFO ✓✓✓✓	gifts, incentives and prizes for delivery in the UK
VALUE ✓✓✓	and overseas. You can send flowers, chocolates, fruit,
EASE ✓✓✓✓	wine, and a range of themed hampers, Edinburgh
	crystal, or simply send a gift voucher. It's fast and easy
	to use, with some good offers too. Delivery depends on
	type of order placed.

www.allpresent.com

GIFTS FOR THE DISCERNING

ORIGIN UK	An Amazon-style shop offering gifts in the form of
INFO ✓✓✓✓	chocolates, drinks and bakery items such as cakes
VALUE ✓✓	and biscuits all beautifully boxed. They also sell
EASE ✓✓✓✓	flowers and cards; delivery costs vary according
	to what you buy.

www.fortnumandmason.co.uk

EXQUISITE GIFTS

ORIGIN UK	A wide range of gift chocolates, hampers and more
INFO ✓✓✓✓	from one of the leading luxury stores, UK residents
VALUE ✓✓	have a wider choice including condiments, teas and
EASE ✓✓✓✓	wines. Carriage is £7 for UK residents unless you're
	a F&M account holder then it's free when you
	spend £50.

See also:
www.champershampers.co.uk – family run
    hamper business.
www.fifthsense.com – odd design but a wide range
    and good value.
www.hamper.com – good design and a wide range
    of products.
www.hampers.uk.com – a wide range of hampers
    large and small.

Meat and fish

www.realmeatco.sageweb.co.uk

WELFARE WITHOUT COMPROMISE

ORIGIN UK	Produces meat in a caring and compassionate way,
INFO ✓✓✓✓	they are against things like livestock markets for
VALUE ✓✓	example. You can buy online or visit one of the
EASE ✓✓✓✓	approved list of butchers. The shop is split into several
	areas featuring different meat products, its easy to use
	but the minimum order is £35.

www.traditionalbutcher.co.uk

A TRADITIONAL BUTCHER

ORIGIN UK	John Miles is based in Herefordshire and knows a
INFO ✓✓✓✓	thing or two about meat. You can buy meats and deli
VALUE ✓✓✓	products online, there's a good range and delivery is
EASE ✓✓✓✓	charged at cost. They seem to take a great deal of care

on quality. See also **www.meat-at-your-door.com** who offer a wide range of meats and you get a 5% discount if you spend more than £100.

www.fresh-fish-online.co.uk

FRESH FISH DELIVERED

ORIGIN UK	A Devon company who own their own trawlers will
INFO ✓✓✓✓	deliver overnight so that your fish is very fresh. They
VALUE ✓✓✓	also deliver frozen, shell fish and smoked fish. Delivery
EASE ✓✓✓✓	costs vary but it's free if you spend over £60.

Middle Eastern cookery

www.al-bab.com/arab/food.htm

MIDDLE EAST CUISINE

ORIGIN UK	An excellent overview of Arab cuisine from Arab
INFO ✓✓✓✓	Gateway with links to key sites covering all the major
VALUE ✓✓✓✓✓	styles. See also the enjoyable Nadia's Middle Eastern
EASE ✓✓✓✓	Cookery site at **http://twdg.com/cooking/home.html**

www.arabicslice.com

STEP BY STEP ARABIC CUISINE

ORIGIN UK	A well designed and well written cookery site featuring
INFO ✓✓✓✓	the best of Arabic food with simple step-by-step
EASE ✓✓✓✓	recipes, lots of explanation and illustrations.

Miscellaneous food sites

www.leapingsalmon.co.uk
STRESS IS FOR OTHER FISH

ORIGIN UK
INFO ✓✓✓✓✓
VALUE ✓✓✓
EASE ✓✓✓✓

This well publicised site is about providing creative and inspirational products to make gourmet cooking fun and achievable in the home. Each meal kit is created for two people by a top chef with step-by-step instructions; order your meal the day before and it gets delivered overnight so that the food is as fresh as possible. They deliver anywhere in the UK for £4.50. Same day delivery is available in London. It really works.

www.reluctantgourmet.com
GOURMET COOKING FOR BEGINNERS

ORIGIN US
INFO ✓✓✓✓✓
EASE ✓✓✓✓

Basically a beginner's cookery book, it's well designed and easy to follow with a glossary, guide to techniques, equipment, tips and recipes.

www.cheftalk.com
THE FOOD LOVER'S LINK TO PROFESSIONAL CHEFS

ORIGIN UK
INFO ✓✓✓✓✓
EASE ✓✓✓✓

Excellent site devoted to articles and discussion about food with tips and advice from the top chefs. There's a good links section, recipes and a recommended restaurant guide.

www.expatboxes.com
FOOD PARCELS FOR THOSE LIVING ABROAD

ORIGIN UK
INFO ✓✓✓
VALUE ✓✓✓
EASE ✓✓✓✓

OK so you miss HP sauce, childhood sweet favourites and proper salad cream; relief is at hand here. You can get your rations in the form of specially selected hampers or they will tailor make and shop the High Street for you. Delivery costs are high.

Recipes, general food sites and magazines

www.kitchenlink.com
WHAT'S COOKING ON THE NET

ORIGIN US
INFO ✓✓✓✓✓
EASE ✓✓✓

A bit clunky to use, but it has so many links to other key foodie sites and food-related sections that it has to be the place to start your online food and drink experience. The design can make it irritating to use and it's got a little slow, but persevere and you'll be rewarded with a resource that is difficult to beat.

Other American sites worth checking out are these. All have loads of recipes and it's just a matter of finding one you like.

ww.cyber-kitchen.com – excellent for links and specialised subjects.

www.chef2chef.net – outstanding cookery portal site with masses of links.

www.cookeryonline.com – very messy design but pretty comprehensive.

www.foodstop.com – excellent articles about food.

www.goodcooking.com – another excellent food site, with some good food writing.

www.ichef.com – good search facility, nice design.

www.meals.com – good for meal planning and recipes.

www.netcooks.com – hundreds of recipes submitted by the public.

www.recipezaar.com – the world's smartest cookbook.

www.ucook.com – the ultimate cookery shop with recipes added.

www.yumyum.com – good fun.

www.tudocs.com
THE ULTIMATE DIRECTORY OF COOKING SITES

ORIGIN US
INFO ✓✓✓✓✓
EASE ✓✓✓✓

The main difference with Tudocs is that it grades each cookery site on its site listing. The listing is divided up into 19 sections, such as meat, beverages, low fat and ethnic. British cookery is in the ethnic section. See also **www.cookingindex.com**

http://epicurious.com

WORLD'S GREATEST RECIPE COLECTION

ORIGIN US
INFO ✓✓✓✓✓
EASE ✓✓✓✓

Owned by Condé Nast, this massive site combines articles from their magazines with information generated by the Epicurious team, the site has been tidied up but there's still plenty of advice on topics such as recipes, cooking tips, TV, restaurant reviews, live-chat, forums, wine and kitchen equipment. It's fast, easy to navigate and international in feel.

www.foodlines.com

FOR THOSE WITH A PASSION FOR FOOD

ORIGIN CANADA
INFO ✓✓✓✓
EASE ✓✓✓✓

It's easy to find the right recipe at this comprehensive site with a modern touch. There are some good recipes, as well as food quizzes and food jokes.

www.allrecipes.com

THE HOME OF GREAT RECIPES

ORIGIN US
INFO ✓✓✓✓✓
EASE ✓✓✓✓

This site gets its own review because it's not overly cluttered, it's just got loads of recipes which can be found easily and each is rated by people who have cooked them.

http://cookbook.rin.ru

COOKERY ART

ORIGIN RUSSIA
INFO ✓✓✓✓✓
EASE ✓✓✓✓

Really interesting cookery site; all the usual recipe sections but some unusual ones including exotic and erotic!

Vegetarian and organic

www.organicfood.co.uk

A WORLD OF ORGANIC INFORMATION

ORIGIN UK
INFO ✓✓✓✓✓
EASE ✓✓✓✓

A very informative site which gives the latest news on organic food. There are sections on why you should shop organic, recommendations on retailers, lifestyle tips, shopping and chat. There's also links to key related sites.

www.organicsdirect.co.uk
ORGANIC FOOD DELIVERED NATIONWIDE

ORIGIN UK
INFO ✓✓✓✓
VALUE ✓✓✓✓
EASE ✓✓✓✓

An award-winning site, this company offers a wide variety of organic food and other related products. The whole thing is well put together with the emphasis on ethical living and it's much better value than supermarkets, delivery (UK) is free if you buy a veg box otherwise it is £5.95.

www.theorganicshop.co.uk
GOOD VALUE ORGANIC FOOD

ORIGIN UK
INFO ✓✓✓✓
VALUE ✓✓✓✓✓
EASE ✓✓✓✓

Excellent organic store with some great introductory offers, charity donations and free delivery if you spend up to a certain amount on food and wine.

See also:

www.crueltyfreeshop.com – the animal-friendly super-store who sell a wide range of products but a limited amount of foodstuffs.

www.organicdelivery.co.uk – a good organic food retailer with some good offers.

www.simplyorganic.net – the organic supermarket, a range of around 2,500 products.

www.freshfood.co.uk
THE FRESH FOOD COMPANY

ORIGIN UK
INFO ✓✓✓✓
VALUE ✓✓✓✓
EASE ✓✓

Another combined supermarket and information site with a wide range of produce to choose from, this one has a recipe section too. They have a subscription system, which delivers your chosen goods on a regular basis. Delivery charges are included in the prices quoted for the mainland UK, if you live offshore then you pay a surcharge.

www.vegsoc.org
THE VEGETARIAN SOCIETY

ORIGIN UK
INFO ✓✓✓✓✓
VALUE ✓✓✓
EASE ✓✓✓✓

This is the official site of the UK branch with sections on news, new veggies, environment, business opportunities, recipes and the Cordon Vert school, youth with virtual schoolroom, health, membership info and online bookstore. Each section is packed with information, written in plain English, and there is a search engine for information on any veggie topic.

www.vegweb.com

VEGGIES UNITE!

ORIGIN US
INFO ✓✓✓✓✓
EASE ✓✓

If you're a vegetarian this is a great place, though not a great design. There are hundreds of recipes, plus features, chat and ideas in the VegWeb newsletter.

www.vegansociety.com

AVOIDING THE USE OF ANIMAL PRODUCTS

ORIGIN UK
INFO ✓✓✓✓
VALUE ✓✓✓
EASE ✓✓✓✓

The official site of the Vegan Society, promotes veganism by providing information, links to other related sites and books. You can't shop for food from the site (although you can get vegekit) but it does recommend suitable retailers. If you want to shop go to www.veganstore.co.uk who offer over 800 suitable products.

See also:

www.earthsave.org – a worthy organisation who promote vegetarianism by helping you choose the right way to eat.

www.living-foods.com – devoted to the subject of eating only raw foods.

www.veggieheaven.com – UK restaurant guide for vegetarians and vegans with over 170 listed.

Drink: non-alcoholic

www.whittard.co.uk

SPECIALITY TEAS DELIVERED WORLD-WIDE

ORIGIN UK
INFO ✓✓✓✓
VALUE ✓✓✓✓
EASE ✓✓✓✓

An excellent site dedicated to their selection of teas and coffee's, it's easy to use and they will ship throughout the world. Delivery is £3.50 for the UK – free if you spend £50 or more.

See also:

www.realcoffee.co.uk – coffee delivered to your door the day after roasting from the Roast and Post Coffee company.

www.redmonkeycoffee.com – modern online coffee retailer with free UK delivery.

www.tea.co.uk – great looking site from the Tea Council with lots of facts and reasons given why we should drink more of the stuff.

Drink: beer

www.camra.org.uk

THE CAMPAIGN FOR REAL ALE STARTS HERE

ORIGIN UK

INFO ✓✓✓

EASE ✓✓✓✓

A comprehensive site that has all the news and views on the campaign for real ale. Sadly, it only advertises its *Good Beer Guide* and local versions, with only a small section on the best beers. Includes sections on beer in Europe, cider and festivals.

www.realbeer.com

THE BEER PORTAL

ORIGIN US

INFO ✓✓✓✓

EASE ✓✓✓✓

Over 150,000 pages dedicated to beer, with articles, reviews, links and shopping all wrapped up in a well designed site. See also the very good www.beerhunter.com which is home to expert Michael Jackson author of the World Beer Guide and for the unusual try www.beersofeurope.co.uk who offer a huge range from their shop.

Drink: wine and spirits

There are many web sites selling wine and spirits, these are the best so far.

www.berry-bros.co.uk or www.bbr.co.uk

THE INTERNET WINE SHOP

ORIGIN UK

INFO ✓✓✓✓

VALUE ✓✓✓

EASE ✓✓✓✓

This attractive and award-winning site offers over 1,000 different wines and spirits at prices from £4 to over £4,000. There is a great deal of information about each wine and advice on the different varieties. You can also buy related products such as cigars. Delivery for orders over £120 is free; otherwise it's £9 for the UK. They will deliver abroad and even store the wine for you.

www.winecellar.co.uk

NOT JUST WINE AND GOOD VALUE

ORIGIN UK

INFO ✓✓✓✓

VALUE ✓✓✓✓

EASE ✓✓✓

They also sell spirits as well as wine and, while the choice isn't as good as some online wine retailers, Wine Cellar are good value. Use the search facility to find the whole range which isn't obvious from the home page. Delivery is free for orders of 12 bottles or more; otherwise it's £4.99.

www.wine-lovers-page.com

ONE OF THE BEST PLACES TO LEARN ABOUT WINE

ORIGIN US

INFO ✓✓✓✓✓

VALUE ✓✓✓✓

EASE ✓✓✓

Highly informative for novices and experts alike, this site has it all. There are categories on learning about wine, reading and buying books and tasting notes for some 80,000 wines. Also within the site there's a label decoder, a list of Internet wine shops, wine writers archive, wine search engine and much more.

www.winespectator.com

THE MOST COMPREHENSIVE WINE WEB SITE

ORIGIN UK

INFO ✓✓✓✓✓

EASE ✓✓✓

From *Wine Spectator* magazine you get a site packed with information. There are eleven comprehensive sections, including news, features, a wine search facility, forums, weekly features, a library, the best wineries, wine auctions and travel. The dining section has a world restaurant guide, tips on eating out, wine matching and a set of links to gourmet food.

www.wine-pages.com

A GREAT BRITISH NON-COMMERCIAL WINE SITE

ORIGIN UK

INFO ✓✓✓✓✓

EASE ✓✓✓

Most independently written wine sites are poor, however wine expert Tom Cannavan has put together a strong offering, which is updated daily. It's well written, informative and links to other good wine sites and online wine merchants.

www.wineanorak.com

THE WINE ANORAK

ORIGIN UK

INFO ✓✓✓✓✓

EASE ✓✓✓✓

For another good British independent wine site, try the Wine Anorak, it's just a great wine magazine, with lots of advice, articles, issues of the day and general information on wines and regions.

www.jancisrobinson.com

TV WINE EXPERT

ORIGIN UK
INFO ✓✓✓
EASE ✓✓✓

Jancis Robinson has a bright site with wine news, tips, and features on the latest wines and information on her books and videos.

www.ozclarke.com

OZ ON OZ

ORIGIN UK
INFO ✓✓✓✓
VALUE ✓✓✓✓
EASE ✓✓✓

Lots about Oz and what he's up to plus information on how to get his books and CD-ROM. There's also his wine magazine to browse, which includes tips on tasting, producer profiles, wine basics and the latest news.

www.superplonk.com

MALCOLM GLUCK

ORIGIN UK
INFO ✓✓✓✓✓
EASE ✓✓✓✓

Excellent site from Malcolm Gluck, the author of the Superplonk books; there are offers and tips on where to buy good value high quality wines. Sometimes slow to download.

Other wine sites worth checking out are:
www.cephas.co.uk – superb images of wines and vineyards around the world.
www.internetwineguide.com – a good, if advert laden, all rounder.
www.madaboutwine.com – easy to use, good value wine shop, with help and advice.
www.majestic.co.uk – lots of offers and a well designed site.
www.vintageroots.co.uk – excellent for organic wines, spirits and beers.
www.wineontheweb.com – good wine magazine with audio features.
www.winepros.co.uk – a very informative site with lots of reviews, advice, links and chat.
www.wine-searcher.com – a wine search engine, type in the wine you want and up pops a selection from various retailers from around the world and UK, all suppliers are vetted for quality and service.

www.drinkboy.com

ADVENTURES IN COCKTAILS

ORIGIN US
INFO ✓✓✓✓
EASE ✓✓✓✓✓

You can't shop from this site, but it contains virtually everything you need to know about cocktails including instructions for more than 100. There is also a section in the making on party games. See also www.idrink.com who enable you to create cocktails from over 160 ingredients.

www.barmeister.com

THE ONLINE GUIDE TO DRINKING

ORIGIN US
INFO ✓✓✓✓
EASE ✓✓✓✓

Packed with information on everything to do with drink, there are over 1,700 drink recipes available and about 500 drinking games. If you have another, then send it to be featured in the site.

Eating out

www.goodguides.com

HOME OF THE GOOD PUB GUIDE

ORIGIN UK
INFO ✓✓✓✓
EASE ✓✓✓✓

Once you've registered it has an easy-to-use regional guide to the best pubs, which are rated on food, beer, value, good places to stay and good range of wine. You can also get a listing by award winner. It also houses the Good Guide to Britain, which is a good resource for what's on where. See also www.greatbeer.co.uk one man's passion and guide to over 200 pubs in the UK.

www.dine-online.co.uk

UK-BASED WINING, DINING AND TRAVEL REVIEW

ORIGIN UK
INFO ✓✓✓✓
EASE ✓✓✓✓

A slightly pretentious, but a sincere attempt at an independent eating out review web site. It has a good and expanding selection of recommended restaurants, covers wine and has some well-written feature articles. It relies heavily on reader recommendation, so there's a good deal of variation in coverage and review quality.

www.theaa.com/getaway/restaurants/ restaurant/home.jsp

AA RESTAURANT SEARCH

ORIGIN UK
INFO ✓✓✓✓✓
EASE ✓✓✓✓✓

Nestled away in the AA site is a little known gem in its hotels section – an excellent regional restaurant guide to the UK. Each of the 4,000 listed is graded and there are comments on quality of food, ambience, an idea of the price and, of course, how to get there.

www.viamichelin.co.uk

MICHELIN

ORIGIN UK
INFO ✓✓✓✓
EASE ✓✓✓✓

A revamped site from Michelin with improved route finding and a good restaurant and hotel guide. Really annoying intrusive pop-up adverts though.

www.gofortea.com

TEA TIME

ORIGIN UK
INFO ✓✓✓✓
EASE ✓✓✓✓

A site devoted to finding the best spots for the traditional British afternoon tea, though it does concentrate on hotels rather than tea shops.

Other restaurant review sites worth looking at before you go out are:

www.conran.com/eat – a guide to Terence Conran's restaurants with online booking and some special offers, nice design too.

www.cuisinenet.co.uk – book online at selected restaurants, nice design.

www.local-restaurant.com – good restaurant finder.

www.restaurantreview.co.uk – good design, but London only.

www.toptable.co.uk – co-ordinates free booking at over 1,100 restaurants, nice design too.

www.ukrestaurantguide.com – good for links and finding a restaurant but slow and not comprehensive.

Free Stuff

Free stuff is exactly what the term suggests, and these are sites whose owners have trawled the Net or been offered free services, software, trial products and so on. It's amazing what you can find but as most sites are American some offers won't apply.

www.allforfree.co.uk

DELIVERED DAILY IN YOUR E-MAIL

ORIGIN UK
INFO ✓✓✓✓✓
VALUE ✓✓✓✓✓
EASE ✓✓✓✓

All for free will let you know all the latest 'free' news with their e-mail service. There's a lot here, the highlights being how to ensure that you are getting the most out of government services, free Internet access, free magazines and where to go for the best competitions. Members get even more tips and information.

www.free.com

GET SOMETHING FOR NOTHING

ORIGIN US
INFO ✓✓✓✓✓
VALUE ✓✓✓✓✓
EASE ✓✓✓✓✓

One of the best and largest sites of its type, there are literally hundreds of pages of free goodies waiting to be snapped up. Very wide-ranging and very much geared towards the US, but with over 9,000 links you should find something.

www.freeinuk.co.uk

JUST THE UK

ORIGIN UK
INFO ✓✓✓✓✓
VALUE ✓✓✓✓✓
EASE ✓✓✓✓

Not just free stuff but also excellent internet offers from British sites, good design, but not that easy to navigate. The Top 10 section is great.

Other sites worth looking into are these listed below, but most are American so some offers may not apply for the UK.

www.1freestuff.com – one of the oldest and probably best categorised.

www.find-a-freebie.co.uk – very well categorised and extensive selection.

www.freeandfun.com – the usual long list, don't see what's fun about it though.

www.freebielist.com – a well categorised listing - easy to use and good links.

www.thefreesite.com – more of the same, nice layout.
www.thefreezone.co.uk – an excellent collection of
   link pages.
www.totallyfreestuff.com – massive selection.

Furniture

*Believe it or not it's becoming quite common to order items of
furniture for the home over the Net, or at least to browse online
catalogues before venturing out into the stores.*

www.mfi.co.uk
MFI HOMEWORKS

ORIGIN UK	MFI offer a nicely designed site with all the best
INFO ✓✓✓✓	aspects of online shopping and a wide range of
VALUE ✓✓✓	surprisingly good furniture for home and office
EASE ✓✓✓✓	available for order online or via a hotline. Delivery
	is included in the price.

www.habitat.net
DESIGN OVER CONTENT

ORIGIN UK	A clever, beautiful if slightly irritating web site giving
INFO ✓✓✓	an overview of what Habitat are about and what they
VALUE ✓✓✓	stock; you can't order online though you can check
EASE ✓✓✓	store availability.

www.mccord.uk.com
MCCORDS CATALOGUE

ORIGIN UK	McCords offer a huge range of furniture, gift ideas
INFO ✓✓✓✓✓	and accessories for the home via their online catalogue.
EASE ✓✓✓	It's very quick, easy to use, good value and delivery is
	£3.95 per order. Straightforward returns policy.

www.furniture123.co.uk
SMART PLACE TO BUY FURNITURE

ORIGIN UK	This company has a well laid out web site offering
INFO ✓✓✓✓	a good range of furniture, many offers, tips and
VALUE ✓✓✓✓	free delivery.
EASE ✓✓✓✓	

www.heals.co.uk

STYLISH CONTEMPORARY DESIGN

ORIGIN UK
INFO ✓✓✓✓
VALUE ✓✓✓
EASE ✓✓✓✓

Heals has a beautifully designed web site which gives information about the store and inspiration for the home. There's an online store which stocks primarily gifts and home accessories, but there's a special services section where you can get information on furniture and interior design.

www.conran.com

TERENCE CONRAN STYLE

ORIGIN UK
INFO ✓✓✓
VALUE ✓✓✓
EASE ✓✓✓✓

As well as information on all his restaurants, this site has an online shopping facility that allows you to buy Conran-designed accessories as well as stuff for the home including a good range of furniture and kitchen products.

www.ancestralcollections.co.uk

REPRODUCTIONS FROM THE BEST HOMES

ORIGIN UK
INFO ✓✓✓✓
VALUE ✓✓✓
EASE ✓✓✓✓

If you've ever fancied a Regency stool or any decent piece of antique furniture but couldn't run to the expense, then this company will supply you with a reproduction. They have a wide range of products not just furniture and are great for unusual gifts too.

www.amazingemporium.com

REPRODUCTIONS FROM THE BEST HOMES

ORIGIN UK
INFO ✓✓✓✓
VALUE ✓✓✓✓
EASE ✓✓✓✓

A web site that has developed well with a wide range of high quality beds and furniture on an attractive site with good pictures and descriptions of the products. They've expanded into gifts too and offer good value for money.

Other furniture retailers that may be worth a virtual visit are:
www.bedbathandhome.co.uk – excellent for soft furnishings with delivery from £2.99.
www.cjfurniture.com – contemporary furniture.
www.davidlinley.com – posh contemporary classics.
www.mufti.co.uk – more posh beautifully designed furniture.

www.new-heights.co.uk – simple, stylish solid wood.
www.sofaworkshopdirect.co.uk – well designed with
quality photos of the sofas and what looks like a
good online service.

Gambling and Betting Sites

*Gambling sites abound on the Internet and they often use some of
the most sophisticated marketing techniques to keep you hooked;
new screens pop up as you click on the close button tempting you
with the chance to win millions. All the gaming sites are monitored
by gaming commissions but above all be sensible, it's easy to get
carried away. You should be aware that some carry spyware,
programs that monitor your online activity.*

www.national-lottery.co.uk

IT COULD BE YOU

ORIGIN UK
INFO ✓✓✓✓
EASE ✓✓✓✓

Find out about Camelot, good causes, the National
Lottery and whether you've won. Also, find out
whether your premium bonds are worth anything at
www.nationalsavings.co.uk you need your bondholder
number handy.

www.gamblehouse.com

YOUR ONLINE GAMBLING GUIDE

ORIGIN UK
INFO ✓✓✓✓✓
EASE ✓✓✓✓

A very good place to start, they review online casinos
and rank them according to whether they are licensed,
make payments quickly, offer good odds, variety and
quality of games and lastly customer service. Lots of
pop-up adverts though.

These are the casinos and gambling sites we liked:
www.24ktgoldcasino.com – good graphics and fast
response times make this great fun, but you need a
decent PC to download the software. There are 40
or so games and you can either play for fun or for
money.
www.888.com – claims to be the world's most popular
online casino, great design.

> **www.entercasino.com** – the Gamble House number one casino, need we say more.
>
> **www.galagames.co.uk** – good graphics, lots of games and less fussy than most.
>
> **www.intercasino.com** – easy to use and they've got 35 games to choose from.
>
> **www.pogo.com** – from EA Games lots to choose from, lots of prizes to play for.

www.oddschecker.co.uk

COMPARE THE ODDS

ORIGIN UK
INFO ✓✓✓✓✓
EASE ✓✓✓✓

A great way to ensure you get the best deal from the online bookmakers, you just choose the sport and the event, then you get a read out of the latest odds and from a selection of bookies – you can click on the bookmaker to visit and place your bet. It's continually being updated; we'd say the site was a must for the committed gambler.

www.ukbetting.com

LIVE INTERACTIVE BETTING

ORIGIN UK
INFO ✓✓✓✓
EASE ✓✓✓✓

Concentrating on sports betting, this is a clear, easy-to-use site; take a guest tour before applying to join. You need to open an account to take part, using your credit or debit card, bets are £1 minimum. See also the popular **www.bluesq.com** also offers a similar service, but with a football bias and special bets on things like soap operas and political elections. Also worth a visit is **www.bet365.co.uk** who cover a wide variety of areas and offer some good deals.

www.mybetting.co.uk

FREE BETTING

ORIGIN UK
INFO ✓✓✓✓✓
VALUE ✓✓✓✓✓
EASE ✓✓✓

My betting works as a collation site for free bets and offers from bookmakers around the Internet. It takes a minute or so to get used to the design but once you're on board it's easy to get yourself a few free bets, albeit at the price of a registration or two.

www.racingpost.co.uk

THE RACING POST

ORIGIN	UK	A combination of news, racing and betting on a clearly
INFO	✓✓✓✓	laid out and well-designed site. Also features grey-
EASE	✓✓✓✓	hounds and information on bloodstock.

www.ladbrokes.co.uk

UK'S NUMBER 1 BOOKMAKER

ORIGIN	UK	Ladbrokes offer a combination of news, information
INFO	✓✓✓✓	and betting, which is geared to sport with excellent
EASE	✓✓✓✓	features on racing, golf and the other major sporting

events. There's even a casino, lotteries, a fantasy league
and a sort of bingo game called balls!

www.willhill.com

THE MOST RESPECTED NAME IN BOOKMAKING

ORIGIN	UK	The best online betting site in terms of speed, layout
INFO	✓✓✓✓	and design, it has the best event finder, results service
EASE	✓✓✓✓✓	and betting calculator. The bet finder service is also

very good and quick. All the major sports are featured
and there is a specials section for those out of the ordinary flutters. Betting is live as it happens.

See also:

www.paddypower.com – a strong site from Ireland's
biggest bookmaker with betting on horses, football
and other top sports – even politics.

www.sportingindex.com – excellent and wide ranging
spread betting site with offers and competitions.

www.victorchandler.com – horse racing specialist but
covers other sports too.

www.tote.co.uk

BET ON THE HORSES, LIVE

ORIGIN	UK	Devoted to horse racing, the Tote fairly successfully
INFO	✓✓✓✓	attempts to bring you the excitement and feel of live
VALUE	✓✓✓✓	betting online. It explains what the bets mean and has
EASE	✓✓✓✓	a very good set of links relating to horses and racing.

www.thedogs.co.uk
GONE TO THE DOGS

ORIGIN UK
INFO ✓✓✓✓✓
EASE ✓✓✓✓

Everything you need to know about greyhounds and greyhound racing. You can adopt or get advice on buying a dog, find the nearest track, get the latest results and learn how to place bets. You can't gamble from the site but they provide links.

www.betasyouclick.com
THE ONLINE GAMBLER'S DIRECTORY

ORIGIN US
INFO ✓✓✓
EASE ✓✓✓✓

A betting and gambling directory with links to web sites from around the world, which offer sports books, casinos, financial spread betting, lotteries and competitions.

Games

There's a massive selection of games on the Internet, here's just some of the very best ones; from board games to quizzes to your everyday 'shoot 'em up' type. There are more games for Macs listed on page 19.

It's worth remembering that before downloading a game from a site it's wise to check for viruses. If you've not got anti-virus software on your PC then check out our section on Security on page 320.

Finding games

http://gamespotter.com
GAMES SEARCH ENGINE

ORIGIN US
INFO ✓✓✓✓
EASE ✓✓✓✓

A really handy site where you can get links to virtually every type of game whether it be a puzzle or action. Alternatively, you can use the search facility to find something. Each game on the list is reviewed as well.

Games magazines

www.avault.com

THE ADRENALINE VAULT

ORIGIN US
INFO ✓✓✓✓
EASE ✓✓✓✓

A comprehensive games magazine with demos, reviews and features on software and hardware – good looking too. There's also a good cheats and hints section.

www.gamespy.com

GAMINGS HOMEPAGE

ORIGIN US
INFO ✓✓✓✓
EASE ✓✓✓✓

Lots here, apart from the usual reviews and features. There are chat and help sections and links to the arcade section with some 300 demos plus free games to play. See also **www.gamespot.co.uk** which offers lots of info as well.

www.gamers.com

A MOMENT ENJOYED IS NOT WASTED

ORIGIN US
INFO ✓✓✓✓
EASE ✓✓✓✓

A great-looking site with all the features you'd expect from a games magazine but it has more in the way of downloads and games to play. There is also a chat section and competitions.

www.gamesdomain.co.uk

THE GAMES DOMAIN

ORIGIN US
INFO ✓✓✓✓
EASE ✓✓✓✓

A strong combination of freebies, competitions, good links, news and reviews make this site a great place to start online gaming. It's clear, fast and easy to use.

www.happypuppy.com

GAMES REVIEWED

ORIGIN US
INFO ✓✓✓✓✓
EASE ✓✓✓✓

Happy Puppy has been around a while now reviewing games in all the major formats. Each is given a thorough test, then it's rated and given a review. There are also links to related games sites. It's all packaged on a really good web site which is quick and user-friendly.

www.gamefaqs.com
GAMES FREQUENTLY ASKED QUESTIONS
ORIGIN US
INFO ✓✓✓✓
EASE ✓✓✓✓

All information is free and donated, there are FAQs and tip sheets on any number of games, and it seems to be regularly updated.

www.game-sector.co.uk
FOR THE GAMERS BY THE GAMERS
ORIGIN UK
INFO ✓✓✓✓
EASE ✓✓✓✓

Easy on the eye design, latest news and reviews with links and surveys. We don't normally include sites looking for funding at time of our visit, but this one deserves to succeed.

Games to play

www.barrysworld.com
GAMES ONLINE
ORIGIN UK
INFO ✓✓✓✓✓
EASE ✓✓✓

Barrysworld specialise in providing online servers for players to play their games and you can take part in several from this site. There's also more information and links than you'll ever need, which makes it a little daunting at first, but it's also helpful and very well written.

www.boxerjam.com
ONLINE GAMESHOW
ORIGIN UK
INFO ✓✓✓✓✓
VALUE ✓✓✓✓
EASE ✓✓✓✓

Excellent site devoted to giving the user access to original and traditional games played online, for cash and prizes.

www.classicgaming.com
GAMING THE WAY YOU REMEMBER IT
ORIGIN US
INFO ✓✓✓
EASE ✓✓✓✓

Probably one for older gamers but there's some good stuff on here so it's at least worth a look and it's amazing how new some of the games are.

www.gamehippo.com

OVER 1000 FREE GAMES

ORIGIN US
INFO ✓✓✓✓✓
EASE ✓✓✓✓

Enough to keep you occupied for hours with games of every type from board to action to puzzles and sports. There's also a really good set of links to other sites. It's worth checking out **www.freeloader.com** which has a more modern selection available, but you have to register and jump through a few hoops to get them.

See also the oddly designed **www.download-game.com** who also offer a large number including old favourites, and Sean O'Connor's site **www.windowsgames.co.uk** where there's a small selection of high quality games to download.

www.gamearchive.com

PINBALL MACHINES

ORIGIN UK
INFO ✓✓✓
EASE ✓✓✓✓

A site devoted to pinball machines and similar games put together by real fans. There's also a selection of video games and links to similar sites, however, there are no console games. See also **www.videogames.org**

www.gamebrew.com

JAVA GAMING

ORIGIN US
INFO ✓✓✓✓
EASE ✓✓✓✓

Gamebrew specialise in Java games and there are some brilliant ones to download and play here. The Java program gives gaming an extra edge with brilliant graphics in particular. Send them to your friends. The site has some really annoying pop-up ads.

http://games.yahoo.com

YAHOO!

ORIGIN US
INFO ✓✓✓✓
EASE ✓✓✓✓

This popular search engine has its own games section. Here you can play against others or yourself online. The emphasis is on board games, puzzles and quizzes although there are other games available plus links to games sites.

www.graalonline.com

THE GRAAL KINGDOMS

ORIGIN UK
INFO ✓✓✓✓
EASE ✓✓✓✓

Set in a mythical realm, this is a good multi-player game with lots of levels and a high degree of interactivity and customisation.

www.worldogl.com
ONLINE GAMING LEAGUE

ORIGIN US
INFO ✓✓✓✓
VALUE ✓✓✓✓
EASE ✓✓✓✓

Join a community of gamers who play in leagues for fun. You can play all the major online games and compete in the leagues and ladders if you like. To quote them: 'What matters is that people are meeting and interacting with other people on the Internet via our services and their game.'

www.neoto.com
COUCH-POTATO HEAVEN

ORIGIN US
INFO ✓✓✓✓
EASE ✓✓✓✓

Exciting-looking games site with good graphics. It's especially good for puzzle solving, quizzes and just basically silly games.

www.planetquake.com
THE EPICENTRE OF QUAKE

ORIGIN US
INFO ✓✓✓✓
EASE ✓✓✓✓

Quake is the most popular game played on the Internet, and this slightly slow site gives you all the background and details on the game. It's got loads of links and features as well as reviews and chat.

www.shockwave.com
SHOCKWAVE GRAPHICS

ORIGIN US
INFO ✓✓✓✓✓
EASE ✓✓✓✓

Shockwave's fantastic site offers much more than games, there are cartoons, greeting cards and music too. Click on 'games' and you get access to five sections: action, adventure, sports, jigsaws and board games plus two sections of arcade games. The graphics are superb.

www.lysator.liu.se/tolkien-games
LORD OF THE RINGS

ORIGIN SWEDEN
INFO ✓✓✓✓✓
EASE ✓✓✓

Get immersed in Tolkien's Middle Earth with some 100 games. It's got action games, quizzes and puzzles, strategy games and, of course, role playing games.

www.wireplay.com
THE GAMES NETWORK

ORIGIN US
INFO ✓✓✓✓✓
VALUE ✓✓✓✓
EASE ✓✓✓✓

A new look site that was being rebuilt when we visited, it still had all the old features but improvements were being made. Worth keeping an eye on because quality will be high when it's back.

www.zone.com

MICROSOFT GAMES ZONE

ORIGIN US
INFO ✓✓✓✓
EASE ✓✓✓✓

With over 100 games to choose from you shouldn't be disappointed. They range from board and card games to multi-player strategy and simulation games, there's a good kids' section too.

www.atitd.com

A TALE IN THE DESERT

ORIGIN US
INFO ✓✓✓✓✓
EASE ✓✓✓✓

Based on Ancient Egypt this is one of the outstanding multi-player role playing games, with great graphics and lots of features.

www.orisinal.com

JUST FOR FUN

ORIGIN US
INFO ✓✓✓✓
EASE ✓✓✓✓

A selection of high quality silly and funny games using a very original and text free format and design.

www.popcap.com

100% JAVA

ORIGIN US
INFO ✓✓✓✓✓
EASE ✓✓✓✓✓

An excellent site with very high quality games to download onto the PC, Palm or Mac and also to play on the web.

www.sodaplay.com

BUILD YOUR OWN....

ORIGIN UK
INFO ✓✓✓✓
ASE ✓✓✓✓

A really interesting and different gaming experience. Here you can design your models and send them to the 'zoo' for display and use by others. You can race them and exchange them with friends too.

Game manufacturers and console games

www.dreamcast.com

DREAMCAST FROM SEGA

ORIGIN US
INFO ✓✓✓✓
EASE ✓✓✓✓

Get the latest information on what's coming, try it out or play online; you can also get the latest technology.

www.gamecube.com

THE GAME CUBE

ORIGIN UK   The ever developing game consul from Nintendo
INFO ✓✓✓✓✓ has a typically original site where you can learn
EASE ✓✓✓✓   all about it and the games that go with it.
See also **http://cube.ign.com**

www.hasbro.com/games/

HASBRO GAMES

ORIGIN US   A commercial site from one of the biggest
INFO ✓✓✓✓ manufacturers with a useful list of what they produce.
EASE ✓✓✓✓

www.nintendo.com

OFFICIAL NINTENDO

ORIGIN US   Get the latest news from Nintendo and its spin-offs –
INFO ✓✓✓✓✓ N64, Game Boy and Game Cube. There's also infor-
EASE ✓✓✓✓   mation on the hardware and details of the games new
and old. For a site with wider Nintendo info go to the
excellent **www.nintendojo.com**

http://uk.playstation.com

OFFICIAL PLAYSTATION SITE

ORIGIN US   Looks good with games information, information on
INFO ✓✓✓✓ the hardware, previews, new release details and a
EASE ✓✓✓✓   special features section featuring reviews by well-
known gamers. There's also a chat section and a shop.

Also check out:
www.absolute-playstation.com
www.playstation.com
www.psxextreme.com

www.pocketgamer.org

GAMES FOR POCKET PCS

ORIGIN UK   OK, so you've bought your handheld PC, you've
INFO ✓✓✓✓ impressed the boss, now, what do you really use it for?
VALUE ✓✓✓   Oh yes, play games! There's a lot here for most
EASE ✓✓✓✓   different types of operating systems, if not, then there
are links to related sites. If you still can't find what
you're looking for, try **www.handango.com**

www.planetxbox.com

XBOX

ORIGIN US
INFO ✓✓✓✓
VALUE ✓✓✓✓
EASE ✓✓✓✓

Part of the Gamespy network, this site gives background on Microsoft's toy, with the latest game news, reviews, demos and previews too. See also www.xbox.com www.xboxweb.com and www.playmore.com who offer some exclusive previews.

www.station.sony.com

SONY ONLINE GAMES

ORIGIN US
INFO ✓✓✓✓✓
VALUE ✓✓✓✓
EASE ✓✓✓✓✓

Sony have put together an exceptional site for online gaming, and with over 6 million members, it's one of the most popular. It's well designed and easy to use. There are lots of games to choose from. Providing you can put up with the adverts, it's a real treat to use.

www.segaweb.com

SEGA AND DREAMCAST

ORIGIN US
INFO ✓✓✓✓
EASE ✓✓✓✓

News, reviews, cheats and much more including chat and a letters section. For the official site with links and information on the products go to www.sega-europe.com

Fantasy league and strategy games

www.dreamleague.com

PLAY FANTASY SPORT

ORIGIN US
INFO ✓✓✓✓
VALUE ✓✓✓✓
EASE ✓✓✓✓

Dream League offer fantasy games in several sports including football, formula 1 and cricket. Even with the sports you can play foreign leagues. It's easy to register and join in – and it's free.

www.fantasyleague.com

FANTASY FOOTIE

ORIGIN UK
INFO ✓✓✓✓✓
VALUE ✓✓
EASE ✓✓✓

Be a football manager, play for yourself, in a league, or even organise a game for your workplace or school. Get the latest team news on your chosen players and how they're doing against the rest. It's also worth checking out http://uk-fantasyfootball.20m.com

www.thedugout.net

CHAMPIONSHIP MANAGER

ORIGIN UK	An excellent site devoted to Championship Manager
INFO ✓✓✓✓✓	and soccer gaming, you can discuss the game, get up
EASE ✓✓✓✓	to speed with the latest tactics, get the low down on

the players and generally join in. There are also links
to related sites.

www.primagames.com

PRIMA

ORIGIN US	The largest fantasy game publisher offers a site packed
INFO ✓✓✓✓	with reviews, demos and articles. You can also buy
EASE ✓✓✓✓	a book on virtually every strategy game. See also

www.strategy-gaming.com which is pretty
comprehensive.

www.gamesworkshop.com

WAR GAMING

ORIGIN UK	A comprehensive offering covering war games
INFO ✓✓✓✓✓	including collecting, painting and gaming itself. There's
EASE ✓✓✓✓	also forums, chat and links to the major games.

Cheats, hints and tips

www.computerandvideogames.com

THE CHEAT STATION

ORIGIN US	Select the console or game type that you want a cheat
INFO ✓✓✓✓✓	on, then drill down the menus until you get the specific
EASE ✓✓✓✓	game or cheat that you want. There are cheats for

thousands of games so you should find what you're
looking for. If you can't, check out **www.xcheater.com**
who have a smaller selection, but you never know
your luck.

See also:
www.cheatextreme.com – great for Play Station cheats.
www.cheatheaven.com – a one-stop site for cheats in
   over 1200 games covering most consoles. Good
   search facility, but some annoying adverts and pop-
   ups.
www.playstation2-cheats.co.uk – cheats for PS2.

Games shops

If you know which game you want, then it's probably better to use a price checker such as Kelkoo (http://uk.kelkoo.com) to find the best price on the game. They will put you through to the store offering the best all round deal. If you want to browse, then these are considered the best online stores for a wide range of games:

www.chipsworld.co.uk – good for Sega and Nintendo. (UK)

www.game.uk.com – a good comprehensive offering. (UK)

www.gameplay.com – Gameplay is one of the most visited games sites. Once a magazine site, it's now transformed into a well designed store, browsable by platform and good value. (UK)

www.gamesstreet.co.uk – part of the Streets Online group, one of the top shops on the Internet – good kids' section. Delivery costs start at £1. Good value too. (UK)

www.telegames.co.uk – around 5,000 types of game in stock, covering all makes. Also has a bargain section. (UK)

www.ukgames.com – excellent range and good prices. (UK)

Miscellaneous

www.etch-a-sketch.com

REMEMBER ETCH-A-SKETCH?

ORIGIN UK
INFO ✓✓✓
EASE ✓✓✓

For those of you who don't remember back that far, Etch-a-Sketch is a rather annoying drawing game. It's been faithfully recreated here and it's still just as difficult to do curves. There are also a few other simple games and some links to children's games sites.

www.wargames.co.uk

WAR GAMES FORUM

ORIGIN UK
INFO ✓✓✓
EASE ✓✓✓

All you need to know about war-gaming on one site, albeit a slow one. There are links to specialist traders and to every aspect of the game from figurines to books to software.

Board and card games

www.chess.co.uk
ULTIMATE CHESS

ORIGIN UK
INFO ✓✓✓✓
EASE ✓✓✓

Massive chess site that's got information on the game, news and views, reviews and shopping. There are lots of links to other chess sites and downloads. Also info on Backgammon, Go, Poker and Bridge.

See also:
www.bcf.ndirect.co.uk – for the British
    Chess Federation.
www.chessclub.com – for the Internet Chess
    club who had over 2,000 players online
    when we visited, including 19 grandmasters.

www.gammon.com
BACKGAMMON

ORIGIN US
INFO ✓✓✓✓
EASE ✓✓✓

If you like backgammon, here's the place to start. There are links to live game playing and masses of related information. Also check out www.bkgm.com

www.msoworld.com
BOARD GAMES, PUZZLES AND QUIZZES

ORIGIN US
INFO ✓✓✓✓
VALUE ✓✓✓✓
EASE ✓✓✓✓

The ultimate site of its type, there are over 100 board games and masses of quizzes and tests.

www.monopoly.com
MONOPOLY

ORIGIN US
INFO ✓✓
EASE ✓✓✓✓

A pretty boring site, it offers a history plus information on where you can buy, along with tips on how to play and how you can get involved in tournaments.

www.thehouseofcards.com
LOADS OF CARD GAMES

ORIGIN US
INFO ✓✓✓✓
EASE ✓✓✓✓

Huge number of card games to play and download with sections on card tricks, history, links and word games – there's not much missing here. See also www.pagat.com for an alternative.

www.playsite.com

EASY TO PLAY

ORIGIN	US	A collection of straightforward multi-player online
INFO	✓✓✓✓	games, specialising in cards and board games.
EASE	✓✓✓✓	

www.solitairegames.com

SOLITAIRE

ORIGIN	US	Play online or download a game onto your PC, there
INFO	✓✓✓✓	are plenty to choose from and it's quick. There's also
EASE	✓✓✓✓	a good set of links to other online card games.

Crosswords, puzzles and word games

www.cluemaster.com

CROSSWORDS AND WORD PUZZLES

ORIGIN	UK	1,000 pages of puzzles, word games and crosswords,
INFO	✓✓✓✓	all free. The site is pretty straightforward, although
EASE	✓✓✓✓	you have to register to get the best out of it.

www.crosswordsite.com

ALL CROSSWORDS

ORIGIN	UK	Hundreds to chose from, with the option either to
INFO	✓✓✓	print off or fill in online. There are four levels of diffi-
EASE	✓✓✓✓	culty with the hardest being quite tough. See also
		www.crossword-puzzles.co.uk

www.fun-with-words.com

THE WORDPLAY WEBSITE

ORIGIN	US	Dedicated to amusing English, the Fun with Words site
INFO	✓✓✓✓	offers games, puzzles and an insight into the sorts of
EASE	✓✓✓✓	tricks you can play with the language.

*Other crossword and puzzle sites worth checking out
are listed below*

http://crosswords.about.com – links and tips from this
giant reference site.

www.canopia.com – odd design but a good choice of
puzzles and crosswords.

www.lovatts.com.au – plenty to chose from at this
Australian magazine.

Quizzes and general knowledge

www.thinks.com

FUN AND GAMES FOR PLAYFUL BRAINS

ORIGIN UK

INFO ✓✓✓✓✓

EASE ✓✓✓✓

Massive collection of games, puzzles and quizzes with something for everyone, it's easy to navigate and free.

www.mensa.org.uk

THE HIGH IQ SOCIETY

ORIGIN UK

INFO ✓✓✓✓

EASE ✓✓✓

Mensa only admit people who pass their high IQ test – see if you've got what it takes. The site which has been upgraded, has a few free tests and, if eligible, you can join the club.

www.queendom.com

SERIOUSLY ENTERTAINING

ORIGIN US

INFO ✓✓✓✓

EASE ✓✓✓✓

Excellent site for all sorts of brain tingling tests, the major difference is that it also offers personality profiles and psychometric tests so that they may be useful in getting on in your career or just keeping your brain healthy. See also www.emode.com

www.uselessknowledge.com

MASSIVE TRIVIA

ORIGIN US

INFO ✓✓✓✓✓

EASE ✓✓✓✓

Useless information and trivia by the ton plus quizzes and tests just to see how good you really are.

Check out these sites:

www.coolquiz.com – several different types of quiz from sports to movies and quotes. Nice wacky design. (USA)

www.quiz.co.uk – a couple of hundred questions in several unusual categories including kids, nature, food and sport. (UK)

www.quizyourfriends.com – a fun quiz creation site.

www.test.com – mainly serious tests, but you can find out your IQ and find out how creative you are. Visit the family section to take tests on entertainment and sports amongst others. You have to pay for some of the tests. (USA)

Gardening

There are several high quality British gardening sites, but many of the best sites are still based in America, so bear this in mind for tenderness, soil and climate advice. Those recommended give good general information and good links to specialist sites. Due to regulations on importing of seeds and plants, these can't be imported from outside the UK.

www.gardenworld.co.uk
THE UK'S BEST

ORIGIN UK	Described as the UK's best garden centre and horticul-
INFO ✓✓✓✓✓	tural site. It includes a list of over 1,000 garden
VALUE ✓✓✓	centres, with addresses, contact numbers and e-mail
EASE ✓✓✓✓	addresses. Outstanding list of links to other sites on

most aspects of gardening. Truly comprehensive with sections on wildlife, books, holidays, advice, societies and specialists, it now also has the addition of a link to the RHS plant finder service – excellent.

www.greenfingers.com
COMPREHENSIVE GARDENING

ORIGIN UK	There's so much here it takes a while to find your way
INFO ✓✓✓✓✓	around. It features sections on gardens to visit, finding
EASE ✓✓✓✓	a gardener, tips, chat, what's on, weather reports, a

plant selector and articles written by celebrities and well known gardeners. It's also got an excellent selection of online shops and links to related sites.

www.expertgardener.com
GARDENING COMMUNITY

ORIGIN UK	Essentially a chat site devoted to gardening, but there's
INFO ✓✓✓✓✓	advice and articles from award-winning gardeners too,
EASE ✓✓✓✓	which combined with good design, makes this site

stand out. There are links to a good selection of online shops, plus a magazine as well as access to chat rooms and communities on various subjects from urban gardening to plantaholics corner.

www.gardenweb.com
GARDEN QUESTIONS ANSWERED

ORIGIN UK
INFO ✓✓✓✓✓
EASE ✓✓✓✓

Probably the best site for lively gardening debate; it's enjoyable, international, comprehensive and has a nice tone. There are several discussion forums on various gardening topics, garden advice, plant dictionary and competitions. Using the forums is easy and fun, and you're sure to find the answer to almost any gardening question.

www.kew.org.uk
ROYAL BOTANIC GARDENS

ORIGIN UK
INFO ✓✓✓✓
VALUE ✓✓✓✓
EASE ✓✓✓✓

Kew's mission is to increase knowledge about plants and conserve them for future generations. This site gives plenty of information about their work, the collections, features and events. There are also details of the facilities at the gardens, conservation, educational material and lots of links to related sites.

www.rhs.org.uk
ROYAL HORTICULTURAL SOCIETY

ORIGIN UK
INFO ✓✓✓✓✓
EASE ✓✓✓✓

An excellent site from the RHS which features a plant finder service covering some 70,000 plant types, a garden finder and an event finder. There's also advice and information about the RHS, an opportunity to buy advance tickets to their shows and a seed catalogue.

Other gardening advice sites well worth trying are:
www.carryongardening.org.uk – award winning site with all the usual features plus some celebrity input. Good for links and the idea exchange feature.
www.e-garden.co.uk – one of the best; there's lots here for everyone, covering a much wider range of topics and regions than most, all packaged in a compact site.
www.gardenforum.co.uk – outstanding gardening forum site, good if you're a novice to using forums and chat sites.
www.gardenguides.com – a useful American resource site with loads of information on every aspect of gardening. It has lots of tips, handy guides, and a free online newsletter.

www.gardenlinks.ndo.co.uk – links to gardening sites in 44 categories, a good place to start searching for something specific.

www.garden-uk.org.uk – a gardener's web-ring and chat room which is great for links to other related and specialist sites. It's quite slow though and the site needs a re-design.

www.gonegardening.com – nice design, wide ranging magazine and shop.

www.plants-magazine.com – very good garden magazine, broad in scope but particularly strong on new plants.

Gardening stores

www.dig-it.co.uk
GARDENING IN STYLE

ORIGIN UK
INFO ✓✓✓✓
VALUE ✓✓✓
EASE ✓✓✓✓

This is a beautifully designed garden shop and magazine, although sometimes the graphics overlap. The magazine section offers features, tips and well-written articles, while in the consultancy bit you can get online advice or e-mail a gardening expert. The shop offers a wide range of plants and gardening equipment and related products, delivery to mainland UK is £4.95 or £10.95 if you live on the islands or in Northern Ireland.

www.crocus.co.uk
GARDENERS BY NATURE

ORIGIN UK
INFO ✓✓✓✓
VALUE ✓✓✓✓
EASE ✓✓✓✓

A good-looking site full of ideas enhanced by excellent photographs, there are some good articles and features, but it's basically a gorgeous shop with thousands of plants and products to choose from and some good offers. Delivery to England and Southern Scotland starts at £5.95 (£1 for seeds), if you live elsewhere you need to contact them to see if delivery is possible for a surcharge.

www.blooms-online.com

ONE-STOP GARDENER'S RESOURCE

ORIGIN	UK
INFO	✓✓✓✓
VALUE	✓✓✓
EASE	✓✓✓✓

A beautiful site that will supply all your garden needs and desires. In addition to ordering your seeds and buying your garden furniture, there's a great plant search where you can find plants of specific size and colour for that difficult hole in the border. There are DIY projects and a design service too, a gardener's club and advice. Delivery cost depends on your order, alternatively you can pick up at their nearest store.

Other gardening shops worth checking out are:
www.burncoose.co.uk – nice design, searchable plant catalogue with some good offers.
www.earth-to-earth.com – supplies natural and environmentally friendly products.
www.e-garden.co.uk – nice looking site with a magazine and shop, a little slow, but with some good offers.
www.gardencentre.co.uk – not a great design but some good offers and ideas.
www.glut.co.uk – the Gluttonous Gardener provides unusual presents for every gardener.

Garden design

www.dreamgardens.co.uk

TURNING DREAMS INTO REALITY

ORIGIN	UK
INFO	✓✓✓✓
VALUE	✓✓✓
EASE	✓✓✓

Complete Anne and Suze's questionnaire from which you'll get a suggested ideal garden, it's easy to use and full of good ideas, but the real design costs from £25 per border. For more ideas try **www.creativegardener.com** which is devoted to providing inspiration for your garden.

Organic gardening

www.hdra.org.uk
HENRY DOUBLEDAY RESEARCH ASSOCIATION

ORIGIN UK
INFO ✓✓✓✓✓
EASE ✓✓✓

The leading authority on organic gardening, this site offers a superb resource if you're into gardening the natural way. It's particularly good if you're growing vegetables, with fact sheets and details on why you should garden organically. See also **www.soilassociation.org** for advice on growing organic food plus the latest news on their campaigns.

For information, compost lovers should go to **www.oldgrowth.org/compost** and for shopping go to the excellent **www.greengardener.co.uk**

British wildflowers and plants

www.nhm.ac.uk/science/projects/fff
FLORA AND FAUNA

ORIGIN UK
INFO ✓✓✓✓✓
EASE ✓✓✓✓

Using the postcode search, find out the plants that are native to your area, where to get seeds and then how to look after them once they're in your garden. Sponsored by the Natural History Museum.

www.british-trees.com
FORESTRY AND CONSERVATION

ORIGIN UK
INFO ✓✓✓✓
EASE ✓✓✓✓

Information on British trees which, while comprehensive, it has got a good set of links and a list of books and magazines. A little slow. For information on how to care for trees go to **www.trees.org.uk**

www.wildflowers.co.uk
BRITISH WILDFLOWERS

ORIGIN UK
INFO ✓✓✓
EASE ✓✓✓

An online store specialising in British wildflowers with advice on how to grow them; there's also a search engine where you can find the plants you need using common or Latin names.

Specific plants and specialists

www.herbnet.com
GROWING, COOKING HERBS, GOOD LINKS

ORIGIN US
INFO ✓✓✓✓
EASE ✓✓✓

An American network specialising in herbs, with links to specialists, trade and information sites. It can be hard work to negotiate, but there's no doubting the quality of the content. See also the excellent Breckland nursery site at **http://herbs.get-the-web.com**

www.discoveringannuals.com
ANNUALS GALORE

ORIGIN UK
INFO ✓✓✓✓
EASE ✓✓✓✓

Based on the successful book, this site offers information on hardy annuals, half-hardy annuals, biennials and seed-raised bedding plants of all kinds. There's an A–Z listing on the plants and it tells you where you can buy them.

www.windowbox.com
CONTAINER GARDENING

ORIGIN US
INFO ✓✓✓✓
VALUE ✓✓✓✓✓
EASE ✓✓✓✓

A really good American site which is well worth a look if you're into container gardening in any form, it's well laid out and very well written with great ideas for unusual plant combinations. Worth a long browse.

www.rareplants.co.uk
RARE PLANT NURSERY

ORIGIN UK
INFO ✓✓✓✓
VALUE ✓✓✓✓✓
EASE ✓✓✓✓

A site developed by a specialist nursery, which is well illustrated, and pretty comprehensive, it offers information on the plants and can supply plants world-wide. Delivery costs vary.

www.rosarian.com
ROSES

ORIGIN UK
INFO ✓✓✓✓✓
EASE ✓✓✓✓

As this is a generalist guide we wouldn't normally review such a specialist site, but it's so well-designed in terms of how an online magazine should look for its audience, that we couldn't resist including it. If you love roses or just need information on them, drop in here for a good, long browse. See also **www.davidaustinroses.com** the outstanding rose specialist.

Seed specialists

www.chilternseeds.co.uk
SEED SPECIALIST

ORIGIN UK	Choose from over 5,000 different types of seeds with
INFO ✓✓✓✓✓	many unusual plants, supplied fresh and including
VALUE ✓✓✓✓	organically grown seeds. Very easy to find the right
EASE ✓✓✓✓	plant, excellent.

See also:

www.suttons-seeds.co.uk – comprehensive offering
  with a money back guarantee and an easy to
  use site.
www.thompson-morgan.com – huge range, good
  advice and good value too.
www.unwins-seeds.co.uk – find your local stockist,
  but no online shop.

Gardening peripherals and equipment

www.lawnmowersdirect.co.uk
BUY A LAWNMOWER ONLINE

ORIGIN UK	A retailer specialising in mowers and other power
INFO ✓✓✓✓✓	tools, you can browse by make and it's quick and easy
VALUE ✓✓✓✓	to use, if a little basic. Delivery within the UK is free, if
EASE ✓✓✓✓	you spend more than £50.

www.lightingforgardens.co.uk
LIGHT UP YOUR GARDEN

ORIGIN UK	A specialist that offers advice, ideas and a wide range
INFO ✓✓✓✓	of products to light up your garden, all on a nicely
EASE ✓✓✓✓	designed site.

www.agriframes.co.uk
GARDEN STRUCTURES

ORIGIN UK	A wide range of non-plant garden products from
INFO ✓✓✓✓	pergolas to watering cans from probably the UK's
VALUE ✓✓✓	leading supplier; it could be a much more user-
EASE ✓✓✓	friendly site.

www.simplygardeningtools.co.uk

GARDEN TOOLS

ORIGIN UK
INFO ✓✓✓✓
VALUE ✓✓✓✓
EASE ✓✓✓✓

A messy, bright site offering a wide range of tools and equipment and free delivery in the UK, plus a money back guarantee. For a more high class approach to garden tools try **www.hortus-ornamenti.com** but they do charge for delivery.

TV tie-ins and celebrities

www.bbc.co.uk/gardening

GARDENING AT THE BEEB

ORIGIN UK
INFO ✓✓✓✓
EASE ✓✓✓✓

A set of web pages from the BBC site which offer a great gardening magazine, with celebrities mixed with helpful advice and features such as plant profiles, ask the expert and what to expect in the month ahead. See also **www.gardenersworld.beeb.com**.

www.barnsdalegardens.co.uk

GEOFF HAMILTON'S GARDEN

ORIGIN UK
INFO ✓✓✓✓
VALUE ✓✓✓
EASE ✓✓✓✓

To many people the real home of Gardener's World, this site tells you all about Barnsdale and has features about the garden, Geoff and his work. There's also an online store selling a limited range of products and a good set of gardening site links.

www.alantitchmarsh.com

ALAN TITCHMARSH

ORIGIN UK
INFO ✓✓
EASE ✓✓✓✓

Part of the Expert Gardener site with competitions, biographical details, sponsored events and some gardening details.

Other important gardeners:
www.bethchatto.co.uk – find out about her garden and shop for plants too.
www.capability-brown.org – an overview of his work.
www.gertrudejekyll.co.uk – devoted to the work of this amazing woman.

Visiting gardens

www.gardenvisit.com

GARDENS TO VISIT AND ENJOY

ORIGIN UK
INFO ✓✓✓✓
EASE ✓✓✓✓

With over 1,000 gardens listed world-wide, this site offers information on all of them and each is rated for design, planting and scenic interest with Sissinghurst scoring top marks. There's also information on the history of gardening, tours and hotels with good gardens.

See also:
www.edenproject.com – for the grandest garden scheme of them all. **www.greatbritishgardens.co.uk** – good regional reference and guide.
www.museumgardenhistory.org – based in Lambeth, this site offers details of the museum and the famous Tradescant family.
www.nationaltrust.org.uk – offering information on their gardens and places of interest.

www.ngs.org.uk

NATIONAL GARDEN SCHEME

ORIGIN UK
INFO ✓✓✓
EASE ✓✓✓✓

This is basically the famous yellow book converted into a web site with details on over 2,000 gardens to visit for charity and the work they undertake with the money they earn from your support.

Gardeners with special needs

www.thrive.org.uk

NATIONAL HORTICULTURAL CHARITY

ORIGIN UK
INFO ✓✓✓✓
EASE ✓✓✓✓

This charity exists to provide expert advice on gardening for people with disabilities and older people who want to continue gardening with restricted mobility. The site gives information on how the charity works and links to related sites. See also **www.gardenforever.com** who offer lots in the way of horticultural therapy.

Gay and Lesbian

www.rainbownetwork.com

LESBIAN & GAY LIFESTYLE

ORIGIN UK
INFO ✓✓✓✓✓
EASE ✓✓✓✓

A very well thought out magazine-style web site catering for all aspects of gay and lesbian life. It primarily covers news, fashion, entertainment and health, but there's a travel agency as well. There are also forums and chat sections, classified ads as well as profiles on well-known personalities.

For other good gay/lesbian sites try:
www.blackberricafe.com – sisterhood chat site.
www.channel4.com/entertainment/tv/showcards/S/ so_graham_norton.html – Channel 4's site for Graham Norton – So excellent!
www.gaybritain.co.uk – brilliant graphics, a gay portal site.
www.gaylifeuk.com – well rounded magazine site with support and advice sections.
www.gaysports.com – wide ranging sports site.
www.gaytravel.co.uk – gay travel guide, UK-oriented but with some good world-wide information.
www.glinn.com – the gay gateway to the web.
www.kenric.co.uk – the long running lesbian support and social site.
www.navigaytion.com – a travel specialist.
www.proudparenting.com – interesting site aimed at helping gay and lesbian parents and their children.
www.queercompany.com – this site used to be one of the most highly rated, it's due to make a comeback soon so keep an eye on it.
www.uk.gay.com – British page from the big American magazine site.

Genealogy

www.sog.org.uk

THE SOCIETY OF GENEALOGISTS

ORIGIN UK
INFO ✓✓✓✓
EASE ✓✓✓✓

This is the first place to go when you're thinking about researching your family tree. It won't win awards for web design, but it contains basic information and there is an excellent set of links you can use to start you off. See also the excellent **www.cyndislist.com** where you'll find almost 100,000 links in 150 categories to help with your family research.

www.pro.gov.uk

PUBLIC RECORD OFFICE

ORIGIN UK
INFO ✓✓✓✓✓
EASE ✓✓✓✓

To quote the introduction 'The Public Record Office is the national archive of England, Wales and the United Kingdom. It brings together and preserves the records of central government and the courts of law, and makes them available to all who wish to consult them. The records span an unbroken period from the 11th century to the present day'. The site is easy to use, the information is concisely presented and easy to access. It also has information on how you can access the 1901 census.

See also **www.familyrecords.gov.uk** which can help enormously with tracing your family tree, the links selection is excellent.

www.census.pro.gov.uk

1901 CENSUS

ORIGIN UK
INFO ✓✓✓✓✓
VALUE ✓✓✓
EASE ✓✓✓

This site has reopened after unanticipated huge demand shut it down. You can search but for detailed information you have to pay using a rather odd system. Mapping is also available from the site to help with place names or boundary changes.

www.accessgenealogy.com

GENEALOGY WEB PORTAL

ORIGIN US
INFO ✓✓✓✓
EASE ✓✓✓✓

A massive number of links and access to web rings from a number of different countries give this site 'must check out' status. It is biased towards an American audience but it's very useful none-the-less. See also another portal site **www.genealogyportal.com** which is less cluttered.

www.everton.com

GENEALOGICAL HELPER

ORIGIN US
INFO ✓✓✓
EASE ✓✓✓✓

No we haven't gone mad and put a football team in the wrong section, Everton is the name of one of the best magazines devoted to genealogy. It's an attractive site which has articles and features on the subject along with tips on how to conduct your search.

www.origins.net

DEFINITIVE DATABASES

ORIGIN UK
INFO ✓✓✓✓
EASE ✓✓✓✓

This site has information provided from the Society of Genealogists' records, from Scotland going back to 1553 and from England going back to 1568, and unlike many other sites in this area, it's also well designed and easy to use. There are also search tips, access to discussion groups and a new section devoted to Ireland.

www.brit-a-r.demon.co.uk

THE OFFICIAL BRITISH ANCESTRAL RESEARCH SITE

ORIGIN UK
INFO ✓✓✓
VALUE ✓✓
EASE ✓✓✓✓

For £495 they will research one surname or line, for £895 two or a minimum of 7 hours work for £195. They guarantee results to four generations. Not as much fun as doing it yourself though.

www.genuki.org.uk

VIRTUAL LIBRARY OF GENEALOGICAL INFORMATION

ORIGIN UK
INFO ✓✓✓
EASE ✓✓✓✓

An excellent British-oriented site with a huge range of links to help you find your ancestors. There is help for those starting out, news, bulletin boards, FAQs on genealogy and a regional search map of the UK and Ireland.

www.ancestry.com

NO 1 SOURCE FOR FAMILY HISTORY

ORIGIN US
INFO ✓✓✓
VALUE ✓✓
EASE ✓✓✓✓

Find out about your ancestors for a subscription beginning at $29.95 per year. This US-oriented site has 1 billion names and access to 3,000 databases. It offers some information for free, but for real detail you have to join. It's especially good if you're searching for someone in the US or Canada. Linked to this is the chat site **www.familyhistory.com** where you can visit surname discussion groups.

www.surnameweb.org
ORIGINS OF SURNAMES

ORIGIN US
INFO ✓✓✓✓✓
EASE ✓✓

A great place to start your search for your family origins. On top of the information about your name, there are thousands of links and they claim 2 billion searchable records.

Other useful sites that may help in your family research:

www.bbc.co.uk/education/beyond/factsheets/surnames/surnames_intro.shtml – a BBC factsheet on how to trace your ancestors.

www.bigfamily.co.uk – useful shop devoted to genealogy.

www.englishorigins.com – information for people tracking their relatives from an excellent database, it costs though.

www.familysearch.org – The Church of Jesus Christ and the Latter-day Saint's excellent research site with good step-by-step information.

www.genforum.com – a huge number of forums devoted to specific family names, US oriented.

www.gengateway.com – claims to have the number one family tree making software.

www.rootsweb.com – free genealogy site supported by Ancestry.com with interactive guides and research tools.

Government

www.ukonline.gov.uk
THE ENTRY POINT FOR GOVERNMENT INFORMATION

ORIGIN UK
INFO ✓✓✓✓✓
EASE ✓✓✓✓

A massive web site devoted to the workings of our government, it is a superb resource if you want to know anything official both at a national and a local level. Use the index or the search facility to navigate, as it's easy to get side-tracked. There are several major sections – in 'Citizenspace' you can have your say and take part in decision making, there's life stage support and advice in 'Yourlife', in 'Do It Online' there's information on achieving things online from booking a driving test to help with debt recovery. There's also a newsroom and a quick search facility.

Other key links:

http://europa.eu.int – The European Union.

http://younggov.ukonline.gov.uk – a good site aimed at explaining the workings of government to 11-18 year olds.

www.bopcas.soton.ac.uk – a service that announces when government documents are published.

www.clicktso.com – the Stationery Office bookstore.

www.congress.org – an excellent overview of the U.S. Congress and how it works.

www.conservatives.com – Conservative party.

www.europarl.eu.int – how the European Parliament works.

www.hrw.org – Human Rights Watch tells you where the corrupt governments are, where they get it just wrong.

www.labour.org.uk – Labour party.

www.libdems.org.uk – Liberal Democrats.

www.parliament.uk/commons/hsecom.htm – what's on in the House of Commons.

www.parliamentlive.tv – the workings of Parliament broadcast live. Comes with a calendar of events too. See also www.scottishparliamentlive.com

www.royal.gov.uk – for the monarchy.

www.ukmeps.info – Information on Members Of European Parliament.

www.ukmps.info – A definitive non-political portal for United Kingdom Members of Parliament.

www.un.org – United Nations.

Greetings Cards

www.bluemountain.com

E-CARDS

ORIGIN US
INFO ✓✓✓✓
VALUE ✓✓
EASE ✓✓✓✓

Blue Mountain has thousands of cards for every occasion; it's easy to use but you have to subscribe to get the best designs. There are all sorts of extras you can build in like music, cartoons and even voice messages.

http://cards.webshots.com
YOUR PHOTOS INTO CARDS

ORIGIN US
INFO ✓✓✓✓✓
VALUE ✓✓✓
EASE ✓✓✓

Part of the Corbis site, there's a great deal to choose from in the form of photographic cards and you can also create your own.

See also:
www.egreetings.com – big range, busy design that gets on your nerves after a while.
www.greeting-cards.com – massive range and geared to the American market, not all free.
www.moonpig.com – personalised humorous cards to create and buy.
www.regards.com – nice design and the best bit is that it's free!

www.nextcard.co.uk
3D CARDS

ORIGIN UK
INFO ✓✓✓
EASE ✓✓✓

Send free three-dimensional cards using this site, there are great pictures of animals, sunsets and mountain scenery to choose from.

www.cybercard.co.uk
REAL CARDS TO REAL PEOPLE

ORIGIN UK
INFO ✓✓✓✓
VALUE ✓✓
EASE ✓✓✓✓

Create your card and message and they'll send it for you, all for £2.95.

www.charitycards.co.uk
CONTRIBUTIONS TO CHARITY

ORIGIN UK
INFO ✓✓✓✓
VALUE ✓✓✓✓✓
EASE ✓✓✓✓

Buy your cards here and give money to charity, this is traditionally a Christmas thing but Charitycards have turned it into an all year round possibility. There are also discounts available and free postage if you buy in quantity and they also sell stamps.

Health Advice

*Here are some of the key sites for getting good health advice,
featuring online doctors, fitness centres, nutrition and sites
that try to combine all three. As with all health sites, there is no
substitute for the real thing and if you are ill, your main port
of call must be your doctor. Dietary advice sites are listed on
page 144, specialist sites aimed at men, on page 230 and for
women, on page 452. The advice for parents, page 274 and
teens, page 376 may also be useful.*

General health

www.nhsdirect.nhs.uk

NHS ADVICE ONLINE

ORIGIN UK
INFO ✓✓✓✓✓
EASE ✓✓✓✓

NHS Direct is a telephone advice service and this is the
Internet spin-off, it comprises of an excellent guide to
common ailments with the emphasis on treating them
at home, a health magazine with monthly features,
audio clips on a wide range of health topics and a
superb selection of NHS-approved links covering
specific illnesses or parts of the body. There's also
health information and an A–Z guide to the NHS.

www.bupa.co.uk

BUPA HOMEPAGE

ORIGIN UK
INFO ✓✓✓✓✓
EASE ✓✓✓✓

Health fact-sheets, special offers on health cover,
health tips and competitions are all on offer at this
well-designed site. You can also find your nearest
BUPA hospital and instructions on referral. See also
www.ppphealthcare.co.uk who have over 150 fact-
sheets available on a wide range of health conditions.
See also www.privatehealth.co.uk a portal site
devoted to all things to do with private health.

www.healthfinder.com

A GREAT PLACE TO START FOR HEALTH ADVICE

ORIGIN US
INFO ✓✓✓✓✓
EASE ✓✓✓

Run by the US Department of Health, this provides
a link to more or less every health organisation,
medical and fitness site you can think of. In several
sections you can learn about hot medical topics, catch

the medical news, make smart health choices, discover what's best for you and your lifestyle and use the medical dictionary in the research section. The site is well designed, fast once it's fully downloaded and very easy to use.

www.patient.co.uk
FINDING INFORMATION FROM UK SOURCES

ORIGIN UK
INFO ✓✓✓✓✓
EASE ✓✓✓✓✓

This excellent site has been put together by two GPs. It's essentially a collection of links to other health sites, but from here you can find a web site on health-related topics with a UK bias. You can search alphabetically or browse within the site. All the recommended sites are reviewed by a GP for suitability and quality before being placed on the list. For a second opinion you could visit www.surgerydoor.co.uk which is more magazine-like in style with up to the minute news stories. It's comprehensive and has an online shop. Also try the well-designed www.netdoctor.co.uk who describe themselves as the 'UK's independent health web site' and offer a similar service.

www.embarrassingproblems.co.uk
FIRST STEP

ORIGIN UK
INFO ✓✓✓✓✓
EASE ✓✓✓✓✓

An award-winning and much-recommended site that works well; it's what the Internet should be about really. The site helps you deal with health problems that are difficult to discuss with anyone; it's easy to use and comprehensive. Younger people and teenagers should also check out www.coolnurse.com which is an excellent American site with similar attributes.

www.drkoop.com
THE BEST PRESCRIPTION IS KNOWLEDGE

ORIGIN US
INFO ✓✓✓✓✓
EASE ✓✓✓✓

Don't let the silly name put you off, Dr C. Everett Koop is a former US Surgeon General and is acknowledged as one of the best online doctors. The goal is to empower you to take care of your own health through better knowledge. The site is very comprehensive covering every major health topic and is aimed at all, including both young and old.

www.mayohealth.org

RELIABLE INFORMATION FOR A HEALTHY LIFE

ORIGIN US
INFO ✓✓✓✓✓
EASE ✓✓✓✓

Mayo has a similar ethic to Dr Koop but is less fussy and very easy to use. However, the amount of information can be overwhelming, as they claim the combined knowledge of some 2,000 doctors in the 21 'centers'. Essentially it's a massive collection of articles that combine to give you a large amount of data on specific medical topics. There are also guides on how to live a healthy life, first aid and a newsletter, plus information on specific medical conditions and diseases.

www.cellscience.com

MEDICAL DICTIONARY

ORIGIN UK
INFO ✓✓✓✓
EASE ✓✓✓✓

The dictionary covers Aids, HIV, cancer, cystic fibrosis and diabetes. It's easy to use and contains listings for links, hospitals and charities as well as other essential information.

www.quackwatch.com

HEALTH FRAUD, QUACKERY & INTELLIGENT DECISIONS

ORIGIN US
INFO ✓✓✓✓
EASE ✓✓✓

Exposes fraudulent cures and old wives tales, then provides information on where to get the right treatment. It makes fascinating reading and includes exposés on everything from acupuncture to weight loss. Use the search engine or just browse through it; many of the articles leave you amazed at the fraudulent nature of some medical claims.

The following sites also offer good health information:
http://medlineplus.gov – a health information centre from the U.S. National Library of Medicine.
www.24dr.com – a site from a UK doctor, lots of help with self diagnosis and what appears to be a good medical encyclopedia.
www.bbc.co.uk/health – good all rounder covering lots of topics, good links.
www.dr-ali.co.uk – a popular all round health advisory site run by the high profile Dr Ali. You have to register to get the best out of it.

www.e-med.co.uk – your own private doctor everywhere you go is the strap line for this site, it costs
£20 to join then £15 per consultation.

www.gmc-uk.org – home of the General Medical
Council, the place to go if you have a problem with
a doctor.

www.medterms.com – a straightforward glossary of
medical terms.

www.nice.org.uk – the National Institute of Clinical
Excellence provides 'robust and reliable guidance
on current health best practise'.

www.studenthealth.co.uk – written by doctors,
sensible and funny with some good competitions.

www.allcures.com
UK'S FIRST ONLINE PHARMACY

ORIGIN UK	After a fairly lengthy but secure registration process
INFO ✓✓✓✓	you can shop from this site which has all the big
EASE ✓✓✓	brands and a wide range of products. There are

also sections on toiletries, beauty, alternative medicine
and a photo-shop. You can arrange to have your
prescriptions made up and sent to you with no
delivery charge.

See also:
www.academyhealth.com – who deliver free in the UK.
www.mypharmacy.co.uk – good basic health site
from a real pharmacist, with a shop stocking a
relatively wide range of products.
www.pharmacy2u.co.uk – who have lots of offers
and cover lots of health areas, even a section on
embarrassing problems.

Fitness and exercise

www.netfit.co.uk
DEFINITIVE GUIDE TO HEALTH AND FITNESS

ORIGIN UK	Devoted to promoting the benefits of regular exercise
INFO ✓✓✓✓✓	with a dedicated team who put a great deal of effort
EASE ✓✓✓✓	into the site. You can gauge your fitness, there's

information on some 200 exercises, tips on eating
and dieting, nutrition and links to useful (mainly
sport) sites.

www.hfonline.co.uk

HEALTH & FITNESS MAGAZINE

ORIGIN UK   A spin-off site from the magazine, which offers the
INFO ✓✓✓✓   latest health news and advice, it's attractive and it's
EASE ✓✓✓   quite comprehensive.

www.fitnessonline.com

PROVIDING PERSONAL SUPPORT

ORIGIN US   This good-looking site is from an American magazine
INFO ✓✓✓✓✓   group. It takes a holistic view of health offering advice
EASE ✓✓✓   on exercise, nutrition and health products. In reality
what you get is a succession of articles from their
magazines, all are very informative but getting the
right information can be time-consuming.

*The following sites also offer good advice and
fitness information:*
www.exercise.co.uk – a good health equipment
     store with information on exercise and the right
     equipment to use and buy.
www.exercisegroup.com – natural body building.
www.fitnesspeak.co.uk – the best prices for gym
     equipment.
www.getfitta.co.uk – with the Territorial Army.
www.workout.com – over 500 exercises, lots of
     information too. You've got to join to get the
     most out of it.

Alternative medicine and therapies

www.altmedicine.com

ALTERNATIVE HEALTH NEWS

ORIGIN US   Keep up-to-date with the latest therapies and trends
INFO ✓✓✓✓   with articles and features from some of the key figures
EASE ✓✓✓✓   in the world of alternative medicine. The site is
supplemented by an excellent medical search engine,
an overview of the major philosophies and associated
healing techniques plus a good set of related links.

www.therapy-world.co.uk
THERAPY WORLD MAGAZINE

ORIGIN UK
INFO ✓✓✓✓
EASE ✓✓✓✓

A well put together magazine covering many different types of therapies with a good overview of all of them and some interesting articles.

www.medical-acupuncture.co.uk
ACUPUNCTURE

ORIGIN UK
INFO ✓✓✓✓
EASE ✓✓✓✓

A good looking site with information from the British Medical Acupuncture Society on the nature of acupuncture and where to find a practitioner in your area. There are also good links and information on courses.

www.drlockie.com
HOMEOPATHY MADE EASY

ORIGIN US
INFO ✓✓✓✓
VALUE ✓✓
EASE ✓✓✓✓✓

An interesting, clear and simple site that offers sensible advice at all levels. Click on any of the medicine jars to get to the relevant sections on everything from basic information, products and links.

www.homeopath.co.uk
ONLINE HOMEOPATHIC SERVICES

ORIGIN UK
INFO ✓✓✓✓
VALUE ✓✓✓✓
EASE ✓✓✓✓

An excellent and attractive site that offers a directory of practising homeopaths in the UK plus information on college courses and a bookshop. In addition there is access to an online pharmacy via ThinkNatural where you can buy homeopathic medicines.

See also:

www.alternativemedicines.co.uk – use the ailment search to find the right alternative products.

www.drweil.com – the vitamin guru has a site that offers much in advice and his own brand of balanced living.

www.homeopathyhome.com – slightly confusing but comprehensive.

www.homeopathy-soh.org – home of the Society of Homeopaths.

www.trusthomeopathy.org – home of the British Homeopathic Association.

www.ukselfhelp.info – a listing of almost 800 self-help groups and nearly 700 links to self-help sites.

www.massagetherapy.co.uk

GETTING THE RIGHT TYPE OF MASSAGE

ORIGIN	UK	A useful and informative site giving information on where to go to get the right type of massage for you. Lots of guidance and advice on the different type of therapies and where to find a practitioner.
INFO	✓✓✓✓	
EASE	✓✓✓	

www.pilates.co.uk

PURELY PILATES

ORIGIN	UK	Keep up with the latest information on pilates; find out what it can do for you and where to find a qualified instructor. There's also a newsletter and an events listing.
INFO	✓✓✓✓	
EASE	✓✓✓	

www.thinknatural.com

THINK NATURALLY

ORIGIN	UK	A nicely designed site with a mass of information on every aspect of natural health including a comprehensive shop with loads of special offers and a very wide range of products.
INFO	✓✓✓✓	
VALUE	✓✓✓✓	
EASE	✓✓✓✓	

www.yogauk.com

YOGA

ORIGIN	UK	Welcome to the yoga village where you can get information on yoga in the UK, subscribe to their magazine, or browse the links section, which has a comprehensive list of stores.
INFO	✓✓✓✓	
EASE	✓✓✓	

See also:
www.calmcentre.com – calming experiences from Paul Wilson.
www.interconnections.co.uk – up to date information on living holistically.
www.mydailyyoga.com – simple yoga exercises.
www.yogaplus.co.uk – who offer courses and workshops.
www.yogatherapy.org – using yoga to cure.

Sites catering for a specific condition or disease

Here is a list of the key sites relating to specific diseases, addictions and ailments, we have not attempted to review them, but if you know of a site we've missed and would like it included in the next edition of this book please e-mail us at
goodwebsiteguide@hotmail.com

Alcohol and drug abuse
www.al-anon-alateen.org
www.alcoholconcern.org.uk
www.alcoholics-anonymous.org
www.wrecked.co.uk
Allergies
www.allergy.co.uk
www.allergy-info.com (sponsored by Zyrtec)
Alzheimers and dementia
www.alzheimers.org.uk
www.dementia.ion.ucl.ac.uk
Aids and HIV
www.avert.org
www.hiv-development.org
www.hivstopswithme.org
www.tht.org.uk
Anxiety
www.anxieties.com
www.healthanxiety.com
Arthritis
www.aboutarthritis.com
www.arc.org.uk
Asthma
www.asthma.org.uk
Autism
www.nas.org.uk
Backpain
www.backpain.org
Blindness
www.rnib.org.uk
www.sense.org.uk
Bowels and bladder
www.continence-foundation.org.uk
www.ibsnetwork.org.uk
www.incontact.org

Brain disease and injury
www.bbsf.org.uk
www.headway.org.uk
Breast Cancer Campaign
www.bcc-uk.org
Bullying
www.bullying.co.uk
Cancer
www.bowelcancer.org
www.cancerresearchuk.org
www.cancer.gov
www.dipex.org (prostate cancer)
Cerebral palsy
www.scope.org.uk
Chiropody
www.feetforlife.org
Deafness
www.britishdeafassociation.org.uk
Dental
www.bda-dentistry.org.uk
www.dentalwisdom.com
www.gdc-uk.org
Depression
http://www.depressionalliance.org
Dermatology
www.skinhealth.co.uk
Diabetics
www.diabetes.org.uk
www.diabetic.org.uk
Digestion
www.digestivecare.co.uk
Disabled
www.disability.gov.uk
www.radar.org.uk
Drugs
www.acde.org
www.release.org.uk
Eczema
www.eczema.org
Epilepsy
www.epilepsy.org.uk
www.epilepsynse.org.uk

Feet
www.drfoot.co.uk
Fertility
www.ifconline.org
Fibromyalgia
www.ukfibromyalgia.com
Gambling
www.gamblersanonymous.org.uk
Heart
www.bhf.org.uk
www.familyheart.org
High blood pressure
www.hbpf.org.uk
Kidney problems
www.kidney.org.uk
Liver problems
www.britishlivertrust.org.uk
Lupus
www.lupusuk.com
Meningitis
www.meningitis-trust.org
Mental health
www.mentalhealth.com
www.mind.org.uk
www.youngminds.org.uk
Migraine
www.migraine.org.uk
www.migrainetrust.org
Multiple sclerosis
www.mssociety.org.uk
Older people
www.elderabuse.org.uk
Osteopathy
www.osteopathy.org.uk
Plastic surgery
www.baaps.org.uk
Repetitive Strain Injury
www.rsi.org.uk
Sexually Transmitted Diseases (STDs)
www.playingsafely.co.uk
Smoking
www.ash.org.uk

Solvent abuse
www.canban.com
Spina bifida
www.asbah.org
Stress
www.isma.org.uk
www.stressrelease.com
Stroke
www.stroke.org.uk

www.self-help.org.uk
THE SELF HELP DATABASE
ORIGIN UK   A portal site devoted to providing a searchable
INFO ✓✓✓✓✓   database of self help and patient organisations in
EASE ✓✓✓✓   the UK. There are currently over 1,000 on file.

History and Biography

The Internet is proving to be a great storehouse, not only for the latest news but also for cataloguing historical events in an entertaining and informative way; here are some of the best sites.

www.thehistorychannel.com
THE BEST SEARCH IN HISTORY
ORIGIN US   Excellent for history buffs, revision or just a good
INFO ✓✓✓✓✓   read, the History Channel provides a site that is
EASE ✓✓✓   packed with information. Search by key word or
               timeline, by date and by subject, get biographical
               information or speeches. It's fast and easy to get
               carried away once you start your search.

www.historyworld.net
HISTORY WORLD
ORIGIN UK   An outstanding site containing timelines, articles,
INFO ✓✓✓✓✓   quizzes and tours all designed to educate and bring
EASE ✓✓✓✓   history to life in an engaging and stimulating way,
               and it's successful.

www.historytoday.com

WORLD'S LEADING HISTORY MAGAZINE

ORIGIN UK
INFO ✓✓✓✓
EASE ✓✓✓✓

Contains some excellent articles from the magazine, but probably the most useful bit is the related links section, which offers many links to other history sites.

www.newsplayer.com

RELIVE THE LAST CENTURY

ORIGIN UK
INFO ✓✓✓✓✓
VALUE ✓✓
EASE ✓✓✓✓

Relive the events of the past hundred years, witness them at first hand as they happened. A truly superb site with real newsreel footage worth the £25 annual subscription fee. See also the BBC's excellent site **www.bbc.co.uk/onthisday** where you can see what happened on a particular day in history. Strongly biased to the 20th century with film clips and eye witness reports.

www.ukans.edu/history/VL

HISTORY LINKS

ORIGIN US
INFO ✓✓✓✓✓
EASE ✓✓✓

The folks at the University of Kansas love their history and have put together a huge library, organised by country and historical period. It's got an easy-to-use search engine too. For modern history go to **www.fordham.edu/halsall/mod/modsbook.html**

http://history.about.com

HISTORY AT ABOUT.COM

ORIGIN US
INFO ✓✓✓✓✓
EASE ✓✓✓

A massive archive including bringing history to life by using the eyewitness accounts of people who were actually there. This site is excellent for most periods of history.

www.pepysdiary.com

DIARY OF SAMUEL PEPYS

ORIGIN UK
INFO ✓✓✓✓✓
EASE ✓✓✓✓

Put together by an aficionado of Pepys, this is updated daily with an entry from the diaries on the day he wrote them over 340 years ago. Apart from the fascinating social history there's lots of annotation, explanation and cross referencing too as well as audio readings, which all help to picture the scene.

www.thebanmappingproject.com

THEBES AND THE VALLEY OF THE KINGS

ORIGIN US   A great and genuinely interesting site devoted to life
INFO ✓✓✓✓✓ in ancient Thebes in what is now Egypt, with over
EASE ✓✓✓✓   200 interactive maps, narrative tours and 3D
features. Outstanding.

www.documentsonline.pro.gov.uk

DOWNLOAD YOUR HISTORY

ORIGIN UK   From the Public Record Office, this site gives you
INFO ✓✓✓✓   the chance to see digitised versions of over 800,000
EASE ✓✓✓✓   wills, ancient documents and other important
academic papers.

www.pbs.org/commandingheights

GLOBAL ECONOMY

ORIGIN US   An outstanding site devoted to the explanation of
INFO ✓✓✓✓✓ how the global economy works, great for students
EASE ✓✓✓✓   of politics and history alike.

For more general history sites try these:
http://perseus.csad.ox.ac.uk – the Perseus Digital
    Library, a great site featuring a history timeline and
    archive.
www.historylearningsite.co.uk – great for school, it
    covers Key Stage 3 and upwards.
www.historyplace.com – biased towards the US but
    has some great historic photos.
www.ibiscom.com – containing a large catalogue of
    historical recollections both ancient and modern,
    and take the 'history through the eyes of those who
    lived it' approach.
www.hmc.gov.uk – home of the Historical
    Manuscripts Commission who are responsible for
    looking after and advising on the upkeep and use of
    historical documents.
www.spartacus.schoolnet.co.uk – a useful history
    encyclopedia.

Good sites on specific periods or subject areas:
www.angelcynn.org.uk – excellent site on how the
    Anglo-Saxons lived.
www.greatwar.co.uk – a well laid out site on the 1914-
    18 war.

www.pastforward.co.uk/vikings – a directory of all
   things Viking.
www.regia.org – Anglo-Saxons, Vikings and Normans.
www.roman-empire.net – excellent site covering all
   aspects of the Roman Empire with a good kids
   section.
www.tudorhistory.org – a who's who of Tudor times
   with background on what it was like to live then.

Other types of history sites

www.biography.com
FIND OUT ABOUT ANYONE WHO WAS ANYONE

ORIGIN US
INFO ✓✓✓✓✓
EASE ✓✓✓

Over 25,000 biographical references and some 4,000
videos make this site a great option if you need to
find out about someone in a hurry. There are special
features such as a book club and a magazine. There
is a shop but at time of going to press they don't
ship to the UK.

See also:
http://almaz.com/nobel/nobel.html – a fascinating site
   about the people who have won the Nobel prize.
www.fordham.edu/halsall – a messy site, presenting
   copies of history source books that are freely
   available for use.
www.royalty.nu – the world of royalty, historical
   and recent.
www.rulers.org – an amazing database providing a list
   of the rulers of every country going back to 1700.
www.s9.com/biography – a biographical dictionary
   covering the lives of over 28,000 people!

www.francisfrith.co.uk
HISTORY IN PHOTOGRAPHS

ORIGIN UK
INFO ✓✓✓✓
VALUE ✓✓✓✓
EASE ✓✓✓✓

This remarkable archive was started in 1860 and
there are over 365,000 photographs featuring some
7,000 cities, towns and villages. The site is very well
designed with a good search facility. You can buy
from a growing selection of shots, different sizes

are available and it's good value too. See also
www.photolondon.org.uk where you'll find an
excellent photo archive of the capital.

www.old-maps.co.uk

FREE OLD MAPS

ORIGIN UK	Access to mapping as it was between 1846 and 1899,
INFO ✓✓✓✓	just type in your town and you get a view of what it
EASE ✓✓✓✓	looked like in those times. The quality is variable

but it's fun to try and spot the changes. See also
www.alangodfreymaps.co.uk

www.museumofcostume.co.uk

COSTUME THROUGH THE AGES

ORIGIN UK	Excellent site showing how the design of costume has
INFO ✓✓✓✓	changed through the ages. There's a virtual tour and
VALUE ✓✓	links to other museums based in Bath.
EASE ✓✓✓	

www.yesterdayland.com

YOUR CHILDHOOD REVISITED

ORIGIN US	A modern history site devoted to those things that
INFO ✓✓✓✓✓	made up our childhood, mainly aimed at those of
EASE ✓✓✓✓	us who are in our thirties and forties. It provides a

great nostalgia trip covering areas such as toys,
TV programs, arcade games, fashion and music.

www.blackhistorymap.com

BLACK AND ASIAN HISTORY ACROSS THE UK

ORIGIN UK	A beautifully designed and important site, which
INFO ✓✓✓✓✓	graphically describes how Black people and Asians,
EASE ✓✓✓✓	have contributed to British history. Search by region,

use the timeline or category headings. It's well
written and very informative with a wide range
of contributions, there's also a selection of videos.

www.findagrave.com

FIND A GRAVE!

ORIGIN US	Find graves of the rich and famous or a long lost
INFO ✓✓✓✓✓	relative, either way there's a database of over 3
EASE ✓✓✓✓	million to search. It really only covers the USA.

www.the-reenactor.co.uk

TAKE PART IN A BATTLE

ORIGIN UK	OK so you feel the urge to play at being a Viking
INFO ✓✓✓✓	for the day, well here's where to start where there
EASE ✓✓✓	are some 100 societies to join and play a part in.

The site is divided into sections according to time period and you can find out where events are being held plus the latest news.

Hobbies

www.yahoo.co.uk/recreation/hobbies

IF YOU CAN'T FIND YOUR HOBBY THEN LOOK HERE

ORIGIN UK	Hundreds of links for almost every conceivable
INFO ✓✓✓	pastime from amateur radio to urban exploration,
VALUE ✓✓	it's part of the Yahoo service (see page 317); also
EASE ✓✓✓	try www.about.com/hobbies who have a similarly

large list but with an American bias.

See also:
www.allcrafts.net – a wide-ranging directory covering all the major crafts and many minor ones. Very good links pages.
www.ehobbies.com – they don't ship outside the USA, but are worth a visit anyway for information and links.
www.hobbyseek.net/cgi-search/Great_Britain – a German site with good links to modelling sites.
www.hobbywebguide.com – a modest list with some good hobby sites.

www.save-on-crafts.com

SAVINGS EVERYWHERE YOU LOOK

ORIGIN US	An excellent craft supply and interiors store covering
INFO ✓✓✓✓	an extensive range of crafts and merchandise. It's
VALUE ✓✓✓	well worth a browse and good for the unusual
EASE ✓✓✓✓	but shipping is expensive.

www.cass-arts.co.uk
ONE STOP SHOP FOR ART MATERIALS

ORIGIN UK
INFO ✓✓✓
VALUE ✓✓✓✓
EASE ✓✓✓✓

A huge range of art and craft products available to buy online, also hints and tips and step-by-step guides for the novice. There is an online gallery and a section of art trivia and games. The shop has a decent search engine which copes with over 20,000 items, delivery is charged according to what you spend.

www.sewandso.co.uk
SHOP AT THE SPECIALISTS

ORIGIN UK
INFO ✓✓✓✓
VALUE ✓✓✓✓
EASE ✓✓✓✓

This site offers a huge range of kits and patterns for cross-stitch, needlepoint and embroidery. In addition, there's an equally large range of needles and threads, some 15,000 products in all. There are some good offers and delivery starts at £1 for the UK, but the cost is calculated by weight. It's also worth checking out the specialist pages at About.com http://knitting.about.com and http://sewing.about.com

www.horology.com
THE INDEX

ORIGIN US
INFO ✓✓✓
EASE ✓✓✓

The complete exploration of time, this is essentially a set of links for the committed horologist. It's pretty comprehensive, so if your hobby is tinkering about with clocks and watches, then this is a must.

www.royalmint.com
THE VALUE OF MONEY

ORIGIN UK
INFO ✓✓✓✓✓
VALUE ✓✓✓
EASE ✓✓✓✓

The Royal Mint's web site is informative, providing a history of the Mint, the coins themselves, plus details on the coins they've issued. You can buy from the site and delivery is free.

See also:
http://coins.to – US coins and much more from the Austin Coin Collecting Society.
www.coinclub.com – good for information and links.
www.coinlink.com – a good directory devoted to all things numismatic.

www.tclayton.demon.co.uk/coins.html – Tony
Clayton's informative home page on coins.
www.telesphere.com/ts/coins/faq.html – commonly
asked questions about coin collecting.
www.tokenpublishing.com – owners of *Coin News*.

www.stanleygibbons.com

STAMPS ETC.

ORIGIN UK
INFO ✓✓✓
EASE ✓✓✓✓

The best prices and a user-friendly site for philatelists,
you can buy a whole collection or sell them your own.
Their catalogue is available online and you can take
part in auctions.

See also:
www.corbitts.com – auctioneers for stamps, coins,
notes and medals.
www.duncannon.co.uk – for accessories and albums.
www.postcard.co.uk – home of the Postcard Traders
Association.
www.robinhood-stamp.co.uk – for good prices and
range.
www.stampsatauction.com – a good auction site
devoted to stamps.
www.ukphilately.org.uk/abps – information on
exhibitions and events at the Association of
British Philatelic Societies.

www.towerhobbies.com

EXCITING WORLD OF RADIO CONTROLLED MODELLING

ORIGIN US
INFO ✓✓✓
VALUE ✓✓✓
EASE ✓✓✓✓

An excellent, clearly laid out site offering a vast range
of radio-controlled models along with thousands of
accessories and parts. The delivery charge depends
on the size of the order.

www.brmodelling.com

BRITISH RAILWAY MODELLING

ORIGIN UK
INFO ✓✓✓✓
EASE ✓✓✓✓

A high quality magazine site devoted to model
railways, it includes a virtual model set for you to
play with and articles on specific types of trains and
railways. There's also a forum where you can chat to
fellow enthusiasts.

See also:
www.corgi.co.uk – home of the leading model
   car maker.
www.modelboats.co.uk – a model boats magazine.
www.toysoldier.freeuk.com – informative site
   devoted to toy soldiers.
www.ukmodelshops.co.uk – a directory mainly
   railways oriented.
www.wingsandwheels.co.uk – model aircraft
   specialists.

www.ontracks.co.uk
MODEL AND HOBBY SUPERSTORE

ORIGIN UK	They sell over 35,000 models and hobby items, but
INFO ✓✓✓	it's tricky to find what you want as the site is a bit
VALUE ✓✓✓✓	messy with lots of annoying graphics. Having said
EASE ✓✓✓	that there are some good special offers and delivery
	prices are reasonable.

www.woodworking.co.uk
WORKING WITH WOOD

ORIGIN UK	A good amateur site offering loads of information
INFO ✓✓✓✓	about all aspects of wood working. There's a
EASE ✓✓✓	gallery of work from featured craftsmen plus
	advice for beginners.

Humour

*The 'Net has become home to an amazing array of funny sites,
here's just a few of the best. You should be aware that most
aren't suitable for children.*

Jokes, links and directories

www.comedy-zone.net
COMPLETE COMEDY GUIDE

ORIGIN UK	Excellent and wide-ranging comedy site with lots
INFO ✓✓✓✓✓	of links and competitions, alongside quotes, jokes
EASE ✓✓✓	and chat.

For other comedy portals and loads of jokes go to:

http://uk.dir.yahoo.com/entertainment/humour –
Yahoo's excellent listing devoted to humour
and bizarre sites.

www.bored.com – a great directory of humour sites.

www.funnybone.com – huge database with lots
of rude jokes.

www.funnymail.com – lots of jokes well categorised
with good features such as tests, top 10 jokes of all
time, newest jokes and so on.

www.funs.co.uk – lots here from jokes to games.

www.humorlinks.com – massive portal for all things
funny.

www.humournet.co.uk – categorised jokes, links and
funny pictures.

www.jokecenter.com – hundreds of jokes, vote for
your favourites.

www.jokepost.com – hundreds, all well categorised.

www.jokes2000.com – e-mail you the latest jokes.

www.jokes.com – typical jokes directory but these are
rated, tame, racy etc...

www.kidsjokes.co.uk – 12,000+ jokes, great for the
family.

www.weirdwebbed.com – a directory of the weirdest
web sites.

www.funny-downloads.com

THE BEST IN MULTI-MEDIA HUMOUR

ORIGIN US
INFO ✓✓✓✓✓
VALUE ✓✓✓
EASE ✓✓✓✓

What used to be Olley's Place has transformed into
a subscription only site costing £3 per annum. For
that you get access to a superb selection of funny
video clips and comedy downloads, there is some
free content though and you should be aware that
most of it is adult oriented.

In a similar vein see also the very entertaining
www.videoparodies.com who offer loads of
parodies on the pop video theme and more;
and there's also **www.cyberparodies.com**
both offer the classic 'Oops I've farted again' by
Britney. **www.ebaumsworld.com** is also worth
checking out, it offers a huge amount of adult
humour and currently it's free. Another directory of
fun clips is the wonderfully named **www.spongi.com**

www.pickthehottie.com

PICK THE HOTTIE!

ORIGIN US
INFO ✓✓✓✓
EASE ✓✓✓✓✓

Probably the best of many sites where people post photos of themselves and their friends (or enemies) the idea being that you vote for the hottest-looking people and the ugliest too.

www.uebersetzung.at/twister

TONGUE TWISTERS

ORIGIN AUSTRIA
INFO ✓✓✓✓
EASE ✓✓✓✓

An international collection of tongue twisters, over 2,000 in 87 languages when we last visited, nearly 400 in English – 'Can you can a can as a canner can can a can?' as they say.

British humour

www.britcoms.com

BRITISH COMEDY LINKS

ORIGIN UK
INFO ✓✓✓✓
EASE ✓✓✓✓

If you want to find a link to a British comedy show or comedian, then start here. The sites are selected for quality and there's also a broader selection of links for you to browse. You can also sign up for their newsletter. For traditional humour check out **www.britishcomedy.org.uk**

www.comedybutchers.com

SURREAL BRITISH COMEDY

ORIGIN UK
INFO ✓✓✓✓✓
EASE ✓✓✓✓

A really good attempt at creating a web site that shows off surreal adult comedy in the traditional British style, you click on various rooms within a floating town to get clips and sketches.

Stand-up comedy

www.chortle.co.uk

GUIDE TO LIVE COMEDY IN THE UK

ORIGIN UK
INFO ✓✓✓✓
VALUE ✓✓✓✓
EASE ✓✓✓✓

Chortle provides a complete service, listing who's on, where and when – also whether they're any good or not. There's also a comic's A–Z so that you can find your favourites and get reviews on how they're performing, or not, as the case may be.

www.comedyonline.co.uk

STAND UP COMEDY IN YOUR AREA

ORIGIN UK
INFO ✓✓✓✓
EASE ✓✓✓✓

News, links, interviews, clubs and listings; its all here at this comprehensive and well put together site, so if you're looking to check out a new comedian or just want to see an old favourite, start here. See also www.jongleurs.co.uk whose entertaining site has audio clips and details of what's on and when at their clubs.

Comedy magazine and satirical sites

www.theonion.com

AMERICA'S FINEST NEWS SOURCE

ORIGIN US
INFO ✓✓✓✓✓
EASE ✓✓✓✓

A great send-up of American tabloid newspapers, this is one of the most visited sites on the Internet and easily one of the funniest. See also the equally good Framley Examiner at www.framleyexaminer.com

www.private-eye.co.uk

PRIVATE EYE

ORIGIN UK
INFO ✓✓✓
EASE ✓✓✓

A pretty average effort really considering the wealth of material that must be available, there are a few of the best cartoons and features, but it's only updated every couple of weeks or so.

www.viz.co.uk

NOT FOR CHILDREN

ORIGIN UK
INFO ✓✓✓✓
EASE ✓✓✓✓

A very good reflection of what you get in the real thing with lots of games and downloads, you can even contribute to Roger's Profanisaurus.

www.thespark.com

TAKE THE SPARK TESTS

ORIGIN UK
INFO ✓✓✓✓
EASE ✓✓✓✓

The Spark consists of a humorous news magazine and a few other jokey bits and bobs plus lots of annoying adverts, but its main feature, and the reason why millions visit, is for the tests. From the popular personality test, through bitch and bastard tests to the wealth test, all are good for a laugh and of course very accurate. Dare you take the 'Death test' or the new 'Cut-throat' test though?

www.b3ta.com

WE LOVE THE WEB

ORIGIN UK	A messy site that catalogues all that is unusual and
INFO ✓✓✓✓	fun, they'll e-mail you with their latest finds and it's
EASE ✓✓✓	a great place to find the unashamedly silly.

www.bizarremag.com

BIZARRE MAGAZINE

ORIGIN US	The magazine is devoted to 'life in the extreme' and
INFO ✓✓✓	the site reflects this with a selection of pictures and
EASE ✓✓✓✓	stories. It's all geared to getting you to subscribe.
	Be aware that the content is adult oriented.

www.whitehouse.org

THE WHITE HOUSE

ORIGIN US	A great mickey-take on the US presidency, very
INFO ✓✓✓✓✓	clever and vicious too.
EASE ✓✓✓✓	

TV comedy

www.comedycentral.com

THE HOME OF SOUTH PARK AND MORE

ORIGIN US	Great for South Park and selected American TV
INFO ✓✓✓✓	shows, but also with clips and background
EASE ✓✓✓✓	information and stand up comedy too.

www.thesimpsons.com

HOME OF THE SIMPSONS

ORIGIN US	The official site with biographies, background, quizzes
INFO ✓✓✓✓	and more, plus the ever-present merchandise store. If
VALUE ✓✓	you are a real fan then go to the Simpsons archive at
EASE ✓✓✓✓	www.snpp.com

Urban legends

www.snopes2.com
URBAN LEGENDS

ORIGIN US
INFO ✓✓✓✓✓
EASE ✓✓✓✓

An outstanding collection of all those stories and myths that have that edge of unlikely truth about them. Well categorised and with a good search facility it's easy to find your favourites. See also **www.urbanlegends.com** another catalogue of unlikely stories from urban folklore.

www.darwinawards.com
FATAL MISADVENTURES

ORIGIN US
INFO ✓✓✓✓
EASE ✓✓✓✓

The Darwin Awards have been going several years now and their site is packed with stories, urban legends and personal accounts of those who have 'improved our gene pool by removing themselves from it in really stupid ways'.

Miscellaneous

www.losers.org
THE WEB'S LOSERS

ORIGIN US
INFO ✓✓✓✓
EASE ✓✓✓✓

A site that catalogues and rates the saddest sites and sights on the web, note that some of the content is strictly adults only. Still, it's one of the most fascinating giggles available, all web site designers should see this.

www.strangereports.com
PRANKS ONLINE

ORIGIN US
INFO ✓✓✓✓
EASE ✓✓✓✓

Play pranks on your friends using the service available here, with trick web sites and fake news reports it's almost irresistible but beware their revenge…

www.freakydreams.com
DREAM INTERPRETED

ORIGIN US
INFO ✓✓✓✓
EASE ✓✓✓✓

You just type in the description of your dream and an 'accurate' interpretation pops up in seconds.

www.joecartoon.com

FREAKY CARTOONS

ORIGIN US
INFO ✓✓✓✓
EASE ✓✓✓✓

Follow the gruesome, messy adventures of Joe, download the cartoons and send them to your friends and buy the T-shirt - he's a legend after all. Superb animation and very funny, but you need patience for the downloads.

www.emilystrange.com

ENTER THE WORLD OF EMILY STRANGE

ORIGIN UK
INFO ✓✓✓✓
EASE ✓✓✓✓

Another animated site with outstanding illustrations that's worth a visit just to look at the design, if nothing else. Emily is a popular icon with teenagers and here you can participate in her freaky adventures.

www.user-error.co.uk

EXCUSE GENERATOR

ORIGIN UK
INFO ✓✓✓
VALUE ✓✓✓
EASE ✓✓✓

Apart from the excellent excuse generator which is very handy, there's also a virtual makeover section, articles on the unusual universe we live in and, if you're in a disagreement with someone over some fact or other, they'll help you settle your bet.

www.createafart.com

FARTS

ORIGIN US
INFO ✓✓✓✓
EASE ✓✓✓✓✓

Create your fart based on duration, smelliness, type and density – well no one said we had to make this book a sophisticated one...

www.museumofhoaxes.com

HOAXES

ORIGIN US
INFO ✓✓✓✓
EASE ✓✓✓

The world's greatest hoaxes and April Fools are catalogued here, makes entertaining browsing and is sometimes unbelievable.

www.smalltime.com/dictator

GUESS THE DICTATOR

ORIGIN UK
INFO ✓✓✓✓
EASE ✓✓✓✓

You think of dictator or TV sit-com character, answer the questions put to you and the site will guess who you are thinking of...it's spookily accurate.

www.optillusions.com

OPTICAL ILLUSIONS

ORIGIN US
INFO ✓✓✓✓
EASE ✓✓✓✓

A good selection of optical illusions to download, plus links to other similar and funny sites. The visit is completely spoiled by the large amount of adverts, both pop-ups and banners.

www.emotioneric.com

EMOTIONAL ERIC

ORIGIN US
INFO ✓✓✓
EASE ✓✓✓✓

A cult site in the U.S. Eric will act out any emotion in any situation, you just have to place your request.

www.snapbubbles.com

VIRTUAL BUBBLE WRAP

ORIGIN US
INFO ✓✓✓✓
EASE ✓✓✓✓

How comforting, just when you have the urge to pop and there's no bubble wrap to hand, just come here for the nearest substitute.

Internet Service Provision

There are so many Internet Service Providers (ISPs) that it would be impossible to review them all and it's moving so fast that any information soon becomes outdated. However, help is at hand and here are some sites that will help you chose the right one for you.

www.net4nowt.com

THE PLACE TO START LOOKING FOR THE BEST ISP

ORIGIN UK
INFO ✓✓✓✓✓
EASE ✓✓✓✓✓

This is a directory of Internet service providers offering news and advice on the best ones. There is an up-to-date critique on each ISP with comments on costs and reliability. There is also a good summary table featuring all the ISPs, which proves useful for comparisons.

www.ispreview.co.uk

INTERNET NEWS

ORIGIN UK
INFO ✓✓✓✓✓
EASE ✓✓✓✓✓

Find out what's really going on at this impressive site – they are especially good at exposing the worst performers. There's plenty in the way of news, offers and a top 10 ISP list. Also check out **www.thelist.com** which is international.

Jobs and Careers

There are several hundred sites offering jobs or career advice but it's largely a matter of luck if you come across a job you like. Still, it enables you to cover plenty of ground in a short space of time without trawling the newspapers. These sites offer the most options and best advice.

Career guidance

www.careerguide.net

ONLINE CAREER ADVICE RESOURCE

ORIGIN UK
INFO ✓✓✓✓✓
EASE ✓✓✓

This is a comprehensive service with many sections on job hunting, vacancies, CVs, careers advice and professional institutions that can help.

www.careers-portal.co.uk

AWARD WINNING CAREERS SERVICE

ORIGIN UK
INFO ✓✓✓✓✓
EASE ✓✓✓✓

An excellent portal site that is part of the National Grid for Learning, with lots of advice on universities, jobs and how to apply. There's a very useful careers directory and it's all geared to helping you choose the right career. See also **www.get.hobsons.com**, a careers and jobs site aimed at graduates.

www.careers-gateway.co.uk

THE CAREER GATEWAY

ORIGIN UK
INFO ✓✓✓✓✓
EASE ✓✓✓✓

Great advice and lots of information. For example, how to launch a proper career, evaluate your options and read articles to help you decide what you can do with your life. There's a virtual career show, quizzes designed to help and advice for HR professionals too.

www.reachforthesky.co.uk

CAREER ADVICE FROM SKY TV

ORIGIN UK
INFO ✓✓✓✓
EASE ✓✓✓✓

Sky has put together a great web site that doesn't just look good. However, it's developed into more of a teen magazine, but there is a good deal of advice here plus some fun too.

www.careersolutions.co.uk

HELP TO GO FORWARD

ORIGIN UK
INFO ✓✓✓✓✓
EASE ✓✓✓✓

A good place to start if you're not sure what you want to do next with your career, don't know where to start or you've been made redundant. Using the site enables you to narrow your options and clarify things. The list of links is logically laid out and very helpful.

www.careerstorm.com

WHERE DO YOU GO FROM HERE?

ORIGIN HOLLAND
INFO ✓✓✓✓
EASE ✓✓✓✓

A site that will help you make decisions about your next career steps by a series of quizzes and questionnaires designed to find out what you're really good at. It's interesting anyway, and it costs nothing.

www.icg-uk.org

INSTITUTE OF CAREER GUIDANCE

ORIGIN UK
INFO ✓✓✓✓
EASE ✓✓✓✓

A useful place to go for basic advice and resource information on what to do wherever you are in your career, it has a good links section too. Limited use for non-members though.

Job finders

www.transdata-inter.co.uk/jobs-agencies

DIRECTORY OF JOB SITES

ORIGIN UK
INFO ✓✓✓✓✓
EASE ✓✓✓✓✓

Don't let the long URL put you off, this is an excellent place to start on your search. The Directory lists all the major online employment agencies and ranks them by the average number of vacancies, the regions they cover, whether they help create and store CVs and what industries they represent. Clicking on the name takes you right to the site you need.

www.jobs.co.uk

JOB SEARCH ENGINE

ORIGIN UK
INFO ✓✓✓✓
EASE ✓✓✓✓✓

With this facility you can search all the major jobs sites in one go, it's easy to use and quite accurate providing you have a defined job title. They also offer all the usual features such as CV help and advice. See also www.jobsearch.co.uk

www.gisajob.co.uk

SEARCH FOR YOUR NEXT JOB HERE

ORIGIN UK
INFO ✓✓✓✓
EASE ✓✓✓✓✓

The largest of the UK online job sites with over 86,000 vacancies. You can search by description or sector or get advice on your career. It's good for non-senior executive types.

www.workthing.com

IT'S A WORK THING

ORIGIN UK
INFO ✓✓✓✓✓
EASE ✓✓✓✓

One of the best-looking job sites with a reputation to match, this site must be one of the first to visit when job hunting across a wide range of industries. Registered users can set up an e-mail alert when a job matching their search criteria appears. They also work with businesses to develop their people skills and recruitment; you can also get advice on training and personal development too.

www.monster.co.uk

GLOBAL JOBS

ORIGIN UK
INFO ✓✓✓✓✓
EASE ✓✓✓✓✓

With over 1 million jobs available world-wide there are plenty to chose from. The site is well-designed and easy to use with the usual help features. At time of writing there were over 17,000 UK jobs listed in over 20 categories.

www.stepstone.co.uk

EUROPEAN INTERNET RECRUITMENT

ORIGIN UK
INFO ✓✓✓✓
EASE ✓✓✓✓

Regarded as one of the best, Stepstone has a huge number of European and international vacancies. It's quick, easy to use and offers lots of timesaving cross-referencing features. You can also register your CV. For other overseas jobs see **www.overseasjobs.com**

Other job finder sites worth checking out:
www.doctorjob.com – graduates only need apply.
www.jobpilot.co.uk – good for European jobs, over 47,000 listed.
www.reed.co.uk – some 126,000 vacancies from a wide range of categories.
www.totaljobs.co.uk – 30,000 jobs listed in a wide range of sectors.

These government run sites might also be useful:

www.aimhigher.gov.uk – how to get the qualifications to get the job you really want.

www.connexions.gov.uk – an advice service aimed at 13–19 year olds.

www.dfes.gov.uk – the Dept of Education has lots of helpful advice.

www.jobcentreplus.gov.uk – information about job centres and how to go about finding a job.

www.worktrain.gov.uk – jobs, training, voluntary work, it's all here.

Other careers and related sites

www.i-resign.com/uk
THE INS AND OUTS OF RESIGNATION

ORIGIN UK
INFO ✓✓✓✓✓
EASE ✓✓✓

Pay a visit before you send the letter, it offers a great deal of advice both legal and sensible. The best section contains the funniest selection of resignation letters anywhere. There are also jobs on offer, links to job finder sites and a career guide service.

www.freelancecentre.com
SELF EMPLOYED

ORIGIN UK
INFO ✓✓✓✓
VALUE ✓✓✓
EASE ✓✓✓✓

Great for anyone thinking of going it alone, or are looking for help if you're already working for yourself. There's plenty of advice here – good deal of it is absolutely free.

www.homeworking.com
WORKING FROM HOME

ORIGIN UK
INFO ✓✓✓✓✓
EASE ✓✓✓✓

A site full of advice and information for anyone considering or actually working from home. There are links, directories and classified ads, as well as forum pages where you can share experiences with other home workers.

www.eoc.org.uk
EQUAL OPPORTUNITIES COMMISSION

ORIGIN UK
INFO ✓✓✓✓✓
EASE ✓✓✓✓

A very informative site and it's where to go if you think you are being discriminated against.

www.queendom.com
SERIOUSLY ENTERTAINING

ORIGIN UK
INFO ✓✓✓✓✓
EASE ✓✓✓✓

Apart from the fun tests there's a serious side to this site that allows you to take the sort of tests you're likely to face when applying for a job. See also www.emode.com

Legal Advice and the Law

We all need help with certain key events in life: marriages, moving house, making a will or getting a divorce. Maybe you need advice on lesser issues like boundary disputes or problems with services or property? Here are several good sites that could really make a difference.

www.compactlaw.co.uk
LEGAL INFORMATION FOR ENGLAND AND WALES

ORIGIN UK
INFO ✓✓✓✓✓
VALUE ✓✓✓✓
EASE ✓✓✓✓

An extremely informative and useful site that covers many aspects of the law in a clear and concise style, there are usable documents – you can download some free, others to buy, case histories, news, tips and plenty of fact-sheets. Formally **www.lawrights.co.uk**

www.uklegal.com
LEGAL RESOURCES AT YOUR FINGERTIPS

ORIGIN UK
INFO ✓✓✓✓✓
EASE ✓✓✓✓

This site offers a superb selection of links to everything from private investigators to barristers to legal equipment suppliers.

www.family-solicitors.co.uk
FAMILY LAW REFERENCE

ORIGIN UK
INFO ✓✓✓✓✓
EASE ✓✓✓✓

Excellent resource for everyday legal issues covering everything from wills to neighbourhood disputes. Great for links too with an excellent search facility for finding a family law solicitor near you. See also **www.solicitors-online.com**

www.desktoplawyer.net

THE UK'S FIRST ONLINE LAWYER

ORIGIN UK
INFO ✓✓✓✓
VALUE ✓✓✓
EASE ✓✓✓✓

This site is quite straightforward if you know what you need and have read through the instructions carefully. First you register, then download the software (Rapidocs) enabling you to compile the document you need. The legal documents you create will cost from £2.99 upwards depending on complexity. The range of documents available is huge and there are more being added. See also **www.everyform.net** who have some 900 free forms to download.

www.legalservices.gov.uk

GOVERNMENT ADVICE

ORIGIN UK
INFO ✓✓✓✓✓
EASE ✓✓✓

The replacement for legal aid, this is the official line on legal matters with guidance on how to access legal assistance, where to get information and news on latest changes to the Community Legal Service and Criminal Defence Service. It could be a lot more user-friendly. For Scottish legal aid go to **www.slab.org.uk**

See also:
www.divorce-online.co.uk – fast track divorces and good advice.
www.emplaw.co.uk – the low down on British employment law.
www.lawassure.co.uk – subscribe to excellent personal legal advice and related services.
www.lawpack.co.uk – legal book specialist.
www.lawscot.org.uk – the Law Society of Scotland.
www.legaladvicefree.co.uk – excellent all rounder that provides the answer to many legal questions.
www.legalpulse.com – well designed site along the lines of Desktop Lawyer although not as comprehensive.
www.legalshop.co.uk – affordable solutions to your legal problems; a good site, with a business section too.

www.dumblaws.com
THE DAFTEST, STUPIDEST LAWS

ORIGIN US
INFO ✓✓✓✓
EASE ✓✓✓✓

Did you realise that in England placing a postage stamp that bears the Queen's head upside down is considered treasonable, or that in Kentucky it's illegal to fish with a bow and arrow? These are just a couple of the many dumb laws that you can find on this very entertaining site. It's now been expanded to include dumbest criminals, dumbest warnings and place names.

Magazines

Where to buy and subscribe to your favourite magazines.

www.magazinecity.co.uk
THE WEB'S LARGEST SUBSCRIPTION SOURCE

ORIGIN US
INFO ✓✓✓
VALUE ✓✓✓
EASE ✓✓✓

A site dedicated to magazine subscriptions, it's fairly slow but easy to use, however, it is annoying that most prices are quoted in dollars. See also the very similar and equally slow **www.subscription.co.uk** who at least quote prices in pounds, a better alternative is probably **www.newsstand.co.uk** who have turned into a subscription only retailer.

See also:
www.actualidad.com – newspapers of the world and links to their sites.
www.whsmith.co.uk – some good offers on subscriptions which are available to UK addresses only.
www.worldofmagazines.co.uk – 3,000 mags featured but they provide information only; however, they will point you in the direction of the nearest stockist.

Men

Maybe not what you think, these are just a few sites especially for blokes, lads and real men.

Magazines

www.fhm.co.uk
FHM MAGAZINE

ORIGIN UK
INFO ✓✓✓✓
EASE ✓✓✓✓

A good reflection of the real thing, with sections on everything from serious news to the lighter side, with the usual blokey features, it suffers from lots of advertising though.

www.gqmagazine.co.uk
GENTLEMEN'S QUARTERLY

ORIGIN UK
INFO ✓✓✓
EASE ✓✓✓✓

A stylish site, which gives a flavour of the real magazine, it contains a few stories, competitions, fashion tips and the odd feature.

www.sharpman.com
SHARP!

ORIGIN UK
INFO ✓✓✓✓
EASE ✓✓✓✓

While a little odd, it's good fun and there's some useful advice. Split into six key sections:
Dating – with tips on conversation and repartee.
Health – how to keep in tip-top condition.
Work – getting the best out of the Internet.
Travel – staying sharp abroad.
Grooming – looking the part.
Toys – the best advice on windsurfing.

www.fathersdirect.com
A MAGAZINE FOR FATHERS

ORIGIN UK
INFO ✓✓✓✓
VALUE ✓✓✓
EASE ✓✓✓✓

Written by fathers for fathers, this entertaining e-zine has all the advice and support you need if you're a new dad or you're trying to fit in both work and kids. There are competitions, a rant section where you can let off steam and a games room. Rather twee graphics let it down somewhat and it needs to be updated a bit more regularly.

See also:

www.askmen.com – a very good American men's magazine covering almost every topic you're likely to need.

www.dullmen.com – the dullest website from the National Council for Dull Men, very funny too.

www.modernman.com – nicely designed men's magazine site from the US with loads of interesting articles and features.

Health

www.menshealth.co.uk

MEN'S HEALTH MAGAZINE

ORIGIN UK
INFO ✓✓✓✓✓
EASE ✓✓✓✓

Lots of advice on keeping fit, healthy and fashionable too. There's also an excellent section on the number one topic – sex, plus others on wealth, health, sport and a shop that sells subscriptions and recommends the latest gear.

www.menshealthforum.org.uk

STOP MOANING!

ORIGIN UK
INFO ✓✓✓✓✓
EASE ✓✓✓✓

An excellent all-rounder revealing the truth behind the state of men's health and lots of discussion about specific and general health issues facing men today – good for links too.

Other men's health sites:

www.impotence.org.uk – the Impotence Association.

www.malehealth.co.uk – comprehensive site where you can check the state of your health and your health knowledge; excellent links and advice make up the picture.

www.orchid-cancer.org.uk – promotes the awareness of testicular and prostate cancer.

www.vasectomy-clinic.co.uk – no scalpel vasectomy – honest!

Shopping

www.firebox.com

WHERE MEN BUY STUFF

ORIGIN UK
INFO ✓✓✓✓
VALUE ✓✓✓
EASE ✓✓✓✓

An online shop aimed totally at boy's toys, with it's own bachelor pad containing all you need for the lifestyle. There's masses of games, videos, toys and, of course, the latest gadgets. Delivery costs vary. See also **www.big-boys-toys.net** and **www.boysstuff.co.uk** both are worth a visit if you can't find what you want at Firebox.

www.condomsdirect.co.uk

CONDOMS UK

ORIGIN UK
INFO ✓✓✓✓
VALUE ✓✓✓✓
EASE ✓✓✓✓

Many different types of condoms are available to buy, and you get free delivery if you spend more than £10 – there's even a price promise and the assurance of a fast and discreet service. It's also worth checking out **www.condomania.com**

www.giftsforbirds.co.uk

SO YOU DON'T KNOW WHAT TO BUY...

ORIGIN UK
INFO ✓✓✓✓
VALUE ✓✓✓✓
EASE ✓✓✓✓

Full of ideas for clueless men, and it comes with a reminder service built in for those important dates. You can even type in a price and it'll suggest appropriate presents. Delivery costs are built in, along with enough wrapping paper to cover the gift.

Motorcycles

www.bmf.co.uk

BRITISH MOTORCYCLISTS FEDERATION

ORIGIN UK
INFO ✓✓✓✓
EASE ✓✓✓✓

At this site you can join the BMF, get involved with their activities or just use the site for information or for their magazine *Rider*. You can also get club information and e-mail them on any issues. For the international governing body go to **www.fim.ch/en**

www.motorcycle.co.uk

THE UK'S MOTORCYCLE DIRECTORY

ORIGIN UK   Essentially a list of links by brand, dealer, importer,
INFO ✓✓✓   classics, gear, books and auctions. For more informa-
EASE ✓✓✓✓   tion on clubs go to **www.motorcycle.org.uk**

www.moto-directory.com

THE WORLD MOTORCYCLE DIRECTORY

ORIGIN US   US-oriented, but links to over 800 sites ensure that
INFO ✓✓✓✓   you'll know what's going on in motorcycling and find
VALUE ✓✓✓   the information you need.
EASE ✓✓✓✓

www.motorworld.com

ALL YOU NEED TO KNOW ABOUT MOTORCYCLES

ORIGIN US   Good coverage of both machines and events with
INFO ✓✓✓✓   multimedia features. Although the site is American
EASE ✓✓✓   there's a good British section.

www.motorcycle-search.co.uk

FREE CLASSIFIED ADS

ORIGIN UK   A good, fast site with a good selection of used bikes,
INFO ✓✓✓✓   luggage, clothing, parts and accessories. See also
EASE ✓✓✓✓   Bike Exchange at **www.biketrader.co.uk** who also
             offer other services such as insurance and finance.

www.fowlers.co.uk

WHERE TO GET YOUR GEAR

ORIGIN UK   A good shop and information site dedicated to motor-
INFO ✓✓✓✓   cycles, clothing and accessories, they seem intent on
VALUE ✓✓✓✓   providing good customer service too. See also
EASE ✓✓✓✓   **www.bikeadelic.co.uk** which has on the face of it a
             better design, but some links didn't work when we
             visited it. Also worth a visit is **www.customlids.co.uk**
             who offer a wide range of clothing, albeit from a
             messy site.

See also:
www.mag-uk.org – home of the Motorcycle Action
    Group dedicated to campaigning on behalf of
    motorcyclists in the UK.

www.motorcycleshow.co.uk – details of the motor
cycle show.

www.scootermania.co.uk – if you love scooters here's
where to go.

www.umgweb.com – owned by the auctioneer E-bay,
here you can find used motorcycles for sale.

Movies

*All you need to know about films and film stars including where to
go to get the best deals on DVDs and videos. For information on
film stars also check out the Celebrities section on page 57.*

http://uk.imdb.com

INTERNET MOVIE DATABASE

ORIGIN US
INFO ✓✓✓✓✓
VALUE ✓✓✓✓
EASE ✓✓✓✓

The best and most organised movie database on the
Internet. It's very easy to use and every film buff's
dream with lots of features and recommendations,
plus games, quizzes, chat and movie news. Another
good database site is www.allmovie.com which has
a really good search engine.

www.aintitcoolnews.com

AIN'T IT JUST COOL

ORIGIN US
INFO ✓✓✓✓✓
EASE ✓✓✓

A renowned review site that can make or break a
movie in the US, it's very entertaining and likeable,
albeit a bit messy. Harry Knowles' movie reviews are
by far the best bit of the site, although they can go on
a bit. You can search the archive for a particular
review or contribute a bit of juicy gossip by e-mailing
Harry direct.

www.corona.bc.ca/films

COMING ATTRACTIONS

ORIGIN US
INFO ✓✓✓✓
EASE ✓✓✓✓

An excellent site that previews upcoming movie
releases, giving background information on how films
were made (or are progressing), gossip and links. You
can join in with your own film ratings or just read the
articles, which are generally well written. Not perfect
but it's very entertaining.

See also:

www.mrqe.com – the Movie Review Query Engine, just enter the film title and reviews from magazines from all round the world pop up, along with lots of adverts too!

www.metacritic.com – a site that compiles reviews from around the world, and gives the reviewed movies a score based on them. Also covers games and music.

www.rottentomatoes.com – a comprehensive review site and store.

www.empireonline.co.uk

THE UK'S NUMBER ONE

ORIGIN	UK	An epic of a site with masses of information and
INFO	✓✓✓✓✓	background on the latest movies and the stars.
EASE	✓✓✓✓	There's also quizzes, a shop and forums where you

can put across your views. It can be a little slow, but it's worth the wait.

www.insidefilm.com

FILM FESTIVAL DIRECTORY

ORIGIN	US	Comprehensive news on the film festival with a
INFO	✓✓✓✓	calendar and features on awards.
EASE	✓✓✓✓	

www.eonline.com

E IS FOR ENTERTAINMENT

ORIGIN	US	This is one of the most visited entertainment news sites
INFO	✓✓✓✓✓	and it has a reputation for being first with the latest
VALUE	✓✓✓✓	gossip and movie news. It's vibrant, well designed and
EASE	✓✓✓✓	has a tongue in cheek style which is endearing; sadly

some of the reporters prattle on though.

www.variety.com

VARIETY MAGAZINE

ORIGIN	US	The online version of the show business stalwart
INFO	✓✓✓✓✓	magazine has an excellent and entertaining site with
EASE	✓✓✓✓	all the hot topics, news and background information

you'd expect plus biographies and international film news.

For more gossip see:

www.ew.com – *Entertainments Weekly* has a really
  attractive site with lots of features.

www.hollywood.com – over one million pages of
  gossip, news and trailers.

www.hollywoodreporter.com – all the latest gossip
  and you can subscribe to the magazine.

www.bollywood.com

LINKING BOLLYWOOD FANS WORLD-WIDE

ORIGIN INDIA All the latest gossip, supposition and intrigue, plus
INFO ✓✓✓✓✓ chat, poetry, ratings and reviews at this sweeping site.
EASE ✓✓✓✓ There are also fashion tips, a movie club, a Hollywood
section and sport – massive in fact.

www.oscars.com

THE ACADEMY AWARDS

ORIGIN US Stylish and as glitzy as you'd imagine it should be,
INFO ✓✓✓✓ this is the official tie-in site for the Oscars. There's an
EASE ✓✓✓✓ archive and even some games to play. For the Golden
Globes go to **www.goldenglobes.org**

www.bafta.org

BRITISH ACADEMY OF FILM & TELEVISION ARTS

ORIGIN UK A site giving all the information you need on the
INFO ✓✓✓✓ BAFTAs, their history and how it all works.
EASE ✓✓✓✓

www.bfi.org.uk

BRITISH FILM INSTITUTE

ORIGIN UK A top site from the BFI packed with information on
INFO ✓✓✓✓✓ how the film industry works with archive material,
EASE ✓✓✓✓ links and how to make movies. Refreshing that there's
not much mention of Hollywood! For the American
Film Institute go to **www.afi.com** where you'll find
an excellent site.

www.britmovie.co.uk

DEDICATED TO BRITISH CINEMA

ORIGIN UK A site devoted to the history of British cinema and its
INFO ✓✓✓✓✓ wider contribution to film-making in general. There's
EASE ✓✓✓✓ a great deal of information, links and background and

it's all well cross-referenced, although it could do with a search facility.

www.indiewire.com
INDEPENDENT CINEMA

ORIGIN UK
INFO ✓✓✓✓
EASE ✓✓✓✓

An enthralling site covering independent cinema, the films, people and gossip. It stands out as a site that genuinely feels like it's contributing positively to an industry. See also **www.exposure.co.uk** who cover the low budget end of film making.

Cinemas

Listed below are the major cinema companies and their sites.

www.cineworld.co.uk – straightforward and easy-to-use guide.

www.odeon.co.uk – book online at this attractive site.

www.showcasecinemas.co.uk – lots here to see and do.

www.uci-cinemas.co.uk – good looking site with all the usual information and previews.

www.warnervillage.co.uk – excellent site with online booking.

Movie humour

www.moviesounds.com
LISTEN TO YOUR FAVOURITE MOVIES

ORIGIN US
INFO ✓✓✓✓
EASE ✓✓✓✓

Download extracts from over 50 movies, it's a little confusing at first but once you've got the technology sorted out it's good fun.

http://rinkworks.com/movieaminute
DON'T HAVE TIME TO WATCH IT ALL?

ORIGIN US
INFO ✓✓✓✓
EASE ✓✓✓✓

Summaries of the top movies for those who either can't be bothered to watch them or just want to pretend they did, either way it's really funny.

www.moviecliches.com
THE MOVIE CLICHÉ LIST

ORIGIN US	Clichés listed by topic from aeroplanes to wood,
INFO ✓✓✓	there's something for everyone here...
EASE ✓✓✓✓	

www.moviebloopers.com
BLOOPERS GALORE

ORIGIN US	A catalogue of mistakes and continuity errors from
INFO ✓✓✓✓	many of the world's greatest films – rather than be
VALUE ✓✓✓	funny though, it just makes you wonder how long
EASE ✓✓✓✓	some people study films to spot such small errors!
	There are also reviews and quizzes.

Film companies

Some of the best web sites are those that promote a particular film. Here is a list of the major film producers and their web sites, all of which are good and have links to the latest releases. Most have clips, downloads, screensavers and lots of advertising.

> www.disney.com
> www.foxmovies.com
> www.miramax.com
> www.paramount.com
> www.spe.sony.com
> www.uip.com
> www.universalpictures.com
> www.warnerbros.com

Buying movies

It's probably best to start with visiting a price checker site first such as www.kelkoo.com (see page 295) but these are the best of the movie online stores.

www.blackstar.co.uk
THE UK'S BIGGEST VIDEO STORE

ORIGIN UK	The biggest online video and DVD retailer, it claims to
INFO ✓✓✓✓	be able to get around 50,000 titles. Blackstar is very
VALUE ✓✓✓✓	good value, boasts cheap delivery prices and has a
EASE ✓✓✓✓	

reputation for excellent customer service. If you want to shop around try www.blockbuster.com who have a less packed site and offers on a wide variety of films.

www.dvdstreet.infront.co.uk

FOR DVD ONLY

ORIGIN UK
INFO ✓✓✓✓
VALUE ✓✓✓✓
EASE ✓✓✓✓

Part of the Streets Online group, this is a great value and easy-to-use site that only sells DVD. There are lots of other movie-related features too, such as the latest news and gossip or reviews. Delivery is £1 for the UK

www.movietrak.com

RENT A DVD MOVIE

ORIGIN UK
INFO ✓✓✓✓
VALUE ✓✓✓
EASE ✓✓✓✓

The latest films are available to rent for £3.25 (plus 50p p&p) for seven days. Pick the title of your choice and it's dispatched the same day, you then return it seven days later in the pre-paid envelope. The range offered is excellent covering eleven major categories plus the latest releases, coming soon and a good search facility too.

www.in-movies.co.uk

IT'S IN THE MOVIES

ORIGIN UK
INFO ✓✓✓✓
VALUE ✓✓✓
EASE ✓✓✓✓

The latest trailers, short films, competitions and DVD rental are just some of the things you can see and do here at this good-looking site. DVD rental is £7.99 a month but you can take out as many as you like, you can also buy DVDs from their shop.

www.reel.com

OVER 100,000 MOVIES

ORIGIN US
INFO ✓✓✓✓
VALUE ✓✓✓
EASE ✓✓✓✓

Here is a mixture of news, gossip, interviews, event listings and US-style outright selling. The content is good and you can get carried away browsing. The search facility is very efficient but shipping to the UK costs a minimum of $6. The shop sells DVD and CDs.

See also:

www.discshop.com – a wide-ranging DVD shop that sells hardware too.

www.dvdoptions.com – rent your favourite DVDs from £3.25 for 7 nights.

www.dvdpopcorn.com – a good looking UK based DVD shop with some good offers and prices include postage and packing.

www.dvdreview.com – great for reviews, but the shop doesn't supply the UK.

www.mymovies.net – a good review and film store with a movie club.

www.play.com – a strong selection of DVDs and CDs too with some good offers.

www.play.com – nice design with some good offers, sells games and CDs too.

Memorabilia

www.vinmag.com
POSTERS, CARDS AND T-SHIRTS

ORIGIN	UK	Vintage magazines, stand-up cutouts, posters, T-shirts
INFO	✓✓✓✓	and magazine covers complete the picture from this
VALUE	✓✓✓	established dealer. Shipping to the UK starts at around
EASE	✓✓✓✓	£2, but it depends on how much you spend.

www.asseenonscreen.com
AS SEEN ON SCREEN

ORIGIN	UK	At this site you can buy what you see on the screen,
INFO	✓✓✓✓✓	your favourite star's shirt or dress can be replicated
VALUE	✓✓✓	just for you. You can also search by star, film and TV
EASE	✓✓✓✓	show.

www.propstore.co.uk
PROPS FOR SALE

ORIGIN	UK	An extensive selection of props and replicas await you
INFO	✓✓✓✓	here with everything from snow globes to clothing.
VALUE	✓✓	Each piece is unique and has been bought from the
EASE	✓✓✓✓	relevant film company and a provenance is provided.

See also:

www.efilmposters.com – who sell posters from a good site.

www.memomine.com – for Hollywood memorabilia.

www.ricksmovie.com – some 11,000 posters and related items for sale.

www.vinylandfilmposters.co.uk – film and music related posters.

Music

Before spending your hard earned cash on CDs it's worth investigating MP3. MP3 technology allows the compression of a music track into a file, which can be stored and played back.

An MP3 player can be downloaded free onto your PC from several sites, the best being the original at www.mp3.com or the popular www.real.com and its RealPlayer. It takes minutes to download the player and if you play CDs on your PC it will also record them.

You'll then be able to listen to samples available on music stores. Once you've joined the MP3 revolution, there's an amazing amount of free music available, start at either web site where there are excellent search facilities.

> *Other good MP3 players can be found at:*
> **http://sonique.lycos.com** – the Sonique Player is good looking with lots of options.
> **www.liquidaudio.com** – the Liquid player is great and works well with Windows XP. **www.listen.com** – the Rhapsody player is adequate but there's probably more music choice on the site.
> **www.winamp.com** – the Winamp play is versatile and easy to use.

Other sites with lots of MP3 downloads that are worth checking out are listed below. Also have a look at www.100topmp3sites.com who list all the good MP3 sites including specialist ones.

> **www.artistdirect.com** – great design, with the latest music news and tunes from over 100,000 artists.
> **www.eatsleepmusic.com** – free karaoke! You need RealPlayer to play.
> **www.eclassical.com** – many free classical greats and many more to buy.
> **www.emusic.com** – over 6,700 artists, great but you have to pay.
> **www.icrunch.co.uk** – offers exclusive DJ mixes, live performances and prides itself on quality alternative music.
> **www.listen.com** – good for previewing a wide variety of music.

www.mp3.com – the original and still one of the best.
www.mp3-mac.com – MP3 for Mac users.
www.musicnet.com – the combined might of AOL,
Bertlesmann, EMI and Real providing top name
downloads from three of the five major labels.
www.real.com – quality and range but you have to
subscribe.

Downloading free music

*Much has been written about the effect on the music industry that
downloading free music has had at the expense of copyright, with
some suggesting that it's damaging to the industry by taking away
musicians' livelihood, while others say it stimulates sales by
enabling potential customers to sample music they wouldn't
have heard otherwise.*

*The following sites are basically different file-sharing programs
that allow users to exchange files easily whether it is music or not.
It's best to read up on the subject before downloading any of the
programs, but once you're up to speed it couldn't be easier.*

*Please be aware that some may contain adult material including
pornography (music files aren't the only things traded) and most
carry some sort of spyware so that they can adapt to your tastes
and advertise accordingly.*

*Some of these sites are also prone to change often, as regulations
are introduced to block their activities, it's also quite difficult to
establish their origin in some cases. You must be aware that the
legal aspects surrounding music file sharing are unclear and if
you're not sure about using them then I suggest you go to the pay
sites and keep your eye on the press.*

http://opennap.sourceforge.net
CONNECTING PEOPLE

ORIGIN US
INFO ✓✓✓✓
EASE ✓✓✓

A variant of the original Napster program this is
freeware and you can select some of the many
specialist and general servers which hold music,
(see **www.napigator.com** for a server list) then use
the program to search them for the music you like.

www.gnutella.com

THE GNUTELLA NETWORK

ORIGIN US
INFO ✓✓✓✓
EASE ✓✓✓

Sounds like something you spread on toast, but is basically a mini search engine and file sharing system on one site. It consists of a network of thousands of computer users, all of whom use Gnutella software 'clones' which link them directly to other users to find music, movies and other files. Also check out **http://gnucleus.sourceforge.net**

www.imesh.com

OVER 40 MILLION USERS...

ORIGIN ISRAEL
INFO ✓✓✓✓
EASE ✓✓✓✓

The latest version of iMesh is really a Napster clone; you type in an artist and song, and then a list of available matches from a centralised server appears. Since it's an Israeli site, it's likely to be immune from U.S. copyright lawsuits, so it'll probably be around for a while yet. Supposed to be spyware free.

www.madster.com

IT'S MAD...

ORIGIN US
INFO ✓✓✓✓
EASE ✓✓✓

This used to be Aimster, it combines AOL's instant message service with the ability to search for files and trade them with other users of the network, of Gnutella or even of Napster. It includes encryption software, so nobody can monitor your files while they're in transit and will even tell you which other AOL messenger buddies use it. Again it claims to have no spyware attached.

See also:

www.musiccity.com – uses the FastTrack file sharing system, their version is called Morpheus, it's quite secure, but lots of ads. Good design, lots of unsigned bands.

www.rootnode.org – this file-sharing network gets around legal shenanigans by concentrating on live recordings that are made available with the permission of the original artists. It's a good music magazine too.

www.winmx.com – a very flexible file-sharing program that does not contain spyware.

Buying music

*It's as well to start by checking prices of CDs through price
comparison sites such as those listed on page 295. These will take
you to the store offering the best combination of price and postage.
All the stores listed below offer good value plus a bit extra.*

www.hmv.co.uk

HIS MASTERS VOICE ONLINE

ORIGIN	UK	Excellent features and offers on the latest CDs and
INFO	✓✓✓✓✓	videos. There are sections on most aspects of music
VALUE	✓✓✓	as well as video, DVD and games with a good search
EASE	✓✓✓✓	facility. You can listen to selections from albums before

buying if you have RealPlayer. Spoken word or books
on tape are available as well.

www.cd-wow.com

OUTSTANDING VALUE

ORIGIN	UK	A very easy site to use with some great offers on CDs
INFO	✓✓✓✓	and there's free delivery too. Probably the best site
VALUE	✓✓✓✓✓	for value at time of writing.
EASE	✓✓✓✓	

www.cduniverse.com

WIDE RANGE AND GREAT OFFERS

ORIGIN	US	There is a massive range to choose from and some
INFO	✓✓✓✓	good discounts; delivery normally takes only five days.
VALUE	✓✓✓✓	You can also buy games, DVDs and videos. Excellent,
EASE	✓✓✓✓	but can be quite slow, and delivery is very expensive.

www.secondsounds.com

THE USED CD STORE

ORIGIN	UK	With a huge range to choose from and prices from as
INFO	✓✓✓✓	low as £1.99 you can't really go wrong, they guarantee
VALUE	✓✓✓✓✓	mint condition or your money back. You can browse
EASE	✓✓✓	by artist or through the bargain bins, delivery starts at

a £1 and of course they are interested in buying from
you too. See also www.eil.com

www.minidisco.com
HOME OF THE MINIDISC

ORIGIN US
INFO ✓✓✓✓
EASE ✓✓✓✓

The minidisc is alive and well here with some good offers on the players and information on the latest developments. Delivery to Europe takes about a week, costs vary. See also **www.minidisc.org** which is a messy site but contains everything you need to know about minidiscs.

For more great offers on CDs try these sites:
www.101cd.com – renowned for offering good value, choose from 1.6 million titles.
www.amazon.co.uk – as good as you'd expect from Amazon.
www.audiostreet.co.uk – some good prices, free delivery in UK when you spend over £29.
www.cdnow.com – one of the originals but now part of Amazon.
www.eil.com – specialists in rare and collectible CDs and vinyl.
www.recordstore.co.uk – choose from thousands of vinyl records, CDs, T-shirts, record bags and assorted DJ gear.
www.secondsounds.com – a large used CD specialist with a 30 day refund scheme.
www.timelesstracks.com – devoted to the music of the 50s, 60s, 70s and 80s with some excellent prices on CDs.
www.towerrecords.co.uk – wide variety and some good offers – better service than you get from the real store.
www.virgin.net/music – average music store with reviews.

www.htfr.co.uk
HARD TO FIND RECORDS

ORIGIN UK
INFO ✓✓✓✓
VALUE ✓✓✓
EASE ✓✓✓

Although they specialise in new and deleted house, garage, techno, electro, disco, funk, soul and hip-hop vinyl, they will try and find any record previously released. They also offer a complete service to all budding and serious DJs. See also **www.popetc.com** who offer a wide range of memorabilia, vinyl and rare CD singles.

Bands, groups and stars

http://ubl.artistdirect.com
THE ULTIMATE BAND LIST

ORIGIN US
INFO ✓✓✓✓✓
VALUE ✓✓✓✓
EASE ✓✓✓✓

It is the place for mountains of information on groups or singers. It has a totally brilliant search facility, and you can buy and download from the site as well, although the prices are not as good as elsewhere. For a similar, but better organised site try www.allmusic.com where you can also get excellent information and videos.

www.eartothesound.fsnet.co.uk
REVIEWS AND RATINGS

ORIGIN US
INFO ✓✓✓✓
VALUE ✓✓✓✓
EASE ✓✓✓✓

They call themselves the ultimate review site and it's great, except that they concentrate almost entirely on rock music, so if that's your poison, then it's perfect.

www.onehitwondercentral.com
A CATALOGUE OF ONE HIT WONDERS

ORIGIN US
INFO ✓✓✓✓
EASE ✓✓✓✓

US-oriented information site on those who only triumphed once, never to be seen again. It's arranged by decade and you get some interesting titbits in the artist profiles.

Music TV, awards and magazine sites

www.bbc.co.uk/totp
TOP OF THE POPS

ORIGIN UK
INFO ✓✓✓✓✓
VALUE ✓✓✓
EASE ✓✓✓

The Top of the Pops site is a bright and busy magazine with loads of good features and articles as well as competitions, trivia and lots of information.

www.cdukweb.com
UK'S NUMBER ONE MUSIC SHOW

ORIGIN UK
INFO ✓✓✓✓
VALUE ✓✓
EASE ✓✓✓✓

Considering their boast, the web site is a bit of a disappointment with not much in the way of information or interaction. There are some quizzes, competitions and you can download a few things but it has none of the buzz of the show.

www.grammy.com

THE GRAMMY AWARDS

ORIGIN US	An overview of the awards, who won what and when,
INFO ✓✓✓✓	and then where to buy their music. For the Brit awards
EASE ✓✓✓✓	go to www.brits.co.uk where you'll find a similar site.
	The MOBO awards are celebrated at www.mobo.net

www.mtv.co.uk

MUSIC TELEVISION

ORIGIN UK	MTV offers loads of info on events, shows and the
INFO ✓✓✓✓	artists as well as background on the presenters and
VALUE ✓✓✓✓	creative bits like movie and music video clips.
EASE ✓✓✓	Great design.

www.music-mag.com

NEWS AND REVIEWS

ORIGIN UK	A good, cool-looking all rounder covering all aspects
INFO ✓✓✓✓	of modern music in a straightforward style, it has a
EASE ✓✓✓✓	really good section on clubbing and the latest dance
	news. There's also a good links section and hundreds
	of ring-tones and logos to download. It has a pretty
	annoying registration process.

www.nme.com

NEW MUSICAL EXPRESS

ORIGIN UK	If you're a rock fan then this is where it's at. There's
INFO ✓✓✓✓✓	all the usual information, it's well laid out and easy
EASE ✓✓✓✓	to access. The archived articles are its greatest asset,
	featuring 150,000 artists and every article, feature
	and review they've ever published plus full UK
	discographies, pictures, e-cards, ring-tones and
	links to the best web sites.

www.q4music.com

Q MAGAZINE

ORIGIN UK	A music magazine site that reflects its parent magazine
INFO ✓✓✓✓✓	extremely well. It has 20,000 reviews, plus features
EASE ✓✓✓✓	and articles that cover most aspects of music, it
	doesn't miss much.

www.popworld.com
WHERE POP COMES FIRST

ORIGIN UK
INFO ✓✓✓✓
EASE ✓✓✓

Brilliant site that concentrates on pop, it's fun and has great graphics. You have to register to join but once you're in you get access to competitions, features on your favourite bands, clips from Popworld TV, fashion tips and much more. You need the latest Flash download from Macromedia to get the best out of it.

www.rollingstone.com
ROLLING STONE MAGAZINE

ORIGIN US
INFO ✓✓✓✓
EASE ✓✓✓

The archetypal music magazine has an excellent site with all the features you'd expect to see including reviews, photos, articles on the bands, downloads, links and games.

www.thebox.co.uk
SMASH HITS YOU CONTROL

ORIGIN UK
INFO ✓✓✓✓
EASE ✓✓✓✓

Similar to Q but with added features such as the ability for you to select a tune to be played on their TV channel and you can influence their overall selection by voting for your favourite songs.

Sites for specific types of music

BLUES

www.darkerthanblue.com
HOME OF BLACK MUSIC

ORIGIN UK
INFO ✓✓✓✓✓
EASE ✓✓✓✓

Very well-designed site dedicated to black-influenced music and musicians, it has all the latest news, gig guides, artist features and downloads as well as sections on reggae, garage, soul and hip-hop.

www.bluesworld.com
HOMAGE TO THE BLUES

ORIGIN US
INFO ✓✓✓✓
EASE ✓✓✓✓

If you're into the blues then this is your kind of site. There are interviews, memorabilia, 78 auctions, bibliographies, discographies and lists of links to other blues sites. You can order CDs via affiliated retailers and if the mood takes you, order a guitar too.

CLASSICAL AND OPERA

www.gramophone.co.uk

GRAMOPHONE MAGAZINE

ORIGIN UK
INFO ✓✓✓✓✓
EASE ✓✓✓✓

An outstanding site with features, reviews, competitions, shop and concert listings; there's also an awards section plus the editor's choice with the top recommendations.

www.classicalmusic.co.uk

CLASSICAL MUSIC REVEALED

ORIGIN UK
INFO ✓✓✓✓✓
EASE ✓✓✓

Excellent for lovers of classical music, with articles, guides, reviews and concert listings, you can play in a fantasy concert or just browse the excellent links section.

www.operabase.com/en

OPERA BASE

ORIGIN US
INFO ✓✓✓✓
EASE ✓✓✓

This site offers opera listings, information on festivals and provides background to the history of opera. For the *Opera* magazine site go to **www.opera.co.uk** which offers articles and links.

Other key classical music sites:
www.aria-database.com – information on over 1,000 arias.
www.choralnet.org – excellent site devoted to choral music.
www.classical.net – great for information and links.
www.classicallink.com – a very good portal site.
www.eclassical.com – download MP3s, many are free.
www.mdcmusic.co.uk – good offers on CDs.
www.orchestranet.co.uk – excellent selection of links.

COUNTRY

www.thatscountry.com
COUNTRY MUSIC SCENE

ORIGIN CANADA
INFO ✓✓✓✓
EASE ✓✓✓✓

A good overview of country music with offers and
links as well as information on the artists and bands.

See also:
www.cmdn.net – country music dance.
www.countrymusic.org.uk – a very naff site that
covers the UK scene.
www.countrystars.com – good all rounder with a
messy design but the shop does supply the UK.

DANCE AND BEAT

www.anthems.com
DANCE, HOUSE AND GARAGE

ORIGIN UK
INFO ✓✓✓✓✓
VALUE ✓✓✓
EASE ✓✓✓

Great design combined with brilliant content, there's
everything here for dance fans, news, information and
samples of the latest mixes or if you're feeling rich you
can buy them too, although you'll probably find
cheaper elsewhere. For alternative views of the dance
scene try www.fly.co.uk who have a real urban look to
their site, while for links to over 500 dance-related
sites and a complete listing of new releases go to
www.juno.co.uk

www.burnitblue.com
LIVING AND BREATHING DANCE MUSIC

ORIGIN UK
INFO ✓✓✓✓✓
EASE ✓✓✓✓

Concentrating on dance and club culture this coolly
designed site offers up all the information you need to
keep up with the scene; it's been critically acclaimed as
one of the best sites of its type.

See also:
www.crasher.co.uk – details on nearly 900 clubs listed.
www.garagemusic.co.uk – reviews and samples plus
the latest on the UK scene, annoying adverts though.

FOLK

www.folkmusic.net

FOLK ON THE WEB

ORIGIN UK
INFO ✓✓✓✓
EASE ✓✓✓✓

A straightforward site from *Living Traditions* magazine, a collection of articles, features, reviews and news.

See also:
www.folking.com – a good all round site with news, downloads and shopping.
www.frootsmag.com – a magazine site with news, information and reviews.
www.thetraditionbearers.com – a project aimed at keeping alive our traditional songs.

HIP HOP AND RAP

www.sohh.com

SITE OF HIP HOP

ORIGIN US
INFO ✓✓✓✓
EASE ✓✓✓✓

Voted the best of its kind by *Rolling Stone* this site offers all you'd expect in terms of news, reviews, forums, interviews and samples. It also has links to shops and other related sites.

See also:
www.britishhiphop.co.uk – the story of British Hip Hop and artist listing and discography.
www.hiphopville.com – where to go for all the gear.
www.rapsheet.com – wide ranging and well put together site offering much of what SOHH does.

INDIE

www.playlouder.com

INDIE MUSIC

ORIGIN US
INFO ✓✓✓✓
EASE ✓✓✓✓

Great graphics and excellent design make Playlouder stand out from the crowd; it covers the Indie music scene in depth with all the usual features, but with a bit more style. Another really well designed web site covering Indie music in great depth is Channel Fly www.channelfly.com – take your pick!

JAZZ

www.jazzonln.com

JAZZ ONLINE

ORIGIN US
INFO ✓✓✓✓✓
EASE ✓✓✓✓

Whether you need help in working your way through the minefield that is jazz music, or you know what you want, Jazz Online can provide it. Its easy format covers all styles and it has a brilliant search facility. There is a good chat section and you can ask 'Jazz Messenger' just about anything. You can't buy from the site but there are links to Amazon's music section.

See also:
www.allaboutjazz.com – well organised, slightly dull but very comprehensive.
www.jazzcorner.com – a beautifully designed jazz magazine site and directory.
www.jazzimprov.com – a messy but thorough offering.
www.jazzreview.com – lots of reviews and discussion plus a photography section and downloads.

KARAOKE

www.streamkaraoke.com

SING ALONG

ORIGIN US
INFO ✓✓✓✓
VALUE ✓✓✓✓
EASE ✓✓✓✓

Over 1,500 tunes to download but you have to subscribe which is from $8 a month depending on which package you take. See also **www.singtotheworld.com**

REGGAE

www.reggaetrain.com

REGGAE TRAIN A COME

ORIGIN US
INFO ✓✓✓✓✓
EASE ✓✓✓✓

An excellent and comprehensive portal site devoted to all things reggae, with several hundred links.

See also:
www.reggaefusion.com – a huge site devoted to Jamaican music.

www.reggaereview.com – a monthly web magazine
from California.

www.reggaetimes.com – a good site connected with
Reggae Times, lots of reviews and links.

ROCK MUSIC

www.rocksite.com

INFORMATION THAT ROCKS

ORIGIN US
INFO ✓✓✓✓
EASE ✓✓✓✓

Devoted to rock music, there are band listings, tour
news, reviews plus links and a musicians directory.
All this wrapped up in an appropriately designed site.

For more try:

www.history-of-rock.com – a good overview
of the roots of rock and roll.

www.rockhall.com – the Rock and Roll Hall
of Fame has an outstanding site dedicated to
celebrating only the best.

www.rockhaven.co.uk – a UK-oriented rock
portal site.

www.rocknrollzone.com – a good, colourful
portal and news site.

Music information

www.clickmusic.co.uk

EVERYTHING YOU NEED TO KNOW ABOUT MUSIC

ORIGIN UK
INFO ✓✓✓✓✓
EASE ✓✓✓✓

This is great for all music fans. It has quick access to
details on any particular band, tickets, and downloads,
gigs or gossip. Shopping is straightforward using their
'Best 10' listings, just click on the store or use the
search engine to find something specific. The search
engine needs improving though. See also
www.musites.com where you can find a rather
variable but improving music search engine.

www.dotmusic.com
ALL THE MUSIC NEWS

ORIGIN UK
INFO ✓✓✓✓
VALUE ✓✓✓
EASE ✓✓✓✓

Get the latest 'insider' views from the music industry, with reviews, charts, chat and a good value online shop where you buy tickets and books too. These combined with great design make this an excellent site. There are sections on each major music genre and a broadband section where you can watch the latest pop videos.

www.musicsearch.com
THE INTERNET'S MUSIC SEARCH ENGINE

ORIGIN US
INFO ✓✓✓✓
EASE ✓✓

Musicsearch is a directory site with over 20,000 links to reviewed music sites, the search facility has improved and you can offer up sites to be included.

www.bl.uk/collections/sound-archive/cat.html
BRITISH LIBRARY SOUND ARCHIVE

ORIGIN UK
INFO ✓✓✓✓✓
EASE ✓✓✓

This catalogue contains over two and a half million entries, there are only a few sounds you can listen to online, but more are being put on the site. You can find out how to get a listening appointment and order copies of the sounds, music or oral recordings.

See also:
http://musiccrawl.com – a basic music and
  MP3 search engine.
www.hitsquad.com – a well-categorised portal
  site aimed primarily at musicians.
www.thisdayinmusic.com – what happened on
  a particular day plus quizzes and competitions.
www.vitaminic.co.uk – a music club, excellent
  portal and host to many specialist music sites.
  You have to join to get the best out of it.

Learning music

Long-winded though the site URL is, it's worth visiting
www.si.umich.edu/chico/mhn/enclpdia.html *where you can find a music encyclopaedia in which you can sample the sound of many instruments.*

www.happynote.com/music/learn.html

LEARN MUSIC WITH A GAME

ORIGIN US
INFO ✓✓✓✓
EASE ✓✓✓✓

You download the game, which helps you learn the basics, but the more you learn and the better you get the higher the score. See also www.abachamusic.com.au and www.musicnotes.net who also offer fun ways to learn music.

Sites for specific instruments

GENERAL

www.harmony-central.com – all sorts of instruments reviewed and rated.

www.music4worship.co.uk – a music store covering a wide range of musical instruments.

www.musicianshop.com – another musical instrument store, especially good for guitarists.

www.starland.co.uk – musical instruments by mail order, some good offers too.

STRINGS

www.aic.se/basslob – playing the bass.

www.guitar.com – good all rounder, all you need to know.

www.guitarsite.com – masses of information.

www.guitarstrings.co.uk – a guitar specialist shop

www.sitar.co.uk – comprehensive plus good links.

www.violin-world.com – complete resource for all string instruments.

PERCUSSION

www.drummersweb.com – drummer's delight.

www.drumnetwork.com – online shop includes a virtual drum kit and the latest hot licks!

www.rhythmweb.com – the place to go for all things percussive.

WIND

http://kristin.newdream.net/flute – the flute resource.

www.saxophone.org – great for info and links.

www.wfg.sneezy.org – woodwind.

ELECTRONIC
http://nmc.uoregon.edu/emi – great introduction to electronic music and instruments.
www.etcetera.co.uk – download all the latest sampling and music creation software here.
www.synthzone.com – excellent source for articles, links and reviews for all things to do with electronic music making.

KEYBOARD
www.pianonanny.com – complete piano course.
www.pianoshop.co.uk – masses of links, pianos for sale and information on learning.

For aspiring bands

www.taxi.com
FOR UNSIGNED BANDS

ORIGIN US
INFO ✓✓✓✓
EASE ✓✓✓✓

Looking to get a music contract for your band? You should start here, there's loads of information, contacts and links that will help you on the rocky road to success and stardom – well that's the theory anyway!

For more places to find something new and get help if you're in a band, see also:
www.2bdiscovered.com – good use of video footage as well as sound, but you have to register to use it.
www.audiogalaxy.com – for sampling new and some existing bands.
www.bpi.co.uk – the British Phonographic Industry and what they do.
www.burbs.co.uk – British Underground Rock Bands, home of the UK's real music scene.
www.getoutthere.bt.com – tomorrow's new young talent.
www.iuma.com – massive selection of unsigned groups all well categorised.

www.joescafe.com/bands
BAND NAMES

ORIGIN UK
INFO ✓✓✓✓
VALUE ✓✓✓✓
EASE ✓✓✓✓

So you can't think of a name for your band? Here is the 'Band-o-matic' which will offer all sorts of never before used band names in seconds. This time we got Snurge and the Clown Hammers.

Sheet music

www.sunhawk.com
DOWNLOAD SHEET MUSIC

ORIGIN US
INFO ✓✓✓✓
VALUE ✓✓✓
EASE ✓✓✓✓

Well-designed site where you can download music from a wide variety of styles including pop, Christian, country, Broadway, jazz and classical, you have to pay but there are some freebies.

See also:
www.musicroom.com – a huge range and free postage in the UK.
www.sheetmusicplus.com – US-oriented but a wide range and some new stuff.

Lyrics

www.lyrics.com
THE WORDS TO HUNDREDS OF SONGS

ORIGIN US
INFO ✓✓✓✓
EASE ✓✓✓✓

There are songs from hundreds of bands and artists including Oasis, Madonna, Britney Spears and Queen, you'll have to ignore the directory section that makes up most of the page, there's an A–Z listing at the bottom. Hopefully they'll redesign soon.

Other good lyric sites:
http://home.iae.nl/users/kdv/en/ring.htm – a web ring for lyrics.
www.britishacademy.com – support and advice for songwriters.
www.execpc.com/~suden – songs from the 50s, 60s and 70s.
www.letssingit.com – big archive plus karaoke!

www.kissthisguy.com

MISHEARD LYRICS

ORIGIN US	Mr Misheard lists all those lyrics that you thought
INFO ✓✓✓✓	were being sung but in reality you were just not quite
EASE ✓✓✓✓	listening properly. This time we liked 'Mamma mia,

here I go again' misheard as 'Diarrhoea, here I go
again' but there are hundreds more.

Concerts and tickets

www.liveconcerts.com

WELCOME TO THE CYBERCAST

ORIGIN US	Watch live concerts online! A great idea but let down
INFO ✓✓✓✓	by 'Net congestion'. You'd think it was designed just
VALUE ✓✓✓	to sell RealPlayer though, which you'll need to see the
EASE ✓✓✓✓	concerts and listen to the interviews and recordings.

It's actually very good for sampling different types
of music and you can buy CDs as well.

See also:
www.live-online.com – the digital jukebox.
www.pollstar.com – the concert hotwire!

www.bigmouth.co.uk

UK'S MOST COMPREHENSIVE GIG GUIDE

ORIGIN UK	UK-based, with lots of links to band sites, news,
INFO ✓✓✓✓	events listing and information on what's up and
EASE ✓✓✓✓	coming. Great search facilities and the ability to buy

tickets make this a really useful site for gig lovers
everywhere. It's geared to rock and pop though.

www.ticketmaster.co.uk

TICKETS FOR EVERYTHING

ORIGIN UK	Book tickets for just about anything and you can run
INFO ✓✓✓✓✓	searches by venue, city or date. The site is split into
VALUE ✓✓✓✓	five key sections:
EASE ✓✓✓✓	Theatre – theatre, drama and musical

Performing arts – comedy, classical and opera
Music – gigs, jazz, clubs, rock and pop.
Family – shows, anything from Disney on Ice
   to air shows.
Sports – tickets for virtually every sporting occasion.

www.concertphoto.co.uk
PHOTOS OF YOUR FAVOURITE BANDS

ORIGIN UK
INFO ✓✓✓✓
VALUE ✓✓✓
EASE ✓✓✓✓

OK so you've been to the gig and you didn't take a camera, well the chances are that Pete Still has a photo available for you to buy from this great web site. There are hundreds of bands to choose from both old and new and he's covered the major festivals too. Costs vary according to size and quantity.

Nature and the Environment

The Internet offers charities and organisations a chance to highlight their work in a way that is much more creative than ever before; it also offers the chance for us to get in-depth information on those species and issues that interest us.

www.panda.org
THE WORLD WIDE FUND FOR NATURE

ORIGIN UK
INFO ✓✓✓✓
EASE ✓✓✓✓

Called the WWF Global Network, this is the official site for the WWF. Information on projects designed to save the world's endangered species by protecting their environment. You can find out how to support their work or how to get involved; there is also a good kids' section, the latest news and information on the key projects. An American organisation called the National Wildlife Fund has a similar excellent site at www.nwf.org

www.nhm.ac.uk
THE NATURAL HISTORY MUSEUM

ORIGIN UK
INFO ✓✓✓✓✓
EASE ✓✓✓✓

A superb user-friendly web site that covers everything from ants to eclipses. You can get the latest news, check out exhibitions, take a tour, browse the Dinosaur database or explore the wildlife garden. There are details on the collections, galleries, educational resources and contacts for answers to specific questions. See also the Smithsonian National Museum of Natural History who also has a great site at www.mnh.si.edu

www.bbc.co.uk/nature

WILDLIFE EXPOSED

ORIGIN UK
INFO ✓✓✓✓
EASE ✓✓✓✓

A brilliant nature offering from the BBC with sections on key wildlife programmes and animal groups. The information is good and enhanced by video clips. Also visit **www.bbcwild.com** the commercial side of the BBC wildlife unit with over 120,000 wildlife images available to buy. It's aimed at commercial organisations but offers prints for personal use starting at £20 each. It is a great place to browse just for the remarkable images in the premium selection alone.

Other nature sites worth checking out are...

http://wcs.org/ – home of New York's Wildlife Conservation Society who have a very informative site.

www.enature.com/ – an American magazine site with a huge amount of information and features on all aspects of nature.

www.ewg.org – an excellent and detailed site from the Environmental Working Group, dedicated to the fight against pollution.

www.kalama.com/~mariner/qserwild.htm – basically just a list of good sites devoted to nature; it has a US bias.

www.naturephotographers.net – a magazine devoted to wildlife photography with a great selection on shots and advice.

www.virtualparks.org – just stunning photography from the parks of Canada and the US.

www.wri.org – World Resources Institute promoting effective campaigning for a far better world.

www.naturenet.net

UK COUNTRYSIDE, NATURE AND CONSERVATION

ORIGIN UK
INFO ✓✓✓✓✓
VALUE ✓✓
EASE ✓✓✓✓

Ignore the rather twee graphics and you'll find a great deal of information about nature in the UK. Their interests include: countryside law, upkeep of nature reserves, voluntary work, education and environmental news. You can also search the site for specifics and there is a good set of links to related sites.

See also:

www.englishnature.org.uk – supply maps, photos and
information on all our nature reserves and explains
why reserves are so important - all on an excellent
site.

www.phenology.org.uk – how to help with this 'study
of the times of recurring natural phenomena
especially in relation to climate change' going
on in a woodland near you.

www.wildlifetrust.org.uk – who care for over 2,000
of Britain's nature reserves.

www.foe.co.uk

FRIENDS OF THE EARTH

ORIGIN UK
INFO ✓✓✓✓
EASE ✓✓✓✓

Not as worthy as you might imagine, this site offers
a stack of information on food, pollution, green
power, protecting wildlife in your area and the
latest campaign news.

http://earthobservatory.nasa.gov

THE EARTH FROM ABOVE

ORIGIN US
INFO ✓✓✓✓✓
EASE ✓✓✓✓

Really outstanding photography and detailed
information on the environment presented in an
interesting and thought provoking way. Owned by
NASA, the site offers sections on the atmosphere,
land and air as well as the latest news stories.

www.envirolink.org

THE ONLINE ENVIRONMENTAL COMMUNITY

ORIGIN US
INFO ✓✓✓✓✓
EASE ✓✓✓✓

A huge site focused on personal involvement in
environment issues. There are several sections
including: organisations, educational resources, jobs,
governmental resources, actions you can take to help
and environment links. There is also a good search
facility on environment-related topics. For more real
campaigning go to the Greenpeace site
www.greenpeace.org where you can find out about
their latest activities and how to get involved. For
more campaign work check out the International
Fund for Animal Welfare who do a great deal of
work protecting animals and their environment. Find
out how you can help by going to **www.ifaw.org**

www.environment-agency.gov.uk
WHAT THE GOVERNMENT IS UP TO

ORIGIN UK
INFO ✓✓✓✓
EASE ✓✓✓✓

The Environment Agency's site offers information on the latest initiatives and news of the latest research. It also helps with recycling and gives out information on how to improve the environment and how you can contact them with any issues you have.

See also:
www.defra.gov.uk – the Department for Environment, Food and Rural Affairs has a newsy site that offers lots of information and does it pretty well when you consider the size of their brief.
www.forestry.gov.uk – Forestry Commission has details of its work and how you can help sustain our woods and forests.

www.planetdiary.com
WHAT'S REALLY HAPPENING ON THE PLANET

ORIGIN US
INFO ✓✓✓✓✓
EASE ✓✓✓✓

Every week Planetdiary monitors and records world events in geological, astronomical, meteorological, biological and environmental terms and relays them back via this web site. It's done by showing an icon on a map of the world, which you then click on to find out more. Although very informative, a visit can leave you a little depressed.

http://library.thinkquest.org/C003603
FORCES OF NATURE

ORIGIN US
INFO ✓✓✓✓✓
EASE ✓✓✓✓

An amazing site that covers all the known natural disasters, giving background information, simulations and multimedia explanations with experiments for you to try at home.

See also:
www.earthquake.com – check out the most recent seismic activity.
www.fema.gov/kids – great for young kids.
www.geographyiq.com – comprehensive.
www.naturalhazards.org – interesting site with basic information on natural phenomena and links.

www.coralcay.org

HOW YOU CAN JOIN IN

ORIGIN UK
INFO ✓✓✓✓
EASE ✓✓✓✓

In Coral Cay's words its aim is 'providing resources to help sustain livelihoods and alleviate poverty through the protection, restoration and management of coral reefs and tropical forests'. Sign up for an expedition or a science project in Honduras or the Philippines.

See also:

www.ecoclub.com – a network providing a wealth of information about all aspects of ecotourism.

www.ecotourism.org – American site with useful links.

www.ecovolunteer.com – if you want to give your services to a specific animal benefit project.

Animals

www.arkive.org.uk

RAISING AWARENESS OF ENDANGERED SPECIES

ORIGIN UK
INFO ✓✓✓✓✓
EASE ✓✓✓✓

Sponsored by the Wildscreen Trust, this site's aim is to catalogue and picture all the world's endangered species. Each animal and plant has a page devoted to it giving details on how and where it lives, including pictures and movie clips. You can help by donating pictures and film. See also **www.umich.edu/~esupdate/** for the endangered species update which has detailed information on species in danger, albeit on a cluttered site.

www.uksafari.com

BRITAIN'S WILDLIFE

ORIGIN UK
INFO ✓✓✓✓✓
EASE ✓✓✓✓

A good overview of the UK's wild animals with a section on each and tips on wildlife gardening, a photogallery and lots of additional stuff like film clips, facts and figures and information on nature sites.

www.wdcs.org

WHALE AND DOLPHIN SOCIETY

ORIGIN UK
INFO ✓✓✓✓
EASE ✓✓✓✓

All the latest news and developments in the fight to save whales and dolphins. There's also information on them, how and where they live, a 'Sightings and Strandings' section and details of how to book a whale-watching holiday.

See also:

www.cetacea.org – an excellent site where you can
get background info on every species of dolphin,
whale and porpoise.

www.flmnh.ufl.edu/fish – the University of Florida's
Department of Ichthyology has a good site where
you can find an overview of all things fishy plus
links and a good selection of photographs.

www.seawatchfoundation.org.uk – here you can
learn more about cetaceans, and their sightings
around the UK.

www.africam.com

ALWAYS LIVE, ALWAYS WILD

ORIGIN S. AFRICA

INFO ✓✓✓✓✓

EASE ✓✓✓✓

Web cameras have come a long way and this is one of
the best uses of them. There are strategically placed
cameras at water holes and parks around Africa and
other of the world's wildlife areas, and you can tap in
for a look at any time. You have to register to get the
best out of it, but even a quick visit is rewarding.

See also:

http://elephant.elehost.com – an excellent elephant
only site.

www.lioncrusher.com – all large carnivores and a
good picture archive.

www.wildnetafrica.com – the wildlife portal has lots of
all aspects of African animals and how to see them.

www.rainforestlive.org.uk

THE RAINFOREST – LIVE!

ORIGIN UK

INFO ✓✓✓✓

EASE ✓✓✓✓

A largely educational site about rainforests and their
importance. It gives a good illustrated overview of the
subject plus chat, links, competitions and colouring
pages for the very young.

See also:

http://ths.sps.lane.edu/biomes/rain3/rain3.html –
a long URL but worth a visit for the information
it contains. It also offers possibly the worst
combination of background and text colours
I've seen, so be prepared!

www.rainforest.org – home of the Tropical Rainforest
Coalition with up-to-date information on rainforest
destruction and how you can help.

www.rainforest-alliance.org – excellent for
information and links to related sites.

www.rainforestconcern.org – home of a charity
which aims to protect the world's rain forests.
The site gives an overview of the problems faced
and details on how you can help.

www.ran.org – Rainforest Action Network, another
group devoted to saving the rainforest, this one is
American. You can't help asking why these
charities don't get together?

www.bugbios.com

BUGS AND INSECTS

ORIGIN US   A beautifully designed site exposing insects as miracles
INFO ✓✓✓✓✓   of nature, with amazing macro-photography,
EASE ✓✓✓✓   information and links. For great photography see
           www.virtualinsectary.com

http://butterflywebsite.com

BUTTERFLYING

ORIGIN US   Not that great design wise but an interesting site on
INFO ✓✓✓✓✓   butterflies. Although it's biased towards the US, it
EASE ✓✓✓   does have sections that cover Britain and also has
           a very good links section.

www.birds.com

ALL ABOUT BIRDS

ORIGIN US   An online directory and guide to birds covering both
INFO ✓✓✓✓   wild and pets, biased to America but excellent except
EASE ✓✓✓✓   that it's a bit too commercial.

See also:

www.birdsofbritain.co.uk – a strong monthly
web magazine for British bird watchers.

www.ornithology.com – a good, if serious site
dedicated to wild birds.

www.rspb.org.uk – the Royal Society for the
Protection of Birds have a nice site detailing
what they do, and how you can help.

www.prehistoricplanet.com

PREHISTORIC PLANET

ORIGIN US	A great site put together by some dinosaur enthusiasts.
INFO ✓✓✓✓✓	It's got information on what the planet looked like in
VALUE ✓✓✓	prehistoric times, you can ask a palaeontologist a
EASE ✓✓✓✓	question or just browse the many articles.

See also:

www.bbc.co.uk/dinosaurs – excellent Walking with Dinosaurs site with lots of features.

www.dinodata.net – easy to use and information packed.

www.dinosaur.org – a messy and unstructured site, but packed with dino facts and links.

www.becominghuman.org

HUMAN ORIGINS

ORIGIN US	A superb site detailing the progress of human
INFO ✓✓✓✓✓	evolution, showing our development in an interactive
VALUE ✓✓✓	and enthralling way. Beautifully illustrated throughout,
EASE ✓✓✓✓	however it can be a little slow, so best seen by
	broadband users.

For other sites that feature our evolution and our nearest relatives try:

www.archaeologyinfo.com/evolution.htm - good site on human evolution, the Hall of Skulls is great for showing our development through time.

www.gorilla.org - home of the Gorilla Foundation and Koko.

www.iup.edu/~rgendron/links.htmlx - great for links on evolution and human origins.

www.janegoodall.org - very well put together site featuring the work of this pioneer with biographical details and information on chimpanzees and how you can help preserve them.

Zoos and safari parks

www.safaripark.co.uk

SAFARI ONLINE

ORIGIN UK
INFO ✓✓✓✓
EASE ✓✓✓

A detailed site on the UK's safari parks including open-ing times, animal information and facts on endangered species. At www.zoo-keeper.co.uk you get information on the most common zoo animals and some back-ground about what it's like to work with them.

www.sandiegozoo.org

SAN DIEGO ZOO

ORIGIN US
INFO ✓✓✓✓
EASE ✓✓✓✓

Probably the best zoo site. You can get conservation information, check out the latest arrivals and browse their excellent photo gallery. The highlight is definitely the Panda Cam.

Other good zoo sites:
www.bristolzoo.co.uk – good looking and fun for kids.
www.dublinzoo.ie – slow but good content.
www.londonzoo.co.uk – excellent and comprehensive zoo site, also covers Whipsnade Wildlife Park.
www.marwell.org.uk – masses to see and do.
www.seaworld.com – information on holidays and the attractions at their three zoos.

www.bornfree.co.uk

ZOO CHECK

ORIGIN UK
INFO ✓✓✓✓
EASE ✓✓✓✓

Zoo Check is a charity whose mission is to promote Born Free's core belief that wildlife belongs in the wild. They expose the suffering of captive wild animals and investigate neglect and cruelty. They want tighter legislation and the phasing out of all traditional zoos. If you want to know more then this is where to go.

News and the Media

The standard of web sites in this sector is usually very high making it difficult to pick out one or two winners, just find one which appeals to you and you won't go far wrong.

www.sky.co.uk/news
WITNESS THE EVENT

ORIGIN UK	Sky News has fast developed a reputation for
INFO ✓✓✓✓✓	excellence and that is reflected in their web site. It has
EASE ✓✓✓✓	a well rounded news service with good coverage across

the world as well as the UK. You can view news clips, listen to news items or just browse the site. There are special sections on sport, business, technology and even a few games.

www.bbc.co.uk/news
FROM THE BBC

ORIGIN UK	As you'd expect the BBC site is excellent – similar to
INFO ✓✓✓✓✓	Sky but without the adverts. You can also get the news
EASE ✓✓✓✓	in several languages and tune into the World Service or

any of their radio stations.

www.itn.co.uk
INDEPENDENT TELEVISION NEWS

ORIGIN UK	A corporate site where you get information on what
INFO ✓✓✓	they do plus links to their news sites, which are clear
EASE ✓✓✓✓	and to the point.

www.teletext.com
TELETEXT NEWS

ORIGIN UK	Excellent and clear layout makes Teletext's site stand
INFO ✓✓✓✓	out, it has lots of added features and links too.
EASE ✓✓✓✓✓	

www.cnn.com
THE AMERICAN VIEW

ORIGIN US	CNN is superb on detail and breaking news with
INFO ✓✓✓✓✓	masses of background information on each story. It
EASE ✓✓✓✓	has plenty of feature pieces too. However, it is biased

towards the American audience. For a similar service try **www.abcnews.com**

www.telegraph.co.uk

NEWSPAPERS ONLINE

ORIGIN UK
INFO ✓✓✓✓
EASE ✓✓✓✓

The Telegraph has the best site for news and layout with all its sections mirrored very effectively on the site.

Other major newspapers with sites worth a visit include:

www.dailymail.co.uk – not so much the paper as a portal for Associated Newspapers, which is disappointing, but there are some good articles and features.

www.guardian.co.uk – clean site with lots of added features and guides.

www.thesun.co.uk – very good representation of the paper with all you'd expect.

www.fish4news.co.uk

LOCAL NEWS MADE EASY

ORIGIN UK
INFO ✓✓✓✓✓
VALUE ✓✓✓
EASE ✓✓✓✓

An outstanding web site, just type in your postcode and back will come a collated local 'newspaper' with regional news headlines, sport and links to the source papers sites and small ads.

www.whatthepaperssay.co.uk

WHEN YOU'VE NOT GOT TIME

ORIGIN UK
INFO ✓✓✓✓✓
EASE ✓✓✓✓

Can't be bothered to sift through the papers? At this site you can quickly take in the key stories and be linked through to the relevant newspaper site too. You can also sign up to its daily e-mail bulletin so you need never buy a paper again. See also the colourful **www.thepaperboy.com** which has a good search facility.

http//:ask.elibrary.com

RESEARCH WITHOUT THE LEGWORK

ORIGIN US
INFO ✓✓✓✓
VALUE ✓✓
EASE ✓✓✓✓

A subscription only site which has access to over 600 newspapers on a searchable database. It can be tailored to your needs and includes books, maps and photos too. The subscription cost is $79.95 per annum.

www.newsnow.co.uk
NEWS NOW!

ORIGIN UK
INFO ✓✓✓✓✓
EASE ✓✓✓

A superb news gathering and information service that you can tailor to your needs and interests. The layout is confusing at first but it allows you to flick between latest headlines from 3,000 leading news sources without visiting each site separately, you can then read their choice of stories in full on the publishers' web sites. It's updated every 5 minutes!

www.ananova.co.uk
NEWS ON THE MOVE

ORIGIN UK
INFO ✓✓✓✓
EASE ✓✓✓✓

Ananova has been changed a few times and in the latest guise you get a well put together site that is much clearer than some. They've also teamed up with Orange to produce a mobile text messaging news service.

www.moreover.com
DYNAMIC CONTENT

ORIGIN US
INFO ✓✓✓✓✓
EASE ✓✓✓✓

With real time news and rumour reporting, Moreover has become the news site of choice for many business people and journalists as it enables them to target the type of news and information they are looking for, saving time and effort all round.

www.salon.com
RESPECT

ORIGIN US
INFO ✓✓✓✓✓
EASE ✓✓✓✓

One of the most respected Internet news magazine sites often quoted in the media. The operation is very slick and, although the stories are biased towards the US, it's well worth a browse, especially the archive which has some real gems. You have to register to get the best out of it.

Other news sites worth a visit are...
www.anorak.co.uk – humorous newspaper reviews.
www.economist.co.uk – business, world events and in depth reports.
www.positivenews.org.uk – for a positive spin on the news.

www.private-eye.co.uk – some of the best features
from the mag, but not much news if truth be told.
www.theregister.co.uk – for technology news.

www.drudgereport.com

NOW FOR THE REAL NEWS

ORIGIN US
INFO ✓✓✓✓✓
EASE ✓✓

One of the most visited sites on the web. It's a pain to
use, but the gossip and tips about upcoming features in
the papers make it worthwhile. One of its best features
is its superb set of links to other news sources.

www.foreignreport.com

PREDICT THE FUTURE

ORIGIN UK
INFO ✓✓✓✓
EASE ✓✓✓

Owned by Janes, the Foreign Report team attempt to
pick out trends and happenings that might lead to
bigger international news events. Browsing through
their track record shows they're pretty good at it too.

www.wwevents.com

WORLD EVENTS

ORIGIN UK
INFO ✓✓✓✓
EASE ✓✓✓✓

Details of events that are happening in the world
today, tomorrow and this weekend all available at
the touch of a button, it really is that simple. You
can search by country or even region and county.

One Stop Web Sites

*Here's a list of outstanding sites that seem to have something for
everyone. Some are magazine like in style while others are basically
extended reference sites, in fact once you've found a favourite it's
difficult to leave!*

www.about.com
www.aol.co.uk
www.bbc.co.uk
www.handbag.com
www.msn.co.uk
www.sify.com
www.tesco.co.uk
www.waitrose.com
www.whsmith.co.uk
www.zoom.co.uk

Organiser and Diary

www.organizer.com
ORGANISE YOURSELF
ORIGIN US
INFO ✓✓✓✓
EASE ✓✓✓✓

An American site that is just what it says it is, an organiser that allows you to list all your commitments and it will send e-mail reminders in good time.

www.opendiary.com
THE ONLINE DIARY FOR THE WORLD
ORIGIN UK
INFO ✓✓✓✓
EASE ✓✓✓

Your own personal organiser and diary, easy to use, genuinely helpful and totally anonymous. Simply register and away you go but follow the rules faithfully or you get deleted. Use it as you would any diary, go public or just browse other entries.

See also:
www.livejournal.com – download your own journal and customise it to suit.
www.webdiary.net – flexible diary for business users.
www.yourorganiser.com.au – good looking site, easy to use with a group organiser facility.

Over 50s

If you're over 50 then you're part of the fastest growing group of Internet users, and some sites have cottoned on to the fact with specific content just for you.

www.idf50.co.uk
I DON'T FEEL FIFTY
ORIGIN UK
INFO ✓✓✓✓✓
EASE ✓✓✓

Graham Andrews is retired and this is his irreverent and opinionated magazine site. It's very positive about the power of being over 50 and it has a great deal of motivational advice on how to get the best out of life combined with a superb set of links to useful sites.

See also:
www.theoldie.co.uk – *The Oldie* magazine, which is great fun.
www.togs.org – where devoted fans of Terry Wogan meet.

www.50connect.co.uk

LIVE LIFE TO THE FULL

ORIGIN UK
INFO ✓✓✓✓✓
EASE ✓✓✓✓

A very strong portal site with masses of information and links covering a wide range of topics. It's incredibly useful, however, there are plenty of annoying adverts to go with it.

See also:

http://ourworld.compuserve.com/homepages/ Smilne6/silv.htm – A long-winded URL, but you are rewarded with a good set of links to sites for senior citizens.

www.age-net.co.uk – another portal site but one that takes a magazine-style approach.

www.lifes4living.co.uk – an upbeat site dedicated to chat and links, some good offers too.

www.seniority.co.uk – a very comprehensive offering covering all you are likely to need with advice and links. Not exactly the most inspiring design though.

www.silversurfers.net – not the easiest site to get to grips with but it has a huge number of links in over 50 categories.

www.ageconcern.co.uk

WORKING FOR ALL OLDER PEOPLE

ORIGIN UK
INFO ✓✓✓✓✓
EASE ✓✓✓✓

Learn how to get involved with helping older people, get information and practical advice on all aspects of getting old. You can also make a donation. There are also over 100 links to related and special interest sites.

www.arp.org.uk

ASSOCIATION OF RETIRED PERSONS

ORIGIN UK
INFO ✓✓✓✓✓
EASE ✓✓✓✓

ARP's mission is to change the attitude of society and individuals towards age in order to enhance the quality of life for people over 50 – and this site goes a long way to achieving that. It has great design and plenty of features aimed at helping you get the most out of life. It's excellent for a place to chat if nothing else.

www.helptheaged.org.uk
HELP THE AGED

ORIGIN UK
INFO ✓✓✓✓✓
VALUE ✓✓✓
EASE ✓✓✓✓

Find out how you can get involved in their work, what they do plus the latest news. You can also go to 'home shopping' and buy all sorts of useful gadgets to make life easier.

www.hairnet.org
TECHNOLOGY EXPLAINED

ORIGIN UK
INFO ✓✓✓✓
VALUE ✓✓✓
EASE ✓✓✓✓

So you've bought the PC and now you need to know how to work it properly? Hairnet explains all through a series of forums and specific courses designed to help you get the most from technology.

> *See also:*
> **www.seniornet.org** – a pretty boring but
> comprehensive guide.
> **www.technomum.co.uk** – one woman's story of
> how she got to grips with the Internet.

www.u3a.org.uk
LIFELONG LEARNING

ORIGIN UK
INFO ✓✓✓✓
EASE ✓✓✓✓

An organisation working to improve the lives of older people through the concept of life long learning, learning for the pleasure of it. The site offers details of the subjects covered and how to contact the relevant groups.

www.age-exchange.org.uk
MAKE YOUR MEMORIES MATTER

ORIGIN UK
INFO ✓✓✓✓
EASE ✓✓✓✓

Share your experiences and pass them on, Age Exchange aims to 'improve the quality of life for older people by emphasising the value of their memories to old and young, through pioneering artistic, educational, and welfare activities', they are also active in improving care for older people. This site gives details of how you can join in.

www.saga.co.uk/travel

HOLIDAYS FOR THE OVER 50S

ORIGIN UK
INFO ✓✓✓✓✓
VALUE ✓✓✓
EASE ✓✓✓✓

A superbly illustrated and rich site from Saga who've been specialising in holidays for older people for many years. Here you'll find everything from top quality cruises to weekend breaks.

See also:
www.takeaholiday.co.uk – Direct Reader holidays
specialise in the over 50s.
www.travel55.co.uk – a great database of travel sites
specialising in travel for older people.

Parenting

As a source of advice the Internet has proved its worth and especially so for parents. As well as information, there are great shops and useful sites that filter out the worst of the web and give advice on specific problems. Some of the education web sites, page 100, also have useful resources for parents as do the health sites, page 196. In addition, there is loads of useful stuff for parents about taking children on holiday and activities to do with the children in the UK in the travel section, page 434.

Advice and information

www.babyworld.co.uk

BE PART OF IT

ORIGIN UK
INFO ✓✓✓✓✓
EASE ✓✓✓✓

Babyworld is an online magazine that covers all aspects of parenthood. There's excellent advice on how to choose the right products for your baby and for the pregnancy itself. The layout is much improved and it's easier to find information.

www.babycentre.co.uk

A HANDS-ON GUIDE

ORIGIN UK
INFO ✓✓✓✓✓
EASE ✓✓✓✓

A superb site with a massive amount of information and links to all aspects of pregnancy, childbirth and early parenthood. The content is provided by experts and you can tailor-make your profile so that you get the right information for you. There's also a series of buying guides to help you make the right decision on baby shopping.

www.babyzone.com

PARENTAL ADVICE

ORIGIN US
INFO ✓✓✓✓✓
EASE ✓✓✓

This massive, comprehensive, American site on parenting gives a week-by-week account of pregnancy, information on birth and early childhood. The shop is not open to UK residents, but they have a good set of links to UK stores and community activities. See also the similarly well-put-together **www.parentsoup.com**

www.raisingkids.co.uk

FROM BIRTH TO...

ORIGIN UK
INFO ✓✓✓✓✓
EASE ✓✓✓✓✓

An excellent and information laden site devoted to helping parents get through the minefield of child raising with sections on every life stage. You can also ask an expert, and amongst many sections there's advice on travel, education and safety. Excellent.

www.ukparents.co.uk

YOUR PARENTING LIFELINE

ORIGIN UK
INFO ✓✓✓✓
VALUE ✓✓✓
EASE ✓✓✓✓

Chat, experiences, stories and straightforward advice make this site worth a visit – there are competitions, links and a good online shop.

www.tigerchild.com

A BALANCED SOURCE OF INFORMATION

ORIGIN UK
INFO ✓✓✓✓✓
VALUE ✓✓✓
EASE ✓✓✓✓

Covering health, leisure, education, childcare and parenting, this attractive and well laid out site offers unbiased and straightforward information with over 1,000 links throughout. The shop is actually a directory with a review for each retailer.

www.all4kidsuk.com

IF YOU'RE LOOKING FOR SOMETHING TO DO

ORIGIN UK
INFO ✓✓✓✓✓
EASE ✓✓✓✓

This aims to be a comprehensive directory covering all your parental needs from activities to schools. It's got an easy-to-use search engine, where you can search by county if you need to.

www.miriamstoppard.com

MIRIAM STOPPARD LIFETIME

ORIGIN UK
INFO ✓✓✓✓
EASE ✓✓✓✓

An excellent web site from the best selling author with lots of advice on being a parent, how to cope with pregnancy and keeping you and your family healthy. New information is continually being added, so it's very up-to-date and will become a great resource for parents.

www.babydirectory.com

A—Z OF BEING A PARENT

ORIGIN UK
INFO ✓✓✓
EASE ✓✓✓✓

The Baby Directory catalogue is relevant to most parts of the UK. It lists local facilities plus amenities that care for and occupy your child. The quality of information varies by area though.

www.gingerbread.org.uk

SUPPORT FOR LONE PARENT FAMILIES

ORIGIN UK
INFO ✓✓✓
EASE ✓✓✓

Gingerbread is an established charity run by lone parents with the aim of providing support to lone parents. The site is fun to use and well designed, the best aspect being that it's available in several languages.

Other useful sites:
www.allkids.co.uk – a well categorised portal site covering all things for children.
www.fnf.org.uk – support for dads at Families Need Fathers.
www.ncb.org.uk – home of the National Children's Bureau who provide support for children's charities and support organisations.
www.oneparentfamilies.org.uk – advice for single parents.

www.tommys.org

PREMATURE BIRTH, MISCARRIAGE & STILLBIRTH

ORIGIN UK
INFO ✓✓✓✓
EASE ✓✓✓✓

Information on getting through some of the tragedies that occur in pregnancy plus details on how you can help.

Childcare

www.bestbear.co.uk

MARY POPPINS ONLINE

ORIGIN UK
INFO ✓✓✓✓
EASE ✓✓✓✓

Select your postcode and they will provide you with a list of reputable childcare agencies or nurseries in your area. There are also homepages for parents, childcarers and agencies all with information and ideas. There is also a parents' forum. See also **www.sitters.co.uk**

www.daycaretrust.org.uk

CHILDCARE ADVICE

ORIGIN UK
INFO ✓✓✓
EASE ✓✓✓

Daycare Trust is a national childcare charity which works to provide high quality, affordable childcare for all. This site is designed to give you all the information you need on arranging care for your child, there are sections on finance, news and you can become a member.

Shopping

www.bloomingmarvellous.co.uk

MATERNITY, NURSERY AND BABY WEAR

ORIGIN UK
INFO ✓✓✓✓
VALUE ✓✓✓✓
EASE ✓✓✓✓

Excellent online store with a selection of maternity, baby and nurseryware available to buy, or you can order their catalogue. Delivery in the UK is £3.95.

www.mothercare.com

MOTHERCARE

ORIGIN UK
INFO ✓✓✓✓
VALUE ✓✓✓✓
EASE ✓✓✓✓

An attractive site with a good selection of baby and toddler products, also clothing, entertainment and equipment. It's good value and there are some excellent offers, delivery is £3 for the UK. It's not all about shopping though, there are advice sections on baby care, finance, tips on how to keep kids occupied and chat rooms where you can share your experiences.

www.go-help.co.uk

SHOP AND GIVE

ORIGIN UK
INFO ✓✓✓✓
VALUE ✓✓✓✓
EASE ✓✓✓✓

Go-help allows you to raise money for a good cause from your Internet shopping. It's basically a store list set in the usual shopping categories, with each store pledging a certain percentage of the amount you spend with them to your chosen beneficiary be it a school, charity or club.

www.ethosbaby.com

FOR GREEN BABIES

ORIGIN UK
INFO ✓✓✓✓
VALUE ✓✓✓
EASE ✓✓✓

A good store where all products are environmentally friendly, there's not a huge selection but you can order a catalogue. Delivery charges vary according to spend.

See also:
www.allkids.co.uk – a portal site with a good shopping directory.
www.mumsnet.com – a rather advert laden site devoted to product reviews with advice and tips thrown in. You have to subscribe to get the best of it.

Dealing with areas of parental concern

BULLYING

www.bullying.co.uk
HOW TO COPE WITH BULLYING

ORIGIN UK
INFO ✓✓✓✓
EASE ✓✓✓✓

Advice for everyone on how to deal with a bully; there are sections on tips for dealing with them, school projects, problem pages and links to related sites. See also www.successunlimited.co.uk

COMPUTERS AND THE INTERNET

www.cyberpatrol.com
INTERNET FILTERING SOFTWARE

ORIGIN US
INFO ✓✓✓✓
VALUE ✓✓✓
EASE ✓✓✓✓

The best for filtering out unwanted web sites, images and words. As with all similar programs, it quickly becomes outdated but will continue to weed out the worst. You can download a free trial from the site. See also www.netnanny.com whose site offers more advice and seems to be updated more regularly.

www.pin.org.uk
PARENTS' INFORMATION NETWORK

ORIGIN UK
INFO ✓✓✓✓✓
VALUE ✓✓✓
EASE ✓✓✓✓

Provides good advice for parents worried about children using computers. It has links to support sites, guidance on how to surf the Net, evaluations of software and buyer's guides to PCs.

See also:

www.parentsonline.gov.uk – a government site used to promote the benefits to parents of the Internet as an educational tool. Excellent for links.

www.safekids.com – a basic site that is a useful place to go for links and resources if you're worried about your children coming across something unsuitable on the Net.

DRUGS

www.theantidrug.com

TRUTH: THE ANTIDRUG

ORIGIN US
INFO ✓✓✓✓
VALUE ✓✓✓✓
EASE ✓✓✓✓

An outstanding site devoted to the fight against drugs with help for parents and children alike. There's plenty of advice, articles and general information and it's all written in an accessible style, and in several languages.

www.trashed.co.uk

DON'T GET TRASHED

ORIGIN UK
INFO ✓✓✓✓✓
EASE ✓✓✓✓

The NHS's drug site has non-judgemental, factual information on all the major recreational drugs with useful information on what to do in an emergency. For the government's line on drugs and good no-nonsense information go to www.ndh.org.uk – The National Drugs Helpline 0800 776600.

DYSLEXIA

www.bda-dyslexia.org.uk

BRITISH DYSLEXIA ASSOCIATION

ORIGIN UK
INFO ✓✓✓✓
EASE ✓✓✓✓

A good starting point for anyone who thinks that their child might be dyslexic. There is masses of information on dyslexia, choosing a school, a list of local Dyslexia Associations where you can get assessment and teaching, articles on the latest research and educational materials for sale. There is also information on adult dyslexia. www.dyslexia-inst.org.uk who also offer testing and teaching through their centres.

EATING DISORDERS

www.edauk.com

EATING DISORDERS ASSOCIATION

ORIGIN UK
INFO ✓✓✓✓
EASE ✓✓✓✓

If you think you have a problem with eating then at this site you can get advice and information. It doesn't replace going to the doctor but it's a place to start. There are help lines - youth is 01603 765 050, others 01603 621 414.

HEALTH

www.iemily.com

GIRL'S HEALTH

ORIGIN US
INFO ✓✓✓✓
VALUE ✓✓✓✓
EASE ✓✓✓✓

A massive A–Z listing of all the issues and problems you might face, it's easy to use and the information is straight to the point and often accompanied by articles relating to the subject. If you can't find what you need here try **www.prematuree.com** which is especially useful for older teenage girls. See also section on Health Advice page 196 and Teens page 376.

MISSING CHILDREN

www.missingkids.co.uk

UK'S MISSING CHILDREN

ORIGIN UK
INFO ✓✓✓✓✓
EASE ✓✓✓✓

This site is dedicated to reuniting children with their families, the details of those missing are based on police and home office data. You can search by town or date and there's also a section on those who've got back together.

Also try:
www.missingpersons.org – the missing persons helpline – 0500 700 700.
www.salvationarmy.org.uk – for their family tracing service.

RACISM

www.britkid.org

DEALING WITH RACISM

ORIGIN UK
INFO ✓✓✓✓✓
EASE ✓✓✓✓

A game that shows how different ethnic groups live in the Britain of today, full of interesting facts and information. There's a serious side, which has background information on dealing with racism, information on different races and their religious beliefs.

SAFETY

www.childalert.co.uk

CHILD SAFETY

ORIGIN UK
INFO ✓✓✓✓✓
VALUE ✓✓✓
EASE ✓✓✓✓✓

This is about bringing up children in a safe environment; there are tips, product reviews and a shop, stories, links and masses of advice and information. Except for the shop, the site is well-designed and it's easy to find things. See also www.yoursafechild.com

www.childcarseats.org.uk

CAR SAFETY

ORIGIN UK
INFO ✓✓✓✓
EASE ✓✓✓✓

All you need to know about buying, fitting and using child car seats.

SEX

The following sites provide accessible, factual information. The section on Health, page 196, Men page 230 and Women, page 455 may also provide relevant information.

www.lovelife.uk.com now www.playingsafely.co.uk

HERE TO ANSWER YOUR QUESTIONS

ORIGIN UK
INFO ✓✓✓✓✓
EASE ✓✓✓✓

Great site that has lots of information on sex as well as games and links to related sites. The emphasis is on safe sex and AIDS prevention. See also the Terence Higgins Trust at www.tht.org.uk this is the leading AIDS charity.

www.likeitis.org.uk

TELLING IT LIKE IT IS

ORIGIN UK
INFO ✓✓✓✓✓
EASE ✓✓✓✓

A really outstanding site from the Marie Stopes Institute giving good, straight information on all the major issues around sex and puberty that face teenagers today. The 'Cool or Fool' quiz is excellent and there's a 'Dear Doctor…' facility too.

www.fpa.org.uk
FAMILY PLANNING ASSOCIATION

ORIGIN UK
INFO ✓✓✓✓
EASE ✓✓✓✓

Straightforward and informative, you can find out where to get help and there's a good list of web links too. See also the British Pregnancy Advisory service at www.bpas.org

SPEECH

www.speechteach.co.uk
SPEECH THERAPY

ORIGIN UK
INFO ✓✓✓✓
EASE ✓✓✓✓

Information, help and advice on what to do if your child has speech problems or communication difficulties. The site aims to provide a learning resource for parents and teachers alike.

STRESS AND MENTAL HEALTH

www.rethink.org/at-ease
YOUR MENTAL HEALTH

ORIGIN UK
INFO ✓✓✓✓
EASE ✓✓✓✓

At-ease offers loads of good advice on how to deal with stress and is aimed specifically at young people. Go to the A–Z section which covers a large range of subjects from dealing with aggression to exam stress to how to become a volunteer to help others.

www.isma.org.uk/exams.htm
EXAM STRESS

ORIGIN UK
INFO ✓✓✓✓
EASE ✓✓✓✓

Top tips on coping with exams from the International Stress Management Association.

Party Organising

In this new section you'll find all you need to organise the perfect party.

www.partydomain.co.uk
PARTY PARTY!!

ORIGIN UK
INFO ✓✓✓✓
VALUE ✓✓✓
EASE ✓✓✓✓

Probably the best of the party shop sites with a wide range of fancy dress gear, lots of themed party ideas and options plus a party calendar. Shopping is secure with lots of delivery options. **www.thepartystore.co.uk** has a similar offering.

See also:

www.charliecrow.co.uk – a wide range of fancy dress costumes primarily for kids parties.

www.evite.com/ – a US site where you can create your own party invitations.

www.justforfun.co.uk – a good selection but a pretty basic site.

www.kids-party.com – a great resource, find out all you need to hold a kids' party in your area.

www.partypieces.co.uk – very experienced party suppliers with a wide range of products and 48 hour delivery.

www.partyzone.co.uk – specialises in supplying gear and goods for children's parties.

Pets

Here's a selection of web sites devoted to pets, there are shop and information sites and specialists too.

www.pets-pyjamas.co.uk
THE COMPLETE PETS WEB SITE

ORIGIN UK
INFO ✓✓✓✓
VALUE ✓✓✓
EASE ✓✓✓✓

An excellent site split into four sections:
1. Entertainment – quizzes and chat.
2. Services – vet finder, insurance and a funeral service.
3. News and information – topics such as health.
4. Shopping – via their own shop plus **www.animail.co.uk** a more general value-led pet shop and a specialist bookstore.
   There are also subsections on dogs, cats and small animals.

For other good online pet information and stores visit:
www.bluepet.co.uk – specialists in organic food
for pets.
www.mypetstop.com – apparently the only
multilingual website about pets, it's superb
for information and health advice.
www.petpals.com – at home pet care services.
www.petplanet.co.uk – good for the shop and
up-to-the-minute news.
www.petsmiles.com – a good directory site
featuring some 35,000 companies.
www.ukpets.co.uk – a directory of pet shops
and suppliers, plus advice and a magazine
devoted to pets.

www.pethealthcare.co.uk

PET INSURANCE

ORIGIN UK
INFO ✓✓✓✓
VALUE ✓✓✓
EASE ✓✓✓✓

This is a good place to start looking for insurance to
cover your vet's bill. It also has lots of good advice on
how to look after pets and what to do when you first
get a pet. See also **www.petplan.co.uk**

www.naturallypaws.com

COMPLEMENTARY MEDICINE FOR PETS

ORIGIN UK
INFO ✓✓✓✓
EASE ✓✓✓✓

An informative site giving details of how you can
look after your pets using natural foods and
complementary medicines.

www.pets-on-holiday.com

UK HOLIDAYS WITH PETS

ORIGIN UK
INFO ✓✓✓✓
EASE ✓✓✓✓

This site is devoted to finding holiday accommodation
where your pets are always welcome simply arranged
by region, easy. There's also a bookshop and a good
set of links.

See also:
www.defra.gov.uk/animalh/quarantine/index.htm –
animal quarantine and advice on overseas travel.
www.petswelcome.co.uk – pet friendly hotels
throughout the UK.
www.preferredplaces.co.uk – a holiday specialist
with a good pets welcome section.

Animal charities

www.rspca.org
THE RSPCA

ORIGIN	UK
INFO	✓✓✓✓
EASE	✓✓✓

News (some of which can be quite disturbing) and information on the work of the charity plus animal facts and details on how you can help. There's also a good kids' section. It's a good site but a bit tightly packed.

Other charity sites:
www.aht.org.uk – applying clinical and research techniques to help animals.
www.animalrescue.org.uk – fight animal pain and suffering.
www.animalrescuers.co.uk – a directory of centres and people who will help distressed animals.
www.animalsanctuaries.co.uk – index of charities and animal rescue centres.
www.bluecross.org.uk – excellent site with information, help and advice.
www.pdsa.org.uk – Peoples Dispensary for Sick Animals has a good looking site with details on how to look after pets and how you can help.
www.petrescue.com – home of the pet action league.

www.giveusahome.co.uk
RE-HOMING A PET

ORIGIN	UK
INFO	✓✓✓✓✓
EASE	✓✓✓

A nice idea, a web site devoted to helping you save animals that need to be re-homed, it's got a large amount of information by region on shelters, vets and the animals themselves as well as entertainment for kids.

TV-related

www.channel4.com/petrescue
PET RESCUE

ORIGIN	UK
INFO	✓✓✓✓
EASE	✓✓✓✓

Details of the program plus information and links on animal charities and sites, there are also stories, games and chat. See also the excellent BBC web pages on pets which can be found at ww.bbc.co.uk/nature/animals/pets

Sites for different species

BIRDS

www.avianweb.com
FOR BIRD ENTHUSIASTS

ORIGIN US   A massive site devoted to birds, it's especially good for
INFO ✓✓✓✓✓   information on parrots. There are sections on species,
EASE ✓✓✓✓   health and equipment as well as advice on looking
after birds.

See also:
www.birdcare.co.uk – lots of articles and advice on
    avian health.
www.parrot-rescue.co.uk – excellent site devoted to
    rescuing and looking after birds that have out
    grown their owners or need help.
www.rspb.org.uk – mainly wild birds but some
    good advice.

CATS

www.cats.org.uk
HOME OF CAT PROTECTION

ORIGIN UK   A well-designed and informative site, with advice on
INFO ✓✓✓✓   caring, re-homing, news and general advice, an archive
VALUE ✓✓✓   of cat photos and competitions for the best. The online
EASE ✓✓✓✓   shop offers delivery in the UK but charges vary.

See also:
www.crazyforkitties.com – nice site devoted to all
    things cat and kitty.
www.fabcats.org – a charity devoted to cat care.
www.freddie-street.com – fantastic and funny the story
    of the Freddie Street cats, there's some good infor-
    mation in there too.
www.i-love-cats.com – a directory of cat sites.
www.moggies.co.uk – home of the Online Cat Guide,
    not an easy site to use, but has exceptional links to
    pet sites.

DOGS

www.the-kennel-club.org.uk

DOGS OFFICIAL

ORIGIN UK
INFO ✓✓✓✓
VALUE ✓✓✓
EASE ✓✓✓✓

The place to go for the official line on dogs and breeding with information on Crufts and links to related web sites, plus shop and tips on looking after your pooch.

See also:
www.bugsie.co.uk – yes, it's a mobile dog washing service!
www.canineworld.com – an average site with some good links.
www.canismajor.com/dog – an American magazine site.
www.dogs-and-diets.com – comprehensive nutritional information for dogs.
www.howtoloveyourdog.com – a children's guide to caring for dogs.
www.i-love-dogs.com – a directory of web sites devoted to dogs.

www.ncdl.org.uk

NATIONAL CANINE DEFENCE LEAGUE

ORIGIN UK
INFO ✓✓✓✓✓
VALUE ✓✓✓
EASE ✓✓✓✓

Excellent web site featuring the charitable works of the NCDL the largest charity of its type. Get advice on how to adopt a dog, tips on looking after one and download a doggie screensaver. For Battersea Dogs Home go to **www.dogshome.org** who have a well-designed site.

FISH

www.ornamentalfish.org

ORNAMENTAL AQUATIC TRADE ASSOCIATION

ORIGIN UK
INFO ✓✓✓✓
EASE ✓✓✓✓

An excellent site beautifully designed and well executed. Although much of it is aimed at the trade and commercial side, there is a great deal of information for the hobbyist about looking after and buying fish.

See also:

www.aquariacentral.com – a huge site with masses
of information on every aspect of looking after fish.

www.fishlinkcentral.com – a good directory site for
information on fish.

HORSES

www.equiworld.net

GLOBAL EQUINE INFORMATION

ORIGIN UK
INFO ✓✓✓✓✓
EASE ✓✓✓✓

A directory, magazine and advice centre in one
with incredible detail plus some fun stuff too
including video and audio interviews and footage,
holidays and the latest news. The shop consists
of links to specialist traders.

See also:

www.equine-world.co.uk – lots here too including
classified ads, shopping and links.

www.horseadvice.com – a health-oriented site that
supplies a huge amount of information.

RABBITS AND RODENTS

http://www.rabbit.org

HOUSE RABBIT SOCIETY

ORIGIN US
INFO ✓✓✓✓✓
EASE ✓✓✓✓

It's all here, from feeding, breeding, behaviour, health
advice and even info on house-training your rabbit.
Has a nice kids' section and plenty of cute pictures.

See also:

www.rabbitwelfare.co.uk – lots of chat, advice and
links frown the Rabbit Welfare Association.

www.rabbitworld.com – a personal tribute to rabbits,
which also has information on caring for your fluffy
friend.

www.caviesgalore.com – information, forums, games
and names.

www.cavycapers.com – a guinea pig haven on the web!
A nice site too.

www.gerbils.co.uk – home of the National Gerbil Society.

www.rodentfancy.com – good all round site about
the small creatures.

OTHER PETS

www.animalsexoticandsmall.com – an odd site and
e-zine devoted to animal exotica.

www.insectpets.co.uk – a guide to keeping insects
as pets and there's a shop too.

www.petreptiles.com – comprehensive pet reptile
information.

www.ukreptiles.com – an OK directory site for
reptile enthusiasts, good for links.

Photography

www.photographyworld.co.uk
COMMUNITY OF PHOTOGRAPHERS

ORIGIN UK
INFO ✓✓✓✓
VALUE ✓✓✓
EASE ✓✓✓

A very good portal site with links to all aspects of
photography, there's information on everything
from models to lessons.

www.rps.org
THE ROYAL PHOTOGRAPHIC SOCIETY

ORIGIN UK
INFO ✓✓✓
VALUE ✓✓✓
EASE ✓✓✓

An improved site visually, dedicated to the works of
the RPS. There are details on the latest exhibitions and
the collection, you can become a member and get the
latest news about the world of photography. Good for
photographic history links, while the shop has some
related merchandise.

www.nmpft.org.uk
NATIONAL MUSEUM OF PHOTOGRAPHY, FILM
AND TELEVISION

ORIGIN UK
INFO ✓✓✓✓
EASE ✓✓✓✓

Details of this Bradford museum via a high tech
web site, opening times and directions, what's on,
education resources and a very good museum guide.

www.eastman.org
THE INTERNATIONAL MUSEUM OF PHOTOGRAPHY

ORIGIN US
INFO ✓✓✓✓
EASE ✓✓✓✓

George Eastman founded Kodak and this New York-based museum too. This site is comprehensive and amongst other things you can learn about the history of photography, visit the photographic and film galleries, or obtain technical information. Become a member and you're entitled to benefits such as free admission and copies of their *Image* magazine.

www.nationalgeographic.com/photography
HOME OF THE NATIONAL GEOGRAPHIC MAGAZINE

ORIGIN US
INFO ✓✓✓✓✓
EASE ✓✓✓✓

Synonymous with great photography, this excellent site offers much more. There are sections on travel, exhibitions, maps, news, education, and for kids. In the photography section pick up tips and techniques, follow their photographers' various locations, read superb articles and accompanying shots in the 'Visions Galleries'. Good links to other photographic sites.

www.masters-of-photography.com
ONLINE GALLERIES

ORIGIN US
INFO ✓✓✓✓✓
EASE ✓✓✓✓

A simple site with a superb array of galleries devoted to the real masters of the art of photography – you can spend hours browsing here.

www.life.com/Life
LIFE MAGAZINE

ORIGIN US
INFO ✓✓✓✓✓
EASE ✓✓✓✓✓

Life Magazine, it's wonderfully nostalgic and still going strong. There are several sections, features with great photos, excellent articles, and an option to subscribe; however they could do much more and it's a little frustrating to use.

Photo Libraries

www.corbis.com

THE PLACE FOR PICTURES ON THE INTERNET

ORIGIN US
INFO ✓✓✓✓✓
VALUE ✓✓✓
EASE ✓✓✓✓

Another Microsoft product, this is probably the world's largest online picture library. Use the pictures to enhance presentations, web sites, screensavers, or to make e-cards for friends. You can also buy pictures framed or unframed which are good value, but shipping to the UK can be expensive. You can also now buy high quality digital images at $4.50 a go.

See also:
www.freefoto.com – who offer the largest free image database.
www.freeimages.co.uk – 2,500 free quality pictures.
www.webshots.com – which is great for wallpaper and screensavers.

Photographic advice

www.bjphoto.co.uk

THE BRITISH JOURNAL OF PHOTOGRAPHY

ORIGIN UK
INFO ✓✓✓✓
EASE ✓✓✓✓

An online magazine with loads of material on photography. Access their archive or visit picture galleries that contain work from contemporary photographers, find out about careers in photography and where to buy the best photographic gear.

www.betterphoto.com

TAKE BETTER PICTURES

ORIGIN UK
INFO ✓✓✓✓✓
EASE ✓✓✓✓

A very well laid out and comprehensive advice site for new and experienced photographers with a buyer's guide and introductions to and overviews of traditional and digital photography.

See also:

www.photo.net – an American site with lots of advice and reviews.

www.photobuzz.com – the place to discuss digital photography.

www.shortcourses.com – all you need to know about digital photography.

Photography stores

www.jessops.com

TAKE ADVICE TAKE GREAT PICTURES

ORIGIN UK
INFO ✓✓✓✓
VALUE ✓✓✓
EASE ✓✓✓✓

Jessops are the largest photographic retailer in the UK and they offer advice on most aspects of photography plus courses and free software for their digital printing service. They do give you an opportunity to go shopping for your camera and accessories, of course.

See also:

www.bestcameras.co.uk – good range and a clutter free site. Recommended, delivery charges vary though.

www.camerasdirect.co.uk – well designed store, delivery from £9.99.

www.digitaltruth.com – unusual design and very comprehensive equipment shop and portal site.

www.ffordes.com – a good site offering used equipment alongside the new.

www.internetcamerasdirect.co.uk – a good value independent store with reviews and a digital dictionary. Free delivery on orders over £100.

www.photoglossy.com – specialists in paper, material and printing accessories.

www.photographicdirect.co.uk – not just a shop, you can have your say too.

Equipment reviews

www.whichcamera.co.uk

FIND THE RIGHT CAMERA

ORIGIN UK
INFO ✓✓✓✓✓
EASE ✓✓✓

Get advice on the best camera for you then use links to find your local dealer or to the manufacturer direct. The information is very good, there's a good search engine and camera finder service too.

See also:
www.camerareview.com – hundreds of cameras reviewed.
www.dpreview.com – digital photography cameras and equipment reviewed.

Photo storage and development

www.fotango.com
ONLINE DEVELOPERS

ORIGIN UK
INFO ✓✓✓✓
VALUE ✓✓✓
EASE ✓✓✓✓

Fotango will take your film and digitise it, then place your pictures on a secure site for you to view and select for printing the ones you like. The service is quick and easy to use; costs don't seem much different from the high street although single prints can be expensive.

Other sites offering a similar service are:
www.ofoto.com – another online photo album service, you get free postage with your first order of prints.
www.photobox.co.uk – great design, probably the best for digital photo storage.
www.photoscrapbook.com – an American site offering good value.

Miscellaneous photography sites

www.getmapping.com
AERIAL PHOTOGRAPHS

ORIGIN UK
INFO ✓✓✓✓✓
VALUE ✓✓✓
EASE ✓✓✓

Just type in your postcode and get a picture of your home taken from above on a sunny day last year. There are lots of cost options and you can also get a map to go with it.

www.playingwithtime.org
TIME LAPSE PHOTOGRAPHY

ORIGIN US
INFO ✓✓✓✓
EASE ✓✓✓

This site is part of a larger photographic project, here you can see incredible movies filmed with time lapse photography. Excellent.

Price Checkers

Here's a good place to start any online shopping trip - a price comparison site. There are many price checker sites, however, the sites listed here allow you to check the prices for online stores across a much wider range of merchandise than the usual books, music and film.

www.kelkoo.co.uk
COMPARE PRICES BEFORE YOU BUY

ORIGIN	EUROPE
INFO	✓✓✓✓✓
VALUE	✓✓✓✓✓
EASE	✓✓✓✓

Kelkoo is probably the best price-checking site with 18 categories in their shop directory including books, wine, white goods, even cars and second hand goods – they have links with eBay. There are plenty of bargains to be had in fact they keep popping up on every page. In the features section you'll find reviews and news of the latest goods and consumer advice.

www.checkaprice.com
CONSTANTLY CHECKING PRICES

ORIGIN	UK
INFO	✓✓✓✓
VALUE	✓✓✓✓✓
EASE	✓✓✓✓

Compare prices across nearly 60 different product types, from the usual books to cars, holidays, mortgages and electrical goods. If it can't do it for you, it patches you through to a site that can.

Other good sites:

www.buy.co.uk – excellent for the utilities - gas, water and electrical as well as credit cards and mobile phones.

www.dealtime.co.uk – easy-to-use directory and price checker covering a wide range of goods.

www.pricechecker.co.uk – straightforward site, also covers flights and telephone tariffs.

www.price-guide.co.uk – a comprehensive offering including unusually wines.

www.priceoffers.co.uk – not really a checker, but has access to the best bargains, also a regular newsletter covering the latest offers.

www.pricerunner.com – a good all-rounder with a news section giving the latest information on deals and technology updates.

    www.pricescan.com – all the usual, plus watches,
       jewellery, sports goods and office equipment –
       good store finder.
    www.price-search.net – mainly computers
       and gadgets.
    www.pricewatch.co.uk – good for computers
       and personal finance.
    www.unravelit.com – unravel your troubles and get
       the best deal here. Good for utilities and finances.

Property

*Every estate agent worth their salt has got a web site, and in theory
finding the house of your dreams has never been easier. These sites
have been designed to help you through the real life minefield.
For advice on building your own house got to page 92 in the
DIY section.*

www.upmystreet.com

FIND OUT ABOUT WHERE YOU WANT TO GO

ORIGIN UK	Type in the postcode and up pops almost every statistic
INFO ✓✓✓✓✓	you need to know about the area in question. Spooky,
EASE ✓✓✓✓	but fascinating, it's a good guide featuring not only

house prices, but also schools, the local MP, local
authority information, crime and links to services.
It also has a classified section and puts you in touch
with the nearest items to your area.

www.landreg.gov.uk

LAND REGISTRY

ORIGIN UK	An OK site for information on house prices by region,
INFO ✓✓✓	you can also make inquiries about property and land
EASE ✓✓✓✓	values. Could be loads better.

www.conveyancing-cms.co.uk

CONVEYANCING MARKETING SERVICE

ORIGIN UK	Conveyancing is a bit of a minefield if you're new to
INFO ✓✓✓✓	it, this site aims to help with advice and competitive
VALUE ✓✓✓✓	quotes. See also **www.easier2move.com** which is
EASE ✓✓✓	nicely designed and very informative.

www.reallymoving.com

MAKING MOVING EASIER

ORIGIN UK
INFO ✓✓✓✓✓
EASE ✓✓✓✓

A directory of sites and help for home buyers including mortgages, removal firms, surveyors, solicitors, van hire and home improvements. You can get online quotes on some services and there's good regional information. The property search is fast and has plenty to choose from.

For more properties try these sites:

www.arla.co.uk – home of the Association of Residential Letting Agents with lots of useful information.

www.beach-huts.co.uk – great site, providing you want to buy or rent a beach hut.

www.easier.co.uk – free, no hassle advertising, also has a finance section.

www.findaproperty.co.uk – over 60,000 properties listed, biased to the South East.

www.findaproperty.com – over 30,000 properties.

www.flatmate.com – find a flatmate from anywhere in the world.

www.helpiammoving.com – helpful directory of removal and storage companies with information and advice.

www.heritage.co.uk – covers listed buildings for sale only plus information on their upkeep.

www.hol365.com – really good site design and a massive range of services and properties from 6,000 estate agents.

www.homefreehome.co.uk – finding and selling property for no charge.

www.homelet.co.uk – claim to take the risk out of renting by offering sound advice and insurances for both tenants and landlords – good design.

www.houseweb.co.uk – highly rated with comprehensive advice and thousands of properties for sale.

www.itlhomesearch.com – independent home search and advice site that also covers Spain and Ireland – rent or buy.

www.knightfrank.com – world-wide service, easy-to-use site.

www.naea.co.uk – National Association of Estate
Agents with their code of conduct, links and the
latest property news.

www.propertyfinder.co.uk – Britain's biggest house
database.

www.propertylive.co.uk – advice and properties from
the National Association of Estate Agents.

www.rightmove.com – very clear information site
with a good property search engine.

www.smartnewhomes.com – search engine dedicated
to new homes.

www.themovechannel.co.uk – an okay portal site,
each agent or property site gets a review and a
link. Better than it looks at first glance.

www.ukpad.com – details of property auctions in
the UK.

www.ukpropertyshop.com – claims to be the most
comprehensive covering 3,000 towns in the UK.

www.vebra.com – above average property search
engine, much faster than most.

www.home-repo.org

HOME REPOSSESSION

ORIGIN UK	A very useful and informative site that blows the lid
INFO ✓✓✓✓	off the goings on behind what happens when a house
EASE ✓✓✓✓	is repossessed and what you should do if you find
	yourself in arrears. It's assertive and entertaining too.

Property abroad

www.french-property.com

NO.1 FOR FRANCE

ORIGIN UK	If you are fed up with the UK and want to move
INFO ✓✓✓✓	to France this is the first port of call. They offer
EASE ✓✓✓	properties for rent or for sale in all regions and
	can link you with other estate agents.

www.spanish-property-online.com

MOVING TO SPAIN

ORIGIN UK	Avoid all the pitfalls by stopping off for a browse at
INFO ✓✓✓✓	this informative site that covers all you need to know
EASE ✓✓✓	about buying property in Spain.

See also:

www.assertahome.com – excellent site for international moves with lots of advice, information, houses and associated services.

www.fopdac.com – home to the Federation of Overseas Property Developers, a trade association site that has some useful advice and contact information.

www.french-property-news.com – a poorly designed site, but good advice and links.

www.prestigeproperty.co.uk – links with over 100 estate agents in 20 countries.

www.worldclasshomes.co.uk – properties in Spain, Portugal, France, oh, and Arizona…

Radio

You need a decent downloadable player such as RealPlayer or Windows Media Player before you start listening. The downside is that quality is sometimes affected by Net congestion although that's becoming less of a problem these days.

www.mediauk.com/directory

DIRECTORY OF RADIO STATIONS

ORIGIN UK
INFO ✓✓✓✓✓
EASE ✓✓✓✓

Excellent site. You can search by station, presenter or by type, there's also background on the history of radio and articles on topics such as digital radio. The site also offers similar information on television and magazines.

See also:

http://dir.yahoo.com/News_and_Media/Radio/ – Yahoo's list of over 900 stations and related sites.

http://windowsmedia.com – home to Microsoft's media listings, which is very comprehensive.

www.comfm.com – a French site with access to over 4,000 stations.

www.radio-locator.com – a huge directory of radio, US-oriented.

www.spinner.com – a virtual radio which comes with over 175 stations.

www.virtualtuner.com – tune in to a vast number of stations at this good looking site, the top 500 is interesting in itself.

www.radioacademy.org

UK'S GATEWAY TO RADIO

ORIGIN UK
INFO ✓✓✓✓✓
EASE ✓✓✓✓

Radio Academy is a charity that covers all things to do with radio including news, events and its advancement in education and information. It has a list of all UK stations including those that offer web casts. You get more from the site if you become a member.

www.bbc.co.uk/radio

THE BEST OF THE BBC

ORIGIN UK
INFO ✓✓✓✓✓
EASE ✓✓✓✓

Listen to the news and the latest hits while you work, just select the station you want. There's also information on each major station, as well as a comprehensive listing service. Some features such as football commentary on certain matches will be missing due to rights issues. Most of the stations have some level of interactivity, with Radio 1 being the best and most lively, you can also tap into their local stations and of course the World Service.

www.virginradio.co.uk

VIRGIN ON AIR

ORIGIN UK
INFO ✓✓✓✓✓
VALUE ✓✓✓✓
EASE ✓✓✓✓

Excellent, if slightly messy site, with lots of ads plus plenty of stuff about the station, its schedule and stars, there's also a good magazine with the latest music news. You can listen if you have Quicktime, Windows Media Player or RealPlayer.

Other independent radio stations online are:
www.capitalfm.com – Capital Radio.
www.classicfm.com – classical music and background information.
www.coolfm.co.uk – Northern Ireland's number one.
www.galaxyfm.co.uk – good range of dance music.
www.heart1062.co.uk – London's heart.
www.jazzfm.com – live broadcasts, cool site too.
www.lbc.co.uk – the voice of London.
www.wwfm.co.uk – international, pop all-rounder.

Railways

These are sites aimed at the railway enthusiast. For information on trains and timetables see page 440.

www.nrm.org.uk

NATIONAL RAILWAY MUSEUM

ORIGIN UK
INFO ✓✓✓✓
EASE ✓✓✓✓

An excellent museum site packed with information and details on their collection, you can even take a virtual tour. See also Great Western's very informative museum site at **www.steam-museum.org.uk**

http://ukhrail.uel.ac.uk

HERITAGE RAILWAY ASSOCIATION

ORIGIN UK
INFO ✓✓✓✓✓
EASE ✓✓✓✓

This site offers an online guide to the entire heritage railway scene in the UK, including details of special events and operating days for all heritage railways with lots of links world-wide.

www.therailwaystation.co.uk

UK'S BEST RAIL RESOURCE

ORIGIN UK
INFO ✓✓✓✓✓
EASE ✓✓✓✓

A wide ranging site covering all aspects of railway related hobbies from spotting to model making, there's a bookstore, links and classified ads too.

www.narrow-gauge.co.uk

NARROW GAUGE

ORIGIN UK
INFO ✓✓✓✓✓
EASE ✓✓✓✓

The new and improved Narrow Gauge Heaven (formerly Narrow Gauge on the web) steams in with latest news and a better photo gallery plus all the narrow gauge information you'll need. You can also contribute your own articles or just browse.

See also:
www.gensheet.co.uk – keep up to date with timetable changes and diversions.
www.heritagerailway.co.uk – geared to selling the mag but plenty of links and some archive material.
www.railway-technology.com – the latest industry news.

www.rpsi-online.org – Ireland's Railway
Preservation Society.

www.trainspotters.de – a good site from a
German rail fan.

www.trainweb.org – a directory of train and
railway related sites.

www.vintagetrains.co.uk – home of the
Birmingham Railway Museum.

Reference and Encyclopaedia Sites

*If you are stuck with your homework or want an answer to any
question, then this is where the Internet really comes into its own.
With these sites you are bound to find what you are looking for.
For schoolwork also refer to the Education section, page 100.*

www.refdesk.com

THE BEST SINGLE SOURCE FOR FACTS

ORIGIN US
INFO ✓✓✓✓✓
EASE ✓✓✓✓

Singled out for its sheer size and scope, this site offers
information and links to just about anything. Its
mission is 'only about indexing quality Internet sites
and assisting visitors in navigating these sites'. It's
won numerous awards and it never fails to impress.

www.xrefer.co.uk

REFERENCE SEARCH

ORIGIN UK
INFO ✓✓✓✓
EASE ✓✓✓✓✓

Moving towards a library biased subscription service
has toned down the offer that Xrefer once had, but
in the showcase section you can still access data and
information from some 30 reference works, so it's
still very good.

www.knowuk.co.uk

ALL ABOUT BRITAIN

ORIGIN UK
INFO ✓✓✓✓✓
EASE ✓✓✓✓

A subscription service which offers a massive amount
of data about the UK from the arts to the civil service,
education, government, law, travel and sport.
Although most of the information can be accessed
through separate sites, the advantage here is that you
only need the one. Prices aren't listed on the site but
you can contact them for a free trial.

www.about.com

IT'S ABOUT INFORMATION

ORIGIN US
INFO ✓✓✓✓✓
EASE ✓✓✓✓✓

A superb resource, easy to navigate and great for beginners learning to search for information, experts help you to find what you need every step of the way. It offers information on a wide range of topics from the arts and sciences to shopping. Also worth a visit is **www.libraryspot.com** which is similar in scope but has a more literary emphasis. It has an entertaining trivia section for those obsessed by top tens and useless facts.

www.ipl.org

THE INTERNET PUBLIC LIBRARY

ORIGIN US
INFO ✓✓✓✓✓
EASE ✓✓✓

Another excellent resource, there are articles on a vast range of subjects concentrating on literary criticism. Almost every country and its literature is covered. If there isn't anything at the library, there is invariably a link to take you to an alternative web site. It also has sections for young people.

www.allexperts.com

ASK AN EXPERT

ORIGIN UK
INFO ✓✓✓✓✓
EASE ✓✓✓✓

Staffed by expert volunteers, you can ask any question in some thirty three categories from arts to TV, in fact there's an expert covering most subjects or topics no matter how inane. See also the UK's **www.theanswerbank.co.uk** which is also very good.

www.homeworkelephant.co.uk

LET THE ELEPHANT HELP WITH HOMEWORK

ORIGIN UK
INFO ✓✓✓✓✓
EASE ✓✓✓✓

A resource with some 5,000 links and resources aimed at helping students achieve great results. There's help with specific subjects, hints and tips, help for parents and teachers. It's constantly being updated, so worth checking regularly.

See also:
www.homeworkhigh.co.uk – Channel 4's excellent homework help site.
www.kidsclick.org – more than 600 topics and subjects covered.

Encyclopaedias

http://encarta.msn.com
THE ENCARTA ENCYCLOPAEDIA

ORIGIN US
INFO ✓✓✓✓✓
EASE ✓✓✓✓

Even though the complete thing is only available to buy, there is access to thousands of articles, maps and reference notes via the concise version. It's fast and easy to use.

Other useful encyclopaedias:

http://encyclozine.com – wide range of topics covered plus good use of games, quizzes and trivia.

http://i-cias.com/e.o/index.htm – Encyclopaedia of the Orient – for North Africa and the Middle East.

http://plato.stanford.edu – Stanford Encyclopaedia of philosophy.

www.archive.org – an encyclopaedic resource in the making, the 'Wayback Machine' is fun though.

www.babloo.com – interactive encyclopaedia aimed at kids.

www.bartleby.com – one of the best. It offers access to a huge amount of reference work, but also fiction, verse and narrative non-fiction, largely with an American bias.

www.eb.com – Encyclopaedia Britannica for $9.95 per month.

www.ehow.com – instructions on how to do just about anything.

www.elibrary.com – outstanding site with access to huge amounts of data, from newswires to books, maps and images. You have to subscribe though.

www.encyberpedia.com – some 500 links to reference sites.

www.encyclopedia.com – the most comprehensive free encyclopaedia on the net, nice design too.

www.infoplease.com – the biggest collection of almanacs, plus an encyclopaedia and an atlas.

www.si.edu/resource – encyclopaedia and links to the massive resources of the Smithsonian.

www.spartacus.schoolnet.co.uk – Spartacus Encyclopaedia is excellent for history homework.

www.utm.edu/research/iep – the Internet
   Encyclopaedia of Philosophy.
www.wsu.edu/DrUniverse – ask Dr Universe
   a question, any question...

English and words

www.eserver.org

THE ENGLISH SERVER

ORIGIN US

INFO ✓✓✓✓✓

EASE ✓✓✓

A much-improved humanities site, which provides
a vast amount of resource data about almost every
cultural topic, there are some 30,000 texts, articles
and essays available on subjects from the arts, fiction
through to web design.

http://classics.mit.edu

THE INTERNET CLASSICS ARCHIVE

ORIGIN US

INFO ✓✓✓✓✓

EASE ✓✓✓✓

An excellent site for researching into the classics,
it's easy to use and fast, with more than enough
information for homework whatever the level. See
also the excellent **www.bibliomania.com** for a
wider range of resource materials.

www.perseus.tufts.edu

PERSEUS DIGITAL LIBRARY

ORIGIN US

INFO ✓✓✓✓✓

EASE ✓✓✓

An excellent source of data for ancient Classics and
Mythology, history and early science. It also offers
most of Shakespeare and Marlowe and, although it
concentrates largely on pre-1600, it's ever expanding.
See also **www.pantheon.org** which contains over 6,000
definitions covering mythology, legends and folklore.

www.askoxford.com

ASK OXFORD UNIVERSITY

ORIGIN UK

INFO ✓✓✓✓

EASE ✓✓✓✓

A pretty decent effort at making a dry subject
interesting, you can ask an expert, get advice on
how to improve your writing and, of course, use
the famous dictionary and thesaurus.

www.cup.cam.ac.uk/elt/dictionary

CAMBRIDGE UNIVERSITY

ORIGIN UK
INFO ✓✓✓✓
EASE ✓✓✓✓✓

This site has five dictionaries including English, American English, Idioms, Phrasal Verbs and a Learner's dictionary – all free. See also **www.oed.com** where you can find the Oxford English Dictionary which is available by subscription.

www.onelook.com

DICTIONARY HEAVEN

ORIGIN US
INFO ✓✓✓✓✓
EASE ✓✓✓✓

Onelook claim to offer access to almost 750 dictionaries and over 4 million words, at a fast, user-friendly site, it also offers a price checking service for online shopping.

See also:
www.alldictionaries.com – a huge database of dictionaries covering all sorts of subjects.
www.dictionary.com – here you can play word games as an added feature.
www.glossarist.com – essentially a very good portal site for dictionaries by subject.
www.quinion.com/words – International English from a British point of view, new words and phrases analysed.
www.rhymezone.com – type in a word, up pops all those that rhyme with it.
www.word-detective.com – a magazine devoted to words and wordplay.
www.wordspy.com – the latest on how words are being used and new words.
www.yourdictionary.com – very comprehensive, the last word in words, apparently.

www.thesaurus.com

IF YOU CAN'T FIND THE WORD

ORIGIN US
INFO ✓✓✓✓✓
EASE ✓✓✓✓

Based on Roget's Thesaurus, this site will enable you to find alternative words, useful but not worth turning your PC on for in place of the book.

www.visualthesaurus.com

THE VISUAL THESAURUS

ORIGIN US

INFO ✓✓✓✓

EASE ✓✓✓

If you get bored looking up words or looking for alternative meanings for words in the usual way, then check out the Visual Thesaurus. It's fun to use if a bit weird.

http://dictionaries.travlang.com

FOREIGN LANGUAGE DICTIONARIES

ORIGIN US

INFO ✓✓✓✓✓

EASE ✓✓✓✓✓

There are 16 language dictionaries on this site, just select the dictionary you want, and then type in the word or sentence to be translated – it couldn't be simpler. Originally aimed at the traveller, but it's very useful as a translation tool. See also **www.langtolang.com** Where you can translate words in up to seven languages, you can even download on to you mobile, there are quizzes to play too. For an excellent translation service go to **http://babelfish.altavista.com/tr** where you can convert sentences of up to 150 words into many languages.

www.peevish.co.uk/slang

DICTIONARY OF SLANG

ORIGIN UK

INFO ✓✓✓✓

EASE ✓✓✓

A comprehensive dictionary of English slang as used in the UK, with good articles and search facility.

www.acronymfinder.com

WHAT DO THOSE INITIALS STAND FOR?

ORIGIN US

INFO ✓✓✓✓

EASE ✓✓✓✓✓

If you don't know your MP from your MP3 here's where to go, with over 150,000 acronyms you should find what you're looking for.

www.symbols.com

WHAT DOES THAT SYMBOL MEAN?

ORIGIN US

INFO ✓✓✓✓

EASE ✓✓✓✓

Here you can find the meaning of over 4,500 symbols, with articles on their history.

www.techweb.com
THE TECHNOLOGY DICTIONARY
ORIGIN US
INFO ✓✓✓✓✓
EASE ✓✓✓✓

Get the latest business and technology news plus an excellent technology encyclopedia. For a dictionary that specialises in jargon and Internet terms only go to either http://webopedia.internet.com www.jargon.net or www.netdictionary.com for enlightenment.

Numbers and Statistics

www.maths-help.co.uk
E-MAIL YOUR MATHS PROBLEMS
ORIGIN UK
INFO ✓✓✓✓✓
EASE ✓✓✓✓✓

Send your queries to maths-help and they'll e-mail you back the answers in a couple of days. You can also visit the knowledge bank to see past queries and answers. See also www.mathacademy.com for a more bizarre view of maths and also the well put together www.easymaths.com which is much more conventional.

http://www.tractorz.com/Zimmer/Other/metriccalc.htm
CONVERSION CHART
ORIGIN US
INFO ✓✓✓✓
EASE ✓✓✓✓✓

Simply a very useful conversion device for the metric and imperial systems, covering length, temperature, weight, volume, distance and speed.

www.ntu.edu.sg/library/stat/statdata.htm
STATISTICS AND MORE STATISTICS
ORIGIN SINGAPORE
INFO ✓✓✓✓✓
EASE ✓✓✓

Free information and statistics about national economies, not that easy to use at first, but it's all there.

See also:
www.ameristat.org – all you need on the U.S.
from the Population Reference Bureau. Try their
main site too at www.prb.org holds masses of data
on the world and as well as the U.S.
www.cia.gov/cia/publications/factbook – the
CIA's famous fact book albeit a little out of date.
www.citypopulation.de – a really impressive site
with a world population database including

maps and flags.

www.geohive.com/index.html – population
statistics combined with information on other
key economic factors.

www.population.com – which has a huge amount of
data and information.

www.statistics.gov.uk – great for statistics on the UK.

www.atlapedia.com

THE WORLD IN BOTH PICTURES AND NUMBERS

ORIGIN US
INFO ✓✓✓✓✓
EASE ✓✓✓✓

Contains full colour political and physical maps of
the world with statistics and very detailed information
on each country. It can be very slow, so you need
patience, but the end results are worth it.

www.geographyiq.com

THE WORLD LISTED

ORIGIN US
INFO ✓✓✓✓✓
EASE ✓✓✓✓

A great site covering all the information you'd
expect. List freaks will love the rankings pages,
they cover everything from largest to oldest to
richest. Great for homework.

See also:

http://plasma.nationalgeographic.com/mapmachine/ –
home of the *National Geographic's* Map Machine
where you can zoom in to any part of the world.

www.plcmc.org/forkids/mow – where you can find
depicted all the flags of the world.

www.worldatlas.com – a pretty comprehensive
world atlas and gazetteer.

Religion

*In this section we've attempted to list sites that are of interest
and try to explain the philosophy of the religions rather than
the opinions of those who preach.*

www.omsakthi.org/religions.html

RELIGION WORLD-WIDE

ORIGIN US
INFO ✓✓✓✓✓
EASE ✓✓✓

This site provides a clear description of each world
religion including values and basic beliefs with links
to books on each one. See also the World Religion

Gateway at **www.academicinfo.net/religindex.html**
and **www.adherents.com** who offer statistics on
some 4000 religions and religious bodies.

Key religious sites in alphabetical order:
http://shamash.org/trb/judaism.html – a good
   overview of Judaism plus lots of links.
www.al-islam.org – informative site with good
   information and links.
www.buddhanet.net – useful links from this
   non-profit organisation.
www.ciolek.com/wwwvl-Buddhism.html –
   the Buddhist studies virtual library.
www.cofe.anglican.org – home of the Church
   of England.
www.islamonline.net – very comprehensive and
   interesting news and Islamic information site.
www.islamworld.net – a good overview of Islam.
www.jewfaq.org – an encyclopaedia devoted
   to Judaism.
www.methodist.org.uk – the official line
   in Methodism.
www.newadvent.org/cathen/ – the Catholic
   encyclopaedia.
www.panthkhalsa.org – information on the Sikh
   nation.
www.pres-outlook.com – a magazine site covering
   all forms of Presbyterianism.
www.quaker.org.uk – information on what it is to
   be a Quaker.
www.ritualwell.org – ceremonies for Jewish living.
www.russian-orthodox-church.org.ru/en.htm – the
   home site with the latest news.
www.salaam.co.uk – wide ranging site covering all
   aspects of Islamic culture.
www.salvationarmy.org.uk – excellent site with lots
   of background information.
www.scientology.org.uk – comprehensive site on
   Scientology and what it is.
www.ship-of-fools.com – excellent radical
   Christian magazine.
www.singhsabha.com/sikh_links.htm – a Sikh
   links directory.
www.thetablet.co.uk – a well-designed Catholic
   news site.

www.usc.edu/dept/msa/reference/glossary.html – a
   glossary of Islamic terms and concepts.
www.vatican.va – the official site of the Vatican,
   slow but informative, with some content being in
   Italian only.

More general information sites about religion:
http://about.com/religion – about has an excellent
   overview of the major religions and some minor
   ones, it also offers a newsletter and covers areas
   such as spirituality too.
http://religion.rutgers.edu/vri/index.html – Rutgers
   University has made available a library of
   information on the world's religions.
www.bbc.co.uk/religion – the BBC's excellent site
   on religion and ethics.
www.beliefnet.com – a wide ranging and multi-faith
   approach to spirituality.
www.religioustolerance.org – an organisation devoted
   to religions co-operating with each other, it has
   good information on all major faiths.

Science

*The Internet was originally created by a group of scientists who
wanted faster, more efficient communication and today, scientists
around the world use the Net to compare data and collaborate.
In addition, the layman has access to the wonders of science in
a way that's never been possible before, and as for homework -
well now it's a doddle.*

Hard science and the latest thing

www.scirus.com
SCIENCE SEARCH

ORIGIN US   A straightforward and easy to use search engine
INFO ✓✓✓✓✓   devoted to scientific information only.
EASE ✓✓✓✓✓

www.royalsoc.ac.uk

THE ROYAL SOCIETY

ORIGIN UK
INFO ✓✓✓
EASE ✓✓✓✓

An attractive site where you can learn all about the workings of the society, how to get grants and what events they are running. They've improved the content to include more links and more interactivity.

www.scicentral.com

LATEST SCIENCE NEWS

ORIGIN US
INFO ✓✓✓✓✓
EASE ✓✓✓✓

Apart from being a very good portal, this site offers the latest news in the major categories of science, plus a searchable database of articles gleaned from papers and magazines around the world.

See also:
www.bottomquark.com – a messy site with the latest news and discussion.
www.firstscience.com – which is slightly more accessible and colourful.

www.newscientist.com

NEW SCIENTIST MAGAZINE

ORIGIN US
INFO ✓✓✓✓✓
EASE ✓✓✓✓

Much better than the usual online magazines because of its creative use of archive material which is simultaneously fun and serious. It's easy to search the site or browse through back features – the 'Even More Bizarre' bit is particularly entertaining. For a more traditional science magazine site go to *Popular Science* at **www.popsci.com** great for information on the latest gadgets.

www.innovations.co.uk

GADGETS GALORE

ORIGIN UK
INFO ✓✓✓✓
VALUE ✓✓✓
EASE ✓✓✓

Impress your friends with your knowledge of the newest gadgets, innovations or what's likely to be the next big thing. Innovations is well established and has one of the best online stores and a wide range, there's a reward scheme with delivery costs being a flat £2.95.

See also **www.streettech.com** who specialise in the latest hardware and also **www.firebox.com** who have a good selection.

www.21stcentury.co.uk

YOUR PORTAL TO THE FUTURE

ORIGIN UK
INFO ✓✓✓✓
EASE ✓✓✓✓

A stylish site that gives an overview of the latest technology put over in an entertaining way. Whether you're using it for homework or just for a browse, it's useful and interesting, they have 12 categories from cars through to humour, people and technology, they even cover fashion.

www.nesta.org.uk

THE CREATIVE INVENTOR'S HANDBOOK

ORIGIN UK
INFO ✓✓✓✓
EASE ✓✓✓✓

The National Endowment for Science Technology not only helps inventors get their ideas off the ground with support and guidance, but also encourages creativity and innovation. They'll also inspire you, as a visit to this well designed site will show. See also www.inventorlink.co.uk

www.invent.org

THE INVENTOR HALL OF FAME

ORIGIN US
INFO ✓✓✓✓✓
EASE ✓✓✓✓

This outstanding and beautifully designed site is sponsored by Hewlett Packard and features advice on how to patent inventions and details of those who have been inducted into the Hall of Fame. If for no other reason, just go to appreciate the web site design.

www.science-frontiers.com

SCIENTIFIC ANOMALIES

ORIGIN US
INFO ✓✓✓
EASE ✓✓✓

Science Frontiers is a bimonthly newsletter providing digests of reports that describe scientific anomalies – 'those observations and facts that challenge prevailing scientific paradigms'. There's a massive archive of the weird and wonderful, it takes patience but there are some real gems.

www.webelements.com

THE PERIODIC TABLE

ORIGIN US
INFO ✓✓✓✓✓
EASE ✓✓✓✓

So you don't know your halides from your fluorides, with this interactive depiction you can find out. Just click on the element and you get basic details plus an audio description.

Popular science

www.sciencemag.org
SCIENCE MAGAZINE

ORIGIN US
INFO ✓✓✓✓✓
EASE ✓✓✓

A serious overview of the current science scene with articles covering everything from global warming to how owls find their prey. The tone isn't so heavy that a layman can't follow it and there are plenty of links too. You need to register to get the best out of it.

www.sciencemuseum.org.uk
THE SCIENCE MUSEUM

ORIGIN UK
INFO ✓✓✓✓
EASE ✓✓✓✓

An excellent site detailing the major attractions at the museum with 3-D graphics and features on exhibitions and forthcoming attractions, you can also shop and browse the galleries. See also **www.exploratorium.edu** a similar but more child friendly site by an American museum.

www.madsci.org
THE LAB THAT NEVER SLEEPS

ORIGIN US
INFO ✓✓✓✓
EASE ✓✓✓

A site that successfully combines science with fun, you can ask a question of a mad scientist, browse the links list or check out the archives in the library.

www.treasure-troves.com
TREASURE-TROVE OF SCIENCE

ORIGIN US
INFO ✓✓✓✓
EASE ✓✓✓

A really useful growing resource consisting of a number of online encyclopaedias covering the major science topics, the most amazing thing about it is that most of it seems to be the work of one man.

www.howstuffworks.com
HOW STUFF REALLY WORKS

ORIGIN US
INFO ✓✓✓✓✓
EASE ✓✓✓✓✓

A popular site, for nerds and kids young and old; it's easy to use and fascinating, the site has been revamped and there are sections ranging from the obvious like engines and technology, through to food and the weather. The current top ten section features the latest answers to the questions of the day. It's written in a very concise, clear style with lots of cross-referencing. See also **http://howthingswork.virginia.edu** which is less accessible.

www.extremescience.com

ULTIMATE SCIENCE EXPERIENCE

ORIGIN US
INFO ✓✓✓✓✓
EASE ✓✓✓

Not sure that it really lives up to its billing, but is a really entertaining site with lots of useful and useless facts to bamboozle your brain. Features include a time portal where you can learn the effects of relativity and other sections on weather, maps, technology, nature and the Earth. It uses the word 'cool' a lot.

www.voltnet.com

DON'T TRY THIS AT HOME!

ORIGIN US
INFO ✓✓✓✓
EASE ✓✓✓✓

This is literally a high voltage site devoted to electricity and how it works. While there is a serious side, by far the best bit is where they 'stress test' all sorts of objects by sending 20,000 volts through them.

www.world-mysteries.com

WEIRD SCIENCE

ORIGIN US
INFO ✓✓✓✓
EASE ✓✓✓✓

All the mysteries and unexplained phenomena are here, explained and illustrated in a fairly unbiased way. It makes for an interesting browse.

www.improbable.com

THE IG NOBLE AWARDS

ORIGIN UK
INFO ✓✓✓✓
EASE ✓✓✓✓

These awards are for those inventors whose project initially makes others laugh, then makes them think about the science behind it. To quote the site, they 'celebrate the unusual and honour the imaginative'. The site also offers much in the way of unusual scientific gems.

www.discovery.com

THE DISCOVERY CHANNEL

ORIGIN US
INFO ✓✓✓✓✓
EASE ✓✓✓✓

A superb site for science and nature lovers, it's inspiring as well as educational. Order the weekly newsletter, get information on the latest discoveries as well as features on pets, space, travel, lifestyle and school. The 'Discovery Kids' section is very good with lots going on.

http://whyfiles.org
SCIENCE BEHIND THE NEWS

ORIGIN US   If you've ever wondered why things happen and
INFO ✓✓✓✓✓   what's the real story behind what they tell you in
EASE ✓✓✓✓   the papers, then a visit here will be rewarding. With
in-depth studies and brief overviews Why Files is easy
to follow and you'll get the latest news too.

Practical science and science for children

www.doscience.com
EXPERIMENTS FUN AND SERIOUS

ORIGIN US   A slightly messy but entertaining site that has a
INFO ✓✓✓✓   number of experiments to try both at home and
EASE ✓✓✓✓   outside. It's informative and most of the experiments
seem easy to do.

www.planet-science.com
FAST FORWARD TO THE FUTURE

ORIGIN US   A visually gratifying site with lots to offer by way of
INFO ✓✓✓✓✓   helping children (and adults for that matter) to learn
EASE ✓✓✓✓✓   about science in an interactive and entertaining way.

See also:
www.amasci.com – for the science hobbyist.
www.funsci.com – a serious site with many
experiments to try both hard and easy.
www.tryscience.org – aimed at children, with
a few experiments.

Search Engines

The best way to find what you want from the Internet is to use a search engine. Even the best don't cover anywhere near all of the available web sites; so if you can't find what you want from one, try another. These are the best and most user friendly. For children's search engines see page 74.

www.searchenginewatch.com
A GUIDE TO SEARCHING
ORIGIN US
INFO ✓✓✓✓✓
EASE ✓✓✓✓

This site rates and assesses all the search engines and it's a useful starting point if you're looking for a good or specific search facility. There's a newsletter and statistical analysis plus strategies on how to make the perfect search. For a similar site see also **www.searchengineshowdown.com** who do much the same thing but it's less comprehensive.

http://uk.yahoo.com
FOR THE UK AND IRELAND
ORIGIN UK
INFO ✓✓✓✓✓
EASE ✓✓✓

The UK arm of Yahoo! is the biggest and one of the most established search engines. It's now much more than just a search facility as it offers a huge array of other services: from news to finance to shopping to sport to travel to games. You can restrict your search to just UK or Irish sites. It's the place to start, but it can be a little overwhelming at first.

www.mirago.co.uk
THE UK SEARCH ENGINE
ORIGIN UK
INFO ✓✓✓✓✓
EASE ✓✓✓✓✓

Mirago searches the whole web but prioritises the search for UK families and businesses. It's very quick, easy to use and offers many of the services you get from Yahoo! You can tailor your search very easily to exclude stuff you won't need.

For other UK-oriented search sites try:
www.britishinformation.com – well designed and comprehensive.
www.clickclick2.net – odd design and more of a directory.
www.searchsaint.com – good-looking and easy to use.

www.ask.co.uk
ASK JEEVES
ORIGIN US
INFO ✓✓✓✓
EASE ✓✓✓✓✓

Just type in your question and the famous old butler will come back with the answer. It may be a bit gimmicky but works very well, it's great for beginners and reliable for old hands too. See also **www.ajkids.com** which is the child-oriented version.

www.mamma.com

THE MOTHER OF ALL SEARCH ENGINES

ORIGIN US
INFO ✓✓✓✓
EASE ✓✓✓✓

Mamma claim to have technology enabling them to search the major search engines thoroughly and get the most pertinent results to your query – it's fast too, your query comes back with the answer and the search engine it came from. You might also try **www.metacrawler.com** which uses similar technology, and **www.37.com** which is a bit of a mess but can search 37 other search engines in one go.

www.vivisimo.com

CLUSTERING TECHNOLOGY

ORIGIN US
INFO ✓✓✓✓✓
EASE ✓✓✓✓✓

With Vivisimo instead of the usual list, you get your search results back categorised by subject, or clustered. It makes for easy researching and is one of the three search engines I most use. I can't wait for a UK-oriented version.

www.google.co.uk

BRINGING ORDER TO THE WEB

ORIGIN US
INFO ✓✓✓✓
EASE ✓✓✓✓✓

Google is all about speed and accuracy. Using a complicated set of rules they claim to be able to give the most relevant results in the quickest time, in fact they even tell you how fast they are. It's easier to use than most and a mass of information doesn't overload you. At this URL you can limit your search to the UK. You may also want to try the similar **www.teoma.co.uk** (which is my current favourite) for general searches, it seems to be more accurate and you can refine searches more easily.

www.lii.org

THE LIBRARIANS' INDEX TO THE INTERNET

ORIGIN US
INFO ✓✓✓✓
EASE ✓✓✓✓✓

This is a search engine with a difference in that all the source material has been selected and evaluated by librarians specifically for their use in public libraries. This doesn't stop you using it though, and it is very good for obscure searches and research – like putting together a web site guide, for example.

www.dmoz.org

THE OPEN DIRECTORY PROJECT

ORIGIN WORLDWIDE
INFO ✓✓✓✓
EASE ✓✓✓✓

The goal is to produce the most comprehensive directory of the web, by relying on an army (some 36,000) of volunteer editors, and if you want to get involved it's easy to sign yourself up. If it can't help with your query it puts you through to one of the mainstream search engines.

Finding the search engine that suits you is a matter of personal requirements and taste, here are some other very good, tried and trusted ones:

http://uk.altavista.com – limited but very efficient.

www.alltheweb.com – no frills, similar to Google, becoming very popular.

www.bbc.co.uk – a heavily advertised and new search engine that is simple to use.

www.completeplanet.com – chooses from over 100,000 searchable databases.

www.dogpile.com – straightforward and no mess.

www.hotbot.com – good for shopping and entertainment.

www.infoplease.com – good for homework.

www.invisibleweb.com – a pretty OK directory and search engine.

www.iwon.com – US site that's great for prizes and shopping.

www.kidtastic.com – safe search for kids.

www.lifestyle.co.uk – a massive directory of specially selected sites.

www.looksmart.com – good business-oriented site.

www.lycos.co.uk – easy to use and popular, good for highlighting offers.

www.msn.co.uk – searching is just one of the many things you can do here.

www.northernlight.com – specialist news and information search engine that has broadened out into the mainstream.

www.overture.com – straightforward, easy to use, it used to be goto.com.

www.profusion.com – an excellent and fast, advanced search tool.

www.ranks.com – a search engine and directory that ranks sites in each category.

www.scotland.org – small Scotland-oriented site.

Security on the Web

Keeping your computer, its contents and those who use it safe is one of the biggest priorities for any user, albeit unlikely you'll have any problems. Here's a list of sites that will help you keep secure and some protection software that's available for nothing.

www.isr.net
INTERNET SECURITY REVIEW
ORIGIN US
INFO ✓✓✓✓✓
EASE ✓✓✓✓
An exhaustive overview of Internet security with explanations and sections on all the major aspects of the subject.

www.grc.com
SHIELDS UP!
ORIGIN US
INFO ✓✓✓✓
EASE ✓✓✓
Click on the 'Shields Up' logo and follow the instructions. You can then leave the program to run a security revue of your PC – it probably won't make happy reading, it depends on how anxious you are about security. For their check up Mac users can go to **www.symantec.com/mac/security**

www.firewallguide.com
HOME PC FIREWALL GUIDE
ORIGIN US
INFO ✓✓✓✓
EASE ✓✓✓✓
According to my DK Internet Dictionary, a firewall is a piece of filtering software that protects your PC and prevents unknown users from sending material to it. But which is the best one? Find out here. For a good and well regarded firewall program that has a free version available go to **www.zonelabs.com**

www.software-antivirus.com
THE INDEPENDENT ANTI-VIRUS RESOURCE
ORIGIN US
INFO ✓✓✓✓
EASE ✓✓✓✓
All the anti-virus programs reviewed and rated. This site sets out to blow the myth that once you have virus technology installed you're safe, or that the best selling products are actually the best at the job. An authoritative site written by several experienced computer experts.

See also:
http://housecall.antivirus.com – a free virus scanner.
www.grisoft.com – for the free AVG anti-virus scanner.
www.kaspersky.com – home of the top rated anti-
virus program.
www.macafee.com – security specialists.
www.norton.com – where to go for the well known
Norton products.
www.pandasecurity.com – another top rated program.
www.viruslist.com – if you're *really* interested in
viruses then go here where you'll find a virus
encyclopaedia.

www.anti-trojan-software-reviews.com

THE ANTI-TROJAN RESOURCE

ORIGIN US
INFO ✓✓✓✓
EASE ✓✓✓✓

OK so you thought you were protected, but not
entirely. Trojans are programs that pretend to be other
programs and usually hitch a ride into your PC on the
back of e-mail attachments. Go here to find the best
anti-Trojan programs or just ensure that your anti-
virus software does the job on Trojans too.

www.spybot.com

SPYWARE DETECTED

ORIGIN US
INFO ✓✓✓✓✓
EASE ✓✓✓✓✓

As if viruses and Trojans weren't enough, the chances
are that you've got some spyware on your PC sending
information on your surfing activities to one of many
companies who provide marketing data to retailers
for example. This little program will search and
destroy the little so and sos. It's also worth
checking out the ad-aware program which is
available at www.lavasoftusa.com

www.cookiecentral.com

COOKIES EXPLAINED

ORIGIN US
INFO ✓✓✓✓✓
EASE ✓✓✓✓

An excellent site dedicated to explaining the workings
of that mysterious animal the 'cookie' and how you
can deal with them.

Ships and Boats

Boats

www.boatlinks.com

BOATING DIRECTORY

ORIGIN US
INFO ✓✓✓✓✓
EASE ✓✓✓✓

A well categorised directory and the place to start if you're looking for any information on shipping or boating.

http://boatbuilding.com

THE BOAT-BUILDING COMMUNITY

ORIGIN UK
INFO ✓✓✓✓✓
EASE ✓✓✓✓

If you want to repair or build a boat then here's where to go, with features and discussion forums to help you on your way. There's also a very good directory of links to suppliers and resource sites.

www.buyaboat.co.uk

BUY A BOAT MAGAZINE

ORIGIN UK
INFO ✓✓✓✓
EASE ✓✓✓✓

Primarily a vehicle to get you to subscribe to the magazine, the site offers information on brokers and the details of over 14,000 boats for sale. See also the well designed www.boats.com

See also:
www.boatingnews.com – news and classifieds.
www.boatingontheweb.com – an American boating directory.
www.boatlaunch.co.uk – a mapping service showing all the places in the UK where you can launch your boat.
www.uscgboating.org – a good site for advice and information on safe boating.

Ships and Navy

www.royal-navy.mod.uk

THE ROYAL NAVY

ORIGIN UK
INFO ✓✓✓✓
EASE ✓✓✓✓

An excellent site from the Royal Navy giving details of the ships, submarines and aircraft and what it's like to be a part of it all. There's a video gallery featuring highlights from the fleet and details of all the Royal Navy ships. Apart from all the information, you can have a go on the interactive frigate.

www.red-duster.co.uk
RED DUSTER MAGAZINE

ORIGIN UK
INFO ✓✓✓✓
EASE ✓✓✓✓

Red Duster is a merchant navy enthusiasts' site offering lots in the way of history covering sail, stream and shipping lines. There's also a section on the history of customs. To find out what the current merchant navy are up to go to **www.merchantnavyofficers.com** where you find information and links.

www.maritimematters.com
OCEAN LINERS AND CRUISE SHIPS

ORIGIN UK
INFO ✓✓✓✓
EASE ✓✓✓✓

An informative site with data on over 100 ships from the earliest liners to the most modern, each has its own page with quality pictures and some virtual tours. It is also good for news and links to related sites.

Other watercraft

www.hovercraft.org.uk
HOVERCRAFT

ORIGIN UK
INFO ✓✓✓
EASE ✓✓✓✓

If you're into hovercrafts or are just interested, here's the place to look with 3 sections – Britain, Europe and the world, which just about covers it all.

www.jetski.ndirect.co.uk
JETSKI

ORIGIN UK
INFO ✓✓✓
EASE ✓✓✓✓

A comprehensive links site with sections on where to jetski, how to buy one and look after it, dealers, tips and tricks – all to the sound of Hawaii 5-0's theme tune.

www.rontini.com
SUBMARINE WORLD NETWORK

ORIGIN UK
INFO ✓✓✓✓
EASE ✓✓✓✓

A directory site with over 1,000 links all devoted to the world of submarines, it covers everything from navies to models.

See also:
www.nao.rl.ac.uk – home of the Nautical Almanac Office.
www.paddling.net – for buying canoes and kayaks.

www.tpl.lib.wa.us/v2/nwroom/ships.htm – the Tacoma public library has a searchable database of some 13,000 ships.

http://ws1.lr.org/ – Lloyd's register.

Shopping

To many people, shopping is what the Internet is all about, and it does offer an opportunity to get some tremendous bargains. Watch out for hidden costs such as delivery charges, import duties or finance deals that seem attractive until you compare them with what's available elsewhere. For help on finding comparative prices, see the price comparison sites on page 295, in fact, starting your shopping trip at a site like www.kelkoo.com may prove to be a wise move. There is also the new section on Consumer Information on page 78 for the low down on your rights and what to do when things go wrong.

www.tradingstandards.gov.uk
TRADING STANDARDS CENTRAL

ORIGIN UK
INFO ✓✓✓✓
EASE ✓✓✓✓

Find out where you stand and what to do if you think you're being ripped off or someone is not trading fairly – you can even take a quiz about it. There are advice guides to print off or download and there is help and advice to businesses and schools as well as consumers.

Two other consumer sites worth checking out are:
www.consumer.gov.uk – rights advice from the Department of Trade and Industry.
www.howtocomplain.com – advice on how to go about airing your grievances and getting a result.

www.which.net
WHICH? MAGAZINE

ORIGIN UK
INFO ✓✓✓✓✓
EASE ✓✓✓✓

A good place to start your shopping experience but you have to be a member to get the best out of it. There's a good shopping directory plus their product picks section which highlights the 'best in class' on a wide variety of products. There are also the useful sections that you associate with the magazine such as legal advice and personal finance.

www.dooyoo.co.uk

MAKE YOUR OPINION COUNT

ORIGIN UK
INFO ✓✓✓✓
EASE ✓✓✓✓

Media darling Doo Yoo is a site where you, the consumer, can give your opinion or a review on any product that's available to buy, this way you get unbiased opinions about them – in theory. The 'products' range in some 20 categories from books to TV shows and it's easy to contribute. See also **www.ciao.co.uk** where you can actually get paid a small amount of money for your opinion.

www.recallannouncements.co.uk

CONSUMER SAFETY

ORIGIN UK
INFO ✓✓✓✓
EASE ✓✓✓✓

An informative site listing all the latest product recalls covering the USA, UK and Australia, it also offers a consumer guide, an 'Ask the Experts' facility and statistics on recalls. Some of the site can only be accessed if you register.

The virtual high street

www.marks-and-spencer.co.uk

CLOTHES AND GIFTS

ORIGIN UK
INFO ✓✓✓✓✓
VALUE ✓✓✓
EASE ✓✓✓✓

A much clearer, more attractive and faster site than the last time we visited, it has a good selection of products from clothes to gifts for all, as well as fashion advice and a quick order facility. There's not much emphasis on offers, more on quality. Delivery costs start at £2.95.

www.wellbeing.com

BOOTS

ORIGIN UK
INFO ✓✓✓✓✓
VALUE ✓✓✓✓
EASE ✓✓✓✓

A clinical site that offers health advice as well as shopping. There's a comprehensive guide covering health, beauty and baby topics, a good hospital guide, a confidential ask the pharmacist section and a list of specialist stores in your area. The shopping bit is quite understated and is basically split into eight sections; men, fitness, mother and baby, beauty, health, nutrition, gifts and personal care – more recently there's been a move to promote the latest multi-buy offers and their loyalty card. There's also a good search facility, free delivery on some items and you can also use your Advantage card as in the store. You can't return unwanted goods to a Boots shop though; you have to send them back to Wellbeing.

www.whsmith.co.uk

W.H.SMITH

ORIGIN UK
INFO ✓✓✓✓
VALUE ✓✓✓
EASE ✓✓✓✓

The Smiths site has a clean, easy-to-navigate format, with the emphasis on shopping. There is a great deal here though including the usual books, music, mags, games, stationery and DVD. In addition there are details of the latest offers, author features, information on their ISP offer, a store finder, an excellent education zone. Delivery charges start at £1.25, free if you spend over £39 and unwanted goods can be returned to your local store.

www.woolworths.co.uk

WELL WORTH IT

ORIGIN UK
INFO ✓✓✓✓
VALUE ✓✓✓✓
EASE ✓✓✓

A bright and breezy site from Woolworths with all you'd expect in terms of range and prices. They are particularly good on kids' stuff with strong prices on movies, chart music, clothes and games, delivery starts at £1.50 per order.

www.argos.co.uk

ARGOS CATALOGUE

ORIGIN UK
INFO ✓✓✓✓✓
VALUE ✓✓✓✓
EASE ✓✓✓✓

Argos offers an excellent range of products (some 8,000) across fourteen different categories as per their catalogue. There are some good bargains to be had. You can now reserve an item at your local store, once you've checked that they have it in stock. There's a good search facility and you can find a product via its catalogue number if you've a catalogue handy that is. Delivery is £3.95 unless you spend more than £100 in which case it's free. Returns can be made to your local store. It's no wonder that's it's the UK's most popular shopping site.

www.debenhams.com

AWARD WINNING FAMILY SERVICE

ORIGIN UK
INFO ✓✓✓✓
VALUE ✓✓✓✓
EASE ✓✓✓✓

Not a common sight on the high street but Debenhams have a very good site aimed at their retailing strengths: gifts, weddings and fashion. Delivery costs vary.

www.johnlewis.co.uk

NEVER KNOWINGLY UNDERSOLD

ORIGIN UK
INFO ✓✓✓✓✓
VALUE ✓✓✓✓
EASE ✓✓✓✓

A really attractive and usable site with a wide range of products and some good offers too. Delivery costs start at £3.95. Especially good if you haven't got one of their excellent stores near by.

General retailers, directories & online department stores

www.2020shops.com

THE SHOPPER'S FRIEND

ORIGIN UK
INFO ✓✓✓✓✓
VALUE ✓✓✓✓✓
EASE ✓✓✓✓✓

A really likeable site with a great ethic – they don't do cosy deals with other retailers for exposure so the shops they select and rate are there on merit. They are one of the few that give extra information on the shops such as delivery costs, plus some shopping advice. It's fast too.

www.goldfish.com/guides/guide.html

GOLDFISH GUIDES

ORIGIN UK
INFO ✓✓✓✓✓
VALUE ✓✓✓✓
EASE ✓✓✓✓

Another good place for consumer advice and an easy approach to selecting the right store. The Goldfish guides cover a wide range of shopping categories all written by independent journalists. Essentially the idea is that you read up on it, compare prices on it then buy it – simple really. The site is well designed and easy to use.

www.mytaxi.co.uk

SHOP AND SEARCH FOR THE BEST PRICES

ORIGIN UK
INFO ✓✓✓✓
VALUE ✓✓✓✓
EASE ✓✓✓

Personalise your online shopping experience using My Taxi to search retailers' web sites for the best prices on the goods you are interested in. Particularly strong on music and video, less so on other items. The recommended online stores are selected according to safety and service, there is no star rating system; however, they are well categorised.

www.edirectory.co.uk

IF IT'S OUT THERE, BUY IT HERE

ORIGIN UK
INFO ✓✓✓✓
VALUE ✓✓✓✓
EASE ✓✓✓

A nice looking directory with a wide variety of shops and goods to choose from, it has a good reputation for service as well as being topical.

www.shopspy.co.uk

THE GUIDE THAT SHOPS BEFORE IT RATES

ORIGIN UK
INFO ✓✓✓✓✓
VALUE ✓✓✓✓
EASE ✓✓✓

A great idea, the shop spy team actually use the shops on their listing and then report back on things like value, quality of the goods and service then rate them accordingly. The list of more than 500 stores is fairly eclectic and you can easily see the best rated ones. The site could be organised much better though and it's not always that up-to-date.

www.zoom.co.uk

MORE THAN JUST A SHOP

ORIGIN UK
INFO ✓✓✓
VALUE ✓✓✓
EASE ✓✓✓✓

This is an excellent magazine-style site, with lots of features other than shopping, such as free Internet access, e-mail and a dating service. Shopping consists of links to specialist retailers. You can enter prize draws and there are a number of exclusive offers as well. Not always the cheapest, but an entertaining shopping site.

www.virgin.net/shopping

LIFESTYLE AND SHOPPING GUIDE

ORIGIN UK
INFO ✓✓✓✓✓
VALUE ✓✓✓✓
EASE ✓✓✓✓

Virgin's shopping guide is comprehensive covering all major categories while allowing retailers to feature some of their best offers. It also attempts to be a complete service for entertainment and leisure needs with excellent sections on music, travel and cinema in particular.

www.shoppingunlimited.co.uk

INDEPENDENT RECOMMENDATION

ORIGIN UK
INFO ✓✓✓✓
VALUE ✓✓✓✓
EASE ✓✓✓✓✓

Owned by *The Guardian* newspaper, this site offers hundreds of links to stores that they've reviewed. It also offers help to inexperienced shoppers and guidance on using credit cards online. There are also links to other *Guardian* sites such as news and sport.

www.thevirtualmall.co.uk
THE VIRTUAL SHOPPING CENTRE

ORIGIN UK
INFO ✓✓✓✓
EASE ✓✓✓✓✓

Literally browse by floor then click on the shop you want to go into. There's no real advantage in using it other than having all the best stores represented graphically in one place, but there are some good offers to be found.

www.screenshop.co.uk
SHOP ON TV, WEB OR CATALOGUE

ORIGIN UK
INFO ✓✓✓✓
VALUE ✓✓✓✓
EASE ✓✓✓✓

As a shopping channel on Sky, Screenshop was already successful; this well-put-together site shows off the breadth of their range and has some good offers. See also the wide ranging QVC shop at **www.qvcuk.com** which offers some 10,000 products.

www.streetsonline.co.uk
STREETS AHEAD

ORIGIN UK
INFO ✓✓✓✓
VALUE ✓✓✓✓
EASE ✓✓✓✓

One of Britain's most successful online retailers, Streets Online not only offers excellent books, music and movie shops but an entertainment magazine and an exchange service where you can swap your unwanted goods. You can also download trailers, audio clips and e-books.

Ethical shopping

www.crueltyfreeshop.com
CRUELTY FREE SHOP

ORIGIN UK
INFO ✓✓✓✓
VALUE ✓✓✓
EASE ✓✓✓

A wide range of products on sale all of which are guaranteed not to have had any animal cruelty or exploitation in their production. The range is wide and the prices aren't bad either. It can only improve, a good idea that deserves some success.

See also:
www.afrigoods.org – quality gifts from Africa with profits going to the artists who made them.
www.fairtrade.org.uk – home of the Fair Trade Foundation which exists to enable poor artists and workers to get a better deal.
www.getethical.com – who have shopping, advice,

links and a magazine.

www.onevillage.org – A shop specialising in ethnic products and using the Fair Trade system.

www.shopethical.co.uk – who offer a directory of sites that are more aware than most of their social and environmental responsibilities

www.traidcraftshop.co.uk – good selection of crafts, foods and other goods from around the world.

Value for money

www.onlinediscount.com
THE VERY BEST DISCOUNTS

ORIGIN US
INFO ✓✓✓
VALUE ✓✓✓✓
EASE ✓✓✓✓

Online Discount specialise in monitoring Internet stores and highlighting those giving the best discounts in any one of sixteen major categories. You are quickly put through to a list of the key shops and their bargains.

www.priceoffers.co.uk
SUPERMARKETS SORTED

ORIGIN UK
INFO ✓✓✓✓
VALUE ✓✓✓✓✓
EASE ✓✓✓✓

The online guide to high street bargains, check out the site then choose which supermarket to visit for the best offers. There are several sections: the newsletter offering customised updates; an editor's choice of the best bargains; buy one get one free deals; store deals; and lastly a selection found by shoppers willing to share their bargain finds.

www.thesimplesaver.com
WHERE TO GET THE BEST DEAL

ORIGIN UK
INFO ✓✓✓✓
VALUE ✓✓✓✓✓
EASE ✓✓✓✓

What started off as a simple e-mail conversation about where to go for savings has snowballed into a web site and newsletter that lets the whole world know where the best shopping bargains are to be had.

www.gooddealdirectory.co.uk
THE BARGAIN-HUNTER'S BIBLE

ORIGIN UK
INFO ✓✓✓✓
ASE ✓✓✓✓

Based on the book of the same name, this is basically a searchable directory of discount shops and sales. It's easy to use and the information seems comprehensive.

Gift finding

The following sites should help you find the perfect gift, but if you're shopping for the women in your life, there are more gift sites recommended in the Men's section on page 231.

www.hard2buy4.co.uk

GIFT IDEAS

ORIGIN UK
INFO ✓✓✓✓✓
VALUE ✓✓✓✓
EASE ✓✓✓✓

Excellent gift shop with a wide range of unusual products including celebrity items, activities and gifts for men, women and children in separate sections, some good offers too.

See also:

www.blissonline.com – lifestyle enhancing gifts and upmarket presents in a hurry.

www.buyagift.co.uk – activities and experiences for those who have everything.

www.find-me-a-gift.co.uk – gifts, both products and special experiences can be found here, loyalty scheme thrown in too.

www.gotogifts.co.uk – gift ideas in profusion, a bit of a mess design-wise but there's also a reminder service.

www.hawkin.com – odd design but good for range and the unusual.

www.iwantoneofthose.com – for more unusual gifts and stuff you don't need but would really like, it also has a great gift finder.

www.needapresent.com – very good site with some out of the ordinary gifts including the best selling Orgasmatron!

www.powderedwater.co.uk – great design and excellent for designer gifts.

www.pressie.com – offer a free gift wrapping service amongst a wealth of good ideas.

www.thesharperedge.co.uk – some good stuff in amongst the tat.

British shopping

www.british-shopping.com
UK SHOPPING LINKS AND DIRECTORY

ORIGIN UK
INFO ✓✓✓✓
EASE ✓✓✓✓

An excellent comprehensive portal site specialising in British shops, it also has plenty of related links and information. See also www.shops247.com and www.ukonlineshopping.com who both have a comprehensive shop listing.

For more quintessentially British shops check out these sites:
www.brooksandbentley.com – classy British gifts.
www.classicengland.co.uk – the best British products on a fun looking and easy to use site.
www.distinctlybritish.com – a British shop directory with a wide range of food, clothing, gift and children's retailers on offer.
www.harrods.com – a selection of their products available to buy from an attractive looking site.

www.scotsmart.com
SCOTSMART

ORIGIN UK
INFO ✓✓✓✓✓
VALUE ✓✓✓
EASE ✓✓✓✓

A Scottish directory of sites, not just for shopping but covering most areas, you can search by theme or category and the shopping section is split into books, clothing, food, gifts and highland wear. See also www.scotch-corner.co.uk which is Scottish through and through.

The rest

There are hundreds, possibly thousands of online stores and shopping malls, it would be impossible to include them all, but here is a list of some of this year's best reviewed sites and what they do.

THE BEST

www.bobsshopwindow.com – Bob's Shop Window is a comprehensive directory of shops, well categorised but not rated in any way, the site descriptions are provided by the retailers.

www.eshopone.co.uk – posh products and
   cheap prices.

www.eshops.co.uk – great design, loads of shops listed
   in the directory with some excellent offers and a
   good search engine.

www.I-stores.com – a very good store search engine
   and directory.

www.iwant2bshopping.com – a good directory that's
   also full of advice and tips for internet shoppers.

www.mailorderexpress.co.uk – excellent for toy and
   kids' stuff.

www.shopeeze.com – nice design and good prices too.

www.shoptour.co.uk – links to over 1,000 secure
   shops in 14 categories, much improved now with
   a price comparison tool.

http://theukhighstreet.com – a good UK directory,
   with the shops rated by you the customer.

www.ukshopsearch.com – above average search engine
   and quality design make this stand out from the
   crowd, you can also vent your frustrations out on
   the shopping experience in the shoppers forum.

www.worthaglance.com – great looking shop with
   some outstanding bargains.

COULD BE USEFUL

http://orders.mkn.co.uk – a very dull site, Market Net
   simply lists retailers and gives delivery times, good
   for the unusual though.

www.1shop.org – mall supporting small or medium
   sized UK businesses.

www.oneshopforall.co.uk – odd looking shop, good
   for unusual gifts though.

www.shopq.co.uk – massive set of shopping links,
   well categorised on a messy site.

www.shop-shop-shop.co.uk – search the databases
   of over 200 shops, good links.

www.shoppingtrolley.net – lots of shops and
   categories, boring design.

www.sortal.co.uk – very useful directory of UK shops
   sorted into 40 categories.

www.theukmall.co.uk – minimalist design, odd ratings
   and shop selection.

SO YOU CAN'T BE BOTHERED TO SHOP...

www.webswappers.com
SWAP IT!

ORIGIN UK
INFO ✓✓✓✓
EASE ✓✓✓✓

An interesting angle, at this site you can swap almost anything from the smallest item to a car or house! It's all backed by a confidential e-mail service and it looks quite good fun too.

www.anythingforhire.co.uk
HIRE IT!

ORIGIN UK
INFO ✓✓✓✓
EASE ✓✓✓✓

A comprehensive directory of goods and services for hire across the UK, well laid out and easy to use.

Skiing and Snowboarding

These sites tend to include information on both skiing and related travel, so we've moved it from Sports to create a combined section devoted to all things snowy.

www.fis-ski.com
INTERNATIONAL SKI FEDERATION

ORIGIN US
INFO ✓✓✓✓✓
EASE ✓✓✓✓

Catch up on the news, the fastest times, the rankings in all forms of skiing at this site. Very good background information and a live on line section enabling events to be monitored as they happen.

www.ski.co.uk
THE PLACE TO START – A SKI DIRECTORY

ORIGIN UK
INFO ✓✓✓✓
EASE ✓✓✓✓

Straightforward site, the information in the directory is useful and the recommended sites are rated. The sections include holidays, travel, weather, resorts, snowboarding, gear, fanatics and specialist services.

www.1ski.com

COMPLETE ONLINE SKIING SERVICE

ORIGIN UK
INFO ✓✓✓✓✓
VALUE ✓✓✓
EASE ✓✓✓✓

With a huge number of holidays, live snow reports, tips on technique and equipment and the ultimate guide featuring over 750 resorts, it's difficult to go wrong. The site is well laid out and easy to use. There's a good events calendar too.

Other good ski and snowboarding sites:

www.descent.co.uk – specialists in luxury alpine holidays.

www.ifyouski.com – comprehensive skiing site that has a very good holiday booking service with lots of deals.

www.iglu.com – holiday specialists with lots of variety and offers.

www.mountainzone.com – great for features, articles and ski adventurers.

www.natives.co.uk – aimed at ski workers, there's info on conditions, ski resorts, a good job section, where to stay and links to other cool sites all wrapped up on a very nicely designed site.

www.skidream.com – skiing and snowboarding in America and Canada.

www.skisolutions.com – one of the oldest travel companies specialising in skiing holidays, with a huge range of holidays and expertise.

www.snow-forecast.com – weather forecasts for snow areas.

www.snowrental.net – online equipment rental, all seems very easy.

www.boardtheworld.com

SNOWBOARDING

ORIGIN UK
INFO ✓✓✓✓
EASE ✓✓✓✓

Masses of information and links covering the world of snowboarding, the site is well designed and doesn't seem to miss out any aspect of the sport.

See also:

www.boardz.com/snowboard/snowboardcentral.html – the snowboarding e-zine from Boardz.

www.dryslope.co.uk – a good magazine for dry slope snowboarders.

www.goneboarding.co.uk – the UK boarding
  community with lots of information and chat.
www.legendsboardriders.com – online shop
  for snowboarders.
www.snowboardinguk.co.uk – forums and
  snowboarding chat.
www.waxed.com – a great snowboarding e-zine and
  information site.

Software, Upgrades and Debugging

*If you need to upgrade your software then these are the sites to go
to. Shareware is where you get a program to use for a short period
of time before you have to buy it, freeware is exactly what you'd
think – free. Debugging programs fix problems in established
programs that weren't previously identified.*

www.softwareparadise.co.uk
THE SMART WAY TO SHOP FOR SOFTWARE

ORIGIN UK
INFO ✓✓✓✓
VALUE ✓✓✓✓
EASE ✓✓✓

With over 250,000 products and excellent offers make
this site the first stop. It's a bit messy but easy to use,
there's a good search facility and plenty of products for
Mac users. There are links to sister sites offering low
cost software for charities and students.

www.download.com
CNET

ORIGIN US
INFO ✓✓✓✓✓
VALUE ✓✓✓✓
EASE ✓✓✓✓

A superb site covering all types of software and
available downloads. There are masses of reviews
as well as buying tips and price comparison tools; it
also covers handheld PCs, Linux and Macs.

www.softseek.com
ZDNET

ORIGIN US
INFO ✓✓✓✓✓
VALUE ✓✓✓✓
EASE ✓✓✓✓

Another excellent site with a huge amount of resources
to download, it's all a little overwhelming at first but
the download directory is easy to use and there's lots
of free software available.

www.tucows.com
TUCOWS

ORIGIN US
INFO ✓✓✓✓✓
VALUE ✓✓✓✓
EASE ✓✓✓✓

Probably less irritating to use than ZDNet and CNet, the software reviews are also entertaining in their own right, the best thing about it though is that it's quick.

If you feel like shopping around a bit more see also:

http://freshmeat.net – lots of shareware, also good for Linux fans.

http://home.netscape.com/plugins – if you're a Netscape fan then you can improve its performance with 'plug-ins' from this site.

www.completelyfreesoftware.com – hundreds of free programs for you to download, from games to useful desktop accessories if it's available free, then its here. Membership is essential, but free.

www.freewarehome.com – a great selection of free programs including a specialist site aimed at software for children, www.kidsfreeware.com

www.freewarenet.com – a comprehensive collection of freeware.

www.handango.com – a good site specialising in downloads for handheld PCs.

www.neatnettricks.com – an archive of useful tips and downloads with regular updates, you need to subscribe though.

www.vnunet.com – UK-orientated review and download site.

www.winplanet.com – specialises in improving and discussing Windows applications.

www.wired.com – popular technology magazine with all the latest news and reviews.

www.bugnet.com
FIX THAT BUG

ORIGIN US
INFO ✓✓✓
VALUE ✓✓✓✓
EASE ✓✓✓

Subscribe to the Bug Net and they alert you to software bugs, keep you up-to-date with reviews, analysis and the tests they carry out. You can then be sure to buy the right fixes. See also www.annoyances.org which is a good site devoted to fixing problems in Microsoft Windows.

www.winzip.com

MANAGE FILES

ORIGIN US
INFO ✓✓✓✓
EASE ✓✓✓

Winzip allows you to save space on your PC by compressing data, making it easier to e-mail files and unlock zipped files that have been sent to you. It takes a few minutes to download. For Macs go to www.aladdinsys.com

Space

www.space.com

MAKING SPACE POPULAR

ORIGIN US
INFO ✓✓✓✓✓
VALUE ✓✓
EASE ✓✓✓

An education-oriented site dedicated to space; there's news, mission reports, technology, history, personalities, a games section and plenty of pictures. The science section explores the planets and earth. You can buy goods at the space shop with delivery cost dependent on purchase. See also Thinks Space at http://library.thinkquest.org/26220 which is great for photos and links.

www.nasa.gov

THE OFFICIAL NASA SITE

ORIGIN US
INFO ✓✓✓✓✓
EASE ✓✓✓

This huge site provides comprehensive information on the US National Aeronautical and Space Administration. There are details on each NASA site, launch timings, sections for news, kids, project updates, and links to their specialist sites such as the Hubble Space Telescope, Mars and Earth observation. For Britain's place in space go to www.bnsc.gov.uk or www.ukspace.com which is great for links.

www.spacedaily.com

YOUR PORTAL TO SPACE

ORIGIN US
INFO ✓✓✓✓✓
EASE ✓✓✓

A comprehensive newspaper-style site with a huge amount of information and news about space and related subjects. It also has links to similar sister sites covering subjects like Mars, space war and space travel.

www.astronomynow.com

THE UK'S BEST SELLING ASTRONOMY MAG

ORIGIN UK
INFO ✓✓✓✓
VALUE ✓✓
EASE ✓✓✓

Get the news and views from a British angle, plus reviews on the latest books. The store has widened out to include patches, T-shirts and videos as well as the magazine and posters.

www.StarTrails.com

STAR TRAILS SOCIETY

ORIGIN US
INFO ✓✓✓✓
EASE ✓✓✓✓

An entertaining magazine site that covers all aspects of popular astronomy. Features include the daily solar weather, classes on breaking science news and the latest astral headlines.

www.seds.org/billa/tnp

THE NINE PLANETS

ORIGIN UK
INFO ✓✓✓✓✓
EASE ✓✓✓✓

A multimedia tour of the nine planets, stunning photography, interesting facts combined with good text. See also Bill Arnett's other interesting site on Nebulae at **http://seds.lpl.arizona.edu/billa/twn** where there are some beautiful pictures.

www.redcolony.com

MARS

ORIGIN US
INFO ✓✓✓✓✓
EASE ✓✓✓✓

A superb site all about the red planet. There is a synopsis of its history, plus details on past and future space missions with a focus on the colonisation of Mars. There's a great deal of information on things like terra forming and biogenesis, it's all taken very seriously too. See also the equally imaginative **www.exploremarsnow.org** where you can find a plausible manifestation of what a Mars mission could look like, backed up with outstanding graphics.

www.nauts.com

THE ASTRONAUT CONNECTION

ORIGIN US
INFO ✓✓✓✓✓
EASE ✓✓✓

In their words 'The Astronaut Connection has worked to create an educational and entertaining resource for space enthusiasts, young and old, to learn about astronauts and space exploration' and that just about sums up this very informative site.

www.heavens-above.com
IT'S ABOVE YOUR HEAD

ORIGIN US
INFO ✓✓✓✓✓
EASE ✓✓✓✓

Type in your location and they'll give you the exact time and precise location of the next visible pass of the International Space Station or space shuttle. They also help you to observe satellites and flares from Iridium satellites.

www.spaceadventures.com
SPACE TOURISM

ORIGIN US
INFO ✓✓✓✓
VALUE ✓
EASE ✓✓✓✓

OK, so you want to be an astronaut? Well, now you have a golden opportunity, so long as you have $2 million! Having said that there are actually some cheaper options including shuttle tours and a trip to the edge of space.

www.setiathome.ssl.berkeley.edu
GET IN TOUCH WITH AN ALIEN

ORIGIN US
INFO ✓✓✓✓
EASE ✓✓✓

To borrow the official site description 'SETI@home is a scientific experiment that uses Internet-connected computers in the Search for Extraterrestrial Intelligence (SETI).' You can participate by running a free program that downloads and analyses radio telescope data. Millions have participated and 5 billion potential signals have been located; they're pointing their scopes at the most promising now. There's still time for you to be the first!

www.badastronomy.com
DEBUNKING THE MYTHS

ORIGIN US
INFO ✓✓✓✓✓
EASE ✓✓✓

A site devoted to exploring some of the myths and stories that surround astronomy and science fiction. It gives the facts in a straightforward and (because the site owner sometimes gets on his 'high horse') entertaining way.

Sport

One of the best uses of the Internet is to keep up-to-date with how your team is performing, or if you're a member of a team or association, keep each other updated.

General sport sites

www.sporting-life.com

THE SPORTING LIFE

ORIGIN	UK	A very comprehensive sport site, with plenty of advice, tips, news and latest scores. It's considered to be one of the best, good for stories, in-depth analysis and overall coverage of the major sports.
INFO	✓✓✓✓	
EASE	✓✓✓✓	

www.sports.com

SPORTS NEWS AND BETTING

ORIGIN	UK	With a strong international feel, this site offers much in the way of information on all key sports, particularly football, its shop has been replaced with a wide ranging betting service.
INFO	✓✓✓✓✓	
VALUE	✓✓✓	
EASE	✓✓✓✓✓	

www.bbc.co.uk/sport

BBC SPORT COVERAGE

ORIGIN	UK	They may have lost the right to broadcast many sporting events but their coverage at this level is excellent – much broader than most and it's always up-to-date.
INFO	✓✓✓✓✓	
EASE	✓✓✓✓✓	

www.skysports.com

THE BEST OF SKY SPORT

ORIGIN	UK	Excellent for the Premiership and football in general, but also covers other sports very well particularly cricket and both forms of rugby. Includes a section featuring video and audio clips, and there are interviews with stars. You can vote in their polls, e-mail programmes or try sports trivia quizzes. Lots of adverts spoil it.
INFO	✓✓✓✓	
EASE	✓✓✓✓	

www.rivals.net

THE RIVALS NETWORK

ORIGIN UK
INFO ✓✓✓✓✓
EASE ✓✓✓✓

Independent of any news organisations, Rivals is basically a network of specialist sites covering the whole gamut of major and some minor sports, each site hasits own editor who is passionate about the sport they cover. In general its promise is better than the delivery but what there is, is excellent with good quality content and pictures.

www.talksport.net

HOME OF TALK SPORT RADIO

ORIGIN UK
INFO ✓✓✓✓
VALUE ✓✓
EASE ✓✓✓✓

A pretty down-market site where you can listen to sports news and debate while you work. The information comes from *Sporting Life* but it's up-to-date. There's also an audio archive and scheduling information, view the fantastic sports babe and visit the bookstore. There's also a sister site where you can place bets.

http://sport.telegraph.co.uk

THE DAILY TELEGRAPH

ORIGIN UK
INFO ✓✓✓✓✓
EASE ✓✓✓✓

Very comprehensive and well written with lots of archive material. All the major sports are covered and with contributors like Gary Lineker, Mike Atherton, Henry Winter and Sebastian Coe, you know it has authority.

www.sportzine.co.uk

SPORTS SITE DIRECTORY

ORIGIN UK
INFO ✓✓✓✓✓
EASE ✓✓✓✓

Excellent links listing site with each site getting a review or description, covering all the major sports and most of the minor ones, plus news too.

Other good all-rounders, and sites with good links:
http://sportsillustrated.cnn.com – the latest in American sport from CNN.
www.allstarsites.com – directory of several thousand sports sites, you rate the ones you like.
www.EL.com/elinks/sports – list of American-oriented sports links.

> www.sportal.co.uk – good, football-oriented
> magazine site.
> www.sportquest.com – excellent search engine
> and directory.
> www.sportsonline.co.uk – odd looking site with lots of
> links and an OK search engine devoted to UK sport.
> www.sportszine.co.uk – fab search engine and
> directory, all sites are well reviewed and
> well categorised.

www.sportspubs.co.uk
WHERE TO WATCH SPORT

ORIGIN UK
INFO ✓✓✓✓
EASE ✓✓✓✓

A building directory of pubs where you can watch sport. You can search it by sport or by region and there's a good links section too.

www.culture.gov.uk/sport
WHAT THE GOVERNMENT IS UP TO

ORIGIN UK
INFO ✓✓✓✓
EASE ✓✓✓✓

Here's where to go to find the latest policies, what the minister for sport does and how they are helping sport develop in the community at large. Fairly dull site though.

Sites on specific sports

AMERICAN FOOTBALL

www.nfl.com
NATIONAL FOOTBALL LEAGUE

ORIGIN US
INFO ✓✓✓✓
EASE ✓✓✓✓

American football's online bible, it's a huge official site with details and statistics bursting from every page. It's got information on all the teams, players and likely draft picks; there's also information on NFL Europe and links to other key sites. All it really lacks is gossip!

See also:
http://football.espn.go.com/nfl/index– ESPN's site is
authoritative and offers links to other sports.
www.nflplayers.com – for the latest news and background on all the key people in the game plus
nostalgia from ex-players.

ARCHERY

www.archery.org

INTERNATIONAL ARCHERY FEDERATION

ORIGIN UK	Get the official news, events listings, rankings and
INFO ✓✓✓✓✓	records information from this fairly mundane site.
VALUE ✓✓✓✓	For a more entertaining and chatty site try
EASE ✓✓✓✓	www.theglade.co.uk which is basically an online

magazine, devoted to all forms of archery. Lastly, check out **www.archery.net** for chat, links, equipment and advice.

ATHLETICS AND RUNNING

www.iaaf.org

INTERNATIONAL ATHLETICS

ORIGIN UK	The official site of the International Association of
INFO ✓✓✓✓	Athletics Federations is a results-oriented affair with
VALUE ✓✓✓✓✓	lots of rankings in addition to the latest news. There's
EASE ✓✓✓	also a multimedia section where you can see pictures,

listen to commentary or watch video of the key events. There's a good links page and information on the organisation's activities.

www.ukathletics.net

THE GOVERNING BODY

ORIGIN UK	Many official 'governing body' sites are pretty boring
INFO ✓✓✓✓✓	affairs, not so UK Athletics which contains lots of
EASE ✓✓✓	features, is newsy and written with an obvious sense of

enthusiasm. There are details on forthcoming events, reports on aspects of the sport, records, biographies of key athletes and advice on keeping fit. Somehow you get the impression the site is sponsored...

www.runnersworld.com

RUNNER'S WORLD MAGAZINE

ORIGIN US	A rather dry site with tips from getting started through
INFO ✓✓✓✓	to advanced level running. There's lots of information,
EASE ✓✓✓✓	news and records plus reviews on shoes and gear. See

also the less visually exciting but comprehensive **www.runnersweb.com**

www.realrunner.com

A RUNNING COMMUNITY

ORIGIN UK
INFO ✓✓✓✓
EASE ✓✓✓✓

A very well-put-together site with lots of resources to help runners in terms of both equipment and advice. There's an online health check, details of events, marathons and profiles of the athletes. Good design ensures that the site is a pleasure to use. For equipment advice try Runnersworld **www.runnersworld.ltd.uk**

See also:

www.british-athletics.co.uk – a boring site but it has a directory of clubs and regional events. It's good for links to newsgroups though.

www.gbrathletics.com – great for statistics and rankings.

www.marathonguide.com – all you need to know about marathons with news and advice.

www.nuff-respect.co.uk – see what Linford Christie is up to these days.

www.runnersweb.co.uk – a good site covering all aspects of running including marathon training.

www.runtrackdir.com – details of all the UK's running tracks and their facilities.

www.trackandfieldnews.com – all the latest from Track & Field News. US bias.

AUSTRALIAN RULES FOOTBALL

www.afl.com.au

AUSTRALIAN FOOTBALL LEAGUE

ORIGIN AUSTRALIA
INFO ✓✓✓✓✓
EASE ✓✓✓✓

A top quality site covering all aspects of the game including team news, player profiles and statistics as well as the latest gossip and speculation.

BASEBALL

www.mlb.com

MAJOR LEAGUE BASEBALL

ORIGIN US
INFO ✓✓✓✓
EASE ✓✓✓✓

All you need to know about the top teams and the World Series, it's not the best-designed site but there's good information and statistics on the game and the key players as well as related articles and features. If you want to find out more, a good place to try is **www.baseball-links.com** which is easy to use and has over 9,000 links; for the British game try **www.gbbaseball.co.uk**

BASKETBALL

www.nba.com

NATIONAL BASKETBALL ASSOCIATION

ORIGIN US
INFO ✓✓✓✓✓
EASE ✓✓✓✓

A comprehensive official site with features on the teams, players and games; there's also an excellent photo gallery and you can watch some of the most important points if you have the right software. For the official line on British basketball go to **www.bbl.org.uk** or **www.britball.com** which is unofficial but more fun and also covers Ireland. See also **www.basketball.com** who have really extensive coverage including the women's game.

BOWLS

www.bowlsengland.com

ENGLISH BOWLING ASSOCIATION

ORIGIN UK
INFO ✓✓✓✓
EASE ✓✓✓

A straightforward design making it easy to find out all you need to know about lawn bowls in England, including a good set of links to associated sites and even tips on green maintenance.

www.eiba.co.uk

ENGLAND INDOOR BOWLING ASSOCIATION

ORIGIN UK
INFO ✓✓✓✓
EASE ✓✓✓

A pretty basic site giving an overview of the game, links and background information on competitions and rules.

See also:

www.bowlsclub.info – a portal site devoted to lawn bowls.

www.bowlsinternational.com – home of a bowls magazine, good for links.

www.bowlsnews.co.uk – information on some local leagues.

BOXING

www.boxing.com
BOXING NEWS

ORIGIN US
INFO ✓✓✓✓
EASE ✓✓✓✓

A comprehensive site covering world boxing in a pretty newsy way with lots of exclusives and features, there are regular columnists and it's authoritative. There's also chat, links and the latest headlines.

See also:

www.boxinginsider.com – really good looking site with lots of information on the sport plus it's good for chat and stats.

www.boxingzone.co.uk – a boxing equipment retailer.

www.heavyweights.co.uk – who cover the hype around heavyweight boxing.

For the different boxing authorities:

www.aiba.net – the official site from the Amateur International Boxing Association.

www.wbaonline.com – the WBA has an OK looking and functional site.

www.wbcboxing.com – a straightforward site from the WBC.

www.wbu.cc – the World Boxing Union covers the sport well from an unusual site.

www.womenboxing.com – a very comprehensive site devoted to women's boxing.

www.worldboxingfed.com – WBF or Fightshow.com is a really entertaining site with lots of links and info on the sport as well as training tips and where to get equipment.

CLAY SHOOTING

www.clayshooting.co.uk
CLAY SHOOTING MAGAZINE

ORIGIN UK
INFO ✓✓✓✓
VALUE ✓✓✓
EASE ✓✓✓✓

A good introduction to the sport with a beginner's guide to start you off and a good set of links to key suppliers and associated sites. There's also an online shop where you can buy the odd essential item such as global positioning systems and dog food. Serious shooters can go to the comprehensive **www.hotbarrels.com**

CRICKET

www.uk.cricket.org or www.cricinfo.com
THE HOME OF CRICKET ON THE NET

ORIGIN UK
INFO ✓✓✓✓✓
VALUE ✓✓✓
EASE ✓✓✓✓

The best all round cricket site on the Internet, with in depth analysis, match reports, player profiles, statistics, links to other more specialised sites and live written commentary. There's also a shop with lots of cricket goodies, delivery is included in the price. It also looks after the official sites of Lords and the ECB.

http://cricket.khel.com/
WORLD CRICKET

ORIGIN INDIA
INFO ✓✓✓✓
EASE ✓✓✓✓

Khel has gone from being a labour of love to a really professional and commercial site part of the big Indian **www.sify.com** site, although cricket is it's main love (there's women's cricket too) you can also follow football and other sports as well.

www.wisden.com
WISDEN CRICKET MONTHLY

ORIGIN UK
INFO ✓✓✓✓
EASE ✓✓✓✓

Excellent site with the best features from the magazine featuring some of the best cricket journalism you can get as well as statistics and background information on the teams. There's also links, shop directory and quizzes.

www.lords.org

THE OFFICIAL LINE ON CRICKET

ORIGIN UK
INFO ✓✓✓✓✓
EASE ✓✓✓✓

Here you'll find news with plenty of information about the game and players, even a quiz and an excellent section on women's cricket. Good links to governing bodies, associations, the MCC and ECB. If you have RealPlayer, there's access to live games on audio via the BBC.

www.webbsoc.demon.co.uk

WOMEN'S CRICKET ON THE WEB

ORIGIN UK
INFO ✓✓✓✓
EASE ✓✓✓

There are not many sites about women's cricket, this is probably the best, with features, news, fixture lists, match reports and player profiles. Nothing fancy, but it works.

www.theprideside.com

CRICKET TO THE ROOTS

ORIGIN UK
INFO ✓✓✓✓
EASE ✓✓✓✓

A good attempt at encouraging young people to take an interest in cricket with an interactive game played on a really interesting interactive site.

See also:
http://sport.guardian.co.uk/cricket – good looking and up to the minute site from *The Guardian* newspaper.
www.cricketrecords.com – one for the statistics freaks, lots of pop up adverts too.
www.cricketsupplies.com – a good looking online store specialising in cricket gear, delivery is £6 per order.
www.cricnet.co.uk – the Professional Cricketers' Association official site.

CYCLING

These are sites aimed at the more serious sportsman, for more leisurely cycling see page 81 and for holidays turn to page 435.

www.bcf.uk.com

BRITISH CYCLING FEDERATION

ORIGIN UK
INFO ✓✓✓✓
EASE ✓✓✓✓

The governing body for cycling, the site has become more comprehensive, you can get information on events, rules, clubs and rankings, as well as contact names for coaching and development, plus a news service.

www.bikemagic.com

IT'S BIKETASTIC!

ORIGIN UK
INFO ✓✓✓✓
VALUE ✓✓✓
EASE ✓✓✓✓

Whether you're a beginner or an old hand, the enthusiastic and engaging tone of this site will convert you or enhance your cycling experience. There's plenty of news and features, as well as reviews on bike parts and gadgets, a classified ads section and a selection of links to other biking web sites, all of which are rated. It's also worth checking out **www.bikinguk.net** who are big on mountain biking.

www.letour.fr

TOUR DE FRANCE

ORIGIN FRANCE
INFO ✓✓✓✓
ASE ✓✓✓✓

Written in English and French this site covers the Tour in some depth with details on the teams, riders and general background information.

DARTS

www.embassydarts.com

EMBASSY WORLD DARTS

ORIGIN UK
INFO ✓✓✓✓✓
VEASE ✓✓✓✓

Whether you think darts qualifies as a sport or not, this well-designed site gives a great deal of information about the game, its players and the tournament. See also **www.cyberdarts.com** for more information and good links to other darts sites. For some outstanding advice on how to play the game visit the labour of love that is **www.dartbase.com**

EQUESTRIAN

www.bhs.org.uk

BRITISH HORSE SOCIETY

ORIGIN UK
INFO ✓✓✓✓
EASE ✓✓✓✓

A charity that looks after the welfare of horses, here you can get information on insurance, links, riding schools, competitions, events and trials.

www.horseonline.co.uk

A DEFINITIVE RESOURCE

ORIGIN UK
INFO ✓✓✓✓
EASE ✓✓✓✓

Another excellent horse site with lots of news, features and chat, there's also plenty of advice on buying and looking after your horse.

For more information try:

http://horses.about.com – About.com's excellent suite of pages devoted to all things equestrian.

www.badminton-horse.co.uk – background and information on the famous horse trials with lots of extra features and links.

www.britisheventing.com – an attractive text based site with details on the sport and links.

www.equestria.net – Equestrian ISP and news service.

www.horseandhound.co.uk – excellent magazine site from the leading authority.

EXTREME SPORTS

www.extremesports.com

ACTION PACKED

ORIGIN US
INFO ✓✓✓✓
EASE ✓✓✓✓

A buzzy, in-your-face site that puts over what extreme sports is about really well, using good quality photos and the latest news to give the site immediacy. See also the equally exciting www.adrenalin-hit.com which is probably worth a visit just for the design alone.

www.extreme.com

EXTREME SPORTS CHANNEL

ORIGIN US
INFO ✓✓✓✓
EASE ✓✓✓✓

The official site of the Extreme Sports Channel is hi-tech but quite slow, however once downloaded it's got lots to offer in terms of information, shopping and the latest headlines. For branded clothing for extreme sports see **www.extremepie.com**

FISHING

www.fishing.co.uk

HOME OF UK FISHING ON THE NET

ORIGIN UK
INFO ✓✓✓✓✓
VALUE ✓✓
EASE ✓✓✓✓

A huge site that offers information on where to fish, how to fish, where's the best place to stay near fish, even fishing holidays. There's also advice on equipment, a records section and links to shops and shop locations. Shop on-site for fishing books and magazines.

See also:
www.anglersnet.co.uk – good magazine site with lots of information and chat.
www.anglers-world.co.uk – great for fishing holidays.
www.fishandfly.co.uk – another good magazine site, this one devoted to fly fishing.
www.fisheries.co.uk – excellent for coarse fishing and links.
www.nfsa.org.uk – home of the National Federation of Sea Anglers with lots of links and information.
www.nimpopo.com – basic site with over 3,000 tackle bargains.
www.specialist-tackle.co.uk – excellent store for equipment plus much more in the way of chat and information.
www.tackledirectory.com – a store 'run by anglers for anglers'.

FOOTBALL

www.football365.co.uk

FOOTBALL NEWS

ORIGIN UK
INFO ✓✓✓✓✓
EASE ✓✓✓✓

Probably the best of the football e-zines in terms of the combination of looks, quality writing and features, although it can be a bit dense at times.

It's worth having a look at the sites listed below; just pick the one you like best.

www.bootrevolution.com – all about boots.

www.e-soccer.com – hundreds of links and the latest news.

www.guardian.co.uk/football – great writing and irreverent articles, uncluttered design.

www.onefootball.com – an excellent all-rounder with lots of features.

www.philosophyfootball.com – outspoken and fun, comprehensive too, with some good journalism.

www.planetfootball.com – news, information and OPTA statistics and the world game.

www.soccerage.com – excellent for world soccer, in 10 languages.

www.soccerhighway.com – a strange site but good for links.

www.soccernet.com – well put together from ESPN, comprehensive but a bit boring.

www.teamtalk.com

CHECK OUT THE TEAMS!

ORIGIN UK
INFO ✓✓✓✓✓
VALUE ✓✓✓
EASE ✓✓✓✓

The place to go if you want all the latest gossip and transfer information, it's opinionated but not often wrong. They have around 90 journalists on their books and they also cover rugby and racing too. See also www.footballtransfers.net – get the latest transfer gossip and player news.

www.icons.com

THE WORLD'S LEADING FOOTBALLERS

ORIGIN UK
INFO ✓✓✓✓✓
EASE ✓✓✓✓

Keep up-to-date with transfer news, gossip and hear the word from the players themselves. Each has a page or site devoted to them with a biography and other important details like what they think of their team-mates, an interview, achievements to date and the all important gallery.

www.soccerbase.com

SOCCER STATISTICS

ORIGIN UK
INFO ✓✓✓✓✓
EASE ✓✓✓✓

The site to end all pub rows, it's described as the most comprehensive and up-to-date source of British football data on the Internet.

www.fifa.com

FIFA

ORIGIN SWITZERLAND
INFO ✓✓✓✓✓
EASE ✓✓✓✓

This is FIFA's magazine where you can get information on what they do, the World Cup and other FIFA competitions. For the UEFA go to www.uefa.com where you can see how everyone is faring in the Champions League and UEFA cup.

www.footballaid.com

FOOTBALL CHARITY

ORIGIN UK
INFO ✓✓✓✓
EASE ✓✓✓✓

Football aid is a charity that helps good causes by running football events, you can sign on to play for the team of your choice or just send a cheque.

See also:
www.irishfa.com – the Irish Football Association with a pretty standard site.
www.leaguemanagers.com – home of the League Managers Association.
www.ourweecountry.co.uk – a good fanzine covering football in Northern Ireland.
www.premierleague.com – a top site covering the latest news and information.
www.scotprem.co.uk – a comprehensive offering with links too.
www.welsh-football.net – an independent magazine on the Welsh soccer scene.

GOLF

www.golfix.co.uk

GOLF FIX

ORIGIN UK
INFO ✓✓✓✓✓
EASE ✓✓✓✓

A straightforward and informative site with masses of tips and advice on how to improve your game. Alongside this there's all the information you'd expect from a quality sports site with sections on games, fitness and news.

www.golftoday.co.uk

THE PREMIER ONLINE GOLF MAGAZINE

ORIGIN UK
INFO ✓✓✓✓✓
EASE ✓✓✓✓

An excellent site for golf news and tournaments with features, statistics and rankings and also a course directory. It's the best all-round site covering Europe. There are also links to sister sites about the amateur game, shops and where to stay. Golf Today also hosts a comprehensive site on the amateur game; you can find it at **www.amateur-golf.com**

www.golfweb.com

PGA TOUR

ORIGIN US
INFO ✓✓✓✓✓
EASE ✓✓✓✓

The best site for statistics on the PGA, and keeping up with tournament scores, it also has audio and visual features with RealPlayer. For the official word on the tour go to **www.pga.com** while for the European tour go to **www.europeantour.com**

www.golf.com

THE AMERICAN VIEW

ORIGIN US
INFO ✓✓✓✓✓
EASE ✓✓✓✓

Part of NBC's suite of web sites, this offers a massive amount of information and statistics on the game, the major tours and players, both men and women.

www.uk-golfguide.com

GOLF TOURISM

ORIGIN UK
INFO ✓✓✓✓
EASE ✓✓✓

A useful directory of courses and hotels with courses, with links to travel agents for the UK and abroad, you can also get information on golf equipment suppliers and insurance. See also **www.whatgolf.co.uk**

www.onlinegolf.co.uk

GOLF EQUIPMENT

ORIGIN	UK
INFO	✓✓✓✓
VALUE	✓✓✓
EASE	✓✓✓✓

A good looking and comprehensive golf store with lots of offers and a good range, it has a ladies section, a good search facility and you can trial some clubs for 30 days. Delivery is free for standard postage in the UK. See also **www.golfseller.co.uk** who auction second-hand golf equipment.

See also:
http://golfwebcenter.fol.nl – links to all things golf around the world.
www.fade-fashion.com – golfing equipment and gear.
www.golfingguides.net – authoritative reviews of the best golf courses.
www.golflinks.co.uk – a large, UK-oriented site database.
www.grassrootsgolf.com – for summer camps for junior golfers, corporate golf and golf tours.
www.mygolfzone.com – a good all-rounder.

GYMNASTICS

www.gymmedia.com

GYMNASTIC NEWS

ORIGIN	GERMANY
INFO	✓✓✓✓
EASE	✓✓✓✓

A bilingual site giving all the latest news, it covers all forms of the sport and offers lots of links to related sites.

See also:
www.baga.co.uk – for the official UK gymnastics site, which is comprehensive.
www.intlgymnast.com – the latest news from *International Gymnast* magazine.

HOCKEY

www.hockeyonline.co.uk
THE ENGLISH HOCKEY ASSOCIATION

ORIGIN UK
INFO ✓✓✓✓
VEASE ✓✓✓

A slick site covering the English game with information and chat on the players, leagues and teams for both the men's and the women's games. For the Welsh game go to www.welsh-hockey.co.uk and for the Scottish www.scottish-hockey.org.uk neither are great on design but give all the relevant information. For more links to teams and chat sites check out www.hockeyweb.co.uk

HORSE RACING

For sites that cover the gambling side of horse racing go to page 165.

www.racingpost.co.uk
THE RACING POST

ORIGIN UK
INFO ✓✓✓✓✓
EASE ✓✓✓✓

Superb, informative site from the authority on the sport, every event covered in-depth with tips and advice. To get the best out of it you have to register, then you have access to the database and more.

www.racenews.co.uk
RACING, COURSES AND BETTING

ORIGIN UK
INFO ✓✓✓✓✓
EASE ✓✓✓✓

A slightly different spin from *Racenews*, they have three main sections: their news service, a course guide and a tipsters column, there's also an excellent links section covering racing world-wide.

www.flatstats.co.uk
FLAT RACING STATISTICS

ORIGIN UK
INFO ✓✓✓✓
VALUE ✓✓✓
EASE ✓✓✓✓

This site contains masses of detailed and unique statistics – horse, trainer, jockey, sire and race statistics, favourites analysis, systems analysis and much more. You have to be a member to get the best out of it.

See also:
www.attheraces.co.uk – live action, tips and the
latest news plus great design.
www.bhb.co.uk – the British Horse Racing Board's
excellent site.
www.jockeysroom.com – an A–Z of jockeys with
biographies and pictures.
www.rhtresearch.net – statistics and links from the
Racehorse Holdings Trust.

ICE HOCKEY

www.iceweb.co.uk

THE ICE HOCKEY SUPER-LEAGUE

ORIGIN UK   Keep up-to-date with the scores, the games and the
INFO ✓✓✓✓✓   players, even their injuries. Good for statistics as
EASE ✓✓✓✓   well as news.

www.nhl.com

NATIONAL HOCKEY LEAGUE

ORIGIN US   Catch up on the latest from the NHL including a
INFO ✓✓✓✓   chance to listen to and watch key moments from
EASE ✓✓✓   past and recent games.

See also:
www.britnatleague.co.uk – the British National
League information and news.
www.crazykennys.com – ice hockey equipment
suppliers.
www.azhockey.com – home of the Encyclopaedia
of Ice Hockey.

ICE SKATING

www.bladesonice.com

FIGURE SKATING MAGAZINE

ORIGIN UK   From the magazine *Blades on Ice*, this site features
INFO ✓✓✓✓   archive material, the latest news, details of events,
EASE ✓✓✓✓   advice and of course how to subscribe.

See also:
www.iceskatingworld.com – comprehensive US site
   with excellent links and the latest news.
www.iceskating.org.uk – the official site of the
   National Ice Skating Association of the UK, a good
   looking site covering all aspects of ice skating.

MARTIAL ARTS

www.martial-arts-network.com
PROMOTING MARTIAL ARTS

ORIGIN US
INFO ✓✓✓✓
EASE ✓✓✓

Possibly qualifies as the loudest introduction sequence,
but once you've cut the volume or skipped the intro,
the site offers a great deal in terms of resources and
information about the martial arts scene, including
Black Belts magazine. Its layout is a little confusing
and the site is quite slow.

Beginners should go to www.martialresource.com a
good-looking site which explains the background to
each type of martial art and gives hints and tips to
those just starting out. Martial Info
www.martialinfo.com is another slow but
comprehensive site with an online magazine. While at
http://uk.dir.yahoo.com/recreation/sport/martial_arts
you'll find a huge number of links.

www.britishjudo.org.uk
JUDO

ORIGIN UK
INFO ✓✓✓✓
EASE ✓✓✓✓

Judo has a proud tradition in the UK, and if you want
to follow that you can get all the information you need
at the British Judo Association site. It gives a brief
history of judo, a magazine and event information.
For a broader view go to www.judoinfo.com

www.btkf.homestead.com
BRITISH KARATE FEDERATION

ORIGIN UK
INFO ✓✓✓✓
EASE ✓✓✓✓

Information on all forms of the discipline as well as
events listings, fun pages and an online martial arts
club, which is hosted by Yahoo.

MOTOR SPORT

www.crash.net
MOTORSPORT PORTAL

ORIGIN UK   An excellent but very commercial news and directory
INFO ✓✓✓✓✓   site covering the major motor sports and most of the
EASE ✓✓✓   minor ones too. There's an online shop selling motor
sport merchandise among other things and there's a
good photo library.

www.ukmotorsport.com
INFORMATION OVERLOAD

ORIGIN UK   This site covers every form of motor racing; it's got
INFO ✓✓✓✓✓   lots of links to appropriate sites covering all aspects
EASE ✓✓✓   of motor sport. There are also chat sections and
forums plus links to product and service suppliers.

www.linksheaven.com
THE MOST COMPREHENSIVE LINKS DIRECTORY

ORIGIN US   Whatever, whoever, there's an appropriate link. It
INFO ✓✓✓✓✓   concentrates on Formula 1, CART and Nascar though.
EASE ✓✓✓✓

www.autosport.com
AUTOSPORT MAGAZINE

ORIGIN UK   Excellent for news and features on motor sport plus
INFO ✓✓✓✓✓   links and an affiliated online shopping experience for
VALUE ✓✓✓   related products such as team gear, books or models.
EASE ✓✓✓✓

www.MSport-UK.com
UK MOTOR SPORT

ORIGIN UK   A good newcomer covering all aspects of motor sport
INFO ✓✓✓✓   in Britain, highlights include the 'must see' section
EASE ✓✓✓✓   (I wish more sites had one) and the links page. As
they've kept out clutter it's fast to use.

www.itv-f1.com

F1 ON ITV

ORIGIN UK
INFO ✓✓✓✓✓
EASE ✓✓✓✓✓

This web site is excellent, it doesn't miss much and there is plenty of action. There's all the background information you'd expect plus circuit profiles, schedules and a photo gallery. For more news and links to everywhere in F1 go to www.f1-world.co.uk or the eccentric www.f1nutter.co.uk alternatively try www.f1weekly.net

www.fota.co.uk

FORMULA 3

ORIGIN UK
INFO ✓✓✓✓✓
EASE ✓✓✓✓✓

Formula 3 explained plus info on the teams, drivers and circuits, it's the breeding ground for F1 drivers of the future which adds to the excitement reflected in the energy of this site.

www.rallysport.com

COVERING THE WORLD RALLY CHAMPIONSHIP

ORIGIN UK
INFO ✓✓✓✓
EASE ✓✓✓✓

Good for results and news on rallying in the UK and across the world. See also www.rallyzone.co.uk which is a comprehensive international e-zine. You can follow a race stage by stage at http://rally.racing-live.com/en as well as get all the latest news.

www.btccpages.com

BRITISH TOURING CAR CHAMPIONSHIP

ORIGIN UK
INFO ✓✓✓✓✓
EASE ✓✓✓✓

This site offers a great deal of information and statistics on the championship, driver and team profiles, photos and links to other related sites. There are also a number of forums you can get involved with if you feel like chatting to fellow enthusiasts.

www.karting.co.uk

GO KARTING

ORIGIN UK
INFO ✓✓✓✓✓
EASE ✓✓✓✓

A well laid out portal site to all things karting in the UK, with links and directories covering the tracks, manufacturers, events and a photo gallery plus the latest news.

MOTORCYCLING

www.motorcyclenews.com

NEWS AND VIEWS

ORIGIN UK

INFO ✓✓✓✓✓

EASE ✓✓✓✓

A very good magazine-style site giving all the latest news, gossip and event information, there are also sections on buying a bike, where to get parts and the latest gear, off-road biking and a links directory. There's also a chat room and a good classified section.

www.acu.org.uk

AUTO-CYCLE UNION

ORIGIN UK

INFO ✓✓✓

EASE ✓✓✓✓

The ACU is the governing body for motorcycle sports in the UK and this site gives information on its work and the benefits of being a member. There are also links and details of their magazine.

www.motograndprix.com

TRACK AND OFF-ROAD

ORIGIN UK

INFO ✓✓✓✓

EASE ✓✓✓✓✓

A well laid out magazine site, which covers track grand prix and dirt biking in equal measure, even some of the more obscure areas of the sport, such as snowcross, are covered.

www.british-speedway.co.uk

SPEEDWAY

ORIGIN UK

INFO ✓✓✓

EASE ✓✓✓✓

A much improved site giving information on the leagues as well as the latest news, there's also an events calendar and links to related sites.

www.motocross.com

MOTOCROSS

ORIGIN US

INFO ✓✓✓

EASE ✓✓✓✓

An authoritative site covering the sport but it's centred on the US, although it has got some information on the European scene. See also www.motolinks.com

MOUNTAINEERING AND OUTDOOR SPORTS

www.mountainzone.com

FOR THE UPWARDLY MOBILE

ORIGIN US   Thoroughly covers all aspects of climbing, hiking,
INFO ✓✓✓✓✓   mountain biking, skiing and snowboarding with a
EASE ✓✓✓✓   very good photography section featuring galleries
from major mountains and climbers.

www.ukclimbing.com

CLIMBING NEWS

ORIGIN UK   Excellent and very informative site covering all
INFO ✓✓✓✓✓   aspects of climbing, it has plenty of opportunities for
EASE ✓✓✓✓   chat along with the latest news, there's also weather
information and a very good database of climbs with
comments and essential information for each one.

www.rockrun.com

ALL THE RIGHT EQUIPMENT

ORIGIN UK   Excellent equipment shop covering climbing and
INFO ✓✓✓✓✓   walking gear, which is also pretty comprehensive on
VALUE ✓✓✓   the information front too, delivery starts at £3.50 for
EASE ✓✓✓   the UK. See also **www.gearzone.co.uk** who have a
similar offering.

Other good climbing sites:
www.blacks.co.uk – good camping and
equipment store.
www.cruxed.com – nice looking site with advice on
techniques and training, good links.
www.onward-outward.co.uk – a good outdoor
clothing store with a wide range and the best
brands.
www.outdoorgear.co.uk – everything you need for
the outdoors.
www.thebmc.co.uk – good all-round climbing and
hill-walking magazine-style site from the British
Mountaineering Council with good links pages.
www.upandunder.co.uk – Welsh mountaineering store,
good links section.

NETBALL

www.netball.org

INTERNATIONAL FEDERATION OF NETBALL ASSOCIATIONS

ORIGIN UK
INFO ✓✓✓✓
EASE ✓✓✓✓

Get information on the work of the federation and the rules of the game, plus rankings and the events calendar. See also **www.netballcoaching.com** which is good for advice and links.

OLYMPICS

www.olympics.org

BRITISH OLYMPIC ASSOCIATION

ORIGIN UK
INFO ✓✓✓
EASE ✓✓✓✓

A new look site with sections on the forthcoming winter and summer games, information for collectors and also the doping policy, for a history of the games there's the Olympic museum link and links to sports federations and committees.

See also:
www.olympianartifacts.com – good site featuring an Olympic memorabilia store.
www.olympics.com – the official site of the Olympic movement.

ROWING

www.themassive.com

ONLINE ROWING COMMUNITY

ORIGIN UK
INFO ✓✓✓✓
EASE ✓✓✓✓

A wide ranging and popular site offering articles and features by those involved in the sport, club information and chat.

www.ara-rowing.org

AMATEUR ROWING ASSOCIATION

ORIGIN UK
INFO ✓✓✓✓
EASE ✓✓✓✓

This site offers information on the history of the sport, plus the latest news, coaching tips and links.

See also:

www.steveredgrave.com – Steve's official site offers
biographical information, training instruction and
tips, links and background on the sport.

www.total.rowing.org.uk – a good rowing portal site.

RUGBY

www.scrum.com

RUGBY UNION

ORIGIN	UK
INFO	✓✓✓✓✓
EASE	✓✓✓✓

An excellent site about rugby union with impressively
up-to-the-minute coverage, for a similar but lighter
and more fun site go to **www.planet-rugby.com** which
has a comprehensive round-up of world rugby with
instant reports, lots of detail and information on both
union and league.

www.rfu.com

RUGBY FOOTBALL UNION

ORIGIN	UK
INFO	✓✓✓✓
VALUE	✓✓✓
EASE	✓✓✓✓

Masses of features, articles and news from the official
RFU site, it's got team news and information, links and
a shop where you can buy gear – delivery is free for the
UK for orders under £5.

www.irb.org

INTERNATIONAL RUGBY BOARD

ORIGIN	UK
INFO	✓✓✓✓
EASE	✓✓✓✓

For the official line on rugby union, you will find
all the rules and regulations explained, information
on world tournaments, history of the game, fixtures
and results.

www.rleague.com

WORLD OF RUGBY LEAGUE

ORIGIN	UK
INFO	✓✓✓✓✓
EASE	✓✓✓✓

Another very comprehensive site, featuring sections
on Australia, New Zealand and the UK, with plenty
of chat, articles, player profiles and enough statistics
to keep the most ardent fan happy. See also the
magazine site **www.totalrugbyleague.com** and the
well put together fanzine **www.rlfans.co.uk**, both
have loads of information and chat.

SAILING

www.madforsailing.com

THE DAILY SAIL

ORIGIN UK   An informative and well-laid-out site covering all
INFO ✓✓✓✓   aspects of sailing both as a sport and as a hobby.
EASE ✓✓✓✓   There are some really good and well written articles
                  and features such as a crew search facility and
                  weather information.

www.yachtmonster.com

FOR ALL THINGS YACHTING

ORIGIN US   A combination of search engine, site directory and
INFO ✓✓✓✓✓   news round up all devoted to one subject – yachting.
EASE ✓✓✓✓   See also **www.yachtpeople.com** which has an
                  American bias.

www.ukdinghyracing.com

UK DINGHY RACING

ORIGIN UK   Devoted mainly to this one aspect of sailing, it covers
INFO ✓✓✓✓   the sport comprehensively and gives advice on buying
EASE ✓✓✓✓   and hosts links to auctions and specialist shops.

www.ellenmacarthur.com

ELLEN MACARTHUR

ORIGIN UK   An interesting and well put together site where you
INFO ✓✓✓✓   can find out what Ellen is up to as well as
EASE ✓✓✓✓   biographical details.

SKIING AND SNOWBOARDING

Now a section in its own right. See page 334

SNOOKER

www.embassysnooker.com

WORLD CHAMPIONSHIPS

ORIGIN UK
INFO ✓✓✓✓
VALUE ✓✓✓
EASE ✓✓✓✓

An overview of the world championships from their sponsor, the site is comprehensive and there are good features such as a hall of fame, rankings and a look behind the scenes. See also the informative www.worldsnooker.com which is run by the games governing body.

TENNIS AND RACQUET SPORTS

Tennis

www.lta.org.uk

LAWN TENNIS ASSOCIATION

ORIGIN UK
INFO ✓✓✓✓
VALUE ✓✓✓
EASE ✓✓✓✓

An excellent and attractively designed all-year tennis information site run by the Lawn Tennis Association, it has information on the players, rankings and tournament news, as well as details on clubs and coaching courses. There's also an online tennis shop where you can buy merchandise and equipment. See also www.atptour.com which gives a less UK biased view of the game, with excellent sections on the players, tournaments and rankings.

www.wimbledon.org

THE OFFICIAL WIMBLEDON SITE

ORIGIN UK
INFO ✓✓✓✓
VALUE ✓✓
EASE ✓✓✓✓

Very impressive, there's a great deal here and not just in June, but you need to be patient. Apart from the information you'd expect, you can download screensavers, visit the online museum and eventually see videos of past matches. The shop is expensive.

Other tennis sites worth a look:
www.cliffrichardtennis.org – excellent site aimed at encouraging children to take up the game.
www.pwp.com – a comprehensive tennis and racquet sport related store.
www.racquet-zone.co.uk – a good racquet shop.

www.tennis.com – good magazine, with gear guides,
tips and hot news.

www.tennisnews.com – the latest news updated daily
and e-mailed to you.

Badminton

www.badmintonuk.ndo.co.uk

BRITISH BADMINTON

ORIGIN UK
INFO ✓✓✓✓
EASE ✓✓✓✓

A clear, easy-to-use site packed with information about
badminton, how ladders work, directory of coaches,
club directory, rules, but not much news on the game.

See also:

www.badders.com – the Badminton Community
Network, excellent for news and chat.

www.baofe.co.uk – the site of the Badminton
Association of England with all the latest news.

www.intbadfed.org – home of the International
Badminton Federation.

Squash

www.squashplayer.co.uk

WORLD OF SQUASH AT YOUR FINGERTIPS

ORIGIN UK
INFO ✓✓✓✓✓
EASE ✓✓✓✓✓

A really comprehensive round up of the game, with
links galore and a great news section, there's also a
section for the UK, which has club details and the
latest news. See also www.worldsquash.org for a
good site on what's going on world-wide.

Table tennis

www.ettu.org

EUROPEAN TABLE TENNIS UNION

ORIGIN UK
INFO ✓✓✓✓
EASE ✓✓✓✓

Find out about the ETTU, its rankings, competition
details and results plus a section devoted to world
table tennis links. See also www.ittf.com which gives
a worldview.

TEN PIN BOWLING

www.btba.org.uk
BRITISH TENPIN BOWLING ASSOCIATION

ORIGIN UK
INFO ✓✓✓
EASE ✓✓✓✓

The home of the game in the UK with rules, information on clubs and background on what the governing body does. See also **www.bowluk.co.uk** which is a useful directory of bowling centres, shops, links and events.

WATER SPORTS AND SWIMMING

Swimming

www.swimnews.com
SWIMMING NEWS

ORIGIN UK
INFO ✓✓✓✓
EASE ✓✓✓✓

It's up-to-date and offers a wide coverage of news, with other features such as rankings, events calendar, shopping and competition analysis.

Other good swimming sites:
www.learn-to-swim.co.uk – learn to swim holidays.
www.pullbuoy.co.uk – good site that covers the UK scene, you can find unusual features such as a job finder and time converter.
www.swiminfo.com – US magazine site with articles, information and results.
www.swimmersworld.com – pretty average site with news and links.

Surfing

www.coldswell.co.uk
SURFING THE UK COAST

ORIGIN UK
INFO ✓✓✓✓
EASE ✓✓✓✓

Includes forecasts for weather and surf, satellite images, live surf web cams from around the world and a complete directory of surfing web sites.

See also:
www.surfcall.co.uk – slightly odd site but useful
for regional information.
www.surfline.com – check out weather, sea
conditions, the latest gear – all you need before
you go essentially.
www.surfstation.co.uk – for links, shopping and
surf speak.

www.2xs.co.uk
WINDSURFING IN THE UK

ORIGIN UK
INFO ✓✓✓✓
EASE ✓✓✓✓

Where to go windsurfing, plus tips and the latest
sports news, shopping, weather information
and advice.

Water-ski

www.waterski.com
WORLD OF WATER SKIING

ORIGIN US
INFO ✓✓✓✓
EASE ✓✓✓✓

An American site which features information about
the sport, how to compete, news, tips, equipment and
where to ski. See also www.waterski-az.co.uk for news
and information for the UK.

Diving

www.scubauk.co.uk
SCUBA UK

ORIGIN UK
INFO ✓✓✓✓
EASE ✓✓✓✓

A large directory site with lots of links to all the sites
you'd associate with scuba diving, there are sections
on travel, cave diving, product reviews and you can
submit your best photos for the gallery. Good
design too.

See also:
www.bsac.com – the British Sub Aqua Club, a basic
site with info on what they do.
www.cmas2000.org – the World Underwater
Federation with an odd but informative site.
www.divegirl.com – a magazine site about women and
scuba.
www.padi.com – the place to start when you want to
learn to dive.

www.saa.org.uk – home of the Sub Aqua Association
with links and information.

www.ukdiving.co.uk – a good resource site with the
latest news and links.

WRESTLING

www.wwe.com

WORLD WRESTLING ENTERTAINMENT

ORIGIN US
INFO ✓✓✓✓
VALUE ✓✓✓✓
EASE ✓✓✓✓

Whether you think it's sport or soap opera, here you
can keep up with the twists and turns plus all the
action at this exciting site, which has news, clips
and of course a merchandise shop.

See also:

www.amateurwrestlingnews.com – amateur wrestling
scene with U.S. bias.

www.prowrestling.com – all the latest news and
controversy.

www.wrestle-zone.co.uk – the British wrestling scene
covered.

www.wrestlingusa.com – a more serious and credible
magazine site.

SPORTS CLOTHES AND MERCHANDISE

www.sweatband.com

SHOP BY SPORT

ORIGIN UK
INFO ✓✓✓✓
VALUE ✓✓✓✓
EASE ✓✓✓✓

A wide-ranging shop that supplies equipment for
many sports, but it's especially good for tennis,
rugby and cricket. Delivery costs depend on the
weight of your parcel. See also www.newitts.com
which is comprehensive.

www.kitbag.com

SPORTS FASHION

ORIGIN UK
INFO ✓✓✓✓
VALUE ✓✓✓✓
EASE ✓✓✓✓

Football kits and gear galore from new to retro;
covers cricket and rugby too. Costs on delivery vary
according to order. Also offers shopping by brand and
a news service.

www.sportspages.co.uk

TAKING SPORT SERIOUSLY

ORIGIN UK	Book and video specialists, concentrating on sport,
INFO ✓✓✓✓	they offer a wide range at OK prices, even signed
VALUE ✓✓	copies. Great for that one thing you've been unable
EASE ✓✓✓✓	to find.

www.sportsworld.co.uk

SPORT TRAVEL

ORIGIN UK	Specialists in making travel arrangements to sporting
INFO ✓✓✓✓	events; at this site you can book tickets and find out
VALUE ✓✓✓	about future events. The site is a little temperamental
EASE ✓✓	though and not that easy to use.

www.sportingheritage.co.uk

SPORTING GIFTS

ORIGIN UK	A selection of prints, gifts and collectibles available to
INFO ✓✓✓✓	buy from this well laid out site and they cover all the
VALUE ✓✓✓	major sports.
EASE ✓✓	

Stationery

www.stationerystore.co.uk

STATIONERY STORE

ORIGIN UK	A well designed and easy-to-use stationery store
INFO ✓✓✓✓	supplying everything from paperclips to office
VALUE ✓✓✓✓	machinery. There are also sections on green stationery,
EASE ✓✓✓✓	electronics and lots of offers. Delivery is free for
	orders over £40, £4 if below that.

For other stationery stores try:

www.office-world.co.uk – Office World. You can
print off an order form and fax or e-mail it to them
though; delivery is next day and free if you spend
over £30.

www.staples.co.uk – still no online store, but you can
order a catalogue and find your nearest store.

www.whsmith.co.uk/stationery – another good
W.H.Smith site with some offers and multi-buys but
a limited range which does include some of their
fashion stationery.

www.katespaperie.com

POSH PAPER

ORIGIN US
INFO ✓✓✓✓
VALUE ✓✓
EASE ✓✓✓✓

To many people it's just 'paper with bits in' but for those who pay regular homage to the New York stores, Kate's Paperie represents the best in hand made stationery and wrapping paper. Here you can buy online, but shipping can be expensive.

www.greenstat.co.uk

GREEN STATIONERY

ORIGIN UK
INFO ✓✓✓
VALUE ✓✓✓
EASE ✓✓

Green as in environmentally friendly, they supply a wide range of recycled paper products and desk accessories. It's unsophisticated with delivery costs being well hidden and you have to go through an annoying process of making a note of product code numbers for your order form. It's got good links to other environmentally friendly businesses.

See also:
www.reactivated.co.uk – stationery amongst other recycled products.
www.remarkable.co.uk – for pencils made from recycled plastic cups.

Student Sites

There's masses of information for students on the Net. Here are some sites worth checking out. The links are generally very good, so if the topic isn't covered here, it should be easy to track down.

Universities and colleges

www.ucas.co.uk

THE UNIVERSITY STARTING BLOCK

ORIGIN UK
INFO ✓✓✓✓✓
EASE ✓✓✓✓

A comprehensive site listing all the courses at British universities with entry profiles. You can view the directory online and order your UCAS handbook and application form. If you've already applied, you can view your application online. There are links to all the universities plus really good links to related sites. There is good advice too. If you want to study abroad you can try finding a course through **www.edunet.com**

www.nusonline.co.uk
STUDENTS UNITE

ORIGIN UK
INFO ✓✓✓✓
EASE ✓✓✓

Lots of relevant news and views for students on this really good looking site. You need to register to get access to their discounts directory and special offers. Once in, you can send e-cards and use their mail and storage facilities too.

See also these other useful sites:
www.braintrack.com – a comprehensive directory of links to universities world-wide.
www.britishcouncil.org/education – the student section is full of options for further education and training.
www.careers-portal.co.uk – an excellent portal site that is part of the National Grid for Learning.
www.hotcourses.com – a very good database of courses for students of all levels, with career and money advice thrown in.
www.slc.co.uk – home of the Student Loan Company.
www.ucas.ac.uk/student/index.html – UCAS advice and guidance.
www.unn.ac.uk/~iniw2/bestsite.htm – a useful directory of sites for students.

Working abroad and job finding

www.gapyear.com
COMPLETE GUIDE TO TAKING A YEAR OUT

ORIGIN UK
INFO ✓✓✓✓✓
EASE ✓✓✓✓

Whether you fancy helping out in the forests of Brazil or teaching in Europe you'll find information and opportunities here. There's loads of advice, past experiences to get you tempted, chat, bulletin boards, competitions and you can subscribe to their magazine (an old-fashioned paper one).

www.payaway.co.uk
FIND A JOB ABROAD OR WORKING HOLIDAY

ORIGIN UK
INFO ✓✓✓✓✓
EASE ✓✓✓✓

A great starting place for anyone who wants to work abroad. There is a magazine, reports from travellers and you can register with their online jobs service. They've missed nothing out in their links section from embassies to travel health.

www.anyworkanywhere.com
JOBS IN THE UK AND WORLD-WIDE

ORIGIN UK
INFO ✓✓✓✓
EASE ✓✓✓✓

A bright and breezy site with jobs and all the right advice, plus links.

See also:

www.bunac.co.uk – combine work and travel with these programmes from an experienced specialist.

www.prospects.ac.uk – home of the official graduate careers website offering a huge amount of information, which is packed in a pretty dense website.

Discount cards

www.istc.org
INTERNATIONAL STUDENT TRAVEL CONFEDERATION

ORIGIN UK
INFO ✓✓✓✓
VALUE ✓✓✓✓
EASE ✓✓✓✓

Get your student and youth discount card as well as info on working and studying abroad. Also help with such things as railpasses, phonecards, ISTC registered travel agents world-wide, plus e-mail, voice mail and fax messaging. For a European youth card for discounts within the EU go to the cool **www.euro26.org**

Magazines

www.studentuk.com
STUDENT LIFE

ORIGIN UK
INFO ✓✓✓✓✓
VALUE ✓✓✓✓
EASE ✓✓✓✓

A good-looking, useful and generally well-written students' magazine featuring news, music and film reviews, going out, chat, even articles on science and politics. There's also some excellent advice on subjects such as gap years, accommodation and finance. **www.anythingstudent.com** is also worth a look, it covers just about everything although it could be more fun.

Teenagers

Here's a small selection of the best sites aimed at teenagers.
Many of the most hyped sites are just heavily disguised marketing
and sales operations, treat these with scepticism and enjoy the best,
which are done for the love of it. We've also indicated the sort
of age group that the magazines are aimed at. We should add
our thanks to all those who keep writing in to us suggesting
sites for this section.

Teenage magazines

www.globalgang.org.uk
WORLD NEWS, GAMES, GOSSIP AND FUN

ORIGIN UK
INFO ✓✓✓✓
EASE ✓✓✓

See what the rest of the world gets up to at
Global Gang. You can find out what kids in other
countries like to eat, what toys they play with, chat
to them or play games. Lastly you get to find out
how you can help those kids less fortunate than
yourself. *10 plus*

www.girland.com
GIRL AND...

ORIGIN UK
INFO ✓✓✓✓
EASE ✓✓✓✓

An excellent, really attractive and well put together
site aimed at teenage girls, it has chat forums, news
and lots of features, but you have to register, it has
won loads of awards and the environment is
safe. *11 plus*

www.mykindaplace.com
IT'S MY KINDA PLACE

ORIGIN UK
INFO ✓✓✓✓
EASE ✓✓✓

Excellent site for teens, with the latest news, gossip
and celebrity features, aimed squarely at girls it seems
to have everything, including lots of adverts! *11 plus*

www.teentoday.co.uk
FOR TEENAGERS BY TEENAGERS

ORIGIN UK
INFO ✓✓✓✓✓
EASE ✓✓✓✓

Get your free e-zine mailed to you daily or just visit
the site which has much more; games, chat, news,
entertainment, free downloads, ringtones and message
boards. It's well designed and genuinely good with not
too much advertising. *12 plus*

http://www.bbc.co.uk/teens/

E-ZINES FOR BOTH SEXES

ORIGIN UK
INFO ✓✓✓✓✓
EASE ✓✓✓✓

The BBC have replaced *So* mag with a new site that addresses the loves and concerns of the two sexes. Boys get plenty of games, quizzes, cartoons and useless facts while the girls get a dose of celebs, beauty, horoscopes plus some fun and games too. There are excellent advice and information sections for both sexes and both are treated to some brilliant competitions, prizes and fun articles too. *13 plus*

www.alloy.com

ALLOY MAGAZINE

ORIGIN UK
INFO ✓✓✓✓
VALUE ✓
EASE ✓✓✓

On the face of it this is great, it's got loads of sections on everything from personal advice to shopping. But with too many adverts, it all seems to be geared to getting your name for marketing purposes and selling stuff. *13 plus*

www.cheekfreak.com

FOR THE FREAK IN ALL OF US

ORIGIN US
INFO ✓✓✓✓
VALUE ✓
EASE ✓✓✓✓

Best for stories, online diaries and free downloads. It's got chat sections, message boards and a search engine. They deserve a medal for the pranks section, which is brilliant. *13 plus*

www.cyberteens.com

CONNECT TO CYBERTEENS

ORIGIN UK
INFO ✓✓✓✓
VALUE ✓✓
EASE ✓✓✓✓

One of the most hyped sites aimed at teenagers, it contains a very good selection of games, news, links and a creativity section where you can send your art and poems. Don't bother with the shop, which was still being re-designed at time of writing, but on previous visits it was expensive, as is the credit card they offer. *13 plus*

www.dubit.co.uk

GAMES, ARTICLES – THE LOT

ORIGIN UK
INFO ✓✓✓✓
EASE ✓✓✓✓

Dubit combines 3-D graphics with chat, games, video, music and animations in a fun and interactive way. It's a completely different approach to the normal teen magazine. It needs a little patience but it's worth it in the end. Registration is required which is a pity as it is a pain and very slow. *13 plus*

www.terrifichick.com

A FORUM FOR TEENAGE GIRLS

ORIGIN US
INFO ✓✓✓✓✓
EASE ✓✓✓✓

Recommended by Sherry, one of our readers, this excellent site has loads of advice and articles, although at the time of writing the message boards were being worked on and the site hasn't been updated recently. *13 plus*

www.ipl.org/div/teen/

TEEN SPACE

ORIGIN US
INFO ✓✓✓✓✓
EASE ✓✓✓✓✓

Part of the Internet Public Library, these pages offer a directory of links for help and information on everything from careers, homework, issues, fashion and dating. Not really a magazine but useful anyway. *13 plus*

www.spacegirl.org

FUN AND ANGST

ORIGIN US
INFO ✓✓✓✓
EASE ✓✓✓✓

Get it off your chest, check out the issues, read a good book recommendation, have fun, then dress space girl up. Good looking site, lots to do. Shame about Kyle's haircut. *14 plus*

www.mindbodysoul.gov.uk

GET THE LOW-DOWN ON HEALTH

ORIGIN UK
INFO ✓✓✓✓✓
EASE ✓✓✓✓

A health site for teenagers. It covers all you'd expect, all wrapped up in good looking graphics, it's also not too densely written or too patronising. *14 plus*

www.thesite.org.uk

THE SITE

ORIGIN UK
INFO ✓✓✓✓
EASE ✓✓✓✓

This site offers advice on a range of subjects: careers, relationships, drugs, sex, money, legal issues and so on. Aimed largely at 15 to 24 year olds, it's well laid out and very informative. *15 plus*

www.4degreez.com

INTERACTIVE COMMUNITY

ORIGIN US
INFO ✓✓✓✓
VALUE ✓
EASE ✓✓✓✓

A friendly and entertaining site with reviews, poetry, jokes, polls and links to other related sites. You have to become a member to get the best out of it though. *15 plus*

www.missminx.com

UK'S LEADING ALTERNATIVE GRRL SITE...

ORIGIN UK
INFO ✓✓✓✓
EASE ✓✓✓✓

To quote them 'dedicated to shouting about all that is kick-ass and female, mainly in music, and rock-orientated'.*15 plus*

Directories

www.beritsbest.com

SITES FOR CHILDREN

ORIGIN US
INFO ✓✓✓✓✓
EASE ✓✓✓✓

Over 1,000 sites in this directory split into six major categories; fun, things to do, nature, serious stuff (homework), chat and surfing. Each site is rated for speed and content and you can suggest new sites as well. Another similar site to Berits is **www.kids-space.org** which has some really cute graphics and a better search facility.

www.teensites.org

WEB DIRECTORY FOR TEENS

ORIGIN US
INFO ✓✓✓✓✓
EASE ✓✓✓✓

A huge directory of sites covering loads of subjects of interest to teenagers. It's biased to the USA, but if you don't mind that, then it should have everything you need.

Telecommunications

In this section there's information on ADSL and computer-related communications, where to go to buy mobiles, get the best out of them and even have a little fun with them. For phone numbers see the section entitled 'Finding Someone' on page 131.

www.oftel.gov.uk

OFFICE OF TELECOMMUNICATIONS

ORIGIN UK   A useful site that shows the workings of OFTEL with
INFO ✓✓✓✓   the latest news and consumer information surrounding
EASE ✓✓✓✓   the complex world of telecommunication.

ADSL/BROADBAND

*Asymmetric Digital Subscriber Line (ADSL) is a technology for
transmitting digital information at a high bandwidth on existing
phone lines to homes and businesses. It enables you to access the
Internet many times faster than with conventional phone lines.
Unfortunately, access to broadband is limited and its introduction
slower than in other parts of the world.*

www.btopenworld.com

BRITISH TELECOM

ORIGIN UK   Here you can establish whether you are in line to get
INFO ✓✓✓   access to broadband and more or less when. There are
VALUE ✓✓✓   details of the various BT packages, other suppliers and
EASE ✓✓✓✓   also information for business users too.

> See also:
> **www.adslguide.org.uk** – a good guide to everything
> broadband.
> **www.ispreview.co.uk/broadband.shtml** – informative
> pages from the excellent ISP review.
> **www.ntlhome.com/broadband** – supplies most
> of the UK.
> **www.telewest.co.uk** – supplies selected parts of
> the UK.
> **www.theregister.co.uk** – the latest telecom and
> broadband news.

Mobile phones

www.carphonewarehouse.com

CHOOSING THE RIGHT MOBILE

ORIGIN UK   You need to take your time to find the best tariff
INFO ✓✓✓✓   using their calculator, then take advantage of the
VALUE ✓✓✓✓   numerous offers. Excellent pictures, details of the
EASE ✓✓✓✓

phones and the information is unbiased. There's an online encyclopaedia devoted to mobile phone terminology, a shop that also sells handheld PCs and delivery is free too. You can download a wide range of new phone ring tones, from classical to the latest pop tunes.

See also:

www.b3k.net – excellent site with a wide range of phones and accessories, good for the hard to get bits too.

www.expansys.com – dense site with masses of information and competitive prices.

www.miahtelecom.co.uk – Another good site which, apart from some excellent offers, has a simple tariff calculator.

www.mobileedge.co.uk

MOBILE INFORMATION

ORIGIN UK	A really well-designed site with help on buying the
INFO ✓✓✓✓	right mobile, it also offers information on health and
VALUE ✓✓✓	mobiles, links and contact numbers, pre-pay deals,
EASE ✓✓✓✓	global networks, ring tones, shop and much more.

www.anywhereyougo.com

MOBILE NEWS

ORIGIN UK	Excellent for the latest news and developments, good
INFO ✓✓✓✓✓	links and information too.
EASE ✓✓✓✓	

www.yourmobile.com

NEW RING TUNES FOR YOUR PHONE

ORIGIN UK	There are several hundred tunes, icons and logos
INFO ✓✓✓✓	that you can download onto your mobile using
VALUE ✓✓✓✓	text messaging and most are free. See also
EASE ✓✓✓✓	www.toneylogo.co.uk and also www.onmymob.com
	who offer hundreds of free ringtones and logos.

Here's where to find the major phone operators:
www.o2.co.uk
www.orange.co.uk
www.three.co.uk
www.t-mobile.co.uk
www.virginmobile.com
www.vodafone.co.uk

www.bluetooth.com
AFTER WAP COMES BLUETOOTH

ORIGIN US ✓✓✓✓
INFO ✓✓✓✓
EASE ✓✓✓✓

A superb official Microsoft site devoted to Bluetooth technology which is supposed to come into its own soon. Whether it does or not is still open to question but here's where you can find out about it.

www.chatlist.com/faces.html
TEXT MESSAGING

ORIGIN UK
INFO ✓✓✓✓
EASE ✓✓✓

Confused about your emoticons? %-) Here's a list of several thousand for you to choose from.

www.mediaring.com
PC TO PHONE COMMUNICATION

ORIGIN SINGAPORE
INFO ✓✓✓✓
VALUE ✓✓✓
EASE ✓✓✓✓

Media Ring offer a PC to phone service through their My Voiz technology. This enables users to communicate at a much lower cost than phone to phone, it's especially useful if you use the phone a lot.

www.coverfrenzy.com
DESIGN YOUR OWN PHONE COVER

ORIGIN UK
INFO ✓✓✓✓
VALUE ✓✓✓
EASE ✓✓✓✓

You can use one of their images or one of your own to create a unique phone cover, however it costs £18.50. It's available for a wide range of Nokia phones but their range of options is expanding not only to phones but apparently to hairdryers too.

Television

TV channels, listings and your favourite soap operas are all here – some have great sites, others are pretty naff, especially when you consider they're in the entertainment business.

www.itc.org.uk
INDEPENDENT TELEVISION COMMISSION

ORIGIN UK
INFO ✓✓✓✓
EASE ✓✓✓✓

The ITC issues the licences that allow commercial TV stations to broadcast and ensures fair play on advertising, so if you have a complaint about commercial TV then go here first.

www.tvlicensing.co.uk
TELEVISION LICENCE

ORIGIN UK
INFO ✓✓✓✓
EASE ✓✓✓✓

All you need to know about your TV licence, how to pay and how to deal with problems.

Channels

www.bbc.co.uk
THE UK'S MOST POPULAR WEB SITE

ORIGIN UK
INFO ✓✓✓✓✓
VALUE ✓✓✓
EASE ✓✓✓✓

The BBC site deserves a special feature, it is huge with over 300 sections and it can be quite daunting. This review only scrapes the surface. It has sections covering everything from business to the weather and there are also regional sections, a web guide, as well as tips on how to use the Internet and you can subscribe to a newsletter. Their shopping site is now up and running, and you can also obtain full radio and TV listings by signing up to their ISP **www.beeb.net**

www.itv.co.uk
ITV NETWORK

ORIGIN UK
INFO ✓✓✓
EASE ✓✓✓✓

ITV has a pretty straightforward site with links to all the major programs, soaps, topics and categories, their related web sites and a 'what's on' guide, plus a few extras such as quizzes.

www.citv.co.uk
CHILDREN'S ITV

ORIGIN UK
INFO ✓✓✓✓
EASE ✓✓✓

A bright and breezy site that features competitions, chat, safe surfing, features on the programs including all the favourite characters and much more. You need to join to get the best out of it though, and because there's so much on the site, it can be a little slow.

www.channel4.co.uk
CHANNEL 4

ORIGIN UK
INFO ✓✓✓✓
EASE ✓✓✓

A cool design with details of programmes and links to specific web pages on the best-known ones. There are also links to other initiatives such as Filmfour and the 4learning programme.

www.channel5.co.uk

CHANNEL 5

ORIGIN UK
INFO ✓✓✓✓
EASE ✓✓✓

Similar to Channel 4 except it's better designed and has more in the way of games, shopping and competitions. It's also a bit clearer and easier to find your way around.

www.sky.com

SKY TV

ORIGIN UK
INFO ✓✓✓✓✓
EASE ✓✓✓✓

Links to the main Sky sites – news, sport etc, plus information on their digital packages.

www.nicktv.co.uk

NICKELODEON

ORIGIN UK
INFO ✓✓✓✓
EASE ✓✓✓✓

Bright doesn't do this site justice, you need sunglasses! It's got info on all the top programmes plus games and quizzes.

TV fans and viewing

www.sausagenet.co.uk

CULT AND CLASSIC TV

ORIGIN UK
INFO ✓✓✓✓
VALUE ✓✓✓
EASE ✓✓✓✓

An outstanding nostalgia site devoted to popular children's TV programs from the last 40 years. You can download theme tunes or buy related merchandise via the excellent links directory.

www.televisionheaven.co.uk

PRESERVING TV MEMORIES

ORIGIN UK
INFO ✓✓✓✓✓
EASE ✓✓✓✓

An excellent site devoted to archiving reviews and memories of as many TV favourites they can, a visit is very nostalgic and very time consuming. Good for links too.

www.wwitv.com

WORLD WIDE INTERNET TV

ORIGIN US
INFO ✓✓✓✓
EASE ✓✓✓✓

Watch several international channels, the BBC and listen to radio too. Probably best for broadband users. See also the excellent **www.liketelevision.com** which is very much geared to broadband.

www.standroom.com

TICKETS FOR TV SHOWS

ORIGIN UK
INFO ✓✓✓✓
VALUE ✓✓✓
EASE ✓✓✓✓

If you want to watch a TV show being made or be in the audience, then here's where to go for tickets.

TV review and listings sites

www.digiguide.co.uk

THE DOWNLOADABLE GUIDE

ORIGIN UK
INFO ✓✓✓✓
VALUE ✓✓✓
EASE ✓✓✓✓

If you have Sky digital you'll be familiar with this guide, it follows a similar format, although you can customise it. Simply download the program and you get 14 days forward programming for up to 200 channels, masses of links and background information. You then need to access the site for updates. It costs £6.99 per year.

www.radiotimes.beeb.com

THE RADIO TIMES

ORIGIN UK
INFO ✓✓✓✓✓
EASE ✓✓✓✓

Excellent listings e-zine with a good search facility for looking up programme details, plus competitions, links and a cinema guide. There are also sections on the best-loved TV genres – children's, sci-fi, soaps and so on.

See also:
www.ananova.com/tv – concise TV guide from the Ananova news site.
www.onthebox.com – a simple and effective daily TV guide. Lots of pop-up ads.
www.teletext.co.uk/tvplus – great site, a far cry from the listings you get via your television.
www.tvhome.co.uk – a well designed listings site which includes clips too. You need to download RealPlayer though.

Soaps

www.brookside.com
THE OFFICIAL BROOKSIDE WEB SITE

ORIGIN UK
INFO ✓✓✓✓
VALUE ✓✓✓
EASE ✓✓✓✓

You'll get the latest information, gossip or storyline with loads of background info on the cast. There are competitions and you can shop for Brookie merchandise. With the new animated version you can download clips and take a virtual tour, but be patient and the sound effects are really annoying. There are also links to related programs.

www.corrie.net
CORONATION STREET BY ITS FANS

ORIGIN UK
INFO ✓✓✓✓✓
EASE ✓✓✓✓

Corrie was formed in 1999 from several fan's sites and has no connection with Granada, the site is written by volunteer fans who have contributed articles, updates and biographies. There are five key sections. One for Corrie newbies (are there any?) with a history of the Street; a catch up with the story section; what's up and coming; profiles on the key characters; a chat section where you can gossip about the goings on. For another fan's eye view try out **www.csvu.net**

www.dawsons-creek.com
DAWSON'S CREEK

ORIGIN UK
INFO ✓✓✓✓✓
EASE ✓✓✓✓

Everything is here, storylines, interviews, chat and feedback all packaged on a good looking web site.

www.bbc.co.uk/eastenders
THE OFFICIAL EASTENDERS PAGE

ORIGIN UK
INFO ✓✓✓✓✓
EASE ✓✓✓✓✓

A page from the massive BBC site, it's split into several sections: catch up on the latest stories and hints on future storylines; play games and competitions; get pictures of the stars; vote in their latest poll; reminisce and visit the 'classic clips' section; take a virtual tour and view Albert Square with the Walford Cam.

www.hollyoaks.com

THE OFFICIAL HOLLYOAKS WEB SITE

ORIGIN UK
INFO ✓✓✓✓✓
EASE ✓✓✓✓✓

A very cool site with lots on it, you can subscribe to the fortnightly newsletter; peek behind the scenes; catch up on the latest news; chat with fellow fans. There's also the expected photos and downloads to be had.

www.baxendale.u-net.com/ramsayst

NEIGHBOURS WORLD-WIDE FANPAGES

ORIGIN UK
INFO ✓✓✓✓✓
EASE ✓✓✓✓

You can also get them at **www.ramsay-street.co.uk**
This is a labour of love by the fans of Neighbours, it has everything you need: storylines past, present and future; info on all the characters; clips from some episodes; complete discographies of the singing stars; and access to all the related web sites through the links page. Unfortunately, you can't buy Neighbours merchandise from the site.

www.soapweb.co.uk

THE LATEST SOAP NEWS

ORIGIN UK
INFO ✓✓✓✓✓
EASE ✓✓✓✓

Can't be bothered with visiting each site separately? Then try Soap Web. Here you can keep up-to-date on all the soaps, even the Australian and American ones.

www.bbc.co.uk/radio4/archers

THE ARCHERS

ORIGIN UK
INFO ✓✓✓✓✓
EASE ✓✓✓✓

OK so it's not strictly TV but we couldn't think where else this should go. It's a great site with all the information and background you'd wish for including the ability to listen to the last episode and catch up on previous ones.

Theatre

Here's a great selection of sites that will appeal to theatre goers everywhere.

www.whatsonstage.com
HOME OF BRITISH THEATRE

ORIGIN UK
INFO ✓✓✓✓✓
VALUE ✓✓✓
EASE ✓✓✓✓

A really strong site with masses of news and reviews to browse through plus a very good search facility and booking service (through a third party), a real theatre buff's delight.

www.aloud.com
ONLINE TICKET SEARCH

ORIGIN UK
INFO ✓✓✓✓
VALUE ✓✓✓
EASE ✓✓✓✓

You can search by venue, location or by artist, it's fast and pretty comprehensive and there's a hot events section – it mainly covers music and festivals, nowadays though it's good for comedy. The review section is good and you can buy tickets.

www.theatrenet.com
THE ENTERTAINMENT CENTRE

ORIGIN UK
INFO ✓✓✓✓✓
VALUE ✓✓✓
EASE ✓✓✓

Get the latest news, catch the new shows and, if you join the club, there are discounts on tickets for theatre, concerts, sporting events and holidays. You can also search their archives for information on past productions and learn how to become a theatre angel.

www.uktheatre.net
PASSIONATE ABOUT THEATRE

ORIGIN UK
INFO ✓✓✓✓
EASE ✓✓✓✓

Whether you're a fan or an actor this site has much to offer both as a useful source of information and as a good site directory.

www.uktw.co.uk
UK THEATRE WEB

ORIGIN UK
INFO ✓✓✓✓
VALUE ✓✓✓
EASE ✓✓✓✓

A cheerful site offering all the usual information on theatre plus amateur dramatics, jobs, chat, competitions and just gossip.

www.rsc.org.uk

THE ROYAL SHAKESPEARE COMPANY

ORIGIN UK
INFO ✓✓✓✓
EASE ✓✓✓

Get all the news as well as information on performances and tours. You can book tickets online although it's via a third party site.

www.reallyuseful.com

ANDREW LLOYD WEBBER

ORIGIN UK
INFO ✓✓✓✓
EASE ✓✓✓

At this attractive, hi-tech site you can watch video and listen to top audio clips, download screen savers and wallpaper, take part in competitions and chat. There's also a good kids' section plus details on the shows.

www.nt-online.org

THE NATIONAL

ORIGIN UK
INFO ✓✓✓✓✓
EASE ✓✓✓✓

Excellent for details of their shows and forthcoming plays with tour information added. You can't buy tickets online, but you can e-mail or fax for them.

www.officiallondontheatre.co.uk

SOCIETY OF LONDON THEATRES

ORIGIN UK
INFO ✓✓✓✓✓
VALUE ✓✓✓
EASE ✓✓✓✓

The latest news, a show finder service and hot tickets are just a few of the services available at this great site. You can also get a theatreland map, half price tickets and they'll even fax you a seating plan. See also www.thisislondon.co.uk who have a good theatre section.

To book online try the following sites:
www.ticketmaster.co.uk
www.londontheatretickets.com
www.uktickets.co.uk
www.lastminute.com

Travel and Holidays

Travel is the biggest growth area on the Internet, from holidays to insurance to local guides. If you're buying, then it definitely pays to shop around and try several sites, but be careful, it's amazing how fast the best deals are being snapped up. You may find that you still spend time on the phone, but the sites are constantly improving. The amount of information available is staggering and it's no wonder this is the biggest section in the book.

Starting out

www.abtanet.com

ABTA

ORIGIN UK
INFO ✓✓✓✓
EASE ✓✓✓✓

Make sure that the travel agent you choose is a member of the Association of British Travel Agents as then you're covered if they go bust halfway through your holiday. All members are listed and there's a great search facility with links for you to start the ball rolling. See also the Air Travellers Licensing home page **www.atol.org.uk** which is part of the Civil Aviation site.

www.brochurebank.co.uk

BROCHURES DELIVERED TO YOUR HOME

ORIGIN UK
INFO ✓✓✓✓
EASE ✓✓✓✓✓

Holiday brochures from over 150 companies can be selected then delivered to your home, free of charge. The selection process is easy and the site is fast. Delivery is by second class post.

www.tourismconcern.org.uk

ETHICAL TOURISM

ORIGIN UK
INFO ✓✓✓✓✓
EASE ✓✓✓✓

If you're concerned about the impact of your trip, then come here for advice or help with one of their campaigns. It all goes to ensuring that the poorest holiday workers are not exploited.

Travel information, news and tips

www.fco.gov.uk/travel

ADVICE FROM THE FOREIGN OFFICE

ORIGIN UK
INFO ✓✓✓✓✓
EASE ✓✓✓

Before you go, get general advice, safety or visa information. Just select a country and you get a run-down of all the issues that are likely to affect you when you go there, from terrorism to health.

For more travel safety information go to:

www.1000traveltips.org – tips from the very well travelled Koen De Boeck and friends.

www.cdc.gov/travel – official American site giving sensible health information world-wide.

www.etravel.org – masses of tips to browse through from book reviews to flying advice and weather updates.

www.flyingwithkids.com – sensible air travel advice for those travelling with babies and small children.

www.tips4trips.com – all the tips come from well-meaning travellers and are categorised under sections such as pre-planning, what and how to pack, travelling for the disabled, for women, for men or with children.

www.tripprep.com – country-by-country risk assessment covering health, safety and politics; it can be a little out of date so check with the foreign office as well.

www.travel-news.org

TRAVEL NEWS ORGANISATION

ORIGIN UK
INFO ✓✓✓✓
EASE ✓✓✓

A good, travel magazine aimed at British travellers packed with the latest news and information, as well as destination reports and event listings. There are also links to airlines, special offers and specialist holidays.

www.guardian.co.uk/travel

FROM THE GUARDIAN NEWSPAPER

ORIGIN UK
INFO ✓✓✓✓✓
EASE ✓✓✓✓

A good reflection of the excellent *Guardian* weekly travel section with guides, information and inspiration throughout, there's also the latest news and links to sites with offers plus extra features such as audio guides and articles on parts of the UK.

www.vtourist.com

THE VIRTUAL TOURIST

ORIGIN UK
INFO ✓✓✓✓
EASE ✓✓✓

Explore destinations in a unique and fun way. Travellers describe their experiences, share photos, make recommendations and give tips so others benefit from their experience. See also **www.travel-library.com** which is less entertaining but combines recommendation with hard facts very well.

www.budgettravel.com

BUDGET TRAVEL

ORIGIN UK
INFO ✓✓✓✓
EASE ✓✓✓

Masses of links and information for the budget traveller plus advice on how to travel on the cheap. It can be difficult to navigate but the information is very good.

See also:
www.nytimes.com/pages/travel/index.html – travel news and information from the *New York Times*.
www.zyworld.com/brancatelli – excellent site, albeit a little staid, devoted to tips for the business traveller.

Travel services and information

www.johnnyjet.com

TRAVEL PORTAL

ORIGIN US
INFO ✓✓✓✓✓
EASE ✓✓✓✓✓

Very detailed and comprehensive portal site devoted to all things travel-related, it's well categorised but has an American bias. See also **www.thetravelportal.com** who have an excellent set of links from a bigger web directory.

www.webofculture.com/worldsmart/gestures.html
GESTURES OF THE WORLD

ORIGIN UK	Country-by-country, what gestures mean, what not
INFO ✓✓✓✓	to do and what's best to do, all in a concise format.
EASE ✓✓✓✓	Be warned, that you have to go through a really
	laborious registration process to get the information.

www.whatsonwhen.com
WORLD-WIDE EVENTS GUIDE

ORIGIN UK	An easy-to-use site with information on every type
INFO ✓✓✓✓	of event you can think of from major festivals to
EASE ✓✓✓✓	village fêtes.

www.ukpa.gov.uk
UK PASSPORTS

ORIGIN UK	Pre-apply for your passport online and get tips on how
INFO ✓✓✓✓	to get the best passport photo amongst other very
EASE ✓✓✓✓	useful information.

www.hmce.gov.uk
HM CUSTOMS AND EXCISE

ORIGIN UK	All you need to know about visiting the UK, exporting
INFO ✓✓✓✓	and importing and the regulations surrounding what
EASE ✓✓✓✓	you can bring in.

www.visaservice.co.uk
QUICK VISA

ORIGIN UK	This service will get you your visa in double quick
INFO ✓✓✓✓	time, for a price.
VALUE ✓✓✓	
EASE ✓✓✓	

www.travelhealth.co.uk
STAY HEALTHY

ORIGIN UK	An authoritative site with sections on general health
INFO ✓✓✓✓✓	advice, disease prevention, a shop and links. See also
VALUE ✓✓✓	www.travelhealthresource.com
EASE ✓✓✓✓✓	

www.worldtimezone.com
TIME ZONE MAP

ORIGIN	US	Useful time zone mapping, although it's heavily
INFO	✓✓✓✓	advert laden.
EASE	✓✓✓	

www.bananabuzz.com
GET BACK IN TOUCH

ORIGIN	UK	OK so you've had your holiday and lost touch with
INFO	✓✓✓✓	all those friends you've made, here's where to go. It's
EASE	✓✓✓✓	a sort of Friends Reunited for backpackers basically.
		There's also chat and messaging services.

www.goplaces.co.uk
BUYING LUGGAGE

ORIGIN	UK	A wide range and with some good offers this store is
INFO	✓✓✓✓	worth a visit if you have to replace that tatty old case.
VALUE	✓✓✓	
EASE	✓✓✓✓	

www.excessluggage.co.uk
EXCESS LUGGAGE

ORIGIN	UK	For problems concerning excess baggage here's the
INFO	✓✓✓✓	place to go, there are lots of options and it's best to
VALUE	✓✓✓	discuss your requirements with them.
EASE	✓✓✓✓	

Travel money and insurance

www.xe.net/currency
ONLINE CURRENCY CONVERTER

ORIGIN	UK	The Universal Currency Converter could not be easier
INFO	✓✓✓✓✓	to use, just select the currency you have, then the one
EASE	✓✓✓✓✓	you want to convert it to, press the button and you
		have your answer in seconds. See also
		www.oanda.com and you could also try
		www.x-rates.com/calculator.html

www.royalmail.com
CASH FOR THE TRAVELLER

ORIGIN UK
INFO ✓✓✓✓
EASE ✓✓✓✓

Order your currency online at 0% commission, then pick it up and pay at your nearest Post Office, alternatively you can arrange for next day home delivery. They also offer a money transfer service to send money either within the UK or to 55,000 locations in 155 countries which is particularly useful if the recipient doesn't have a bank account. Postal orders can also be bought online and cashed in 47 countres. Other services include travel insurance, medical advice, traveller's tips and passport help including info on which branches will check your completed passport application forms. Really helpful.

www.onlinefx.co.uk
FOREIGN CURRENCY DELIVERED

ORIGIN UK
INFO ✓✓✓✓
EASE ✓✓✓✓

A pretty straightforward and potentially hassle free way of getting your currency, just order with your card and it gets delivered the next working day. There are also other financial services available such as international transfers. See also www.simplyfx.com

www.travelinsuranceclub.co.uk
AWARD WINNING TRAVEL INSURANCE CLUB

ORIGIN UK
INFO ✓✓✓✓
VALUE ✓✓✓✓
EASE ✓✓✓

Unfortunately there isn't one site for collating travel insurance yet, it's a question of shopping around. These sites make a good starting point offering a range of policies for backpackers, family and business travel.

All these companies offer flexibility and good value:
www.columbusdirect.co.uk – good information, nice, but fiddly web site and competitive prices.
www.costout.co.uk – well rated and good value.
www.direct-travel.co.uk – nice design and some good offers too, online quotes.
www.jameshampden.co.uk – wide range of policies, straightforward and hassle free.
www.underthesun.co.uk – good for annual and six monthly policies.
www.world-wideinsure.com – good selection of policies, instant online cover.

Travel shops

www.expedia.co.uk

THE COMPLETE SERVICE

ORIGIN US/UK
INFO ✓✓✓✓✓
VALUE ✓✓✓
EASE ✓✓✓✓

This is the UK arm of Microsoft's very successful online travel agency. It offers a huge array of holidays, flights and associated services, for personal or business use, nearly all bookable online. Its easy and quicker than most, and there are some excellent offers too. Not the trendiest but it's a good first stop. As with all the big operators, you have to register. They've also got sections on travel insurance, mapping, guides, ferries and hotels.

www.lastminute.com

DO SOMETHING LAST MINUTE

ORIGIN UK
INFO ✓✓✓✓
VALUE ✓✓✓✓
EASE ✓✓✓✓

Last Minute has an excellent reputation not just as a travel agent, but as a good shopping site too. For travellers there are comprehensive sections on hotels, holidays and flights, all with really good prices. There is also a superb London restaurant guide and a general entertainment section. Mostly, you can book online, but a hotline is available.

www.thomascook.com

THE WIDEST RANGE OF PACKAGE HOLIDAYS

ORIGIN UK
INFO ✓✓✓✓
VALUE ✓✓✓✓
EASE ✓✓✓✓

This site is easy to use and well laid out and, with over 2 million package holidays to chose from, you should be able to find something to your liking. You can also browse the online guide for ideas or search for cheap flights or holiday deals. Again you have to call the hotline to book.

www.e-bookers.com

FLIGHTBOOKERS

ORIGIN UK
INFO ✓✓✓✓✓
VALUE ✓✓✓✓
EASE ✓✓✓✓

Acclaimed travel agents specialising in getting good flight deals, but also good for holidays, special offers and insurance.

www.travel.world.co.uk

FOR ALL YOUR TRAVEL REQUIREMENTS

ORIGIN UK
INFO ✓✓✓✓✓
VALUE ✓✓✓✓
EASE ✓✓✓✓

A massive, comprehensive site, it basically includes most available travel brochures with links to the relevant travel agent. It concentrates on Europe, so there are very few American sites, but provides links to hotels, specialist holidays, cruises, self-catering and airlines.

www.holidayauctions.net

BID FOR YOUR HOLIDAY

ORIGIN UK
INFO ✓✓✓
VALUE ✓✓✓
EASE ✓✓✓✓

Some amazing bargains are available from these auction sites – you bid in the same way a normal online auction works. It's fully bonded and if you hit a problem call their hotline. They also sell conventional holidays.

www.uk.mytravel.com

SEARCH FOR THE RIGHT DEAL

ORIGIN UK
INFO ✓✓✓✓
VALUE ✓✓✓✓
EASE ✓✓✓✓

This site has got an excellent search engine that enables you to find a bargain or just the right holiday, there are also good offers and the late escapes holiday auction site.

www.priceline.co.uk

LET SOMEONE ELSE DO THE WORK

ORIGIN UK
INFO ✓✓✓✓
VALUE ✓✓✓✓
EASE ✓✓✓✓

You could leave it to someone else to do the travel searching for you, here you provide details of the trip you want and how much you're willing to pay, then they try to find a deal that will match your requirements. If you're flexible about timing then there are some great offers. They cover flights, hotels and car hire. Another site to try is **www.myownprice.com** both this site and Priceline want your credit card details before you agree to any transaction so you may feel more comfortable using a more traditional route.

Online Travel Agents

Here's a selection of well-proven and independent online travel agents sorted by type.

BACKPACKING, ECOTOURISM, ACTIVITY AND ADVENTURE

www.changingworlds.co.uk – it wasn't all up and running but shows outstanding site design and presentation from a company that helps people find worthwhile working holidays.

www.exploreworld-wide.com – adventure holidays from around the world.

www.gvillage.co.uk – specialising in independent travellers and students with some great deals and adventure holidays to the world's most interesting places, excellent round the world trip planner.

www.igougo.com – more of an information exchange for global travellers but you can book trips through them, there are plenty of features and the IgoUgo awards too.

www.inntravel.co.uk – specialists in walking holidays, excellent, informative site.

www.international-academy.com – life changing experiences through sport and travel.

www.madadventurer.com – excellent site design with loads of mad adventures to choose from by way of helping community development in 23 countries.

www.spicemcr.com – vibrant activity and social club with holidays to match.

www.theleap.co.uk – similar approach to Mad Adventurer but based in Africa.

BARGAIN DEALS

www.bargainholidays.com – probably the best for quick breaks, excellent for late availability offers.

www.firstchoice.co.uk – bargains from First Choice holidays. See also the sister site found at **www.travelchoice.co.uk** – discounts for online booking.

www.holiday.co.uk – good deals on package holidays from a very well designed site.

www.packageholidays.co.uk – late bargain holidays and flights from over 130 tour operators including Thomson, Sunworld, Airtours and specialist agents.

GENERAL TRAVEL AGENTS

www.aito.co.uk – offers and information from the Association of Independent Tour Operators, excellent for the unusual.

www.beachtowel.co.uk – good all-round site from an independent travel agent who is ABTA and ATOL covered.

www.firstresort.com – a good general site with some good deals and a price promise, owned by Thomsons.

www.lunn-poly.co.uk – updating the site at time of writing.

www.opodo.co.uk – slick newcomer from some of the major airlines, worth checking out for flight offers.

www.teletext.co.uk/holidays – much better than browsing the TV, you can now get all those offers on one easy-to-use site. There is also lots of useful travel information to help you on your way.

www.thisistravel.co.uk – in association with the newspaper group that publishes the *Daily Mail*, this is a comprehensive offering with some good offers. Lots of pop-up ads too.

www.travelagents.co.uk – another all-rounder, nothing special but competent.

www.travelbag.co.uk – straightforward and easy to use flight and holiday finder.

www.travelcareonline.com – loads of deals and honest information from the UK's largest independent.

www.travelfinder.co.uk – lots of options and great bargains at this simple-to-use site.

www.travelocity.com – one of the oldest online travel agents; it's similar to Expedia and there's a reward scheme too. The trip expert facility is a fun planning tool.

www.travelmood.com – follows the standard site design for an all-rounder, has some good offers though.

www.tripsworld-wide.co.uk – despite the name it specialises in Latin America and the Caribbean. Some beautiful photography enhances the site.

LUXURY AND TAILOR-MADE

www.abercrombiekent.com – one of the most
   experienced luxury travel operators with a
   very competent site.

www.amanresorts.com – exclusive hotels and villas
   in gorgeous locations.

www.audleytravel.com – tailor made itineraries for
   escorted groups.

www.balesworld-wide.com – for something
   special, tailor-made holidays to the exotic parts
   of the world; hi-tech site is excellent but no
   online booking.

www.bridgetheworld.com – a good site from this
   multi-award winning company.

www.carrier.co.uk – luxury holiday specialists, nice
   looking site too.

www.coxandkings.co.uk – a slightly disappointing
   site from one of the oldest travel companies.

www.essentialescapes.com – exclusive luxury
   spa holidays.

www.exsus.com – tailor-made luxury adventures.

www.hayesandjarvis.co.uk – long haul holiday
   specialists, lots to choose from.

www.itcclassics.co.uk – luxury everything basically.

www.jewelholidays.com – Goa, India, Turkey
   and Cambodia.

www.originaltravel.co.uk – holidays for activity
   and well-being, outstanding site design too.

www.pura-aventura.com – active holidays in comfort,
   mainly Latin America and Spain.

www.rbrww.com – opulence and fishing.

www.seasonsinstyle.co.uk – world-wide luxury in the
   world's finest hotels.

www.tailor-made.co.uk – basic site but the holiday
   options look good.

www.world-widejourneys.co.uk – tailor made
   packages, especially experienced in wildlife holidays.

SPECIALIST AGENCIES

www.divechannel.co.uk – excellent site specialising
   in diving holidays and travel.

www.footprint-adventures.co.uk – birding, trekking and wildlife all over the world.

www.golfbreaks.com – a travel agent specialising in holidays for golfing nuts.

www.regaldive.co.uk – learn to dive in the best diving locations.

www.webweekends.co.uk – specialists in weekend breaks both in the UK and abroad.

www.wildlifeworld-wide.com – world-wide wildlife holidays.

VILLAS

www.jamesvillas.co.uk – over 500 villas in the Med.

www.ownerssyndicate.com – a wide choice with some good offers.

www.villa-rentals.com – villas world-wide, some look outstanding.

www.cvtravel.net – passionate about villas, mainly in Europe.

CRUISES

www.cruiseinformationservice.co.uk

CRUISE INFO

ORIGIN UK
INFO ✓✓✓✓
EASE ✓✓✓✓

A trade site put together to encourage people to take cruise holidays. There's an introduction to cruising, information on the cruise lines, a magazine and links to useful sites. There's also information on how to book and what sort of cruise is right for you.

See also:

www.cruisedeals.co.uk – easy to use, a little sparse on info but some good offers.

www.cruise-direct.com – information, advice and good prices.

www.cruiseline.co.uk – a great site from one the UK's leading specialist cruise companies.

www.cruisesandvoyages.com – cruise specialist with a basic site and some good deals.

www.psa-psara.org – useful information from the Passenger Shipping Association.

Airline and flight sites

www.cheapflights.co.uk

NOTHING BUT CHEAP FLIGHTS

ORIGIN UK
INFO ✓✓✓✓✓
VALUE ✓✓✓✓✓
EASE ✓✓✓

You don't need to register here to explore the great offers available from this site; you still need to phone some of the travel agents or airlines listed to get your deal though and some of the prices quoted seem magically to disappear once you've clicked on the link. Having said that, there are obviously some great deals to be had.

www.netflights.com

THE AIRLINE NETWORK

ORIGIN UK
INFO ✓✓✓✓
VALUE ✓✓✓✓
EASE ✓✓✓

Discount deals on over 100 airlines world-wide make The Airline Network worth checking out for their flight offers page alone. It's good for flights from regional airports. They also do all the traditional travel agent things and there are some good holiday bargains too.

www.deckchair.com

RELAX WITH DECKCHAIR

ORIGIN UK
INFO ✓✓✓✓✓
VALUE ✓✓✓✓
EASE ✓✓✓

A much improved site where you can get some good flight bargains as well as plan the rest of your holiday.

For more cheap flight deals try these sites:
www.bargainflights.com – good search facility and plenty of offers, but you need to be patient.
www.dreamticket.com – the usual flight offers, but the site also offers much in the way of information too.
www.easyjet.co.uk – great for a limited number of destinations, particularly good for UK flights. See also **www.easyvalue.co.uk**
www.flightcentre.com – they guarantee to beat any genuine current quoted airfare!
www.ryanair.com – very good for Ireland, northern Europe, Italy and France. Clear and easy to use web site, massive discounts.

www.travelselect.com – good flight selection and
lots of different options available at this very
flexible site.

Airport and airline information

www.worldairportguide.com

WHAT ARE THE WORLD'S AIRPORTS REALLY LIKE?

ORIGIN GERMANY
INFO ✓✓✓✓
EASE ✓✓✓✓

It seems that no matter how out of the way, this
guide has details on every airport – how to get
there, where to park, facilities, key phone numbers
and a map. There are also guides on cities, resorts
and even world weather.

www.baa.co.uk

BRITISH AIRPORT AUTHORITY

ORIGIN UK
INFO ✓✓✓✓
VALUE ✓✓✓✓
EASE ✓✓✓✓

Details on all the major UK airports that are run by
the BAA, you get all the essential information plus
flight data, weather and shopping information.

www.airlinequality.com

RANKING THE AIRLINES

ORIGIN UK
INFO ✓✓✓✓
EASE ✓✓✓✓

An independent ranking of all the world's airlines and
their services, see who's the best and the worst and
why. Each airline is rated using a number of stars (up
to 5) on criteria such as seat quality, catering and staff.

The key airlines:
www.aerlingus.ie – good easy to use site.
www.airfrance.co.uk – plenty of offers.
www.airindia.com – good offers and travel
information and destination guide.
www.britishairways.co.uk – easy to use, efficient site.
www.emirates.com – no frills design and flight
booking facilities.
www.flybmi.com – British Midland, good offers
for European destinations.
www.cathaypacific.com – comprehensive flight
service and guide.
www.virgin-atlantic.com – good online booking
facility with some offers.

www.klm.com – good design with lots of offers.

www.lufthansa.co.uk – masses of information and express booking.

www.quantas.com – straightforward booking facility.

www.ual.com – United Airlines offers a good all round service for this site.

Airport parking

www.bcponline.co.uk

BOOK YOUR SPACE

ORIGIN UK	Easy to use and with some good savings on
INFO ✓✓✓✓	airport car park rates.
VALUE ✓✓✓✓	
EASE ✓✓✓✓	*See also*

www.holidayextras.co.uk who are also good for parking, airport hotels, airport lounges and also has information on getting to airports by public transport.

Hotels and places to stay

www.hotelguide.com

COMPREHENSIVE

ORIGIN UK	With services available in eight languages and
INFO ✓✓✓✓✓	specialist sections such as golfing breaks, this site
VALUE ✓✓✓✓	ranks among the best for finding the right hotel.
EASE ✓✓✓✓	It lists around 85,000 at time of writing.

www.hiphotels.net

FOR THE HIPPEST HOTELS

ORIGIN UK	Excellent for the unusual, it's a directory of the
INFO ✓✓✓✓✓	unique and off-beat with good illustrations of each
EASE ✓✓✓✓	hotel, not much in the way of deals, but then they
	are very special.

www.from-a-z.com

A–Z OF HOTELS

ORIGIN UK	A well-designed British site with over 15,000
INFO ✓✓✓✓	hotels to choose from in the UK, Eire and France
VALUE ✓✓✓	and a further 40,000 world-wide, it's quick and easy
EASE ✓✓✓	to use and there's online booking available plus
	plenty of special discounts.

Other good hotel directory and booking sites:

www.all-hotels.com – 60,000 hotels listed with lots of options, American bias.

www.best-inn.co.uk – another directory of 60,000 hotels, very good for London and links to specialist accommodation.

www.discount25.com – great for hotel discounts, primarily in Spain but also the major European cities.

www.holidayleaders.com – if you need a villa or want self catering.

www.laterooms.co.uk – easy to use directory featuring unsold hotel rooms at great prices.

www.openworld.co.uk – a collection of links to hotel sites, just use the interactive world map.

www.placestostay.com – another with an interactive map, you drill down until you find the place you want to stay, then you get a list of hotels, a description, price and online reservation service.

Travel guides

www.mytravelguide.com

ONLINE TRAVEL GUIDES

ORIGIN US
INFO ✓✓✓✓✓
EASE ✓✓✓

A general American travel site that offers a good overview of most countries, with points of interest, a currency converter, very good interactive mapping and live web cams too. You need to become a member to get the best out of it though.

www.lonelyplanet.com

LONELY PLANET GUIDES

ORIGIN UK
INFO ✓✓✓✓✓
VALUE ✓✓✓✓
EASE ✓✓✓✓✓

A superb travel site, aimed at the independent traveller, but with great information for everyone. Get a review on most world destinations or pick a theme and go with that; leave a message on the Thorn Tree; find out the latest news by country; get health reports; read about the travel experiences of others – what's the real story? They've revamped the site since we last visited, now it's better organised and even easier to find your way around.

http://travel.roughguides.com
ROUGH GUIDES
ORIGIN UK
INFO ✓✓✓✓✓
VALUE ✓✓✓
EASE ✓✓✓✓

Lively reviews on a huge number of places – some 14,000. In addition, there's general travel information, a place to share your travel thoughts with other travellers, or you can buy a guide. Excellent for links and you can get some good deals via the site.

www.fodors.com
FODOR'S GUIDES
ORIGIN US
INFO ✓✓✓✓✓
EASE ✓✓✓

These guides give an American perspective, but there is a huge amount of information on each destination. The site is well laid out and easy to use.

http://kasbah.com
WORLD'S LARGEST TRAVEL GUIDE
ORIGIN UK
INFO ✓✓✓✓
EASE ✓✓✓✓

Clear information, stacks of links and a good search engine should mean that you will find the low down on most destinations. The highlights on each destination are useful and the 'Global Travel Toolbox' provides info, telecommunications, maps, currency and more. Unfortunately, some of the site's links were not working when we visited.

www.packback.com
PACKBACK TRAVEL GUIDE
ORIGIN UK
INFO ✓✓✓✓
VALUE ✓✓✓
EASE ✓✓✓✓

A good looking and useful site with an independent travel guide, a growing membership and a reputation for quality reviews. It includes a discussion forum, travel tools and flight booking.

www.gorp.com
FOR THE GREAT OUTDOORS
ORIGIN US
INFO ✓✓✓✓✓
EASE ✓✓✓

A great title, Gorp is dedicated to adventure, whether it be hiking, mountaineering, fishing, snow sports or riding the rapids. It has an American bias, but is full of relevant good advice, links and information.

www.timeout.com
TIME OUT GUIDE

ORIGIN UK
INFO ✓✓✓✓
EASE ✓✓✓✓

A slick site with destination guides covering many European cites and some further afield such as New York and Sydney. Not surprisingly, it's outstanding for London and you can also book tickets and buy books via other retailers.

www.bradmans.com
BRADMAN'S FOR BUSINESS TRAVELLERS

ORIGIN US
INFO ✓✓✓✓✓
EASE ✓✓✓✓

A really excellent city guide with none of your fancy graphics, just a straightforward listing of countries and sensible information on each one, includes tips on orienting yourself in the city and restaurant reviews.

Other global guides worth checking out are:
http//:about.com/travel – a comprehensive travel
    directory from About.com
www.citysearch.com – a listing for mainly U.S. cities
    with entertainment and orientation guides.
www.officialtravelinfo.com – a directory covering the
    world's official tourism sites.
www.worldinformation.com – not specifically a travel
    guide but there is a mountain of information on the
    world's countries, their culture and advice about
    how to deal with issues like corruption.

Online maps and route finders

www.mappy.co.uk
START HERE

ORIGIN UK
INFO ✓✓✓✓✓
EASE ✓✓✓✓

Mappy has a great-looking site which is easy to use and has lots of added features such as a personal mapping service where you can store the maps you use most. The route finder is OK, doesn't use postcodes but business users can fill in their mileage allowance and Mappy will calculate how much you should claim.

www.multimap.com

GREAT BRITAIN

ORIGIN UK	Outstanding design, easy to use, excellent for the UK,
INFO ✓✓✓✓✓	you can search using postcodes, London street names,
EASE ✓✓✓✓✓	place names or Ordnance Survey grid references.

See also:

http://maps.expedia.co.uk – limited to the US, France, Germany and the UK for detailed maps – modest route finder.

http://maps.msn.com – excellent mapping and route finding service from MSN, incorporating what used to be Map Blast.

www.map24.co.uk/ – easy to use site with functional design, covers UK and Europe.

www.mapquest.com – find out the best way to get from A to B in Europe or America, not always as detailed as you'd like, but easy to use and you can customise your map or route plan.

www.mapsonus.com – it's notoriously difficult to find your way around America, but using the route planner you should minimise your risk of getting lost.

www.ordsvy.gov.uk – a good site with mapping for sale but the interactive mapping was suspended at time of writing.

www.stanfords.co.uk – travel book and map specialists.

www.viamichelin.com – a good all-round travel site with an improved route finder service which is OK.

www.theaa.co.uk

AUTOMOBILE ASSOCIATION

ORIGIN UK	A superb site that is divided into four key sections:
INFO ✓✓✓✓	breakdown cover, route planning and traffic
VALUE ✓✓✓✓✓	information, hotel guide and booking, in addition,
EASE ✓✓✓✓	help with buying a car. There is also information
	on insurance and other financial help.

www.rac.co.uk
GET AHEAD WITH THE RAC

ORIGIN UK
INFO ✓✓✓✓✓
EASE ✓✓✓✓

Great for UK traffic reports and has a very reliable route planner, which seems to be very busy and slow at peak times. There's also a good section on finding the right place to stay, and lots of help if you want to buy a car.

Destinations

Here's an alphabetical list of countries and regions to help you research your chosen destination and plan your holiday.

www.antor.com
ASSOCIATION OF NATIONAL TOURIST OFFICES

ORIGIN UK
INFO ✓✓✓✓
EASE ✓✓✓✓

A useful starting point for information about the 90 or so countries that are members of the association. It also has very good links to key tourism sites. See also www.officialtravelinfo.com

www.embassyworld.com
EMBASSIES AROUND THE GLOBE

ORIGIN US
INFO ✓✓✓✓
EASE ✓✓✓✓✓

Pick two countries one for 'whose embassy', one for 'in what location', press go and up pops the details on the embassy with contact and essential information.

A

www.africaonline.com
AFRICA

ORIGIN S. AFRICA
INFO ✓✓✓✓
EASE ✓✓✓✓

Exhaustive site covering news, information and travel in Africa, with very good features and articles.

www.africatravelresource.com
EAST AFRICA

ORIGIN UK
INFO ✓✓✓✓✓
EASE ✓✓✓✓✓

An exceptional site that specifically covers Burundi, Kenya, Rwanda, Uganda and Tanzania plus the resorts of Lamu and Zanzibar. The level of detail is great but because the site is packaged so well, it doesn't overwhelm. A lesson in how a travel site should be set up.

See also:

http://i-cias.com – excellent information site covering North Africa.

www.africaguide.com – detailed country-by-country guides, discussion forums, shopping, culture and a travelogue feature make this site a good first stop.

www.africanodyssey.co.uk – African and Arabian specialist agents.

www.africansafariclub.com – cruises and safaris a speciality.

www.backpackafrica.com – excellent site for backpackers with over 400 links and advice on where to go and what to see.

www.ecoafrica.com – tailor-made safaris with the emphasis on eco-tourism.

www.onsafari.com – good advice on what sort of safari is right for you.

www.phakawe.demon.co.uk – safaris in Botswana and Namibia.

www.travelinafrica.co.za – budget travel in Southern Africa.

www.vintageafrica.com – awesome safaris and destinations from this specialist travel agent, who will tailor-make holidays if requested.

www.wilderness-safaris.com – specialises in providing safaris that go to pristine wilderness.

www.wildnetafrica.net – an excellent travel and information portal for safaris to south and south-east Africa.

www.arab.net

RESOURCE FOR THE ARAB WORLD

ORIGIN	A wide ranging site covering North Africa and the
SAUDI ARABIA	Middle East with excellent country guides. See also
INFO ✓✓✓✓	http://I-cias.com and www.arabianodyssey.co.uk
VALUE ✓✓✓✓	
EASE ✓✓✓✓	

www.turisme.ad

ANDORRA

ORIGIN ANDORRA	A nice little site extolling the many virtues of this
INFO ✓✓✓✓	tiny country.
EASE ✓✓✓✓	

www.polartravel.co.uk

ARCTIC AND ANTARTICA

ORIGIN UK
INFO ✓✓✓✓
EASE ✓✓✓✓

How to get to the Poles in safety and even enjoy yourself when you get there! See also www.artic-experience.co.uk

www.argentour.com

ARGENTINA

ORIGIN ARGENTINA
INFO ✓✓✓✓
EASE ✓✓✓✓

Outstanding (but very slow loading) travel site with video clips, regional information, history and slide shows of the major cities, even a section on how to tango.

www.asiatour.com

ASIA

ORIGIN PHILLIPPINES
INFO ✓✓✓✓
EASE ✓✓✓✓

Good travel information on all Asian countries. See also www.accomasia.com which concentrates mainly on the Far East.

www.austria-tourism.at

AUSTRIA

ORIGIN AUSTRIA
INFO ✓✓✓✓
EASE ✓✓✓✓

An excellent site covering all you need to know about the country, with information on skiing and summer holidays too.

www.australia.com

DISCOVER AUSTRALIA

ORIGIN AUSTRALIA
INFO ✓✓✓✓✓
EASE ✓✓✓✓

The Australian Tourist Commission offer a good and informative site that gives lots of facts about the country, the people, lifestyle and what you can expect when you visit.

See also:

www.longitude131.com.au – stay in luxury at Ayers Rock or Uluru as it's officially known as now.

www.travelaustralia.com.au – informative site, good for regional information.

www.wilmap.com.au – excellent for Australian maps and links.

B

www.indo.com

BALI ONLINE

ORIGIN INDONESIA   Concentrating on Bali and its top hotels, but there's
INFO ✓✓✓✓   also plenty of information on the rest of Indonesia
EASE ✓✓✓   as well as links to other Asian sites.

www.trabel.com

BELGIUM

ORIGIN BELGIUM   The Belgium Travel Network offers a site packed
INFO ✓✓✓✓   with information about the country and its key towns
EASE ✓✓✓✓   and cities. You can get information on hotels,
                  travelling, an airport guide, flight information and
                  there's also a good links page. See also the well-
                  designed **www.belgium-tourism.net** and
                  www.visitflanders.co.uk

www.brazil.com

BRAZIL

ORIGIN BRAZIL   A straightforward, no-nonsense guide, travelogue and
INFO ✓✓✓✓   listing site for Brazil that also contains information on
EASE ✓✓✓✓   hotels and resorts. The Brazilian embassy in London
                 sponsors an excellent sister site **www.brazil.org.uk**

See also:
www.brazilinfo.com. – detailed information about
  the country and accommodation.
www.helisight.com.br – book your over Rio
  helicopter tour.
www.varig.co.uk – the national airline, good site
  with online booking.

C

www.cambodia-travel.com

HOME OF THE KHMER

ORIGIN CAMBODIA   Wide-ranging site with some interesting spelling!
INFO ✓✓✓✓   There are sections on Angkor Wat, the Khmer
EASE ✓✓✓✓   and the usual accommodation details. See also
                   www.eyeoncambodia.com

www.travelcanada.ca
EXPLORE CANADA

ORIGIN CANADA
INFO ✓✓✓✓✓
EASE ✓✓✓✓

Did you know that the glass floor at the top of the world's tallest free-standing structure could support the weight of 14 large hippos? Find out much more at this wide-ranging and attractive site, from touring to city guides. See also www.canadian-affair.com who offer some excellent low cost flights and tours, and for the outdoor experience of the country go to www.out-there.com

www.turq.com
CARIBBEAN

ORIGIN US
INFO ✓✓✓✓
EASE ✓✓✓✓

All you need to organise a great holiday in the Caribbean. There's information on flights, hotels, cruises, a travel guide and trip reports to the islands, all on a well presented and easy-to-use site.

See also:
www.caribbeandreams.co.uk – UK travel agent specialising in the Caribbean.
www.caribbeansupersite.com – good information.
www.doitcaribbean.com – information, booking and an interactive map.
www.nanana.com/caribbean.html – masses of links.

www.chinatour.com
INFORMATION CHINA

ORIGIN CHINA
INFO ✓✓✓✓
EASE ✓✓✓✓

A comprehensive site stuffed with data on China: where to go and stay, how to get there and what to see, maps and visa application information. See also the China Travel System at www.chinats.com who have a good looking and very polite site where you can book hotels and tours, get travel information and chat to others who've experienced China. For Hong Kong go to www.discoverhongkong.com

www.croatia.hr

CROATIA

ORIGIN CROATIA
INFO ✓✓✓✓
EASE ✓✓✓✓

An excellent site covering the country and its virtues with sections on events, attractions, background, accommodation and an all round travel guide.

www.cubanculture.com

CUBA

ORIGIN US
INFO ✓✓✓✓
EASE ✓✓✓✓

A fast, easy-to-use site with the basic information about Cuba and its heritage. There are lots of useful links too.

www.cyprustourism.org

CYPRUS

ORIGIN CYPRUS
INFO ✓✓✓
EASE ✓✓✓

A pretty basic site about the country, well the Greek run bit anyway.

www.czech-tourism.com

CZECH REPUBLIC

ORIGIN CZECHOSLOVAKIA
INFO ✓✓✓✓
EASE ✓✓✓✓

A good directory site providing information and links in 15 categories from business to the weather including tour operators and a country guide.

D

www.visitdenmark.com

DENMARK

ORIGIN DENMARK
INFO ✓✓✓✓
EASE ✓✓✓✓

The official Danish tourist board site where you can get links to book a holiday and all the advice and information you'd expect from a well-run and efficient looking site. See also **www.woco.dk** for an excellent site on Copenhagen.

E

www.ecuadorexplorer.com

ECUADOR

ORIGIN US
INFO ✓✓✓✓✓
EASE ✓✓✓✓

Very well put together directory site covering all you need for a visit to one of the most beautiful countries on the planet. For specific sites on the Galapagos go to the thorough www.galapagos-travel.com and also the Galapagos Conservation Trust at www.gct.org which is full of information and good for links.

www.egyptvoyager.com

LAND OF THE PHARAOHS

ORIGIN EGYPT
INFO ✓✓✓✓✓
EASE ✓✓✓✓

A superb site with games, snippets of interesting information, in-depth articles and a great photo gallery. You could be forgiven for forgetting that its primary function is to sell holidays – you can even get a lesson on hieroglyphics. For background info go to www.thebanmappingproject.com

See also:
http://touregypt.net – very comprehensive.
www.discoveregypt.co.uk – a well illustrated site from a UK based specialist.
www.peltours.com – great site from this Egypt specialist agent.

www.eurotrip.com

BACKPACKING EUROPE

ORIGIN UK
INFO ✓✓✓✓✓
EASE ✓✓✓✓

Student and independent European travel with in-depth information, facts, reviews, articles, discussion, live reports, links and travel advice on a good looking and well-designed site. See also www.backpackeurope.com

www.eurocamp.co.uk

SELF-CATERING EUROPE

ORIGIN UK
INFO ✓✓✓✓
EASE ✓✓✓✓

The leading self-catering company with over 160 holiday parks in nine countries. Here you can find details of the accommodation and book a holiday and there are some bargains too. See also www.eurocampindependent.co.uk who offer a European campsite reservation service.

www.europeaninternet.com/centraleurope

CENTRAL EUROPE ONLINE

ORIGIN EUROPE
INFO ✓✓✓✓
EASE ✓✓✓

A messy news-based site with comprehensive information on the region. You can get travel information and airline tickets via the links sections.

www.visiteurope.com

EUROPEAN TRAVEL COMMISSION

ORIGIN US
INFO ✓✓✓✓✓
EASE ✓✓✓✓

A site aimed at Americans to encourage them to visit Europe, it's informative and there's a section for each country.

F

www.franceway.com

VOILA LA FRANCE!

ORIGIN FRANCE
INFO ✓✓✓✓✓
EASE ✓✓✓✓

Excellent site giving an overview of French culture, history, facts and figures, and of course, how to book a holiday. You can also sign up for the newsletter.

See also:

www.franceguide.com – official French Government Tourist Office portal site.

www.francemag.com – really informative and useful e-zine devoted to France.

www.francetourism.com – the official French Government Tourist Office site for the US; great information for the UK too.

www.justparis.co.uk – details on how to get there and hotels when you've arrived.

www.logis-de-france.fr – reliable guide to 3,500 hotel-restaurant throughout France.

www.magicparis.com – good Paris guide with
some offers.

www.vive-la-france.org – very comprehensive and
good fun.

G

www.germany-tourism.de

GERMANY – WUNDERBAR

ORIGIN GERMANY   As much information as you can handle with good
INFO ✓✓✓✓✓   features on the key destinations, excellent interactive
EASE ✓✓✓✓   mapping and links to related sites. For further
information try **www.germany-info.org**

www.gibraltar.gi/tourism

GIBRALTAR – THE ROCK

ORIGIN GIBRALTAR   A good site devoted to the area with sections on the
INFO ✓✓✓✓   sights plus travel information.
EASE ✓✓✓✓

www.gnto.gr

GREEK NATIONAL TOURIST ORGANISATION

ORIGIN GREECE   An attractive site with the official word on travelling in
INFO ✓✓✓   Greece, with a good travel guide and information for
EASE ✓✓✓✓   business travellers plus accommodation, advice and
details on what you can get up to.

See also:

www.agn.gr – holidays, information and travel on the
Aegean, the site has a good interactive map with lots
of features. Aimed at US audience.

www.culture.gr – excellent site covering Greek culture
and its legends.

www.filoxenia.co.uk – a specialist, good for unusual
accommodation in Greece.

www.gogreece.com – a search engine devoted to all
things Greek.

www.greekisland.co.uk – an entertaining and personal
view of the Greek islands with over 200 links.

www.gtpnet.com – the Greek Travel Pages with the
latest ferry schedules for island hoppers.

www.islands-of-greece.com – another specialist operator with a good site and features on the better islands.

www.travelalacarte.co.uk – specialists in holidays in the best of the Greek islands.

www.travel-greece.com – masses of links to everything about holidaying in Greece.

H

www.holland.com

HOLLAND IS FULL OF SURPRISES

ORIGIN HOLLAND
INFO ✓✓✓✓✓
EASE ✓✓✓✓

Very professional site offering a mass of tourist information and advice on how to have a great time when you visit. There are sections on how to get there, what type of holiday will suit you and city guides.

I

www.iceland.org

ICELAND

ORIGIN ICELAND
INFO ✓✓✓✓
EASE ✓✓✓✓

Official site of the Icelandic Foreign Service with a wealth of information about the country, the people and its history. It's easy to navigate and there are good links to related sites. See also www.iceland.com and www.icetourist.is both of which are more tourism oriented.

www.indiatouristoffice.org

INDIAN TOURIST OFFICE UK

ORIGIN UK
INFO ✓✓✓✓
EASE ✓✓✓✓

Essential tourist information and advice as well as cultural and historical background on the country and its diverse regions. It has a massive hotel database as well.

www.indiamart.com

INDIA TRAVEL PROMOTION NETWORK

ORIGIN UK
INFO ✓✓✓✓✓
EASE ✓✓✓✓

Basically a shopping site with diverse information including travel, hotels, timetables, wildlife, worship, trekking, heritage and general tourism. It's well organised and easy to use.

See also:

www.hindustantimes.com – full of useful information, news and gossip.

www.indianrailways.com – passenger information and timetables of the largest rail network in the world.

www.india-travel.com – a really strong travel site with lots of information and guidance as well as essential links.

www.indiatraveltimes.com – great for links and the latest news.

www.mapsofindia.com – an excellent site with maps of the country and a rail timetable and route planner.

www.partnershiptravel.co.uk – specialist Indian travel agent.

www.rrindia.com – another good information site offering tour itineraries and hotel booking.

www.tourismindonesia.com

INDONESIA

ORIGIN INDONESIA	A very good overview of the country and its people,
INFO ✓✓✓✓	with lots of useful information about travelling there
EASE ✓✓✓✓	and a good links section.

www.shamrock.org

IRELAND

ORIGIN IRELAND	Wide-ranging site giving you the best of Ireland.
INFO ✓✓✓✓	Aimed at the American market, it really sells the
EASE ✓✓✓✓	country well with good links to other related sites.

See also:

www.12travel.co.uk – Irish holiday specialists with lots of holiday options.

www.camping-ireland.ie – over 100 parks listed for caravanning and camping.

www.heritageireland.ie – exploring the history of Ireland.

www.iol.ie/~discover – a good A–Z travel guide with lots of links.

www.ireland.travel.ie – the very good official Irish Tourist Board site.

www.goisrael.com

ISRAEL

ORIGIN ISRAEL
INFO ✓✓✓✓
EASE ✓✓✓✓

Excellent site with information on the country, its sights and sites, how to get there and how to organise a tour. There's also the latest information on 'the troubles' there from the official tourist board. See also www.infotour.co.il and www.e-israel.com

www.italytour.com

VIRTUAL TOUR OF ITALY

ORIGIN ITALY
INFO ✓✓✓✓
EASE ✓✓✓✓

Good looking, stylish and cool, this site is essentially a search engine and directory but a very good one.

See also:

www.doge.it – a basic but informative site on Venice.

www.emmeti.it – slightly eccentric site with bags of good information, although it takes a while to find it. Very good for hotels, regional info and museums.

www.enit.it – from the Italian State Tourist board another wacky site but useful nonetheless.

www.initaly.com – another eccentric site but generally well organised, informative and useful.

www.itwg.com – Italian hotel reservations with online booking.

www.travel.it – a messy information site but you can book online.

www.tuscanynow.com – villas for rent in Tuscany.

J

www.jnto.go.jp

JAPAN

ORIGIN JAPAN
INFO ✓✓✓✓✓
EASE ✓✓✓✓

This excellent site is the work of the Japanese Tourist Association. There's a guide to each region, the food, shopping and travel info with advice on how to get the best out of your visit.

See also:

www.embjapan.org.uk – Japanese Embassy site, useful but not that up-to-date.

www.jaltour.co.uk – travel agents specialising in Japan.

> www.japan-guide.com – comprehensive information
> site about Japan with links, culture notes, shopping
> and a hotel finder.

www.see-jordan.com

JORDAN

ORIGIN JORDAN
INFO ✓✓✓✓
EASE ✓✓✓✓

An attractive and interesting site from the Jordanian
tourist board, very cultural and informative with good
links and a photo gallery. See also **www.jtehome.com**
where you'll find the attractive site of the Jordan
Travel Exchange.

K

www.visit-kenya.com

KENYA

ORIGIN KENYA
INFO ✓✓✓✓
EASE ✓✓✓✓

A slightly amateurish site with links and information
on travelling in Kenya. There are sections on
Nairobi and the coast as well as the expected
safari information.

See also:
www.kenya.com – good looking site with a safari
  deal finder and information on the country too.
www.kenyaweb.com – a good portal site on all
  things Kenyan.

L

www.lata.org

LATIN AMERICA

ORIGIN UK
INFO ✓✓✓✓✓
EASE ✓✓✓✓

The Latin American Trade Association's text-based site
has a good country-by-country guide to the region plus
links and general information.

*See also the site below and the sites listed under
South America:*
www.journeylatinamerica.co.uk – lots of tour and
  country options from this specialist agent.
www.latinamericatraveler.com – great for links and
  information.

www.lastfrontiers.com – tailor-made itineraries for
holidays across the continent.

www.steppeslatinamerica.co.uk – from the Steppes
group offering tailor made packages.

www.travellatinamerica.com – really comprehensive
travel, directory and news site.

www.lebanon.com

THE LEBANON

ORIGIN LEBANON
INFO ✓✓✓✓✓
EASE ✓✓✓✓

The Lebanon is going through a resurgence and is
successfully rebuilding itself. Here you can find all
the resources you need to organise a visit and see its
many attractions. Also try the official
www.lebanon-tourism.gov.lb

M

www.malaysianet.net

MALAYSIA

ORIGIN MALAYSIA
INFO ✓✓✓✓
EASE ✓✓✓✓

Great for hotels in particular but you'll also find flight
information and hidden away is a pretty good travel
guide to the country. For air travel info see also
www.malaysiaair.com

www.visitmaldives.com

MALDIVES

ORIGIN MALDIVES
INFO ✓✓✓✓
EASE ✓✓✓✓

A good overview of the islands and all the options
available to tourists with links and a section on the
capital Male, plus resort information.

www.visitmalta.com

MALTA

ORIGIN UK
INFO ✓✓✓✓
EASE ✓✓✓✓

A text-heavy but informative site about this beautiful
island, with good details on accommodation and
interactive mapping.

www.tourbymexico.com

MEXICO

ORIGIN MEXICO
INFO ✓✓✓✓
EASE ✓✓✓

A basic site, but there is a travel guide to Mexico plus
information on tours, hotels, health, tips, links and
sights to see. See also the bright and breezy European
gateway into Mexico www.mexicanwave.com/travel

423 | T   Travel and Holidays

http://i-cias.com/morocco
MOROCCO

ORIGIN MOROCCO
INFO ✓✓✓✓
EASE ✓✓✓

A dense and detailed site about Morocco with over 650 articles and 900 photos covering cultural, musical and town by town information. See also www.morocco.com and www.morocco-travel.com both are pretty good.

http://i-cias.com
THE MIDDLE EAST

ORIGIN NORWAY
INFO ✓✓✓✓
EASE ✓✓✓✓

Very good for information on the Middle East, just click on the interactive map, there's travel information on selected countries.

N

www.nepal.com
NEPAL AND THE HIMALAYAS

ORIGIN US
INFO ✓✓✓✓
EASE ✓✓✓

A beautifully presented site showing Nepal in its best light. Business, sport, culture and travel all have sections and it's a good browse too. The travel section is not that comprehensive, it has a basic guide, lots about Everest and access to the useful Sherpa magazine. See also the specialist tour company www.trans-himalaya.ndirect.co.uk and also www.rrindia.com/nepal.html plus www.nepaltravelinfo.com

www.purenz.com
NEW ZEALAND

ORIGIN
NEW ZEALAND
INFO ✓✓✓✓
EASE ✓✓✓✓

A good looking and informative site about the country with a section devoted to recollections and recommendations from people who've visited. See also the comprehensive www.nz.com and www.newzealand.com

www.visitnorway.com
NORWAY

ORIGIN NORWAY
INFO ✓✓✓✓
EASE ✓✓✓✓

The official site of the Norwegian Tourist Board offers a good overview of what you can get up to when you're there, from adventure holidays to lounging

around in the midnight sun to cruising the coast. See
also **www.norway.org** which is the Norwegian
Embassy's site.

P

www.tourism.gov.pk

PAKISTAN

ORIGIN PAKISTAN   A pretty lightweight site but it has all the basic
INFO ✓✓✓✓   information and a good set of links with a travel
EASE ✓✓✓✓   guide built in. See also **www.pak.org** which is a
very comprehensive portal site.

www.enjoyperu.com

PERU

ORIGIN PERU   It's amazing how much there's to see in Peru and this
INFO ✓✓✓✓   site does a good job of reflecting the country's assets.
EASE ✓✓✓✓   Plenty of tourist information and deals. See also the
basic but useful site of the Peruvian embassy
www.peruembassy-uk.com

www.polandtour.org

POLAND

ORIGIN US   Basic overview of the country and tourist facilities
INFO ✓✓✓✓   and travel information.
EASE ✓✓✓

www.polartravel.co.uk

POLAR TRAVEL

ORIGIN UK   How to get to the Poles in safety and even enjoy
INFO ✓✓✓✓   yourself when you get there! See also
EASE ✓✓✓✓   **www.artic-experience.co.uk**

www.portugal-web.com

PORTUGAL

ORIGIN PORTUGAL   A complete overview of the country including business
INFO ✓✓✓✓   as well as tourism with good regional information,
EASE ✓✓✓✓   news and links to other related sites.

See also:

www.portugal.com – a news and shopping site with a good travel section.

www.portugal.org – well designed information site with a good travel section.

www.thealgarve.net – all you need to know about the Algarve.

R

www.russia-travel.com

RUSSIA

ORIGIN RUSSIA
INFO ✓✓✓✓✓
EASE ✓✓✓✓

The official guide to travel in Russia with good information on excursions, accommodation, flights and trains, there's even a slide show, plus historical facts and travel tips. For a traditional approach try **www.themoscowtimes.com/travel**

S

www.sey.net

SEYCHELLES, PARADISE – PERIOD

ORIGIN US
INFO ✓✓✓✓
EASE ✓✓✓✓

A good all-round overview of the Seychelles with background information on the major islands and activities, there's also links to travel agents.

See also:

www.seychelles.uk.com – informative and geared to a British audience.

www.seychelleselite.co.uk – specialists in the Seychelles.

www.seychelles-travel.co.uk – excellent site form another specialist agent.

www.sg

SINGAPORE

ORIGIN
SINGAPORE
INFO ✓✓✓✓
EASE ✓✓✓✓

The shortest URL in the book brings up one of the most detailed and comprehensive sites – all you need to know about the country and its people.

http://satourweb.satour.com

SOUTH AFRICA

ORIGIN
SOUTH AFRICA
INFO ✓✓✓✓
EASE ✓✓✓✓

Official tourist site with masses of information about the country and how you can set yourself up for the perfect visit with suggested itineraries.

See also:
www.gardenroute.org.za – excellent site covering the Garden Route and south coast.
www.southafrica.com/travel – very good portal site with a comprehensive travel section.
www.southafricanaffair.com – tailor-made itineraries, basic site though.

www.southamericanexperience.co.uk

SOUTH AMERICA

ORIGIN UK
INFO ✓✓✓✓
EASE ✓✓✓

Specialists on South America are hard to come by, but at this site you can get tailor-made tours to suit you plus some scant information on the countries and special offers. See also **www.adventure-life.com** and **www.gosouthamerica.about.com** both are very informative and are good for links. Check out the listings under Latin America too.

www.tourspain.es

TOURIST OFFICE OF SPAIN

ORIGIN SPAIN
INFO ✓✓✓✓
EASE ✓✓✓✓

A colourful and award-winning web site that really makes you want to visit Spain. Very good for an overview.

You could also try any of these listed below:
www.costaguide.com – your Costa del Sol companion, lots of information.
www.iberia.com – Iberian airlines site, with helpful advice and offers.
www.majorca.com – great site about the island.
www.okspain.org – nice all round information and travel site.
www.red2000.com – a colourful travel guide, with a good search instrument!

www.lanka.net

SRI LANKA

ORIGIN SL
INFO   ✓✓✓✓✓
EASE   ✓✓✓

An exhaustive site, which isn't easy to navigate, but it has loads of information and news on the country, see also www.slmts.slt.lk for the Ministry of Tourism.

www.sverigeturism.se/smorgasbord

SWEDEN

ORIGIN SWEDEN
INFO   ✓✓✓✓
EASE   ✓✓✓✓

The largest source of information in English on Sweden. It's essentially a directory site but there are sections on culture, history and a tourist guide. For more details of Sweden's cities see the very good http://cityguide.se and www.visit-sweden.com and also www.sweden.com

www.switzerlandtourism.ch

SWITZERLAND

ORIGIN SWITZERLAND
INFO   ✓✓✓✓✓
EASE   ✓✓✓✓

An excellent overview of the country with the latest news, travel information, snow reports and links.

T

www.tanzania-web.com

TANZANIA

ORIGIN TANZANIA
INFO   ✓✓✓✓
EASE   ✓✓✓✓

Find your way round Tanzania with its wonderful scenery, Mount Kilimanjaro, safaris and resorts with this very good and comprehensive online guide from the official tourist board.

www.allaboutzanzibar.com

ZANZIBAR

ORIGIN TANZANIA
INFO   ✓✓✓✓✓
EASE   ✓✓✓✓✓

An outstanding tourist site with concise (then very detailed if your need it) descriptions covering all the information you need, including accommodation and cultural stuff. Other tourism sites could learn a lot from this. See also www.zanzibar.net

www.thailand.com/travel

THAILAND

ORIGIN THAILAND
INFO ✓✓✓✓
EASE ✓✓✓✓

Another excellent portal site, which acts as a gateway to a mass of travel and tourism resources. It covers some of South East Asia too and it has a good search facility. www.tourismthailand.org is the official tourist board site and is very informative, as is www.nectec.or.th/thailand

www.turkey.com

YOUR WINDOW ON TURKEY

ORIGIN US
INFO ✓✓✓✓
EASE ✓✓✓✓

A very well constructed site covering business, tourism, sport, culture and shopping. There's a great deal in terms of advice, tips, maps, but not much in-depth info. For that use the links or go to www.exploreturkey.com which is a good travel guide and www.turkishembassy-london.com for the official line.

U

www.uae.org.ae

UNITED ARAB EMIRATES

ORIGIN UAE
INFO ✓✓✓✓
EASE ✓✓✓✓

A useful guide to the seven states that make up the UAE, it carries historical information as well as the usual travel guide stuff. See also www.godubai.com

www.visituganda.com

UGANDA

ORIGIN UGANDA
INFO ✓✓✓✓✓
EASE ✓✓✓✓

Great site and directory from the Ugandan tourist board with excellent quality pictures.

www.usatourism.com

USA

ORIGIN US
INFO ✓✓✓✓
EASE ✓✓✓

A state-by-state guide to the USA, just click on the interactive map and you get put through to the relevant state site. See also www.areaguides.net which is very detailed.

See also:

www.americanadventures.com – great site devoted
to budget adventure tours. Now merged with
www.treckAmerica.com where they offer an even
broader range of holidays.

www.amtrak.com – rail schedules and fares across
America.

www.disneyworld.com – all you need to know about
the world's number one theme park.

www.gohawaii.com – great site for checking out
Hawaii and it's many attractions.

www.greyhound.com – coach and bus schedules, but
you can't buy tickets online from outside the US.

www.seeamerica.org – an excellent portal to American
travel sites.

www.usahotelguide.com – reserve your room in any
one of 50,000 hotels across the USA.

V

www.vietnamtourism.com

VIETNAM

ORIGIN US	...etnam is the hot destination apparently, here's the
INFO ✓✓✓✓	official tourism site which is informative and good
EASE ✓✓✓	for links.

www.zamnet.zm/tourism-travel.html

ZAMBIA

ORIGIN ZAMBIA	Basic tourist information and directory from the
INFO ✓✓✓	well put together Zamnet portal site.
EASE ✓✓✓	

Travel in Britain

www.visitbritain.com

HOME OF THE BRITISH TOURIST AUTHORITY

ORIGIN UK	Selling Britain using a holiday ideas-led site with lots
INFO ✓✓✓✓✓	of help for the visitor, maps, background stories,
EASE ✓✓✓✓	images, entertainment, culture, activities and a
	planner. There's also a very helpful set of links.

www.informationbritain.co.uk

HOLIDAY INFORMATION

ORIGIN UK
INFO ✓✓✓✓✓
EASE ✓✓✓✓

Where to stay and where to go with an overview of all the UK's main tourist attractions, counties and regions; it has good cross-referencing and links to the major destinations.

www.sightseeing.co.uk

SIGHT-SEEING MADE EASY

ORIGIN UK
INFO ✓✓✓✓
EASE ✓✓✓✓✓

A good looking and very useful site if you're looking for something to do. Just type in what you want to see and where you are, then up pops a listing giving basic information on each attraction, how far it is to get there, entrance fee and a map. One slight criticism: would be better if there was more background information on each attraction.

www.ukholidaybreaks.co.uk

FIND YOUR PERFECT HOTEL

ORIGIN UK
INFO ✓✓✓✓
EASE ✓✓✓✓

A directory of hotels in the UK, you find the one you want by drilling down through a series of maps or select by category. It's easy although results are a bit hit and miss, but it claims to use the latest technology to find just the right break for you.

See also:
www.aboutbritain.com – attractive, well laid out
and comprehensive UK guide.
www.atuk.co.uk – billed as the UK travel
search engine.
www.enjoybritain.com – useful links directory.
www.e-street.com – excellent overview of a dozen
or so English and Irish cities.
www.travelbritain.com – a modest directory site.
www.ukguide.org – well-organised directory with
a UK and a London guide plus mapping.

www.knowhere.co.uk
THE USER'S GUIDE TO BRITAIN

ORIGIN UK
INFO ✓✓✓✓✓
EASE ✓✓✓✓

An unconventional 'tourist guide' which gives a warts-and-all account of over 1,000 places in Britain; it's very irreverent and if you are squeamish or a bit sensitive, then they have a good list of links to proper tourist sites.

For separate countries and regions see also:

CHANNEL ISLANDS

www.alderney.net – a good looking site devoted to the third largest Channel Island.

www.guernseytouristboard.com – slightly dodgy site but there's all the information you need on Guernsey.

www.jerseyhols.com – good looking site with lots of information and info on where to stay and what to do, see also **www.jersey.com** who have a very slick site.

www.sark.info – a lively site with all the information you need plus online booking for ferries.

ENGLAND

www.isle-of-man.com – learn all about this unique island with help on where to stay and, of course, background on the famous TT races.

www.londonhotelreservations.com – some good deals on London hotels.

www.londontown.com – very comprehensive survival and holiday guide rolled into one, with sections on restaurants, hotels, attractions and offers. It is quite slow.

www.simplyscilly.co.uk – specialists in travel to the Scilly islands with info on how to get there and what to do.

www.travelengland.org.uk – nice online guide to everything English, places to visit and accommodation.

NORTHERN IRELAND

www.discovernorthernireland.com – Northern Ireland Tourist Board has an attractive site showing the best that the region has to offer. It has a virtual tour, holiday planner, accommodation, guides, links and special offers.

www.nidirectory.co.uk – basic site, good for links.

SCOTLAND

www.aboutscotland.com – excellent site with information on a broad range of accommodation and sights to see, it's fast too.

www.scotac.com – accommodation by region.

www.scotland.com – nicely illustrated site with a good overview of the country.

www.scotland-info.co.uk – very good online guidebook, covering Scotland by area; it's quite slow but the information is very good.

www.visithebrides.com – a light and airy site with links and information relating to the islands. See also **www.hebrides.com** which offers beautiful photography.

www.visitorkney.com – from the Orkney Tourist Board a very informative and appealing site. See also **www.orknet.com**

www.visitshetland.com – a definite green theme to this site devoted to Shetland, highlighting its outdoor life and spirit of adventure.

WALES

www.cadw.wales.gov.uk – historic monuments in Wales.

www.data-wales.co.uk – not so much a tourist site, but excellent for history and culture and quite funny too.

www.holidays-in-wales.co.uk – holidays in the Welsh countryside with limited online booking, with a good overview of the country.

www.valleyconnection.co.uk – a useful directory devoted to all things Welsh.

THINGS TO DO IN BRITAIN & IRELAND

www.daysoutuk.com

GO TO A GARDEN

ORIGIN UK
INFO ✓✓✓✓✓
EASE ✓✓✓✓

Excellent directory of venues and events with lots of search options, easy to use and you can get discounts to many attractions too.

See also:

www.anothertravel.com – a good looking site, a bit light on information though.

www.daysout.co.uk – similar to Day's Out above but more colourful, it includes a useful section for the disabled too.

www.i-uk.com – useful information on the UK, mainly aimed at visitors.

www.sightseeing.co.uk – a good search engine with travel and facility information.

www.gardenvisit.com

GO TO A GARDEN

ORIGIN UK
INFO ✓✓✓✓
EASE ✓✓✓✓

A basic text-based site, which lists some 1,000 of the UK's gardens open to the public, giving details of each, how to get there and how they rate. It also covers the USA and Europe and there's also an excellent overview of garden history.

www.nationaltrust.org.uk

PLACES OF HISTORIC INTEREST AND BEAUTY

ORIGIN UK
INFO ✓✓✓✓✓
EASE ✓✓✓✓✓

The National Trust's site has an excellent overview of their activities and the properties they own. There is a very good search facility and up-to-date information to help with your visit.

See also:

www.castles-of-britain.com – informative and lively site on the UK's castles.

www.english-heritage.org.uk – excellent, high quality site with information on their properties and an events calendar.

www.hrp.org.uk – pretty boring site devoted to 5 historic royal palaces – the Tower, Hampton Court,

Kensington, Kew and the Banqueting House.
www.statelyhomes.com – comprehensive site devoted
to stately homes, with links and an e-zine to keep
you updated.

www.goodbeachguide.co.uk

THE BEST BEACHES

ORIGIN	UK	From the Marine Conservation Society you can find
INFO	✓✓✓✓	out which are Britain's worst and best beaches. It's
EASE	✓✓✓✓	set out regionally and the site is updated regularly.

WHAT TO DO WITH THE KIDS

www.kidsnet.co.uk

WHAT'S ON AND WHERE?

ORIGIN	UK	Strong design and ease-of-use make this site stand out,
INFO	✓✓✓✓	aligned with a comprehensive database of places and
EASE	✓✓✓✓	attractions. Also has cinema listings, games and book

search facilities which all add to the general excellence.
Good links list too.

For more ideas try:
www.kidstravel.co.uk – nice design but comparatively
little content, still some good ideas and travelling
tips for parents though biased to England.
www.planit4kids.com – covers seven major areas of
the country centred on the major cites, the linked
sites are excellent with plenty to see and do, on top
of all the information you need for a great day out.
They plan to rollout internationally.
www.xkeys.co.uk – specialist in residential camps for
children of all ages, excellent web site with lots of
information and references.

HOLIDAY COTTAGES

www.hidays.co.uk
UK COTTAGES

ORIGIN UK
INFO ✓✓✓✓
EASE ✓✓✓✓

Hidays claims over 22,000 cottages in the UK, Ireland and France. The site is user friendly and you can search using numerous options from those who take pets, even cottages with pools.

See also:
www.cottagesdirect.com – click on the interactive map and away you go, plenty of cottages to choose from.
www.hideaways.co.uk – great for the south of England.
www.holidayrentals4you.com – a wide range of properties to rent in UK, USA and Europe.
www.oas.co.uk/ukcottages – over 1000 cottages available throughout the UK.
www.nationaltrust.org.uk/cottages – holiday cottages with a difference.
www.seasidecottages.co.uk – all within 10 miles of the sea.

Cycling and touring

The following are mostly UK specialists, but some cover further afield too.

www.ctc.org.uk
WORKING FOR CYCLING

ORIGIN UK
INFO ✓✓✓✓✓
EASE ✓✓✓✓

The CTC have a great travel section with routes, tours, offers, links and directories, it's a great place to start your search for the perfect cycling holiday.

Also check out:
www.bicycle-beano.co.uk – Bicycle Beano have a good site covering cycling holidays in Wales and the borders.
www.bikemagic.com – go to the travel pages for an excellent section where Bike Magic have got partners who'll supply flight deals for cyclists or rail travel and holidays.

www.byways-breaks.co.uk – nice looking site, Byways
Breaks arrange cycling and walking holidays in the
Shropshire and Cheshire countryside.

www.cycle-rides.co.uk – a very good selection of
biking tours through Europe and further afield.

www.nationalcyclenetwork.co.uk – details of the
National Cycle Network and how to make the
best use of it.

www.rough-tracks.co.uk – wide range of active
adventure holidays from beginners to experts.

www.scotcycle.co.uk – Scottish Cycling Holidays are
specialists in cycling holidays in Scotland obviously.
Nice site too.

Camping and caravanning

*Many of the sites listed specialise in Britain but some have
information on camp sites abroad too.*

www.camp-sites.co.uk

FIND A SITE

ORIGIN UK	Excellent regional listing of the UK's campsites with
INFO ✓✓✓✓✓	comprehensive details on each site and links to other
EASE ✓✓✓✓	related directories.

See also:

www.eurocampindependent.co.uk – excellent site if
you want to go camping in Europe, some special
offers and you can chat about your experiences too.

www.keycamp.co.uk – European specialist with sites
in seven countries.

www.pjcamping.co.uk – exhaustive selection of tents
and camping equipment for sale, good info but no
online ordering.

www.caravan.co.uk

THE CARAVAN CLUB

ORIGIN UK	Huge listing of sites, advice and practical help with
INFO ✓✓✓✓	details of over 200 sites and some 2,700 other
EASE ✓✓✓✓	certified locations where you can park up. There's also
	a European service, you can join the club on site and
	request any of the fifty or so leaflets they publish.

See also:

http://camping.uk-directory.com – a good regional
sites directory, with retailing links, caravans for sale
and conservation information.

www.campingandcaravanningclub.co.uk – a good
comprehensive offering with information on sites
and technical help and advice too.

www.caravan-sitefinder.co.uk – listing of over 3,000
caravan sites, with background information on a
wide range of topics.

Waterways

www.britishwaterways.co.uk
BRITISH WATERWAYS

ORIGIN UK
INFO ✓✓✓✓✓
EASE ✓✓✓✓

This organisation is responsible for maintaining a
large part of Britain's waterways and this excellent site
details their work and contains interactive mapping of
the routes with a great deal of background information
and events listings and history.

See also:

www.blakes.co.uk – a boating holiday specialist.

www.canalholidays.com – an easy way to book
your narrow boat holiday.

www.canals.co.uk – the biggest canal-related shop
on the Internet, mainly videos, maps and books.

www.gobarging.com – luxury barging in Europe.

www.hoseasons.co.uk – great site from the specialists
in boating holidays, you can book online too.

www.waterways.org.uk – Inland Waterways
Association site, dedicated to keeping canals
open and you can find out about their organised
activities too.

Adventure and activity

Listed below are UK-oriented sites, see also page 398 for international adventure specialists and 351 for info on exteme sports.

www.activitiesonline.co.uk

ULTIMATE RESOURCE FOR LEISURE PURSUITS

ORIGIN UK
INFO ✓✓✓✓
EASE ✓✓✓

A directory of adventure and activity holiday specialists covering everything from extreme sports to gardening. You get a description of the activity, then a list of relevant sites.

www.sportbreak.co.uk

THE SPORTS BREAK DIRECTORY

ORIGIN UK
INFO ✓✓✓✓
EASE ✓✓✓

A good directory, apart from sports it covers all activity holidays including leisure breaks, health clubs, even stag and hen parties. It's easy to use and the information is well put over.

Other adventure holiday sites:

www.activityholsni.co.uk – activity holidays in Northern Ireland have a great site and lots to do.

www.activitywales.co.uk – break out and discover the real Wales with Activity Wales. Use this well-constructed site to suss out which activities to try.

www.activity-scotland.co.uk – lots of things to do in here, nice regional guide as well.

www.adventure.uk.com – Adventure International are experienced adventure holiday specialists based in Bude, Cornwall.

www.adventureholiday.com – ProAdventure specialise in activity holidays in North Wales.

www.leisurepursuits.com – one of the largest sports tour operators and travel agents.

www.pgl.co.uk/holidays – adventure holidays for kids – great site too.

www.trailplus.com – the ultimate adventure, offering lifestyle experiences, adventure camps and much more.

Walking and rambling

www.ramblers.org.uk
THE RAMBLERS' ASSOCIATION

ORIGIN UK
INFO ✓✓✓✓
EASE ✓✓✓✓

News, strong views and plenty of advice on offer here, where you can find out about the Association's activities and even join a campaign. There are features on events and details of *The Rambler* magazine, shopping and holidays.

www.walkingbritain.co.uk
BRITISH WALKS

ORIGIN UK
INFO ✓✓✓✓✓
EASE ✓✓✓✓

Some 2,000 pages of information about walking in Britain, it mainly covers the National Parks but it is expanding to include less well-known areas. They provide decent route maps and photos to guide you. There's also a list of handy links and a good photo gallery.

www.onedayhikes.com
WHERE DO YOU WANT TO HIKE TODAY?

ORIGIN US
INFO ✓✓✓✓✓
EASE ✓✓✓✓

A great site, which is basically a directory of hikes that you can complete in a day, it's not just for the UK either, it covers the whole world. There's excellent information on each hike plus pictures and you get the chance to win a digital camera if you send in a report of a hike you've done and it gets accepted.

www.walkingworld.com
OVER 1500 WALKS

ORIGIN UK
INFO ✓✓✓✓✓
VALUE ✓✓✓
EASE ✓✓✓✓

Each walk has a detailed description and map and it's easy to find a good one. In addition, there's advice on difficulty and what you can expect to see. The walks cost £1.50 or you can become a member for £14.95 per annum, then they're free.

For more sites for hikers try:
www.bwf-ivv.org.uk – the British Walking Federation organise a wide range of activities and you can find out about them here.

www.gelert.com – equipment for sale, a good looking
site well worth a visit.

www.ramblersholidays.co.uk – Ramblers Holidays
specialise in escorted rambling holidays.

Train, coach and ferry journeys

www.pti.org.uk
PUBLIC TRANSPORT INFORMATION

ORIGIN UK
INFO ✓✓✓✓✓
EASE ✓✓✓✓

An incredibly useful site if you're a frequent user of
public transport or if you're using it to go somewhere
you're not familiar with. It categorises all the major
forms of public transport and lists for each area
useful numbers, timetables, web sites and interactive
mapping to help you. It also includes routes to Europe
and Ireland.

www.kizoom.co.uk
TRAVEL SERVICE TO YOUR PHONE

ORIGIN UK
INFO ✓✓✓
EASE ✓✓✓

Good quality travel information to your mobile phone
sounds great and this is a very well set up and easy-to-
use site. Unfortunately, it only works with a limited
number of WAP phones, so if you've one of those
you're in luck.

www.travelfusion.com
THE TRAVEL COMPARISON PORTAL

ORIGIN UK
INFO ✓✓✓✓✓
EASE ✓✓✓✓

A brilliant idea – pick a journey then compare whether
it would be best to go by coach, car, ferry or by air. It's
simple to use and you can compare by price or speed.
It then connects you with the right operator if you
want to book.

Railway travel

www.rail.co.uk
RAILWAY LINKS

ORIGIN UK
INFO ✓✓✓✓✓
EASE ✓✓✓✓✓

A directory of useful links including timetables,
operators and associated businesses.

www.nationalrail.co.uk

NATIONAL RAIL

ORIGIN UK
INFO ✓✓✓✓✓
EASE ✓✓✓✓

National Rail's site has all the latest information, timetables and links you need to plan a rail journey. It's very comprehensive with up-to-the-minute information on what's going on.

www.thetrainline.com

BUY TRAIN TICKETS

ORIGIN UK
INFO ✓✓✓✓✓
VALUE ✓✓✓✓
EASE ✓✓✓✓

You have to log in first but you can book a ticket for train travel, whether business or leisure, (except sleeper, Motorail, Eurostar and ferry services). They have an up-to-date timetable and the tickets will be sent or you can collect. See also the fast working www.qjump.co.uk which is similar. At both these sites there are a bewildering number of options and prices, a little help with what each ticket type and their relative costs wouldn't go amiss.

See also:

www.eurail.com – details of the Eurailticket, information and prices, but you can't buy online.

www.eurostar.co.uk – online booking plus timetables and offers.

www.eurotunnel.com – online passenger bookings.

www.greatrail.com – escorted railway holidays, world-wide. Well illustrated site.

www.networkrail.co.uk – what was Railtrack, some useful information.

www.trainpain.com – the place to go to complain about trains!

www.traintaxi.co.uk – useful site if you need a taxi once you're off the train, with taxi company contact details and advice on whether there's usually taxis waiting.

www.thetube.com

LONDON UNDERGROUND

ORIGIN	UK
INFO	✓✓✓✓✓
EASE	✓✓✓✓

An excellent and informative site from London Underground with lots of features, articles on visiting London and links to related sites. There's a good journey planner and tube maps too. See also the Tube Planner at **www.tubeplanner.com** which is a straightforward journey planner.

Coaches

www.gobycoach.com

BOOK COACH TICKETS

ORIGIN	UK
INFO	✓✓✓✓✓
VALUE	✓✓✓✓
EASE	✓✓✓

Organise your journey with this easy-to-use web site from National Express, and then book the tickets. Also offers an airport service, transport to events and tours. See also **www.stagecoachbus.com** where you can find information about Stagecoach services and buy tickets.

Ferries

www.ferrybooker.com

BOOK YOUR CROSSING

ORIGIN	UK
INFO	✓✓✓✓✓
VALUE	✓✓✓
EASE	✓✓✓✓

The best ferry site for a wide range of information on crossing times featuring a large number of routes. There is help with planning, special offers, channel tunnel ticket booking and they offer holiday breaks too.

See also:

www.brittany-ferries.co.uk – crossings to France and Spain with online booking and special offers, also cruises and holidays.

www.dfdsseaways.co.uk – details and offers on Scandinavian routes.

www.drive-alive.com – motoring holiday specialists who get good rates on channel crossings as part of their package.

www.ferry.co.uk – great offers on selected crossings.

www.ferrysavers.co.uk – wide range of offers and a good selection of crossings at good prices, you can book online and they offer a price promise too.

www.hoverspeed.com – online booking and all the
information you need to make the fastest channel
and Irish Sea crossings.

www.irishferries.ie – excellent magazine-style site
where amongst all the features you can find
timetables and book tickets.

www.posl.com – P&O Stena Line with online
booking, details of sailings and offers.

www.seafrance.com – bookings and information on
their Calais-Dover service plus some special offers.

Car hire

*It's probably best to go to a price comparison site before going to
one of the car hire companies, that way you should get the best
prices. One of the best is to be found at* **www.priceline.co.uk**

www.holidaycars.co.uk
WORLD-WIDE CAR HIRE

ORIGIN UK	Over 3,000 car hire locations throughout the world
INFO ✓✓✓✓✓	means that this site is well worth a visit on your quest,
VALUE ✓✓✓	you can get an instant online quote and you can book
EASE ✓✓✓✓	too. Very good for the USA. See also Holiday Autos

who have a similar site at **www.holidayautos.co.uk**
and also the competitive **www.pelicancarhire.co.uk**
who specialise in Europe.

Utilities

*Get the best prices on your gas, electricity and water and find out
what the big suppliers are up to as well.*

www.ofgem.gov.uk
GAS AND ELECTRICITY SUPPLIER WATCHDOG

ORIGIN UK	Data on the suppliers and companies providing
INFO ✓✓✓✓✓	comparison information makes for interesting
EASE ✓✓✓✓✓	reading. There's also background on how bills are

made up, complaints and how energy reaches your
home. Excellent.

www.buy.co.uk

CUT YOUR BILLS – COMPARE PRICES

ORIGIN UK
INFO ✓✓✓✓
VALUE ✓✓✓✓✓
EASE ✓✓✓✓✓

Take a few minutes to check the prices of the key utilities and see whether you can save on your current bills, its easy and quick. It also covers phones and loans, and there's also access to *Which?* magazine's energy reports.

See also:
www.servista.com – straightforward and well designed.
www.uswitch.com – compare prices on gas and electricity.
www.unravelit.com – savings on gas and electricity plus numerous other services.

www.natenergy.org.uk

NATIONAL ENERGY FOUNDATION

ORIGIN UK
INFO ✓✓✓✓
EASE ✓✓✓✓

Devoted to saving energy in order to benefit the environment. There's lots of advice and information to help save money too. See also **www.est.org.uk**

Electricity and gas

Here are the main energy sites, who owns them at time of writing and the highlights of the site.

www.amerada.co.uk – one of the best value suppliers with an excellent site, you can even switch to them online.
www.british-energy.com – one of the largest electricity providers with a good-looking but not very useful site.
www.centrica.co.uk – owners of British Gas and the AA, this site aims to give information about the group.
www.esb.ie – good-looking site from an Irish supplier with online sign up available.
www.gas.co.uk – comprehensive service from British gas with account viewing.
www.hydro.co.uk – Scottish Hydro Electric has one of the sites most oriented to its customers.
www.london-electricity.co.uk – straightforward but slow.

> www.nationalgrid.com/uk – the National Grid, the
> Railtrack of power.
> www.nie.co.uk – Northern Ireland Electricity with
> customer information on their service, the rest is
> fairly corporate.
> www.npower.com – nicely designed site with
> online application.
> www.powergen.co.uk – Powergen has a neat site with
> calculators and a switching service.
> www.scottish-southern.co.uk – owner of Swalec, site
> aimed at shareholders.
> www.swalec.co.uk– Swalec, good house move planner.
> www.txuenergi.co.uk – formerly
> www.easternenergy.co.uk – good service, helpful,
> much improved.

www.transco.uk.com

FOR GAS LEAKS

ORIGIN	UK	Transco doesn't sell gas, but maintains the
INFO	✓✓✓	24-hour emergency service for stopping gas leaks
EASE	✓✓✓✓	– call 0800 111 999 to report one.

www.corgi-gas.com

COUNCIL OF REGISTERED GAS INSTALLERS

ORIGIN	UK	CORGI is the gas industry watchdog; the site has
INFO	✓✓✓✓	advice on gas installation and where to find a fitter
EASE	✓✓✓✓	or repairman.

www.calorgas.co.uk

CALOR GAS

ORIGIN	UK	Information on your nearest stockists, how best to
INFO	✓✓✓✓✓	use Calor gas and Autogas, there's also corporate
VALUE	✓✓✓	background and customer services too. You can also
EASE	✓✓✓✓	order it online with payment collected on delivery.

Water

www.ofwat.gov.uk

OFFICE OF WATER SERVICES

ORIGIN	UK	A very poor effort, especially when compared to the
INFO	✓✓✓✓	OFGEM counterparts site, however, you can find out
VALUE	✓✓✓	about what they do and you can contact them for
EASE	✓✓✓✓	advice.

The following are the main water company sites:

www.nwl.co.uk – nice lifestyle site with leisure information and bill paying.

www.nww.co.uk – United Utilities, once North West Water has a well-designed site with help, information and good advice for consumers, with online access to your account. They now supply electricity too.

www.severntrent.co.uk – well it's got the share price, which is nice.

www.swwater.co.uk – lots of information and good advice, bill paying online.

www.thameswater.co.uk – good information and advice.

www.wessexwater.co.uk – good site with bill paying facilities and information, even which reservoirs you can fish in.

The Weather

www.met-office.gov.uk

EXCELLING IN WEATHER SERVICES

ORIGIN UK
INFO ✓✓✓✓✓
EASE ✓✓✓✓

Comprehensive information on Britain's favourite topic of conversation, easy to use, in four sections with interactive maps – world weather and world weather news, UK weather headlines and flash weather warnings. There's also a good selection of links and a mobile phone service.

www.bbc.co.uk/weather

ANOTHER WINNER FROM THE BBC

ORIGIN UK
INFO ✓✓✓✓✓
EASE ✓✓✓✓

Another page from the BBC site, it gives up-to-the-minute forecasts, and is very clear and concise. It features: 5-day forecasts by town, city or post code; specialist reports such as ski resorts, pollution, sun index; world weather and the shipping forecast. There's also a section dedicated to articles on various aspects of the weather and details on making the weather forecast programme.

See also:
www.uk-weather.co.uk – good for links.
www.weather.com – geared to the USA, but
  has some really good articles and features.
www.weather.org.uk – informative UK weather
  information site.

www.weatherimages.org
SEE THE WORLD'S WEATHER – LIVE

ORIGIN US
INFO ✓✓✓✓
EASE ✓✓✓✓

Weatherimages is compiled by a true weather fan.
Split into twenty or so areas of interest, there is plenty
of information and there's loads to see. The best
feature is the network of weather cams from which
you can see the best and worst of the world's weather.

Web Cameras

*One of the most fascinating aspects of the Internet is the ability
to tap into some CCTV or specially set up web cameras from all
around the world. Some sites will contain adult material.*

www.camcentral.com
WEB CAM CENTRAL

ORIGIN US
INFO ✓✓✓✓✓
EASE ✓✓✓

An excellent selection of cameras, chosen for quality
rather than quantity; the wildlife ones are very good
in particular but there's a good search facility too.

See also:
www.camvista.com – web cam shots of the UK and
  the USA from a web cam manufacturer.
www.webcamworld.com – a big directory of web cams.
www.webcam-index.com – lists some 500 sites from
  around the world.

Web Site Design

As it's pretty expensive to get a site designed and built professionally, there's been an explosion in the number of books, software and sites dedicated to helping people put their own sites together. These web sites will help enormously and take you through the world of Hypertext Markup Language, Java and Flash.

http://hotwired.lycos.com/webmonkey
THE WEB MONKEY

ORIGIN US
INFO ✓✓✓✓✓
EASE ✓✓✓✓

A superb resource for all web designers of all skill levels providing everything from basic tutorials to articles from professional designers. The 'How to' library is brilliant and, as you'd expect, the site design is excellent too. See also **www.htmlgoodies.com** who also offer tutorials and lots of tips for those times when things don't go quite the way you want them to.

www.codebeach.com
CODE BEACH

ORIGIN US
INFO ✓✓✓✓
EASE ✓✓✓

Code Beach describe their site as 'your complete guide to free and open source code for ASP, C++, ColdFusion, Java, JavaScript, Palm, Perl, PHP, and Visual Basic' and it is. Each language has a section with tutorials, downloads and links for you to get your head around it all.

Other essential sites:
http://webdeveloper.earthweb.com/webjs – you're going to need this site, it's a great source of those helpful little java programs you find on most sites. Why write your own when you can download one for free.
www.blogger.com – a free web publishing tool.
www.cutandpastescripts.com – a great time saving tool where you can literally cut and paste bits of essential computer graphics.
www.desktoppublishing.com – free web templates and original clip art – excellent.
www.dreamink.com – very good online guide to web site creation and design.

www.dreamweaver.com – home of one of the leading pieces of web creation software, here you can download a trial version, get lots of information and more downloads to improve your site.

www.flashkit.com – animate your site, give it life here.

www.fontfreak.com – over 300 different and unusual fonts.

www.homepagetools.com – a really strong resource of tools and services you can add to your site once you're up and running.

www.htmlgoodies.com – lots to download and lots of help too – well written.

www.internet.com – top tips, news and downloads – a comprehensive offering.

www.jimtools.com – OK, you're site is up and running, now promote it. This site tells you how, with lots of tips and a program that will send your new URL to lots of search engines.

www.learnthenet.com – the usual high standards from About.com.

www.netforbeginners.about.com – the beginners pages from About.com.

www.port41.com – manage and update your website the simple way.

www.spinwave.com – free software to ensure that the pictures you choose fit the site, and load quickly and efficiently too.

www.thecounter.com – find out who visits your site and how often.

www.ultimateresources.co.uk – advice and information on how to make money from your site.

www.useit.com – great place to go for advice from a bone-fide web design guru.

www.webpagesthatsuck.com – examples of how not to do it, a chastening and humourous experience.

Web Site Guides and Directories

If you can't find the site you're looking for in this book then rather than use a search engine, check out one of these web site directories.

www.just35.com

FIND IT THE EASY WAY

ORIGIN UK
INFO ✓✓✓✓✓
EASE ✓✓✓

A very good directory site which is well categorised (maximum 35 sites in each category) and easy to use with each site reviewed and rated. You can also get the latest news and personalise the site.

www.uk250.co.uk

OVER 12,000 SITES IN 250 CATEGORIES

ORIGIN UK
INFO ✓✓✓✓✓
EASE ✓✓✓

Heavily advertised and hyped though this site has been, many people seem to think that it consists of just the top 250 sites, but it's actually a very comprehensive database of Britain's most important and useful '.co.uks' and '.coms'. The sites listed are not reviewed but a one-liner gives a brief description of what they are about. Desperately needs a good search facility.

www.thegoodwebguide.co.uk

GOOD WEB GUIDE

ORIGIN UK
INFO ✓✓✓✓✓
VALUE ✓✓
EASE ✓✓✓✓

The best web sites in several key categories are comprehensively reviewed but you have to subscribe (£30 per annum) or buy the related book (subscription then free to that subject area) to get the best out of it. It's a good site and the books are good (if a little expensive), but the problem for the Good Web Guide team is that you can get all the information at reduced cost elsewhere.

http://cool.infi.net

THE COOLEST SITES

ORIGIN US
INFO ✓✓✓✓
EASE ✓✓✓

Vote for the coolest sites and find out which are considered the best. This has got very commercial now, so lots of deals and adverts get in the way.

www.ukdirectory.co.uk

DEFINITIVE GUIDES TO BRITISH SITES

ORIGIN UK
INFO ✓✓✓✓✓
EASE ✓✓✓✓

A massive database of web sites conveniently categorised into sixteen sections, it is mainly geared to business, but there's leisure too. They don't review, but there are brief explanations provided by the site owners.

www.bored.com

IF YOU'RE BORED

ORIGIN US
INFO ✓✓✓✓
VALUE ✓✓✓
EASE ✓✓✓

Basically a directory of unusual and humorous sites to occupy you when you've nothing better to do, it's quite entertaining really.

Weddings

www.confetti.co.uk

YOUR INTERACTIVE WEDDING GUIDE

ORIGIN UK
INFO ✓✓✓✓✓
VALUE ✓✓✓
EASE ✓✓✓✓

A good looking and busy site, designed to help you through every stage of your wedding with information for all participants. There are gift guides, planning tools, advice, a supplier directory and a shop. They don't miss much.

www.wedding-service.co.uk

UK'S LARGEST WEDDING AND BRIDE DIRECTORY

ORIGIN UK
INFO ✓✓✓✓✓
EASE ✓✓✓

A huge list of suppliers, service providers and information by region, everything from balloons to speechwriters are listed. The site is not that easy on the eye and it takes a little while to find what you want.

www.all-about-weddings.co.uk

GETTING MARRIED IN THE UK

ORIGIN UK
INFO ✓✓✓✓✓
VALUE ✓✓✓
EASE ✓✓✓✓

Excellent for basic information about planning weddings from the ceremony to the reception; it also has a good set of links to related and specialist supplier sites, a travel section and a shop. It's all wrapped up in suitably matrimonial design with love hearts flowing across the screen as you browse.

Other good sites for weddings:

www.allstretchedout.co.uk – luxury limousine hire.
www.bridalplanner.com – well designed and wide ranging, including advice and real life stories plus print off checklists and planners.

www.bridesuk.net – excellent site from *Brides*
magazine; get all the latest in bridal fashion and
a guide to where to go on honeymoon.

www.gwp-uk.co.uk – home to the guild of wedding
photographers with advice on choosing the right
photographer for your wedding.

www.hitched.co.uk – another good all-rounder with
the added feature of a discussion forum where you
can swap wedding stories.

www.lastnightoffreedom.co.uk – everything you need
to organise your stag or hen night.

www.partydomain.co.uk – if you want to organise
your own party then this is the site for you.

www.pronuptia.co.uk – details of the range and stores,
not much else.

www.webwedding.co.uk – lots of expert advice and
inspiration, a bit slow though.

www.weddingguide.co.uk – clean looking site with
shop, directory and advice plus a good search facility.

Women

The following are a few sites of particular interest to women.

Equality issues and politics

www.womens-unit.gov.uk
or www.womenandequalityunit.gov.uk

THE WOMEN AND EQUALITY UNIT

ORIGIN UK
INFO ✓✓✓✓
EASE ✓✓✓✓

'The aim of the Women and Equality Unit is to reduce
and remove barriers to opportunity for all'. Politics
aside, the site provides useful information on how
government policies impact on women's lives, covering
hot topics such as encouraging women to become
more involved in public life, balancing work and
family, domestic violence, money, health and equal
opportunities. Worth visiting for the useful links.
For information on what the UN is doing to promote
gender equality go to **www.un.org/womenwatch** where
there is information on all their initiatives and international treaties. A dry but informative read.

www.aviva.org

INTERNATIONAL FEMINIST WEBZINE

ORIGIN UK
INFO ✓✓✓✓
EASE ✓✓✓✓

If you want information on the political and social issues facing women all over the world, this site has plenty of factual articles, details of meetings and loads of links. There is a nice section on International women's art too.

www.savingwomenslives.org

A GLOBAL PERSPECTIVE

ORIGIN US
INFO ✓✓✓✓
EASE ✓✓✓

An excellent site to visit for a glimpse into the lives of women throughout the world. There are heart-wrenching stories, shocking facts, essays on issues and a newsroom. The US foundation, The National Organisation for Women explore similar issues at **www.now.org**

Working women

www.flametree.co.uk

INSPIRING SOLUTIONS TO BALANCE YOUR LIFE

ORIGIN UK
INFO ✓✓✓✓
EASE ✓✓✓✓

This former magazine site now acts as a specialist consultancy 'working with organisations to respond effectively to the work-life challenge'. If your company needs to improve their flexibility, visit this site. Unfortunately they have abandoned the personal section to concentrate on the corporate.

www.resourceconnection.co.uk

FLEXIBLE WORKING SOLUTIONS

ORIGIN UK
INFO ✓✓✓
EASE ✓✓✓✓

Although not exclusively for women, the flexible working arrangements which are the site's lifeblood are particularly attractive to women. Check out the flexible mum factsheet, get advice on how to convince your boss to be flexible, you can also join their jobshare register. Send in your CV, you never know what's out there.

www.busygirl.co.uk
AURORA WOMEN'S NETWORK

ORIGIN UK
INFO ✓✓✓
EASE ✓✓✓

A more serious site than the name suggests, their aim is to advance women by supporting the business and career needs of women. Amongst its services they offer classroom based and on-line IT training courses, women's investment clubs, networking forums and a women-owned business directory.

www.everywoman.co.uk
NOT JUST FOR BUSINESS WOMEN

ORIGIN UK
INFO ✓✓✓✓
EASE ✓✓✓✓

A really useful site aimed at women business owners, but the 'home' channel provides sound information on personal finance, family and well-being for all women.

www.womanstudent.co.uk
FOR WOMEN IN HIGHER EDUCATION

ORIGIN UK
INFO ✓✓✓✓
EASE ✓✓✓✓

Loads of information for UK and International Students with sections on money and careers, travel, health, leisure and universities. Helpful section for overseas women planning to come to British Universities.

Magazines

www.handbag.com
THE ISP FOR WOMEN

ORIGIN UK
INFO ✓✓✓✓✓
VALUE ✓✓✓
EASE ✓✓✓✓

Described as the most useful place on the Internet for British women, Handbag lives up to that with a mass of information written in an informal style and aimed at helping you get through life. There's shopping and competitions too. For some it's a little too commercial though.

www.ivillage.co.uk
WHERE WOMEN FIND ANSWERS

ORIGIN UK
INFO ✓✓✓✓✓
EASE ✓✓✓✓

All the sections you'd expect in a women's magazine, the difference here is that they are trying to create a community with a range of message boards, advice, a good section on work, even a dating service.

www.blackliving.net
BLACK WOMEN'S NETWORK

ORIGIN US
INFO ✓✓✓✓
EASE ✓✓✓✓

A mainstream magazine for women covering all the usual topics for instance beauty, home, parenting, relationships travel. Although it is an American magazine, it was founded by a woman from Manchester who is concerned about the lack of exposure for black women in the UK, consequently some of the content does specifically mention the UK.

Other general women's e-zines and portals:
http://womensissues.about.com – features on a comprehensive range of women's issues.
www.allthatwomenwant.com – a portal site which offers links to sites covering a vast range of topics. It needs a search engine though.
www.cybergrrl.com – a comprehensive American women's e-zine. Check out the sister site www.femina.com which is a useful search engine for women-friendly sites.
www.icircle.co.uk – part of the Freeserve network calling itself the Women's Channel.
www.newwomanonline.co.uk – good representation of the magazine, particularly liked the lunchbox with daily distractions.
www.workingwoman.com – an online version of the American magazine.

www.e-women.com
THE MULTICULTURAL WOMEN'S PORTAL

ORIGIN UK
INFO ✓✓✓✓
EASE ✓✓✓✓

E-women aims to provide women world-wide with features and links which are relevant to their lives. There are lots of women's magazine-type features, a good range of forums, a shopping directory but less serious comment than when previously visited.

Women's health

Below are a few excellent sources of information on women's health issues, for more general health sites see page 196 and don't rely on websites, see a doctor if you are unwell.

www.womens-health.com
EMPOWERING WOMEN THROUGH KNOWLEDGE

ORIGIN US
INFO ✓✓✓✓✓
EASE ✓✓✓✓

A truly comprehensive look at women's health issues with clear, high quality information. The personal assessments provide a range of linked questionnaires to help you make a self-diagnosis and/or assess your risk of contracting heart disease or osteoporosis for instance. There are good links, a good search engine, although still no update on the newsletter written in 1999!

www.healthywomen.org
EDUCATING WOMEN ABOUT THEMSELVES

ORIGIN US
INFO ✓✓✓✓✓
EASE ✓✓

The layout doesn't do justice to the quality of information on the site provided by the American-based National Women's Health Resource Center. Go to the 'health center' and use the pull-down menu to select a topic such as breast cancer, acupuncture or menopause. The aim is to provide women with good information to help them make informed decisions about their health.

www.womens-health.co.uk
OBS AND GYNAE EXPLAINED

ORIGIN UK
INFO ✓✓✓✓
VALUE ✓✓✓
EASE ✓✓✓

A good starting point for information on obstetrics and gynaecology including pregnancy, infertility, complications and investigations. Has a good search facility and useful links.

www.fpa.org.uk
FAMILY PLANNING

ORIGIN UK
INFO ✓✓✓✓✓
EASE ✓✓✓✓

A really comprehensive web site from the Family Planning Association with information on all aspects of birth control written in a clear and helpful style. There is a useful page entitled 'I need help now' plus good links. For a more campaigning approach, try **www.mariestopes.org.uk** for a rundown on contraception choices and information on related topics such as health screening. You can even arrange for him to have a vasectomy online.

Leisure

www.journeywoman.com
PREMIER TRAVEL RESOURCE FOR WOMEN

ORIGIN US   Dedicated to ensuring safe travel for women,
INFO ✓✓✓✓✓ registering gets you access to the free newsletter plus
VALUE ✓✓✓ lots of advice, guidance and tips from women who've
EASE ✓✓✓✓ travelled, traveller's tales and health warnings.

www.womengamers.com
BECAUSE WOMEN DO PLAY

ORIGIN US   The aim is to provide a selection of reviews and games
INFO ✓✓✓✓ geared specifically to a female audience (although it
EASE ✓✓✓✓ doesn't stop this being an enjoyable site for men to
visit). It has up-to-the-minute reviews, really well-
written articles, lots of content and high quality design.

www.wsf.org.uk
WOMEN'S SPORT FOUNDATION

ORIGIN UK   The voice of women's sport is committed to improving
INFO ✓✓✓✓ and promoting opportunities for women and girls in
EASE ✓✓✓✓ sport at every level. It does this by lobbying and raising
the awareness of the importance of women in sport to
the organisers and governing bodies. Here you can find
out how to get involved or get help.

www.pinknoises.com
PROMOTING WOMEN'S MUSIC

ORIGIN UK   Giving women a voice in the male-dominated
INFO ✓✓✓ international electronic-music scene by providing
EASE ✓✓✓✓ music, profiles of artists, reviews, essays, a message
board and comprehensive links. Truly international
in the artists it features and an invaluable resource
for women DJs and electronic-music freaks.

www.myslexia.co.uk
FOR WOMEN WHO WRITE

ORIGIN UK
INFO ✓✓✓
EASE ✓✓✓✓

Myslexia magazine online unfortunately only provides glimpses at the current issue and some articles from back issues which is a shame as it is a great resource for aspiring and published writers as well as those just interested in women's writing. Pity they don't share more of the writing archive online.

http://digital.library.upenn.edu/women
A CELEBRATION OF WOMEN WRITERS

ORIGIN US
INFO ✓✓✓✓
EASE ✓✓✓

A site with a passion for the work of women writers; the quality and quantity of information on this site is tremendous with links to biographical and bibliographical information about women writers as well as providing complete books written by women.

For other sites on women's writing see:
http://womenwriters.net/links.htm – a guide to internet resources as well as book reviews and features.
www.blackwomen.co.uk – promoting black women in the arts, not just in literature.
www.triangle.co.uk – dedicated to women's writing before 1900.

Stop Press

Here are some sites that came to our notice too late to get into the main body of the book, they will be reviewed properly for the 2005 edition. If you have a favourite site not listed, please let us know by e-mailing goodwebsiteguide@hotmail.com

Books

www.bookcrossing.com A really interesting book review site. The idea is to read the book, review it, then, release it into the community by leaving it somewhere like a park bench where it can be picked up and enjoyed by someone else.

www.greenmetropolis.com A book store where money is donated from the sale of books towards replanting trees.

www.questia.com Claims to be the world's largest online library with over 45,000 books to choose from; however it's a subscription service.

Children

www.koolsun.co.uk A really useful store that sells children's clothes that offer protection from the UV rays from sunlight.

Disability information

www.disabledtravels.com A basic site offering accommodation information. You have to register to get the best out of it.

www.holidaycare.org.uk Information on many accessible hotels and attractions throughout the UK plus some help for overseas travel too.

www.jobability.com A job site for disabled people and is very useful for advice, links and of course the list of available jobs.

Food & Drink

www.lowcarbiseasy.com A very good interactive cook book devoted to low carbohydrate recipes, with lots of features and explanation.

www.brewathome.co.uk Equipment, kits and advice on how to brew many different types of drinks at home.

www.howtobrew.com Free access to the first edition of John Palmer's book on all you need to know about home brewing.

Genealogy
www.genealogylinks.net A great directory site for anyone researching their family tree with over 18,000 links.

Health
www.spinalnet.co.uk An excellent site for people with a spinal injury with information on how to cope plus resources and medical information.
www.uksupplements.co.uk A simple site offering most dietary supplements at good prices; there's also a no quibble money back guarantee.

History
www.ancientmexico.com A beautifully presented site with a full history with maps, timelines and religious details. It can be a little slow.

Jobs
www.deskdemon.co.uk A jobs site aimed at the secretarial community with lots of extras such as financial information and chat.

Law
www.oldbaileyonline.org An amazingly detailed and fully searchable database of trails held at the Old Bailey from 1674 to 1834, with lots of historical background.

Music
www.backstreet.co.uk A London-based rehearsal studio and musical instrument store with a wide range of guitars and accessories for sale.

Nature
www.hedgehog.org.uk All you need to know about hedgehogs at the Prickly Ball Farm Hedgehog Hospital.
www.monkeyworld.co.uk Excellent and informative site from the Monkey World Ape Rescue Centre, devoted to helping endangered primates.

Pets
www.travelpets.com Pet friendly accommodation world-wide, with basic information and advice.

Price checker
www.priceguideuk.com A good, comprehensive and fast price checking site, oriented to the UK.

Space
http://earth.esa.int A site devoted to giving the location of all the ESA satellites orbiting the Earth, including some fantastic images taken from space.

www.dhinds.co.uk and www.telescopehouse.co.uk Two stores specialising in supplying astrological instruments.

Sport
www.bdaa.co.uk The British Disabled Angling Association site is informative and offers much in the way of support.

www.pacgb.com Perhaps a bit specialist but this is a very comprehensive site dedicated to pike fishing.

Travel
www.aitkenspenceholidays.com Gorgeous hotels in Sri Lanka and the Maldives.

www.BedandBreakfast-Directory.co.uk A useful directory site with a multiple search facility.

www.horsebackholidays.com Specialists in holidays on horse back around the world.

www.inthesaddle.com Another agent specialising in holidays on horseback, again world-wide.

www.seasoninstyle.co.uk Specialists in the ultimate luxury holidays, looks fab.

www.SelfCatering-Directory.co.uk Another useful directory site covering the UK.

www.sportingtours.co.uk Specialists in cycling holidays.

www.tastingplaces.com Discover the joys of cooking in exotic and beautiful locations around the world.

www.to-gastronomy.com Moroccan, Italian and French cookery schools in Europe and details on how you can stay and learn how to cook while staying in luxury style.

TV

www.perfectblend.net An excellent site for
Neighbours fans everywhere, with lots of gossip,
reviews and nostalgic features.

Weather

www.its.caltech.edu/~atomic/snowcrystals A site
devoted to snow crystals, how they are formed and
you can even design one.

Web site design

www.extreme-dm.com Designed to help you track
who has entered and used your site.

www.linkdup.com A lesson in site design with sites
reviewed and links to the best designed sites. It just
shows what really can be done with a little effort.

Weddings

www.wrapit.co.uk An attractive and well designed
wedding list site with an excellent selection of gifts.

Index